Routledge Revivals

The League on Trial

First published in 1933, this title explores the inner workings and diplomatic culture of the League of Nations in Geneva, at a time when the increasing strain of international relations was beginning to take its toll and disillusionment towards the League was growing.

Written as a series of short sketches, Max Beer communicates a variety of insights into the League of Nations. Delving into the machinations and bewildering configurations of diplomatic relations that predominated, while at the same time maintaining a very human perspective, this volume represents a unique resource for students of this period in European politics.

The League on Trial
A Journey to Geneva

Max Beer

Translated by
W. H. Johnston

The German original, *Die Reise nach Genf*, published 1932
First published in English 1933
by George Allen & Unwin Ltd

This edition first published in 2014 by Routledge
2 Park Square, Milton Park, Abingdon, Oxon, OX14 4RN

and by Routledge
711 Third Avenue, New York, NY 10017

Routledge is an imprint of the Taylor & Francis Group, an informa business

© 1933 George Allen & Unwin Ltd

All rights reserved. No part of this book may be reprinted or reproduced or utilised in any form or by any electronic, mechanical, or other means, now known or hereafter invented, including photocopying and recording, or in any information storage or retrieval system, without permission in writing from the publishers.

Publisher's Note
The publisher has gone to great lengths to ensure the quality of this reprint but points out that some imperfections in the original copies may be apparent.

Disclaimer
The publisher has made every effort to trace copyright holders and welcomes correspondence from those they have been unable to contact.

ISBN 13: 978-1-138-02388-8 (hbk)
ISBN 13: 978-1-315-77543-2 (ebk)
ISBN 13: 978-1-138-02497-7 (pbk)

MAX BEER

The League on Trial

---- ❖ ----

A Journey to Geneva

Translated by
W. H. JOHNSTON

LONDON
George Allen & Unwin Ltd
MUSEUM STREET

The German original, "Die Reise nach Genf," was published in 1932
FIRST PUBLISHED IN ENGLISH 1933

All rights reserved
PRINTED IN GREAT BRITAIN BY
UNWIN BROTHERS LTD., WOKING

PREFATORY NOTE

OUR object is to know our where and our whither.

We all, who live in the present time, must understand that, while some of us perhaps are free of responsibility for the past, none of us can decline responsibility for the future. It is thirteen years since the Great War ended; for twelve years men have been attempting at Geneva to devise ways for avoiding the next. Where do we stand, and whither does our road lead us?

Is Geneva a place of pilgrimage for the devout and the enthusiastic; or is it the Exchange of skilful profiteers? Will it give us eternal peace, or is it an armistice between battles? Nobody enters the soil of Geneva without hope—and nobody leaves it without a feeling of disquiet; only the diplomats come and go with unshaken calm, even if they carry with them an honest burden of professional cares in their portfolios. They have seen and forgotten so much, they have made use of and despised, they have adored and crucified so many idols, and they stammer in all the tongues of Babel. Why should they not lisp the jargon of peace for a little while?

The nations? The nations are hungry and weary. They toil on the surface of the earth and below, they pay their taxes and debts with a sigh, skim through their papers, spend anxious care upon their children, and, weary of reality, indulge in the intoxication of their brief pleasures. They live in peace, and peace does not enter their thoughts. If Geneva is mentioned, they yawn.

Who knows, and who wants to know, anything of Geneva? It ought to fill the centre of our stage and to carry the problem of the co-operation of nations from dingy offices into the public life of every civic-minded person; and it is the secret science of a few hundred diplomats and a few dozens of professors and experts. Geneva ought to be the new Rome to which every road leads, and in fact it lies far from the beaten path along which the nations carry their burden backwards and forwards. The future is not bright for our children if we can regard with indifference the attempt to teach the nations better manners.

Nothing is more exciting than the cunning stimulation of passions in war: peace is dull. A little frontier incident with two dead recruits is more entertaining than a major conference with two hundred living jurists. Yet surely it is our affair, and the affair of all of us, to make peace a vital part of our lives, and to pay it the tribute of emotion which it deserves, as well as the tribute of passion on which it must feed.

Thirteen years have passed since the exciting Great War ended. For twelve years the Geneva experiment has been attempting to spare us fresh excitement. If the experiment is honest it must arouse our enthusiasm; if not, our indignation. If it is foolish, it may provoke our sarcasm; in no case has it a right to induce our slumbers. If we yawn we are lost.

And therefore, as we approach Geneva, we cease to believe in the virtue of diplomatic secret codes and the magic of logarithmic tables. And therefore—at the risk of annoying a few officials and disappointing a few professors—we will undertake the difficulties of the attempt of producing a simple guide to Geneva without mystery-mongering and without pedantry.

M. B.

GENEVA
February 1932

CONTENTS

CHAPTER		PAGE
	PREFATORY NOTE	7

BOOK I
THE JOURNEY TO GENEVA

I.	THE WOMAN AT THE LEVEL CROSSING	13
II.	THE SIX HUNDRED AND SIXTY-FIFTH DAY	20
III.	THE MESSIAH	33
IV.	THE WOODEN HORSE	47
V.	THE WAR VICTIM	67
VI.	PAPER	85
VII.	THOU SHALT NOT . . .	99
VIII.	THE SIEVE	116
IX.	"A SACRED TRUST OF CIVILIZATION"	132
X.	THE PRISON HOUSE	143
XI.	BETWEEN THE RHINE AND THE KIEL CANAL	158
XII.	THE LAST WORD	168
XIII.	THE STAR OF THE SALÈVE	181

BOOK II
THE HOTEL

XIV.	HOTTOP'S PALACE	191
XV.	COUNTESS TRANI'S ROOM	210
XVI.	LAUGHTER	225
XVII.	MR. SUGIMURA'S MAP	237

CHAPTER		PAGE
XVIII.	COLOURS AT THE FRONT	260
XIX.	HOW IS IT DONE?	293
XX.	A CURIOSITY	314
XXI.	THE WHALE	332
XXII.	PRAYER ON THE ROOF	354
XXIII.	"AFRIQUE DU SUD, ALBANIE, ALLEMAGNE . . ."	374
XXIV.	THE HAMMER	388
XXV.	THE WOMAN AT THE LEVEL CROSSING	405
	ANALYSIS	411
	INDEX	413

BOOK I
THE JOURNEY TO GENEVA

CHAPTER I

THE WOMAN AT THE LEVEL CROSSING

IN a few minutes the train will leave.

At the Friedrichstrasse station in Berlin, Victoria Station in London, the Gare de Lyon in Paris, the Central station in Warsaw, the Statione Termini in Rome; at the Wilson station in Prague, the Western station in Vienna, the Northern station in Madrid, the Southern station in Brussels, the vast halls are filled with clouds and wisps of white smoke, with dull rumblings and shrill whistles. Trollies with chocolate and newspapers are being wheeled up and down, passengers hurry past each other, following their porters. From above a feeble ray of sunshine, or perhaps only the light of a carbon lamp, pierces through the steam and cuts across the vast nave of the cathedral of glass and steel.

Only a few minutes to go.

One spot on the platform has carefully been left clear, a kind of subsidiary chapel within the pious edifice. This spot is occupied by two mingled groups of people who yet are clearly distinguishable: one of them, the group of tall hats and dark coats; the other, that of soft hats and light travelling suits. With some degree of excitement they exchange amiable phrases and the somewhat over-appreciative laughter which people use to fill long minutes of embarrassment. They bow, they shake hands, they raise their hats. The engine whistles; the men of soft hats and light suits emerge from the group and disappear in their compartments, while those of the silk hats and frock coats peer along the coaches for a moment before they rediscover their lost ones at an open window. Conductors hurry past. Doors are slammed. The timid attempt to begin a last conversation at the window is made; but the train starts, and forthwith those left behind lift their hats of state, while those inside, who have already placed their hats in the rack, and thus completed occupation of their travelling home, smilingly raise their hands in token of farewell. Slowly the train gathers speed. Those on the platform hesitatingly accompany it for a few yards and then, assuming a solemn and vague expression, wave their hands, halt, and watch the faces of the others by the shining windows growing indistinct within the ribbon of the moving train. For a few minutes they wait in a cloud of smoke and devotion, stiffly holding their hats with arms half raised. Finally they turn and, forming new groups and entering on new conversations, ascend or else descend the stairs. Passing through the hurrying throng, they find their cars and their chauffeurs in the evening air outside. A serious mien is adopted for the drive through the glittering life of the city. And while they proceed to the pleasant task of governing alone for a while, Havas and Wolff, Reuter and Stefani, Pat and the Czechoslovakian Press Office, Fabra and Belga, report that the deputation left by train for Geneva. "The members of the deputation are . . ." "At the station there were present . . ." the reports run, adding their meed of fame and flattery.

The journey of the nations has commenced: that strange journey which nowadays hardly meets with attention, and which is pursued by thousands from every capital as naturally and regularly as though they were going on business or on holiday. From every quarter of the globe they begin their journey as though it had always been so and always would be so: Prime Ministers and Ministers of Foreign Affairs, diplomats and senior officials, experts on economic, financial and military questions, journalists and observers, some accompanied by their families and others surrounded by a whole swarm of secretaries and typewriters, Press officers and Hughes machines, portfolios, codes, cabin trunks, silk hats, and civil and military decorations. From Sweden, Norway and Denmark, from Finland, Lithuania, Latvia, Estonia and Poland, they hurry to Berlin; from Berlin, where they are joined by the Germans, they hurry through the night through a wide

THE WOMAN AT THE LEVEL CROSSING 15

country groaning under a burden of daily anxiety and need; and so to the frontier at Basle, where they are joined by companions from Holland, Belgium and Luxembourg. Meanwhile the trains are hurrying to Feldkirch from Roumania, Czechoslovakia and Jugoslavia, from Bulgaria and Greece, and from Hungary and Austria. Through the Simplon Tunnel the trains run from Italy, carrying Albanians and Abyssinians, and pilgrims from Siam, Persia, Japan and China, into the high valley of the Rhone. From Paris, where meanwhile the Western world has met by various routes, the International Sleeping Carriage Company jolts hundreds and thousands of pilgrims past the dreaming churches of France to the frontier station at Bellegarde; French and Spanish and Portuguese, English and Irish, and representatives of the Dominions—of Canada, New Zealand, Australia and South Africa, as well as of India—who live in London or else have made their bow there; the deputies of the Ibero-American countries: Bolivia, Chile, Guatemala, Honduras, Columbia, Cuba, Nicaragua, Panama, Paraguay, Peru, San Domingo, San Salvador, Uruguay and Venezuela, and of the coloured Republics of Haiti and Liberia; and with them numerous diplomats from the regions of the north, the east and the south-east, who live as Ministers in Paris, or at any rate consider that the way round via Paris is the shortest way to Geneva. The number grows of cautious tourists from the United States, snoring on the pillows of the Paris Sleeping Car Company, and of worried observers from the U.S.S.R., who, after a brief, unhappy stay in Berlin, are now tossing under the blankets of the Mitropa: a queer and unique company of travellers. For days and weeks they have been crossing the oceans, and have covered hundreds and thousands of miles of the railways of Europe. The ports of the open seas and of the Mediterranean, the capitals of Western and Central Europe, were their first gathering points. And now, by diverse routes, from north and south and east and west, they are hastening towards Switzerland; the many different lines converge; and soon the representatives of the entire world, coming either from Lausanne or else from Bellegarde, will meet, as though for a vast conflict or a vast embrace.

The iron monsters go thundering with darkened windows through the deserted country stations, and few know their meaning and their burden. They do not go rumbling through a startled world accompanied by the exuberant songs of mobilization trains, and no one has thought to chalk on their coaches: To Geneva, towards peace. The magi are pursuing their stars by the regular train, but yet with the stealth of a thief in the night. In the Ministries which they have left behind every messenger can inform the visitor that the gentlemen have proceeded to Geneva; while in the Geneva hotels documents and invitations to luncheons, dinners and receptions accumulate in the pigeon-holes. But of all the travellers hardly one is filled with dreams or emotions at the thought of his journey, once he has left home and has not yet reached the distant goal. The woman at the level crossing waves her flag as for any other train, and when the sun rises over the smoking fields the labourers look up at the passing grandeur as at any other train. Through plains and valleys, past rivers and mountains, they are carried, like so many excursionists, commercial travellers or Congress rubbernecks. Not until the desires of their pacifist organizations are fulfilled, and they wear their own badge in their button-holes, will it be possible to recognize their growing numbers at the frontier stations; and then only will it be seen whether the multitude greets them with cheers, gazes at them with indifferent and barely inquisitive looks, or drives them away with hostile jeers.

What are their own thoughts, while the telegraph poles go whirling past? Are they excited? Do they dream? Or, installed in a corner, are they quietly reading the *Woche* or *L'Illustration*? Do they lay aside their Edgar Wallace with a sigh before turning off the light? Do they think it fun to go to Geneva? Does it bore them? What do they think of? Or are they thinking of nothing at all? And do their thoughts only

THE WOMAN AT THE LEVEL CROSSING 17

wake up as the train rolls into the station, while the travellers rise from their corners, shake straight their trouser creases, and take their hat from the rack? Some, no doubt, are careless and pleased, while others are brooding gloomily: not all faces bear the same look. As we pass through one coach on our journey of investigation we find grave documents on the first-class seats. The agenda of the Geneva consultations balances on the knees of the junior officials. The Minister, who has withdrawn from the noisy conversation by the trembling lamp of the dining-car to the security of his sleeping compartment, peruses the manuscript of his great speech for the Assembly. The Government jurist on his narrow, shaking couch delves into his counter-proposal for the Geneva Committee of Arbitration. The League of Nations expert, for the last time before putting on his pyjamas, opens his case to scan his notes on the Ruthenian Minority Complaint. The journalist has opened his portable typewriter and is tapping for dear life. The train hurtles through the night, the vaulted corridor is empty, and the conductor on his folding seat checks the tickets and diplomatic passports.

What do the travellers expect of their journey? For many clearly their journey is a laborious road towards laborious days. And yet, if they turn wearily before they sleep, or if they meditate while the wheels rumble beneath them, what is it that burdens them? Do they sorrow for the fate of their nations? Do they reach a kind of dream in which they ponder and have the right to ponder the welfare of mankind? Or do they revolve their private problems—the Ministers their parliamentary majorities, the deputies the favour of their party, the diplomats and officials the fulfilment of their instructions, and the journalists the satisfaction of their editors? Is the labourer in the field and the woman at the level crossing right? Are these perplexed voyagers so many commercial travellers and Congress visitors? Are the cheerful voyagers so many excursionists and holiday travellers? However that may be, and whether they are accompanied by the cares of their daily work, or the carelessness of a holiday-maker, surely they must have some sense of their new and special task. Although they travel by ordinary train, surely their journey is no ordinary one, and within themselves they carry a common and mysterious symbol which must differentiate them from all other travellers in the world.

What is the driving force behind these men who are called Ministers, and are diplomats and officials or attachés? Why and whence this journey through the night? The Minister, while thinking over his speech, can look back upon a famous road leading into a distant past: its shining path takes him back to the Roman Empire, the Christian monarchy of the popes and emperors and the vast comprehensive attempts to found a super-national grouping of nations and national power. The Government jurist calculating his formula of arbitration can look back upon the amphictyonic league of Greece, an honourable stage by the way which shines through all the mists which have since arisen. The Foreign Office League of Nations official has only to look up from his papers through the window to see either side of his iron road bordered by flying signals—so many programmes proclaiming an ideal international order. All of them who are now rushing to the distant Swiss town in accordance with a punctual programme from the great and lesser capitals of the world—French and Esthonians, Belgians and Germans—have not left behind them Paris and Riga, or Brussels and Berlin: their journey was prepared, proclaimed and willed in a dark and distant past. They come from a region lying behind their country and time, and the railway stations whence all these trains rush into the world are in sober truth so many temples and cathedrals. Behind them there is more than an agenda: the command and mandate of a thought. Whether they indulge in conversation or concentrate upon their documents, whether they know it or have forgotten it, their journey is the completion of a great and common inheritance, laboriously built

THE WOMAN AT THE LEVEL CROSSING

up during the centuries. Theirs is a great fortune and a great responsibility, for they are allowed to execute the thoughts of lonely pioneers and to fulfil the longing of the nameless masses. They are not surrounded by night; their road is alive with prophetic signs and the progress of their train is filled with secret whisperings. With them fly the shades of the Prophets, who, inspired and ardent, have undertaken the wondrous journey on the wings of the spirit of pity. Their inspiration is uncorporeal, and in their hands they raise the grandiose plans called Utopias, which end to-day in the reality of this railway journey. Their presence is with us, and their blessing and encouragement point out the road they discovered with toil and trouble: they give a soul to the landscape and wings to the train. And as the rushing wheels roll on, and the thunderous melody rises to its crescendo, we seem to hear their salute, pregnant with wisdom.

Prime Ministers and Ministers for Foreign Affairs, diplomats and officials, experts and journalists, and heads of Press Departments, typewriters, cabin trunks and silk hats, are conveyed through the night, and between the country they left behind and their distant destination there is no one to feel the appeal of this journey. But the labourer of the fields is wrong, and the woman at the level crossing ought to stand to attention and present her flag with shining eyes; for no greater majesty ever passed them. Do the children feel it? Perhaps, for suddenly they stop and wave eagerly and gaily at the windows which roll past, dark and unseeing. There is no one in the sleeping train to respond, and yet they wave patiently their cheerful greeting. When the last coach has passed, they turn to their walk toward the growing day.

CHAPTER II

THE SIX HUNDRED AND SIXTY-FIFTH DAY

THE aspirations of the old world had led to no true union among the nations.

But beyond the ocean, in the New World, under a different sky and with different conditions of life, a population freed from their European traditions might find it easier to free themselves from the traditional forms of European constitutional history. Here the nations seemed to approach more closely to the idea of a federal city. The much admired constitution of the United States, with its roots in the world of the Reformation—analogously the old European plans for a league of nations had their roots in the Roman Catholic world—with its Senate, House of Representatives and Supreme Court, was intended to be a last stage on the way to a general Union of Nations, and Benjamin Franklin himself believed that Europe was now ripe for the "Plan of good Henri IV." In the same year which witnessed the Holy Alliance in Europe, Simon Bolivar, the liberator of the Ibero-American races, dreamed of the union of the whole American continent; and surely the prophet of a distant League of Nations would succeed in presiding over the first Pan-American congress in the new Corinth, Panama. It was not to be; and for many years the peoples wandered far from our path, their looks turned inward, and plodding only at the cultivation of their own fields. Here there was no ability to tread a common pilgrim's road. True, a new set of prophets soon appears along our path, scrutinizing the structure of the world from the Catholic-papal, the religious-Socialist, the juridical and the economic standpoint; Joseph de Maistre was the first to coin the phrase "Société des Nations," while Pierre Leroux, the object of Heine's admiring sarcasms, enthusiastically echoed the word. But if they would win the support of the

THE SIX HUNDRED AND SIXTY-FIFTH DAY 21

masses, the prophets must sound a louder note. It no longer sufficed for one of the faithful to hand the torch to the next. The light which hitherto had illuminated a narrow road leading into the future must shine around and throw light upon the landscape in a growing radius.

And indeed the world itself seems to have grown brighter. The age of schools, of new methods of communication, of deliberating bodies and parliaments commences; executive powers have a wider basis, public opinion can form, and the isolated philosopher no longer faces the isolated monarch whom he must convince or controvert alone. The tunnel which attempts to pierce the obstructing mountain is entered not only by individual prophets, but by dense groups of the visionary and enlighted, who consult together, deliberate and conduct propaganda. In 1815 the first Society of Peace was formed in the United States; others followed, forming a powerful federation. The following year witnessed the first European Peace Alliance in England, and in 1830 the Genevese Count de Sellon reported from the distance goal of our journey the foundation of the first Continental pacifist union. Henceforth our journey is enlivened by a growing throng. The groups grow in numbers, carry the torch farther, and form brightly shining constellations; new prophets are awakened, and a friendly familiar circle is formed for others who had been pursuing the lonely path where they could practise a voice destined to appeal more urgently to nations and rulers. In their midst we see the Americans, William Ladds and William Jay, with the popular apostle Elihu Burritt, who crusaded through Europe; the English Macnamara; the Swiss Sartorius, who inspired Sellon's peace prize; Constantin Pequer, and other prizewinners of the French Union. But still there was the urge to grow and comprehend the world; the impulse towards international union led men toward the international communion of all lovers of peace. We witness the spectacle of the first private international Peace Congress, which, meeting in Brussels in the revolutionary year of 1848, and dominated by the kindling words of Burritt, demanded the abolition of war, an arbitrator or supreme international court, the rapid convocation of a congress of nations with representatives of every people, and a system of disarmament in order simultaneously to reduce national expenditure and eliminate a lasting cause of friction and unrest. We are fascinated by that pathetic second Peace Congress which commenced in Paris in the following year, and which was attended by Germans. The President was Victor Hugo, and the tremendous prose poem which he proclaimed before the nations and in which, for the first time, the United States of Europe are mentioned, resounded more powerfully than the proclamation of the Holy Alliance itself.

"The day will come," the poet announced, "when you all, France, Russia, England and Germany, all nations of the Continent, without losing your individual virtues or glorious personalities, will be closely united in a higher unity to found the brotherhood of Europe. . . .

"The day will come when there will be no battlefields save markets open for trade and minds open to thought.

"The day will come when shells and bombs will be replaced by voting papers, by the universal franchise of nations, and by the venerable court of arbitration of a great soveriegn senate, which will be for Europe what the Parliament is for England, the Reichstag for Germany, and the Legislative Assembly for France.

"The day will come when guns will be exhibited in our museums as instruments of torture are to-day, and when people will wonder that such things could be.

"The day will come when two vast groups, the United States of America and the United States of Europe, will stand face to face, clasping hands across the sea, exchanging produce, trade, industry, art and genius, clearing the globe of weeds, colonizing the deserts, improving creation under the Creator's eye, and uniting two omnipotent forces, human fraternity and divine power, to the universal increase of well-being.

THE SIX HUNDRED AND SIXTY-FIFTH DAY 23

"And to bring about this day we need not wait for centuries. We live in an age of speed; we live in a stream of the most tempestuous events and thoughts that ever shook mankind; in our age a year often does the work of a century.

"And we—French and English, Germans, Belgians, Russians, Slavs, Europeans and Americans—what must we do to witness this great day as soon as possible?"

The poet ceased, drew a deep breath, and opened wide his arms: "We must love one another."

The Congress applauded deliriously, deliberated and passed resolutions. These confirmed the postulates of the first Congress, and extended them by condemning war loans and by appealing to clergy and Press. Finally they were solemnly handed over to the President of the French Republic, the future Napoleon III, who was toying with Napoleon's pacifist legacy and would not have been sorry to preside over the first European Peace Conference. The prophets pressed on him with their plans as once they had pressed upon his great-uncle and the Emperor Alexander. Soon the third Congress of the Friends of Peace (1850) carries us to St. Paul's Church at Frankfort, where two years earlier the dream of German unity had been dreamed in vain. Congress follows Congress; in the course of years the movement gains clarity, seeks new methods, and improves and unifies its organization; the question only is whether it will reach its goal. For surely the goal has gradually grown more modest; the dream of a federation of states, although recurrent, tends sometimes to vanish in the vague distance, while the prescription of the Anglo-Saxon school—the immediate prevention of war by arbitration, disarmament and propaganda against war in general—rises more clearly and more soberly before us. The pacifists seek a liaison with exact science, whose function it shall be to smooth their way for the study of judicial means to quell international conflicts. However, a day comes when, in spite of their struggles, one sees them closely ranged with the political opposition of the day. Besides them, nourished on the theories of the St. Simonists, the Socialist movement begins to grow. This movement, too, we find at Geneva, the seat of the first International Labour Congress. Its aim is the union of the proletariat of all countries and the abolition of standing armies: the road pursued by it towards general disarmament leads through anti-militarism in the individual countries. Its everlasting peace implies a previous constitutional and economic revolution. The demand for international *rapprochement* and for disarmament, even if emanating from the bourgeois and aristocratic spheres of pacifism, gradually renders its protagonists suspect not only of propaganda addressed to the existing Powers, but of subversive activities against nation and State. The ruling Powers, on the contrary, consider the preservation of the State more important than the preservation of peace: the bourgeois mass presses towards the fulfilment of national ideals more earnestly than it shrinks from war. There is thus a double process; the idea of peace has been passed on by isolated prophets to growing and multiplying organizations and parties; but at the same time its light is dissipated and we have to fear that there are too many torch-bearers, that the bright sparks tend to become will o' the wisps, and that the roads tend towards a maze.

Every organized movement exaggerates its importance; every persecuted movement exaggerates the achievements to which it has contributed. Are the pacifists justified in rejoicing after their long struggles? One of the main demands of their congresses had been the method of so-called "good offices," which was adopted by the Paris Government Conference of 1856. The great world meeting held by all the peace unions in 1889 at Paris under the chairmanship of the Frenchman Passy was followed by the first meeting of the Inter-Parliamentary Union, which carried the idea of peace into the several parliaments and laid the foundation of an international parliament. At Berne a standing Peace Office and an Inter-Parliamentary Office were arranged, the former being the organ of the international combine of peace unions. Statesmen begin to pay

THE SIX HUNDRED AND SIXTY-FIFTH DAY 25

tribute to the idea of peace—in England Gladstone, Caprivi in Germany—and pacifists can point to the generous words of Leo XIII. Alfred Nobel's sensational will and the American peace prizes excite the attention of public opinion. Inspiring books like Berta von Suttner's *Die Waffen nieder* and von Bloch's *War*, followed later by Norman Angell's *Great Illusion*, shake the public conscience. In the Latin-American States, and again between the United States and England, the idea of arbitration is embodied in actual treaties; and in 1898 it seemed as though after long searching and many prophecies the attempt of allying power with the ideal of peace, having failed in 1815, would at length be realized.

Napoleon III had not succeeded in taking over the testament of Napoleon I. It was now the turn of Nicolas II to enter upon the heritage of Alexander. His startling peace manifesto was addressed to every Government, reminding them of their urgent duty "to put an end to continual armaments and to look for means of avoiding a disaster threatening the whole world." Accordingly he called for a conference "in order to unify the endeavours of all States genuinely endeavouring to carry the great idea of world peace to ultimate triumph over all the elements of dissension." The two Hague Peace Conferences of 1899 and 1907 pass before our eyes dazzled by military and diplomatic uniforms, the first convened by Nicolas II, the second by President Roosevelt; the former attended by twenty-six and the latter by twenty-four States from every part of the world. Neither, however, led to any limitation of armaments, although this was one of the ideals of modern pacifism; and on each occasion the world was destined to rest content with inconclusive resolutions, that of 1907 commencing with the declaration that armaments had increased since that of 1899. The other pacifist ideal, that of the peaceful arbitration of conflicts, seemed to be approaching realization in spite of the restrictions for which German ineptitude and obstinacy were destined to be blamed. The principle of mediation by outside States before the outbreak of hostilities is recognized "so far as circumstances permit" and the formation of international committees of investigation for international disputes was resolved, provided that such disputes did not touch the honour or vital interest of the Powers; while the system of international arbitration was further elaborated by the formation of a so-called permanent Court of Arbitration with optional procedure, and of an international method of litigation. Only in the way of war there was no obstacle, still less any prohibition; its conduct was merely regulated by numerous agreements forming part of a previous series, while attempts were made to humanize it on the analogy of the Red Cross—the work of a citizen of Geneva, Henry Dunant—and of the Geneva Convention of 1864.

Is this much or is this little? On the opening day of the first Congress the German pacifist, Alfred Fried, recalled with emotion Goethe's famous words after the Battle of Valmy, and declared that Berta von Suttner, his neighbour on the Press bench, "must experience a thrill of joy on seeing her ancient ideal so close to realization." And after the conclusion of the Conference he spoke eloquently to posterity in his *Handbuch des Friedens*: "It was a long and weary way from the Congress of Vienna at the beginning of the nineteenth century to the Hague Conference at its end—from the Wars of the Corsican conqueror to the permanent Court destined to be formed at the suggestion of the Emperor of Russia. The demand of those pious men who had formed the first peace societies in America and Europe at the beginning of the century, and of the pacifists of all countries, who for nearly a century proclaimed and preached their faith unwearyingly amid the scornful laughter of their contemporaries, had here been realized; and if it was only a beginning, it was one which pointed hopefully towards the future: a beginning, which at the same time was a turning-point in human affairs."

Of what kind was the future? Walther Schücking, a pacifist and professor of international law, went further than Fried, and on the conclusion of the second Conference went beyond the old idea of arbitration and demanded the full realization of the plan of a League of States. In his pamphlet *Organisation der Welt*, he foretold that "at the present moment the regular meetings of a Conference appear exceedingly probable, if not legally secure." He went on to assure his readers that "this would amount to the World League of States," and thus described the further course of events: "This World League will gradually absorb the subsidiary leagues of States which already subsist between the various civilized States." Behind the World League of States he already sensed the World Federal State.

World League of States: World Federal State: where are we?

We make a pause and draw breath in our headlong career. Have we already reached the goal unawares? We look around us and discover that while books, societies, and parliaments have been championing the idea of peace, the organs of an international administration have been quietly arising on every side—a union of Telegraph administrations in 1865 and a World Postal Union in 1874, both having permanent offices at Berne. Numerous agreements on communications have been concluded meanwhile—on the Danube and Rhine navigation, on signals at sea, lighthouses, railway goods traffic, submarine cables, and publication of tariffs, and by their side commercial agreements have been concluded like the Latin monetary Convention and the metrical Convention with an Office of Weights and Measures at Sèvres. Agreements on legal points have been reached, e.g. on the protection of industrial and intellectual property, both having offices at Berne, as well as agreements on agriculture, police and science. A network of international agreements, the automatic result of the growing technical civilization of the century, has stretched over the world, crowned now by the World League of States of the Hague Conferences. International Law is triumphant: let us be patient for another eight years, until the Third Conference. Another *Hagueiad* will perfect the work.

How is it that we have overlooked all these organizations?

Why do the masses, faced with this work of science and diplomacy, observe a sceptical and sarcastic silence? Beginning, turning-point, World League of States—these terms were familiar in the days of the Holy Alliance, and all that is certain is that, whether our road leads us forward or in a circular track, or, as it often seems to do, backwards, it never opens to us a confident and cheerful prospect. If we turn our backs upon the dreams of Alexander or Nicolas, and look through our windows at reality, we find red conflagrations illuminating a dreary sky, and dimming the candles of the old Congress and the new; while after every peace speech and peace resolution, the despairing cry of murdered peoples strikes our ear. The progress from the Holy Alliance to the First Hague Peace Conference is full of international words and papers: it is also full of national wars. War in Latin America; war of Greeks, English and Russians against the Turks; English wars in Afghanistan and in China; war between Austria and Sardinia, between Prussia and Denmark, and in the Crimea; Anglo-French war against China, Franco-Sardinian war against Austria, Anglo-Franco-Spanish war in Mexico, civil war amidst the States of the North American Union in spite of its model Constitution, war between Germans and Germans despite their Federation, and simultaneously, war between Austria and Italy; war—despite Napoleon III's dreams, and despite all previous acts of fraternization—between French and Germans, war between Russians and Turks, war between England and Afghanistan, war between the United States and Spain, and war between Japan and China. Between the first and the second Hague Conference the striking cordiality with which statesmen and populace had adopted and passed on peace propaganda in England did not prevent the hideous war of annexation against the Boer Republics; and during the same period Russia conducted a sanguinary war with Japan despite the peace manifesto of Nicolas II, while the united nations of Europe fought in China. During the Second *Hagueiad* the most sensitive parts of the old world were shaken by an

Italo-Turkish and by two terrible Balkan wars, fit to provide the nations with a deterrent example of all the horrors of the modern technique of war. Meanwhile the entire century is full of the quasi-anonymous colonial wars of the civilized nations against the natives who are annihilated, annexed or economically exploited.

If the idea of peace was progressing through the world it is certain also that before, behind and around it the armies were marching. World communications, world civilization and world economics were approaching the nations to each other. Meanwhile, the more closely they were bound, the more eager and greedy were they for mutual warfare. The idea of international organization might be triumphant; but while politicians were paying it lip-service, or forming a union for railway goods traffic, the nations were forming huge armed alliances, and the old system of the balance of power was carried to such a pitch of perfection that the world began in sober truth to resemble Swift's imaginary house, which had been constructed so perfectly according to all the laws of equilibrium, that it immediately collapsed when a sparrow alighted on it. While the Second *Hagueiad* was drawing to its conclusion, the greatest and most disastrous, the most hideous, unnecessary and meaningless of all wars broke out, and broke European civilization. It seized Austria-Hungary and the Balkans and laid its hand on Russia, Germany and France, Belgium and England, Japan, Turkey and Italy, and eventually on almost every State of the world. At first men refused to believe in it, and it was thought that it must end within a few weeks or months. But 1914 passed without the international League of States impressing itself upon the belligerents or recalling to them its methods of arbitration. 1915 passed; but the promised Hague Conference did not descend from the clouds to put an end to the horror. 1916 began; spring came, and as the sun rose higher, the war continued to rage. Our road has ceased to exist, the flames burst in upon us and we dimly perceive that they will stretch yet further in space and time.

Another day dawns like all the other days since August 1914. As on each day Berlin, London, Paris, Vienna, Rome, St. Petersburg and Sophia have sent into the world the reports from Headquarters which constitute the essential literature of this period. The English bulletin reports the explosion of mines near Loos, and artillery fire near Gommecourt, Arras and Vimy Ridge, and mentions that the British fire was particularly effective near Fricourt. The French *communiqué* mentions fighting on the left bank of the Meuse, in Avourt and in Mort-Homme wood, and the recovery of a trench between Haudrement wood and Thiaumont farm. The German report announces that Thiaumont ravine was crossed on the right bank of the Meuse, that the enemy was repulsed south of Fort Douaumont and that the French delivered a gas attack. A few hours later, however, the French *communiqué* reports that the German attack was repulsed by machine guns and infantry. The Belgian *communiqué* reports all quiet, while on the Russian front, Germans, Austrians and Russians agree in reporting no change. On the Italian front, however, the Austrians have begun their great offensive, and here more lively descriptions are issued. Vienna reports successes in the Sugana sector, near Asiago in the north, and near Barcarola in the west, further mentioning that an Italian airship dropped bombs on Trieste, while an Austrian submarine fired on factories at Elba and sank the Italian steamer *Washington*. Nevertheless, Rome is in a condition to report sanguinary Austrian reverses, and a brilliant Italian surprise attack carried out by Alpini; adding that bombs were dropped by the enemy at a number of places. Constantinople reports all quiet on the Iraq front, skirmishes in the Caucasus, and bombs dropped by the enemy over Smyrna. London reports that the Turks continue to occupy their positions on the right bank of the Tigris, but that the British artillery interrupted their communications with the left bank, also mentioning fighting in the African colonies. On this day as on every day one *communiqué* follows the other; and in the evening and on the following morning in every town all over the world and even in the neutral countries newspaper readers and their children bend over the big war maps, place the little flags along the lines of the fronts, and observe that the Germans have occupied Belgium and Northern France and are facing Verdun, while the Austrians have crossed their frontiers and are threatening Italy. Germans and Austrians have occupied the whole of Poland and part of the Russian coast, and Germans, Austrians and Bulgarians have seized Montenegro and Serbia.

On the other side of the ocean, in the capital of the greatest neutral Power, the *communiqués* are read and the flags are planted on the maps, where they proclaim the success of the Central Powers. It is the 27th of May 1916; the 665th day of the war; a day like every other day. And it is also the day of the First Annual Meeting to be held at the Belasco Theatre at Washington by the American League to Enforce Peace, which had been founded at Philadelphia in the previous year. We rub our eyes. For 664 days we have been oblivious of the fact that such leagues have been in existence for a century, and that the prophets of the League of Nations have existed for centuries. Apparently this latest league aims at an introduction of a League of Nations; and, more than that, it has already drawn up a programme in which the entry of the United States into a League of Nations is described as desirable. Further, a number of fundamental obligations have been worked out compelling all States members to submit disputes to a judicial court or council of arbitrations, to unite their economic and military forces against any State breaking the peace, and to formulate and codify the rules of international law in periodic conferences. We shrug our shoulders: we are not interested in these neutral games. Nor are we concerned to hear that a former President of the United States, Mr. Taft, is presiding, that the Democratic candidate at a previous presidential election is Vice-President, and that the Presidents of the Chamber of Commerce, of the American Federation of Labour, of Harvard University and numerous other important and well-meaning personalities of the great neutral State are delivering excellent speeches on the necessity of enforcing future peace through a League of Nations. These words, like a thousand others which have been uttered before and during the war, will be heard and forgotten. Already the American Friends of Peace, sated with these excellent addresses, are preparing to sit down to the great concluding banquet which is to form the pleasant crown of their Platonic endeavours: and soon this attempt to save mankind, like many another, will enter into oblivion. Wearily we look forward to the 666th day, and to all the others that will follow it.

But now a movement of respectful anticipation passes through the vast assembly. The chief of the State, President Woodrow Wilson, rises from his seat to deliver the speech of the evening.

CHAPTER III

THE MESSIAH

It is worth while to look more closely at the principal speaker at this neutral League of Nations banquet; for years to come no living man will be more significant than this man with the scholar's mien.

He is a professor, a historian and a reformed Christian; a democrat and an American, and some will call him a hypocrite and others a childish idealist. He will be praised for the strength of character and invincible obstinacy which caused him to pursue his plan tenaciously through all the vicissitudes of his brief rule; he will be blamed for the weakness of character and purblind vanity which allowed him to sacrifice his plan piecemeal. He will be lauded as a citizen of the world who recognized the common interests of all nations beyond the limits of his own, and he will be criticized as an American who camouflaged the political and economic selfishness of his country behind humanitarian ideals. But while his image seems to waver uncertainly, we must ask ourselves whether it is not in fact his age which is uncertainly wavering. In any case Wilson was the elected leader of a great nation which Europe had been admiring for years; for in it Europe, which had long ago forgotten its own ancient dream of peace, saw the native country of the idea of a League of Nations. A personality half scholar and half prophet, a culture derived not from courts, diplomatic salons or chancelleries, but from the quiet gravity of the study, and an ethical and religious fervour which he brought to the exposition of his political ideas, placed him above every other ruler in the eyes of the nations. Above all, he was the unchallenged arbiter, for he was identified with the great neutral country which was not only morally a tribunal whose support was desired by all, while all deprecated its censure, but which also possessed an accumulated power unravaged by war. He was in a position not only to pronounce a verdict but also to ensure the execution of a sentence, and at his will he could change right into wrong and wrong into right. Unlimited possibilities were at his disposal: the masses were ready to believe in him and to support him. The dreadful experiences which the mingled horror and heroism of the war brought vividly before them, the longing for peace which, in spite of the official censorship and of a self-imposed discipline, was daily becoming more evident, would lend a penetrative force to any interference on his part which never lay at the disposal of Alexander of Russia, and which no Metternich could muffle unless by the President's sanction. For once the nations were ready if he was ready.

We soon discover that he is no sentimental pacifist bending tearfully over the sufferings of individuals and lamenting the murder of innocent youth and the tears of anguished mothers. The President is a scholar and a statesman; the war with its train of distress and misery is a calamity; but it is a general, a political calamity. Those who, inspired by the ideal of creating order, succeed in placing themselves above it, are perhaps justified in perceiving in this evil a necessary and beneficent instrument for the creation of a better policy. The President is a statesman and a scholar. Perhaps the times in which we live are the dreamed-of laboratory whence new discoveries will proceed—an institute of pathology where the dead bodies of nations can be dissected in order that the laws of their life can be discovered. The President is a great general; perhaps the scarlet battlefields which stretch beyond the ocean may become the quiet headquarters of peace. This is the lofty height of Wilson's standpoint at the moment when he is preparing to speak at the banquet of the League to Enforce Peace, in whose midst the dream of a League of Nations is about to become reality. And because of the loftiness of this standpoint he diplomatically disregards the obstacles in the way of his plan; he optimistically selects the most favouring conditions for his system; and he calmly asserts that the war had the beneficent effect of changing the intellectual environment of statesmen in every country more rapidly than the course of years might have done otherwise.

"Repeated utterances of the leading statesmen of most of the nations now engaged in war have made it plain that their thought has come to this, that the principle of public right must henceforth take precedence over the individual interests of particular nations . . . (so that) . . . right prevails against any sort of selfish aggression. . . . Henceforth alliance must not be set up against alliance, understanding against understanding, but . . . there must be a common agreement for a common object, and . . . at the heart of that common object must lie the inviolable rights of people and mankind. The nations of the world have become each other's neighbours, it is to their interests that they should understand each other. In order that they may understand each other, it is imperative that they should agree to co-operate in a common cause, and that they should so act that the guiding principles of that common cause shall be even-handed and impartial justice." These are simple words not announcing any novel idea and the manner of their pronunciation and development is diplomatic rather than visionary. But they obtain a strange glamour and a novel power when the President adds: "This is undoubtedly the thought of America. This is what we ourselves will say when there comes proper occasion to say it." This is a weighty pledge given to the world, and it is this which gives their weight to the first three points which the President proceeds to enumerate. First: "Every people has a right to choose the sovereignty under which they shall live." Next: "The small States of the world have a right to enjoy the same respect for their sovereignty and for their territorial integrity that great and powerful nations expect." Thirdly: "The world has a right to be free from every disturbance of its peace that has its origin in aggression and disregard of the rights of peoples and nations." If these are not conditions of peace, they are certainly a foundation of a League; for, so the President proceeds: "I am sure I speak the mind and wish of the people of America when I say that the United States is willing to become a partner in any feasible association of nations formed in order to realize these objects and make them secure against violation."

Having recognized the indissoluble connection between conditions of peace and principles of the League of Nations, the President, whose twofold aim it was to promote the cause of the League and to mediate between the belligerents, was in a position to proclaim two further points for the promotion and safeguarding of peace: "If it should ever be our privilege to suggest or initiate a movement for peace among the nations now at war, I am sure that the people of the United States would wish their Government to move along these lines. First, such a settlement with regard to their own immediate interests as the belligerents may agree upon. We have nothing material of any kind to ask for ourselves, and are quite aware that we are in no sense or degree parties to the present quarrel. Our interest is only in peace and its future guarantees. Second, an universal association of the nations to maintain the inviolate security of the highway of the seas for the common and unhindered use of all the nations of the world, and to prevent any war begun either contrary to treaty covenants or without warning and full submission of the causes to the opinion of the world, a virtual guarantee of territorial integrity and political independence." These sentences resemble many others uttered during the last five hundred years, and they contain a complete outline of the League of Nations in its essentials. The President now concluded with a solemn assurance: "But I did not come here, let me repeat, to discuss a programme, I came only to avow a creed and give expression to the confidence I feel that the world is even now upon the eve of a great consummation, when some common force will be brought into existence which shall safeguard right as the first and most fundamental interest of all peoples and all Governments, when coercion shall be summoned, not to the service of political ambition or selfish hostility, but to the service of a common order, a common

THE MESSIAH

justice and a common peace." And, like Alexander, in the Act of the Holy Alliance, and like Nicolas II in his Manifesto, Wilson made God the guardian of the new age—God to whom all the belligerents at the same moment were praying for victory. "God grant that the dawn of that day of frank dealing and of settled peace, concord and co-operation may be near at hand."

This diplomatic speech with its concluding prayer could not but be the prelude to the, or at any rate to a, League of Nations. True, other statesmen during the course of the war had toyed with the idea of a new international order after they had done with proclaiming their war aims and attacking the enemy; true, the pacifists and students of international law had secretly begun to collect material for the day when peace should be concluded and the next Hague Conference convened. But this does not alter the fact that the birthday of the new era is this 27th of May 1916, this 665th day of the war, a day of victory for Germany, when a League of Nations might have succeeded in obviating the world domination of one of the contending groups—on this day the German group—without the United States being required to cast into the scales any other weight than the plan of a League of Nations. And indeed the League of Nations debate which Wilson initiated on this day was in fact a debate with Germany. (During the entire history of the idea of a League of Nations there had never been any such plan which did not embrace Germany.) In the present instance, however, the task was not only to co-ordinate the inorganic coexistence of States and to present them with a Constitution on the possible analogy of the old German Federation or the older Holy Roman Empire. On this occasion the task was to make peace between the nations and to unite a world torn in two within a League of Nations. A new order, the dream of centuries, was to reconstitute the order among the States which had been ruined in 1914.

Can this task be fulfilled? The Allied statesmen, chiefly the

British, and some of the latter even before Wilson's speech, began to utilize the idea of an international Order of Law in the same way as the question of War Guilt—in order to isolate Germany before the rest of the world. It necessarily followed that the first important German utterance on this capital problem of the war was a polemic delivered by Bethmann-Hollweg on the 9th of November 1916 in reply to a speech delivered by the British Foreign Secretary, Lord Grey. Having refuted the British allegations upon the outbreak of war, he continued: "At last Lord Grey has devoted some attention to the post-war period and the foundation of an international League for the preservation of peace. I should like to make some observations on this point. We have never disguised our doubts on the possibility of ensuring permanent peace by international organizations or courts of arbitration. I will not discuss the theoretical aspect of this programme; practically, however, we must deal with this problem both now and after the end of the war. When the war is over and the world gradually begins to appreciate the full loss of life and property which it has caused there will be a universal demand for peaceful agreements and conciliations to avoid as far as is humanly possible the recurrence of such a terrible catastrophe. This demand will be so powerful and so just that it must lead to some result. Any attempt to find a practical solution will meet with the careful consideration and co-operation of Germany; the more so, if, as we confidently expect, the war will lead to a political situation permitting of the free development of the lesser as well as of the greater Powers." The war aims of the enemy, however, make suspect the international guarantee of peace which Lord Grey had had in mind. "After the war, when Britain, as she hopes, has defeated us and arranged the world according to her desires, the neutrals are to become joint guarantors of the new British World Order," an order embracing, as the Chancellor could reveal from reliable sources, a Russian domination over Constantinople, the Bosphorus and the western banks of the Dardanelles, the division of Asia

Minor among the Allied Powers in accordance with an Anglo-Franco-Russian agreement made in 1915, and annexationist desires of France with regard to Alsace-Lorraine. "Such a policy of might cannot form the foundation of an effective international League of Peace." "It utterly contradicts the ideal State aimed at by Lord Grey and Mr. Asquith, where right is superior to might and all nations belonging to the family of civilized mankind, whether great or small, can develop freely, under equal conditions and in accordance with their natural capacity." But if the Allies retained their programme "the loftiest words on Peace Alliances and the harmonious coexistence of the family of nations are empty and void of meaning." The Chancellor concluded by saying: "The first condition for the development of international relations in the way of arbitration and the peaceful settlement of disputes would consist in the future avoidance of aggressive coalitions. Germany is ready at any moment to join or to lead a League of Nations designed to restrain disturbers of the peace." No doubt these words are partly prophetic; but we listen to them with an interest not unmixed with irritation. "To consider and co-operate—" surely that is too little. "To lead a League of Nations"—surely that is too much. In any case the League of Nations remains for the Chancellor a pawn in the Anglo-German controversy—which is natural enough in November 1916. Already, however, we can observe the imminence of the disaster which is inevitable unless a German leader takes his proper place in good time by the side of the American President, arousing national enthusiasm in the struggle for the coming League. Yet Bethmann-Hollweg was not blind to the ideas of the future; perhaps he was the last German statesman of the victorious phase who, although administering his high office in uniform, was capable of observing statesmanlike moderation in the face of a purely militaristic war policy. He was familiar with the Kantian Law which plagued him only because he possessed a conscience—a conscience which he tried to clear by an excess of frankness destined to be interpreted as cynicisms. But Bethmann-Hollweg was weak and inept. No doubt he had every right to stigmatize the aggressiveness of the enemy as the greatest obstacle in the way towards a League of Nations; but was he called upon to constitute himself the captious critic of a theory? The policy of the enemy was to stifle the idea of the League: why not adopt this idea in the name of his nation? Why not ally himself with the great German prophets, headed by Kant, who had already said more truly and profoundly all that Wilson could possibly say about the League? Or was he morally incapable of preaching an ideal of justice which was also an ideal of renunciation in a country hemmed in on every side and forgetful of everything except the necessities of war? The time was one when the Chancellor needed prophets; had they, who had a kind of life in the powerful pre-war Germany, lost all their lustre? Their modern successors at any rate were without influence; and Professor Walther Schücking, who had hoped that the third Hague Conference of 1915 would bring the World League of States, was instructed in the same year of 1915, by the Deputy G.O.C.I.C., Kassel, to refrain under pain of immediate imprisonment from giving written or oral utterance to his League of Nations ideas or to correspond with neutral scholars on the subject.

No—in this great struggle it was reserved to the neutrals and forbidden to the politicians of the belligerent States to give priority to an Utopian league over concrete terms of peace. Germany, like the rest, considered only the restoration of peace and her immediate interests, and at the utmost thought of providing some legal arrangements to continue the work of The Hague. Accordingly the German offer of peace which was issued on the 12th of December 1916, and in majestic language proclaimed Germany's victory and magnanimous readiness for peace, made no reference whatever to the League. But Wilson remained faithful to his ideal. A few days later, disturbed and irritated by the German step, he addressed to the belligerent States an official offer of peace which in fact

THE MESSIAH

was an offer of mediation. He was supported by almost all the neutrals. The offer began with the optimistic assumption that the belligerents were agreed on the necessity of founding a lasting universal peace organization; the only question which it asked was whether an agreement could be reached on other problems. A deep emotion and a profound hope went through the public opinion of the world; but the Allied Governments repulsed both these peace manifestos, and the German offer met only with furious ridicule. In the Senate Briand described it as an "act of war" and caused the Chamber to prepare a vote of confidence demanding the energetic prosecution of the war. The Russian Duma heard with enthusiasm a martial speech by the Foreign Minister Pokrovsky, who "indignantly declined to break off the struggle and to permit Germany to profit by a last hope of subjecting Europe to her domination." In England Lloyd George obtained power, described the German offer as a trap, and claimed in vigorous language, which he was later to regret when sitting face to face with Clemenceau, that peace was possible only if Germany accepted the Allied conditions. On the 2nd of January 1917 the Allies officially declared that they declined the German offer and would prosecute the war to a victorious conclusion. Ten days later Wilson and the neutral States received the reply to their own offer of mediation. While Germany professed herself ready for a Peace Conference (without, however, revealing the conditions), Briand, in the name of the ten Allied Governments (including Montenegro, which the other nine were later to wipe off the map), declared that peace negotiations were impossible and that the Allies were resolved to fight until they obtained the victory. Although Briand declined to reveal the war aims until the hour for negotiating should have come, he outlined a programme which not only demanded "just compensation and indemnities for all the damage inflicted," but also asked for "the restoration of Belgium, Serbia and Montenegro, the indemnities due to them, and the evacuation of the invaded regions of France, Russia and Roumania." He further demanded "a reorganization of Europe, which must be guaranteed by a stable regime and be based upon the respect for nationalities and for the rights of the great and small nations as well as upon territorial agreements, international arrangements guaranteeing land and sea frontiers against unwarranted assaults, and the restoration of the provinces formerly taken from the Allies by force or against the will of their populations; the liberation of Italians, Slavs, Roumanians, Czechs and Slovaks from foreign domination, and the freeing of populations subjected to the barbarous Turkish tyranny and the elimination from Europe of the Ottoman Empire, so alien to Western civilization." In this manifesto the liberation of Poland had to be content with the modest limits outlined in the proclamation of the Tsar to his Polish subjects; but in exchange the demand for the partition of Germany, long prepared in the Allied war literature, as well as the secret Franco-Russian Treaty, now first emerges behind the phrase that the Allies do not intend "to bring about the extirpation and the political disappearance of the German *peoples.*"

What can the prophet of Washington do with this reply, if he is honest? How can it lead to the necessary identity between the conclusion of peace and a lasting peace, and between the Peace Treaty and the Covenant of the League? The fact that England simultaneously issued an adroit flattery of the Wilsonian plan could afford little consolation.

Ten days after the Allied Note had been presented, on the 22nd of January 1917 Wilson spoke once again of his League of Peace, not before a private pacifist gathering, but before the Senate. Moreover, he spoke with remarkable confidence. Peace, he declared, must be built upon a new foundation; the American people would participate in this work, for the American people had long been prepared for this mission by the spirit informing the principles and aims of its Constitution, and the day of their fulfilment could not be long postponed.

The question of the moment simply was, under what conditions could the United States participate in a League of Peace; and therefore the Messiah once again outlined the foundations of peace based on a league. But this time he struck a louder note than before, and ignored the existence of difficulties. "The treaties and agreements which bring [the war] to an end must embody terms which will create a peace that is worth guaranteeing and preserving, a peace that will win the approval of mankind, not merely a peace that will serve the several interests and immediate aims of the nations engaged." As yet Wilson has a right to continue: "We shall have no voice in determining what those terms shall be," but, although he did not yet possess the power which in all probability he was already seeking, he resolutely continued: "But we shall, I feel sure, have a voice in determining whether they shall be made lasting or not by the guarantees of the universal covenant; and our judgment upon what is fundamental and essential as a condition precedent to permanency should be spoken now, not afterwards, when it may be too late." This once again implies the indissoluble nexus between the details of the impending peace and the organization of the impending League; and it also confirms the voluntary responsibility of America: "No Covenant of co-operative peace that does not include the peoples of the New World can suffice to keep the future safe against war; and yet there is only one sort of peace that the peoples of America could join in guaranteeing. . . . It will be absolutely necessary that a force be created as a guarantor of the permanency of the settlement, so much greater than the force of any nation now engaged, or any alliance hitherto formed or projected, that no nation, no probable combination of nations could face or withstand it. If the peace presently to be made is to endure, it must be a peace made secure by the organized major force of mankind." Can this peace emerge from the present war? That is the question of such vital importance for the future. "Is the present war a struggle for a just and secure peace, or only for a new balance of power? If it be only a struggle for a new balance of power, who will guarantee, who can guarantee, the stable equilibrium of the new arrangement?" And, with a warning and prophetic note, the President exclaims: "Only a tranquil Europe can be a stable Europe. There must be, not a balance of power, but a community of power; not organized rivalries, but an organized common peace." Hence the first condition of a League of Nations must be a "peace without victory." For in fact, "victory would mean peace forced upon the loser, a victor's term imposed upon the vanquished. It would be accepted in humiliation under duress at an intolerable sacrifice, and would leave a sting, a resentment, a bitter memory upon which terms of peace would rest, not permanently, but only as upon a quicksand. Only a peace between equals can last. Only a peace the very principle of which is equality and a common participation in a common benefit. The right state of mind, the right feeling between nations, is as necessary for a lasting peace as is the just settlement of vexed questions of territory, or of racial and national allegiance."

This speech contains all the fine principles which are destined to make the President famous and to haunt diplomatic documents and popular imagination in a hundred interpretations—most of the principles being as yet in the shape of general ideas, but some already applied practically. Great and small nations are to be equal before the law; the longing of mankind is turned towards the freedom to live and not towards the balance of power. No right can exist to transfer nations from one domination to the other, as though they were pieces of property; and hence the world is agreed that a united and independent Poland must be created and all populations must receive guarantees for the inviolable security of their life, worship and industrial and social development.

"Any peace which does not recognize and accept this principle will inevitably be upset. It will not rest upon the affections or the convictions of mankind. The ferment of spirit, of whole populations, will fight subtly and constantly against it, and all the world will sympathize. The world can be at peace only if its life is stable, and there can be no stability where the will is in rebellion, where there is no tranquillity of spirit, and a sense of justice, of freedom, and of right." Further, free access to the sea is demanded: "Where this cannot be done by the cession of territory it can no doubt be done by the neutralization of direct rights of way under the general guarantee." The American demand for the freedom of the seas, a desire shared by Germany, is outlined, and finally the most important principle of any peace based upon a League of Nations, that of the limitation of armaments, is formulated. "There can be no sense of safety and equality among the nations if great preponderating armaments are henceforth to continue here and there to be built up and maintained. . . . The question of armaments, whether on land or sea, is the most immediately and intensely practical question connected with the future fortunes of nations and of mankind."

Perhaps we are startled in places by the hyper-subtle manner of treating certain details. But let us stifle suspicion; for now comes the noblest and finest passage, the confession which we have been awaiting since the days of Napoleon. This passage will show us that the President is willing to be the long foretold fulfiller and powerful ruler who is ready also to be the trustee of nations. He speaks:

"I would fain believe that I am speaking for the silent mass of mankind everywhere who have as yet no place or opportunity to speak their real hearts out concerning the death, the ruin they see to have come already upon the persons and the homes they hold most dear." Once more he summarizes the American thesis in three "points" and finally exclaims: "These are American principles . . . we could stand for no others . . . they are principles of mankind and must prevail."

The speech draws to its end: President Wilson is destined never to deliver a finer; never will he proclaim the new law more effectively, more persuasively and more lucidly, and never, however his name might be reverenced at a later time, would his position be exalted more loftily above nations and rulers. And yet if we scrutinize him more carefully we may ask whether he still bears that clear and simple look which he wore at the great banquet. A kind of veil seems to surround him, although the veil can be pierced by a clear eye. True, the 665th day of war has passed—eighteen months have elapsed since that day. The war maps have not greatly changed, and the *communiqués* are much as they were a year and a half ago. On the eve of the speech the German report merely said: "All quiet on the Western Front; all quiet on the Eastern Front." However, eighteen months have passed: have they been working for the Allies, or for the Central Powers, or for the prophet? The promised League of Nations peace stands like a grandiose mystery among the realities of the moment; but it had been preceded by the Allied reply declining the peace negotiations and the conditions of peace which Wilson needed for his League, and it was to be followed by the declaration of unrestricted submarine warfare which was Germany's reply to the Allied resolve to carry on the war to victory, to the failure of her own peace offer, and to Wilson's efforts at mediation. Will the prophet succeed in realizing his dream?

He met the brutal, domineering gesture of the Allies more cordially than the evasive German note and replied with the pompous League of Nations speech. What would be his reply to the despairing brutality of the German gesture? The prophet of everlasting peace declared war on Germany.

CHAPTER IV

THE WOODEN HORSE

WHO is the powerful ruler who now withdraws from his leading position at the head of mankind to make himself the petulant chief of the greater alliance in order to crush the smaller? We must look at him narrowly, for the fate of the Great War may depend upon this man with the fanatic's mien.

Two enormous obstacles stood in the way of Wilson's programme of peace: the Allied will to conquer, and the will to conquer of the Central Powers. Could there also be two roads for a true prophet of a League of Nations? There was one, the natural method, by which the President could stand superior to the parties in order to control the League of Nations movement and to preserve its meaning and aim from the contaminations of a war-mazed world. The other method was bold and almost fantastic. If the will to conquer of the others threatened to eliminate his dream, the President might attempt himself to lead the conquerors. And indeed the belligerents were continually objecting—Balfour had replied to his last speech to that effect in as many words—that his programme was the dream of a neutral, while the Allies had to shed their blood in order to bring about a reality; and there were even minor neutral Powers who directed an insulting criticism at the greatest of the neutrals. Almost it was a disgrace not to be a belligerent; and if a neutral wished to control the war, he must exchange the convenient privileges of a neutral for the terrible privileges of the belligerents.

Was this to be Wilson's method? A dangerous resolution had to be taken, but once it had been taken there could be no doubt in which camp the prince of peace would plant his banner: even if he was still impartial and took his seat in the chariot of victory only in order to realize his ideal of peace, there could be no hesitation in his choice. The public opinion of his own country, the propagandist and moral influence exercised by British and French on American society, the unhappy fate of Belgium, and the geographical position of the United States all led him to side with the Allies. Yet it is hard to believe that his honourable and heroic path would lead from an urge towards the League of Nations into war, and from war, by cold and inhuman calculation, to the camp which interest indicated. Who can deny that a thoroughly American policy guided by economic, political and sentimental considerations had been tending towards war on the side of the Allies? In any case it was clear that if the President desired to participate in a war from nationalist motives, it was his duty to place before the nation a war ideal worthy of the history and mentality of North America. A nation swayed by a multitude of tendencies—not excluding pro-German tendencies, having nothing in common with the territorial causes and war aims of Europe, having other sources of revenue than the supply of munitions to the Allies, and looking at the great events across the ocean through the spectacles of simple ideals —had to be prepared for entry into war. It might be inferred that Wilson's latest neutral League of Nations speech was in fact a war programme conveying to the Allies not the conditions of peace, but the conditions of an entry into war. It might further be inferred that his first speech before the League for compulsory peace was the first step in an attempt to prepare his countrymen for an active, and perhaps for a warlike, mission in the Great War, destined to lead up, after his re-election, to an entry into a camp which had long been selected. In that case a cold and calculating policy of national interest was the ultimate reason why the discussion of a League of Nations plan by a pacifist society was made the occasion of seizing upon this plan and, instead of allowing it to be forgotten, erecting it into the political programme of a great ruler and a great nation. But, whether its origins were to be looked for in the heart or the head, and whether it was a ruse or an ideal, the American plan now occupied the centre of the stage and implied an obligation to hold fast until the final redemption of the promise. Whether the idea of participating in the war was a part of national policy, or the desperate attempt to fulfil an international duty, the American war was now a factor in world history. The plan for the League of Nations and the war are the two aspects of one divinity.

And now the prophet, who, on the 22nd of January, had so carefully enumerated the postulates of a peace embodying a League of Nations, came before Congress in order to enumerate the postulates for the defeat of Germany. The man who had spoken in the name of the silent masses of the world now proceeded to stimulate the national will to war like any Allied propagandist by skilfully exaggerating the German injuries. He attempted to drive even the other neutrals into war. The Apostle of a righteous peace preaches a war on behalf of right because right is more precious than peace; and for words about peace without victory the demand for a decisive victory is substituted. While a neutral, the Allies had been facing Wilson with suspicion and aversion; will he succeed in imposing upon them his League of Nations? And, above all, the conditions of peace which were the condition of a League of Nations, now that he is a powerful associate? Surrounded by the military leaders of an alliance eager to exterminate its enemies, can he remain the trustee of all the nations? Is not his League of Nations likely to resemble a wooden horse filled with armed men which it will be the function of Wilson to introduce into the enemy fortress? In the whole of our journey, this is the most tragic point. We see with terrible clearness what we knew long ago—that the fate of Germany is closely allied to the fate of the League of Nations. Hundreds of prophets had devised leagues among the nations, but not one programme had excluded Germany; and Wilson's ideal had included Germany more definitely than the visions of the other seers. Now that the prophet is among the warriors, we feel that Germany can no longer win, and with this conviction is coupled the doubt whether the League of Nations will prove an asset to the world. The President launches his wooden horse at the head of the Allied tanks against the German trenches, and in so doing he expels Germany from the diminished League of Nations.

For the moment indeed tanks were more interesting to Wilson than peace. He had dropped the part of neutral mediator, which for the time being passed to the Pope, and it was the latter who made a last attempt on the 1st of August 1917 to obtain for the silent peoples the peace without victory which had once been proclaimed by Wilson. But where the most powerful of temporal rulers among the neutrals had failed, the spiritual power was not likely to be successful. It its reply the German Government expressed "particular sympathy for the leading idea in the message of peace in which His Holiness voiced the clear conviction that in future the weapons of the moral power of right must be substituted for material power," and it further agreed to "definite rules and securities for a simultaneous and mutual limitation of armaments by land, water and in the air," and to the idea that "international differences of opinion should be decided by peaceful methods, specially by that of arbitration, instead of by an appeal to arms." On the other hand, the most violent opposition to his attempt at mediation came from the previous mediator. Wilson angrily exclaimed, in almost the same words which the Allies had once addressed to him, that agreements with the present Governments of the Central Powers were necessarily superfluous and could lead to no lasting peace. "The object of this war is to deliver the free peoples of the world from the menace and the actual power of a vast military establishment controlled by an irresponsible Government which, having secretly planned to dominate the world, proceeded to carry the plan out without regard . . . to the sacred obligations of treaties."

The President adopted the Allied views on the origin of the war and its methods, although only a few months ago he had admitted that all Governments were acting in good faith and inspired by good will and had described it as his privilege to

THE WOODEN HORSE 51

sound a note of impartial truth. But even in the intoxication of war he was unwilling to forget the general foundations of peace without which a League of Nations was impossible. It was indeed merely one of a growing number of ruses when he established a distinction between the German people and its rulers, claiming that it was impossible to negotiate with the latter and undesirable to inflict reprisals on the former. Yet in principle he remained true to his programme. If he repeated once more: "Punitive damages, the dismemberment of empires, the establishment of selfish and exclusive economic leagues, we deem inexpedient and in the end worse than futile, no proper basis for a peace of any kind, least of all for an enduring peace. That must be based upon justice and fairness and the common rights of mankind." But in spite of every endeavour to introduce his old principles into the new policy of war, each successive speech was a more unscrupulous surrender of the essential principle of peace without victory. A speech delivered at Buffalo before the American Federation of Labour on the 12th of November 1917 contained a violent outburst against the dreamers in Russia who were trying to desert the Allied cause; and the idol of the pacifists contemptuously exclaimed: "What I am opposed to is not the feeling of the pacifists but their stupidity. My heart is with them, but my mind has a contempt for them. I want peace, but I know how to get it and they do not."

But the Russian dreamers seized power; and from Tsarskoe Selo Lenin and Trotsky addressed their dangerous rousing call to the belligerent nations: "Down with the winter campaign! Long live peace and fraternity among the nations!" Such sentiments meant a dangerous competition for the President, who was compelled to continue his propaganda campaign against a premature peace and against the German rulers with redoubled violence. In his annual address to Congress on the 4th of December the President voiced his disquiet by attacking the American minority which tried to bring about peace by any compromise, and against the deception of the peoples through formulae like "No annexations, no indemnities," which, so he alleged, were being used by German plotters to deceive the Russian people and to bring about a premature peace.

"Our present and immediate task is to win the war and nothing shall turn us aside from it until it is accomplished." He enunciated concrete conditions of peace going beyond the evacuation of Belgium and Northern France, and demanded the liberation of the peoples of Austria-Hungary, the Balkans and Turkey from the insolent military and economic domination of Prussia. The League of Nations was mentioned only in order to threaten Germany with exclusion; for, although it was admitted that the people had been deceived by its Government and must not be punished, and although no threat was intended to its existence, independence, or peaceful enterprise, it might yet be impossible to admit them to the partnership of nations which must henceforth guarantee the world's peace, should they continue to be obliged to live under ambitious and intriguing masters. "That partnership must be a partnership of peoples, not a mere partnership of Governments."

Meanwhile negotiations commenced at Brest-Litovsk between Germany and Russia, which eventually broke down because the German terms in the East amount to a dictated peace. Once more a decisive opportunity has arisen for the intellectual leader of the Allies to exploit the appeal of his rhetoric and the brilliance of his dialectics. He sides with the Russian dreamers, defending them against the aggressive policy of the Central Powers, and attempting to win over the Russian and with it the German people which, at heart, wants no dictated peace and least of all a dictated peace directed against Russia. Such is the genesis of the most renowned of his great speeches, the one delivered before Congress on the 8th of January and containing the famous Fourteen Points which are an attempt at a compromise between the spirit of peace mediation of December 1916 and the great speech on Allied war aims of

January 1917. A gentler note may now be observed. The demands are: (1) open diplomacy; (2) the freedom of the seas; (3) the abolition of all economic barriers and inequalities; (4) suitable guarantees that national armaments shall be reduced to the minimum compatible with *internal* security; (5) free and impartial arrangement of colonial claims, with due consideration of the interests of the native population; (6) evacuation of all Russian territories and, somewhat vaguely, a regulation of all Russian questions in order to assure for Russia a sincere reception into the league of free nations; (7) the restoration of Belgium in its full independence; (8) the evacuation of occupied French territory; and reparation of the injury done to France in 1871 with regard to Alsace-Lorraine—it being left undecided whether this restoration is to consist in a restoration of these districts, or in a plebiscite; (9) adjustment of the Italian frontier—to which Austria was ready to agree in 1915—a demand softened by the provision that these alterations are to be made according to clearly distinguishable lines of nationality; (10) free development of the Austro-Hungarian peoples, which theoretically could be completed without a partition of the monarchy, and in fact did not prevent the Austro-Hungarian Government from giving a friendly reply to Wilson's declaration; (11) evacuation of Roumania, Serbia and Montenegro, free and secure access to the sea for Serbia, and certain arrangements in the Balkans. This point was formulated cautiously; (12) possibilities of independent development for the non-Turkish peoples within the Turkish empire—a point which, in its general formulation, might appear acceptable; (13) the formation of an independent Polish State. Here it is expressly stated that all regions having an undeniably Polish population must be included. This point again is compatible with an ideal policy of peace, provided that the demand for Polish access to the sea does not lead to any annexationist movement. Finally, the fourteenth point must meet with the approval of the entire world, for it is this point which provides for a League of Nations—"a general association of nations . . . under specific covenants for the purpose of affording mutual guarantees of political independence and territorial integrity to great and small States alike."

But the moment which Wilson considered practicable and appropriate for the promulgation of this programme was one of political and military superiority for the Central Powers, and it is hard to believe that Wilson could hope for a moment that his plan would be adopted *in toto* by the German Government. It contained the principles of a peace by negotiation; but its practical applications presupposed an Allied victory and were blind to any interest save theirs. For Germany it was a programme of renunciation acceptable only in a moment of defeat; accepted now it could only hasten that moment. It was the wooden horse which was being slowly advanced under the walls of the enemy fortress.

Admittedly a statesmanlike appreciation of the hollowness and dangers of the military advantages of the moment might have induced the Germans to initiate a full-dress debate in order to expand the programme of the Fourteen Points, and to illuminate its foundations and applications, including those advantageous to Germany. But given the military mentality of the moment, could any voluntary sacrifice be expected from a powerful State? Did Wilson dream of building up his own principles on a foundation of Allied sacrifices? No doubt the movement in favour of a just peace had grown more powerful in Germany as a concomitant of internal developments. A peace resolution adopted by the majority parties of the Reichstag, headed by Matthias Erzberger on the 20th of July 1917, advocated a peace of lasting reconciliation among the nations, rejected compulsory surrender of territories, and political, economic or financial sanctions, and saluted, however distantly and timidly, the idea of a League of Nations by declaring that the Reichstag would vigorously support the formation of international legal organizations. But although this resolution deprecated annexations on the part of Germany and was referred to with satisfaction by Wilson, none of its supporters

THE WOODEN HORSE 55

could seriously think for a moment of permitting the enemy to annex German territory on any principle, however plausible. Count Hertling, the third Chancellor of the war, a professor like Wilson, but, unlike Wilson, an unimaginative pedant, could hardly be expected to do other than to avoid grappling with the Fourteen Points and to display readiness for peace while keeping a firm grip on the fruits of victory. Obviously he had to agree to the idea of a League of Nations which would obviate the possibility and probability of wars and would promote the peaceful and harmonious coexistence of the nations; but he displayed merely perverted cunning when he added: "If a closer examination of the detail of President Wilson's idea of a League of Nations shows that it was drawn up in a spirit of justice and complete lack of prejudice towards all, His Majesty's Government will be ready to examine the principles of such a League after settling all the pending questions."

Clearly such meaningless phrases were of no use to Wilson. On the other hand, he was himself in the thick of war now and could hardly expect anything else. His real task would have been to draw the enemy to his side and to continue a conversation in which Hertling was willing to participate. In fact he obviously deprecated a favourable development of the conversation; in his reply before Congress on the 11th of February he displayed unnecessary irritation and haughtiness and, while brusquely rejecting Hertling's arguments, gave the Austro-Hungarian Minister a good mark, thus showing that he was not so much concerned to compose differences between his own and the enemy group as to exacerbate the difference between Germany and her Allies which long had been the hope of the Allied Powers. At the same time he flung a new set of Four Points across the ocean. The first emphasized that the future arrangements must render possible a permanent peace; the second demanded that nations and provinces must not be transferred from one Government to the other as though they were inanimate objects or pawns in a game. "The peoples and provinces are not to be bartered about from sovereignty to sovereignty as if they were mere chattels and pawns in a game." The third set up the principle that "every territorial settlement involved in this way must be made in the interest and for the benefit of the populations concerned, and not as a part of any mere adjustment or compromise of claims amongst rival States." The fourth demanded "that all well-defined national aspirations shall be accorded the utmost satisfaction that can be accorded them without introducing new or perpetuating old elements of discord and antagonism that would be likely in time to break the peace of Europe and consequently of the world."

Hertling responded, but clothed his concurrence in stiff and controversial phraseology to which Wilson on this occasion turned a deaf ear; his object being not to reach an agreement with Hertling, but to impress the German masses. For this reason his solemn address at Washington's Tomb at Mount Vernon on the 4th of July 1918 was yet another attack on the old-fashioned Governments of the Central Powers, coupled with flattery for the Central peoples. He proceeded to juggle with a fresh set of Four Points, demanding (1) the destruction, or at least the elimination, of every autocratic power; (2) (expressed with particular vigour) the right of national self-determination; (3) legal foundations for the coexistence of the nations and the respect of treaties; and (4) "The establishment of an organization of peace which shall make it certain that the combined power of free nations will check every invasion of right and serve to make peace and justice the more secure by affording a definite tribunal of opinion to which all must submit and by which every international readjustment that cannot be amicably agreed upon by the peoples directly concerned shall be sanctioned."

Meanwhile the war was drawing to an end; and the idea of a League of Nations, despite its Utopian appearance, was gradually and by devious ways filtering through the world, finding a place in the talk and diaries of soldiers, and becoming the object of numerous drafts and pamphlets, some of them excellent. It was even becoming a subject for Government manifestoes, and some Governments, e.g. the French and the British, considered it advisable to make it the object of official investigations. In fact, however, the League was only an instrument of war for the Allies and their American prophet; for them it was a piece of propaganda for internal and external consumption, while for the Germans it was an object of distrust, the devilish invention of the enemy, designed first to isolate and weaken the Central Powers, and later—if ever the League became a reality—to fetter them politically and economically. In fact, everybody looked to the League to bring victory to his side and nobody to bring salvation to mankind; all had the will to believe in it—and to enforce their will upon the others. A weakening of resistance on one side, far from inducing peaceful sentiments on the other, merely hardened the will to win. Already plans had been devised on every side which the conclusion of peace was to realize. The military and civil leaders of Germany allowed doubts about the future of Belgium to persist far too long, and after the collapse of Russia pursued a fantastic Eastern policy which could find no place in a League of Nations. The Allies had seized Germany's international communications and her colonial empire, and felt no desire to surrender these acquisitions. Complete defeat alone would induce France to conclude a peace which did not restore Alsace-Lorraine, a region which, until the day of its restoration, a poetically exalted public opinion insisted on treating as a part of France compulsorily Germanized. A whole series of secret treaties and obligations bound the Allies to effect numerous other annexations of German territory, to partition Austria, Hungary and Germany, and even to interfere with the life of Allied and neutral States like Persia; and their anarchical madness formed a gloomy contrast to Wilson's bright plans of organization. A few years after the end of the war the President's close collaborator, Baker, was to complete the revelations of the Russian Revolution, and in his memoirs and documents of the Versailles period to reveal the sinister effect of the

Allied war aims policy on Wilson's development, pointing an indignant finger at all the secret treaties which formed the hidden accompaniment to Wilson's public speeches—the France-Anglo-Russian agreement of 1916, which was to ensure for Russia the possession of Constantinople and for Britain certain Turkish possessions as well as advantages in Persia; the Treaty of London of the same date, which purchased Italian participation in the war by territorial concessions in Dalmatia and Tyrol, and by promises of Colonial acquisitions; the Treaty of 1916, which promised Austro-Hungarian territory, with a Serbian population, to Roumania, a territory which Serbia herself had long been claiming; the arrangement made in 1917 between France and Russia, which was to assure the return of Alsace-Lorraine to France, as well as the frontier of the old "principality" of Lorraine, and besides assuring her of the Sarre basin, was to detach the left bank of the Rhine from Germany and arrange for its French occupation until Germany fulfilled her treaty obligations, while the Russians were to be allowed complete freedom of action along their German and Austrian frontiers; and the agreement reached in the same year between Britain and Japan at the cost of China on the division of the German Far-Eastern possessions, the remaining German colonies having already been distributed among the Allies.

"Turkey was by all odds the richest spoil of the war," R. Stannard Baker declares; "the most illuminating of all the exhibits of the old diplomacy—the group of 'secret treaties,' 'arrangements' and 'conversations.'" And he discovers with disgust that the secret negotiations on the subject of Turkey did not cease even with the entry of the United States into the war, or with the acceptance of the Fourteen Points with their precautions against secret diplomacy, or with agreement on Point 12 on Turkey: "The secret conversations . . . kept right on."

Could such war aims be realized otherwise than by a radical victory? Certainly they made impossible the formation of the

THE WOODEN HORSE 59

League of Nations between the European Powers as they existed before the peace. A few weeks before the end of the war Matthias Erzberger gave a skilful if tardy description of the tragic position in a hasty propagandist work entitled *Der Völkerbund*, which outlined an excellent German plan for a League of Nations. "The Allies want a league to stabilize their political and economic predominance; they wish to ensure peace by using such a league as an instrument to enforce their conditions on the other Powers; they want peace through a league dominated by one group of Powers. In Germany too there are circles which consider that the best guarantee for peace would be a German hegemony. . . . They are the same circles who discredit the idea of the League by pointing to its abuse by the Allies, although their aims are the same as those of the Allied propagandists. The principle on which the League is based is the complete equality of nations and their subjection to the same conditions. It is built on the principle of reciprocity, and it becomes meaningless and is doomed to extinction as soon as it is used to ensure the domination of a Power or group of Powers. . . . History shows that all attempts to ensure peace by universal empires have been failures costly in blood. Let us learn the lesson of history."

Could the nations still learn this lesson? Germany gradually had realized that it was to her advantage to negotiate for an equitable peace even at the height of her military power; but for the Allies, in spite of partial relapses or collapses among some of their members, the road to such a peace became progressively more impassable. American support had electrified them; and the war had become the care of a multitude of vested interests. For the Allies a peace by negotiation would have meant a draw, with the painful result that Germany, in spite of some losses, would occupy a position of enormous preponderance amounting to a practical victory. A League of Nations worthy of the name depended on the realization of a single possibility: given the mental disposition of the belligerents, including the Americans, the formation of the League must be preceded by a war of exhaustion, equally weakening both sides and inspiring both sides with an equal desire for peace and even for sacrifices. If neither side was willing or able to lay down arms until the enemy had admitted defeat, the League of Nations would have to depend upon one slender hope, namely, that the winning side would not prove to be men who, in Rousseau's words, "are unjust and greedy, and put their own interests before everything," but that they would have "enough intelligence to understand their own advantage and enough courage to be the architects of their own happiness."

Would Wilson encourage or attempt to compel the nations in this direction? For the last time during the war he outlines his idea of peace against the hopeless background (27th of September 1918): "The constitution of that League of Nations and the clear definition of its objects," so the President, after violent attacks, assured the Governments of the Central Powers, "must be a part, is in a sense the most essential part of the peace settlement itself." He adds, reasonably enough: "It cannot be formed now. If formed now it would be merely a new alliance confined to the nations associated against a common enemy." He wisely adds: "It is not likely that it could be formed after a settlement. It is necessary to guarantee the peace; and the peace cannot be guaranteed as an after-thought." This is the sane and statesmanlike language of peace. The President becomes more aggressive when he insists, "to speak in plain terms again," that peace must be guaranteed because "there will be parties to the peace whose promises have proved untrustworthy, and means must be found in connection with the peace settlement itself to remove that source of insecurity." The nexus between League and peace has ceased to be a fundamental necessity of the League and has become a measure directed against Germany; for, "it would be folly to leave the guarantee to the subsequent voluntary action of the Governments we have seen destroy Russia and deceive Roumania." Here there is a hostile note: the League has become a threat and a penalty for the enemy. Soon, however, there follow five fundamental points worthy of Wilson's best period. First, he tells us "The impartial justice meted out must involve no discrimination between those to whom we wish to be just and those to whom we do not wish to be just." There must be justice "that knows no standard but the equal right of the several peoples concerned." Next, "no special or separate interests of any single nation or any group of nations can be made the basis of any part of the settlement which is not consistent with the common interest of all." Thirdly, the President condemns "Leagues or alliances or special covenants within the general and common family of the League of Nations," while, fourthly, "there can be no special selfish economic combinations within the League, and no employment of any form of economic boycott or exclusion except . . . as economic penalties by exclusion from the markets of the world may be vested in the League of Nations as a means of discipline and control." Fifthly, "all international agreements and treaties of every kind must be made known . . . to the rest of the world," it being added that "special alliances and economic rivalries and hostilities have been the prolific source in the modern world of the plans and passions that produce war. It would be an insincere as well as an insecure peace that did not exclude them in definite and binding terms." There is nothing new here, but the outlines of a true peace based upon a League are clearly drawn.

May we hope once again? What is the meaning of such promises on this 27th of September 1918? On this day the world of navies, armies, trenches, mines, cannons and machine guns, in which millions of men have been living for four years, was shaking in its foundations. The second Battle of the Marne had ended in the failure of the German offensive. Every hour could bring fresh American troops to the French front. Austria-Hungary's desire for peace was well known, and the internal devastation caused among the peoples of the Central Powers by the blockade could no longer be kept a secret. The 27th of September, on which Wilson raised his voice once more, was the beginning of the end. On this day Bulgaria withdrew from her alliance with the Central Powers, and on the following day the German High Command, much against its will, resolved, jointly with Austria and Turkey, to address an offer of armistice to the President, at the same time appealing to his Fourteen Points. Wilson had been waiting for this moment. The new Chancellor, Max von Baden, after a first refusal to sue for peace in such unfavourable circumstances, addressed a note to Wilson on the 3rd of October, in which he solemnly declared that Germany accepted the programme outlined by the President of the United States in his message to Congress on the 8th of January 1918, and in his later speeches, notably that of the 27th of September, as a basis for peace negotiations. The President was requested to bring about the conclusion of a general armistice and a permanent peace. The war period had ended; the period of the League of Nations must begin.

For three years the President had been launching his formulae across the ocean. Three Points, Four Points, Fourteen Points, Four Points, and again Five Points, adapted to varying circumstances and the various aims of the moment, they had flashed high above a struggling world like rockets and sometimes like soap bubbles, only to end in nothing. Now they had become the great and visible pillar of fire leading from war to peace. The Fourteen Points of the 8th of January, as well as the Five Points of the 27th of September, form a bright constellation among the dark confusion in which the various German authorities had been struggling with each other since the collapse of the Balkan front. In the light of this constellation the conflict of opinions urging an armistice on the one hand and a continuation of the war on the other is appeased. If the German nation were faced only by men like Clemenceau, it would resolve to gather all its forces and to pursue the war to the bitter end: its resolve to confess the cause of peace is inseparably connected with the existence of Wilson; and if it was hard to give up long-cherished dreams, there was hope too in the American promises. Hitherto Wilson had been suspect; there was now an unbounded will to believe in him, who had suddenly been identified with reason and courage. Hence there was as yet no feeling of unconditional surrender in Germany; the request for peace was being addressed, not to the French or British, but to the apostle of peace conditions under a League of Nations; these conditions had contributed to prepare the nation for peace; they had been reaffirmed, and it was to their author, towards the trustee of the nations, that Germany turned a face ravaged by war and starvation.

Was Wilson once again standing above the parties? At this moment he stood between them, his back to the Allies and his front toward the Germans. His task was difficult, for he was unwilling to surrender his victory or his programme of peace. As leader in a warlike cause, his first care was to assure practically a theoretical victory, and to dispense peace thereafter. Hence the unparalleled exchange of conversations between the American Secretary of State and the Wilhelmstrasse.

Wilson promised the bewildered Germans that his principles as publicly announced would form the foundation of the peace; but in exchange he took from them piece by piece the power which they possessed, deprived them of their conquests, territories, their arms, and their ruling house and, slowly and methodically, induced a state and a feeling of defeat where defeat had been unknown hitherto. Simultaneously his ideals were launched against the country and broke down the last will to resistance among the populace. This aim was pursued ruthlessly and dispassionately. On the 8th of October he enquired of the Chancellor whether the German Government accepted the President's conditions as laid down in his Congress message of the 8th of January and in subsequent messages, and whether the sole purpose of an entry into discussions would be to reach agreement on practical details of application. The Chancellor agreed, but assumed that the Governments of the Powers associated with the United States likewise accepted the principles of the President's manifestoes; and now the first harsh conditions of an Armistice were introduced into this fundamental question of peace. Wilson turned a deaf ear to this essential assumption, and, using the German acceptance of his principles in order to revert to his speech of the 4th of July, demanded the reduction to practical impotence of every autocratic Power possessing the opportunity of destroying generally, secretly, and at its whim, the peace of the world. Did he intend to carry out his threat of war? At any rate he let it be clearly understood that he was expecting internal upheavals in Germany, and that a thorough realization of peace was conditional on them. The Germans were compelled in reply to come before the head of an alien State with praises of their brand-new system of parliamentary democracy. When Wilson bluntly demanded the resignation of the Kaiser, since otherwise there could be no question of negotiations for peace and Germany would have to surrender at discretion, the Government humbly pointed to the profound changes taking place in the German constitution, and from this abasement proceeded to hint that it was now looking forward to Armistice suggestions leading up to a just peace as outlined in the Presidential manifestos. Germany was broken. On the 5th of November Wilson spoke the last and decisive word. He cabled that the Allies had taken into careful consideration the exchange of notes between the President of the United States and the German Government and that with two provisos, one relating to the freedom of the seas and the other relating to the German obligation for reparations, they were ready to conclude peace with the German Government on the basis laid down in the Congress address of the 8th of January 1918, and in the later speeches of the President. At the same time, however, the German Government was required to send accredited representatives to learn the conditions of an Armistice from Marshal Foch.

The strange deal was concluded: Germany surrendered, but Wilson reaffirmed his points in the name of all the Allies. In the eyes of Germany and of the world his obligation was clear. While the transatlantic conversations were in progress, Max von Baden had explained the position before the Reichstag; at that time, in order to make intelligible the impending sacrifices, he had solemnly declared: "The League of Nations is the core of the President's programme, and it can never be realized unless all the nations rouse themselves to an act of self-abnegation. The realization of a community of nations demands of us as well as of others a surrender of some of the complete independence which hitherto has been the symbol of national sovereignty." With eloquent words the Chancellor attempted to explain to a nation which had been on the verge of victory that rehabilitation and reconstruction were possible only if national egoism "until recently the dominant force in the life of nations" was surrendered. However, he cautiously added: "If in this heavy moment I try to draw consolation and new force for the nation from the idea of the League, yet I do not wish for a moment to obscure the serious obstacles that must be overcome before the idea can be realized." The struggle for the League had ended; but the League still remained to be created, and to be created in the promised form. From now onwards the Germans had the first right to demand a true League of Nations.

While the monarchy was collapsing in Germany the latest German prophet of the League, Matthias Erzberger, was facing the French Marshal in the forest of Compiègne with melancholy eagerness. At this moment—to anticipate a later description by the Foreign Minister, Brockdorff-Rantzau—the idea of the League of Nations seemed to the German armistice delegation to constitute the primary guarantee for a new order in the world. Was Foch thinking of the League of Nations? His only aim was to crush the defenceless enemy compelled to sign his conditions. Did Wilson think of the League of Nations? On this 11th of November on which the "Cease fire" was sounded on every front, and men spoke of peace again, the prophet, with the applause of the world ringing in his ears, delivered yet one more speech before Congress. But he did not enumerate either his old or any new points. He confined himself to some general assurances that the peace desired by the victorious nations would satisfy the longing of the whole world for unselfish justice; and the points which he triumphantly enumerated were those of the French Commander-in-Chief, and contained no mention of a League of Nations. Having completed his enumeration, he looked up from his sheet, gravely surveyed the assembly, and solemnly added: "The war thus comes to an end, for, having accepted these terms of Armistice, it will be impossible for the German command to renew it."

CHAPTER V

THE WAR VICTIM

WHO is the victorious ruler, before whom the whole world is bowing down in admiration? We must carefully scrutinize him, for the fate of the world peace will depend upon this man with the obstinate and irritable mien.

However cold and rigid were the formulae which had flashed from the State Department into the Wilhelmstrasse, the pact which he had once concluded with an indeterminate and nameless world had now been solemnly confirmed between the President and the German nation. Foch, advancing behind the Fourteen and the Four Points, had no difficulty in consolidating his military successes by the easy advance to the Rhine, for his successes had been prepared by American power and American ideology, and his vanguard still consisted in the Fourteen and the Four Points which had made Germany ripe for surrender. The victory had been won by the League of Nations. The military pomps which went to the occupation of Alsace-Lorraine and the Rhineland were arm-chair heroics: the front line was held by the League. Some of these facile conquerors of Germany were soon to raise the petulant and insolent complaint that the pen was spoiling what the sword had won; they had forgotten what every one knew in November 1918—that the pen was aiding the sword as much as the sword was aiding the pen; the last victory lay with the pen, and this victory was now to be marred by the sword.

It could not well be otherwise. From the moment in which the American President, who had wanted to make the peace, allowed the Armistice to be made by the French Marshal, he became as poor as the Germans. The Germans had only his word, and the President had only the word of the Associated Powers. What did he need in order, "with reason and courage," to be victorious over the victory? As a neutral he had required the good will of both parties, and he had not found it. As a belligerent he had required internal neutrality, and this he had been unable to preserve, perhaps because he had never possessed it. As victor he required enemies strong enough to ensure that the method of negotiation and mutual understanding would be followed, and Allies who would be shaken enough to prefer a cessation of hostilities to later and doubtful successes. Both were now wanting, for he had destroyed both. Each American regiment landing in France and reducing the danger of a German victory inevitably reduced the prospects of what will always have to be called the true League of Nations. Having connived at the monstrous Armistice, he was the prisoner of his success, and of his French Allies into whose hands he inevitably surrendered the victory by surrendering the German nation which had trusted him. With the Allies the huge and protracted loss of life soon began to weigh more heavily than the eleventh-hour assistance of the United States, which soon came to be thought of as a mere moral and economic entity. The American soldiers as well as the American doctrines had become superfluous; and the French, having seized the military command of the Allied forces, began to seize the command over the diplomats at the Peace Conference. But if Wilson did not remain master of the Peace Treaty he could not remain master of the League, the two, according to his own doctrine, being indissolubly connected. On the day on which Wilson's points definitively destroyed the German armies, and left the Allied forces as sole supporters of the future League, the League lost its founder—and the founder lost the League army which it is wanting to this day.

Yet surely the President is still rich and strong. If he can no longer rely upon his military power or impose his wish upon the Allied Governments, surely he still exercises an overpowering influence upon the nations, still holds their loyal and trusting attention. May we not hope that the silent masses will become vocal at last and support their former spokesman with a loud call for true and lasting peace? The

President for his part, when crossing the Atlantic in order to transfer the headquarters of peace to the headquarters of the Armistice, may have been counting on such support. Perhaps the adulation and flattery which met him in Paris seemed to be the true voice of the nations; perhaps the narrow nationalist demands which were laid down before him in a thousand petitions seemed to be the solid manifestation of popular trust. In fact, however, the peoples were deaf to the President and the President was deaf to the peoples. Between himself and the masses a wall was built by the Governments which hid from him the few advanced and honest men who tried to recall to the President his mission and to issue a warning against his partners in diplomacy. But the President remained caught in the web of official celebrations, and behind those walls the peoples of the Allied nations remained silent as before, dominated by the methods of censorship and tyranny, propaganda and discipline, which during the war had been used to stifle their longing for peace. Their ideas remained identical with those of their Governments, of whose unclean war aims they were as yet ignorant. At the same time they were living the intoxicating hour of victory, and this victory, which during his neutral period Wilson had always perceived to be an obstacle in the way of his plans and which had been his most violent opponent during his negotiations with the Allied Governments, became a savage enemy when he addressed himself to the nations. The duration of the war, the fact that the greater part of the world had participated in it, that every nation had been involved in it at the front, in the factory and in the home, that it had drained every physical and intellectual force—had everywhere induced a dangerous state of nervous tension. It might serve the cause of lasting peace if the universal longing for peace were imported in its unadulterated state into the peace negotiations. But to calm and cure the shattered nerves of the nations there must be a clear transition from the state of war to the state of peace; instead, the war not only ended with the victory of one side, in itself a disaster, but it brought with it a sensationally rapid change from victory to defeat; and this was a catastrophe. The disease, instead of ending quietly, culminated in a feverish paroxysm. At one stroke the Allied nations, and more particularly France, Belgium, Serbia and Roumania, were raised from utter darkness to a dazzling light, which showed them, whose countries had recently been occupied by the enemy, the advance of their own armies across the hostile frontiers and moving without resistance along the road to Vienna and Budapest, to Strasbourg, and perhaps to Munich and Berlin. Such a victory of supererogation, with all its pomp, its celebrations of liberation, its music and its military splendour, soon shed a brighter radiance on the war aims of the Allied Governments and dimmed the pacifist ideal which had been the support of hours of depression.

The bygone sufferings of this war no longer seemed the inevitable concomitants of every war but the particular troubles of this particular war; the insane international anarchy now appeared to be merely the lunatic caprice of the enemy. The day of peace no longer was the day which ended a war, and the victory was not an escape from threatening danger. On the contrary, it constituted a temptation and a terrible opportunity for abusing the hour of fortune to practise vengeance. The enemy was to suffer for his defeat, or rather, not for his defeat but for a victory which must never be allowed to recur; France, Belgium and all the others were intent to exact payment, not for their victory, but for defeats which must never be allowed to happen again. Woe to the victor vanquished at length was the cry of the victors of the last quarter of an hour, mindful of the four last years. Could the Prophet of the League look for help from these nations?

Meanwhile the Germans had grown ready and more than ready for Wilson's plans. Like the other defeated nations, they had gone through the opposite metamorphosis, the terrific revulsion from victory to defeat. They had fallen from the high estate which the treacherous maps with their flags in France, Belgium, Poland, Russia, the Balkans and the East seemed to

THE WAR VICTIM 71

reflect, and a different paroxysm was threatening them—
revolution, the disease of conquered nations. During the months
which passed before, the Armistice having been signed, the
Allies sat down together to construct their peace, the Germans
were in a dazed state and wavered between the past and an
unknown future. They knew that their ground for hope was
slight, they waited in trepidation and confusion; and yet they
felt a certain confidence. A new era ought to and must commence. Could there be any other compensation for so much
misfortune and misery? The war, now it had definitively been
lost, was cast off like a garment torn in the storm, and the
nation renewed itself by revolution, socialism and pacifism.
In the midst of revolts, starvation and heroic if sporadic revul-
sions against the humiliating end of the war, the majority,
busying itself with the new State and the internal change of
spirit, counted upon the justice of the outside world. The
frontiers were open and the nation disarmed; their only
bulwark, a bulwark which seemed to them almost insur-
mountable, consisted in an exchange of telegrams between the
American and the German Governments on the Fourteen and
the Four Points. Wilson became an ideal figure, regarded with
almost the same trust as Hindenburg and Ludendorff. Confident in the common sense of the enemy, the Germans assumed
that the latter would join them against the threat of Bolshevism
in the same way in which, in July 1914, they had relied upon
the solidarity of the European dynasties with the Habsburgs
against the Serbian assassinators. Realizing what was lost
for good they renounced the Kaiser and the Imperial splendour,
Alsace-Lorraine, and the old flag, and turned to such consola-
tions as might afford them strength and self-confidence—
republican ideas, the dream of a union with German Austria,
and the League. But their clearest experience was that of the
peace, clearest because it was purified by bitterness and undisturbed by shouts of victory; peace without politics, without
calculation and without gain, bare peace which, whatever it
might bring, must be better than the hell of war. However

uncertain the future might be, it was possible to work and hope again, to live and feel like human beings, to breathe a free air, to move freely, and to forget the past. Surely the others whom success allowed to be generous would forget; former enemies would be able to clasp hands, and to work forward together into the future. Was anyone in Germany still angry with the Russians because of their barbarous cruelties in Eastern Prussia? Did anyone ask God to punish England because she had cunningly encircled Germany before the war and cruelly starved her during it? Did anyone charge the Italians with treachery or the French with their brutality to prisoners of war, and the atrocities of their Blacks? Everything was forgotten, even the injuries done to the German nation by the lies of the war. And now, first with incredulous astonishment and then with terror and despair, it was discovered that the late enemies had forgotten nothing, and wished to forget nothing. In spite of the miraculous triumph they were celebrating, the malignant speeches continued about the invasion of Belgium, the deportations, the death of Miss Cavell, the felled fruit-trees of Northern France, the Zeppelin bombs, the Gothas, and Big Bertha. Nothing had been forgotten; their own exaggerations, the propaganda of their Governments, and the protracted fears of four years which, when the German victories were at their height, many had been willing to confess—they all continued to be remembered. The English could not forget their fear of German U-boats and mines, the Belgians their fear of a continuation of the foreign domination, the French their fear of a German advance on Paris and of the final degradation of their country to a second-rate Power. With terror they thought of the abyss from which only a miracle had saved them, and this terror, which persisted in the bravest nations, and blasted all confidence, all understanding of the faults of the enemy, and all sense of domestic guilt, became a spectre which covered the world and demanded the exile of an entire nation to St. Helena.

This terror became embodied in Georges Clemenceau, a

legendary creature, the greatest man of his age beside Lenin and Wilson, inspired by a passionate love for his nation and its aims, a fighter who had never believed in men and only in might, and who, throughout his life, could breathe freely only when his enemy lay crushed on the ground. While he was a journalist he criticized, disturbed and hampered the Government; having become Prime Minister, he put the defeatists against the wall and travelled restlessly between the capital and the trenches in order to watch and encourage the soldiers at the front. His first phase was not influenced by captiousness, nor the second by inhumanity, nor the third by popularity-hunting; always he was urged by anxious fears. If the German peace delegation, called at length to Versailles, was kept behind barbed wire like prisoners and treated with insufferable insolence, untempered by any generosity, such conduct was not dictated by sadism or hybris, but by fear. If his contemporaries in Germany, gradually awakening, cried, "There must never be war again," Clemenceau replied, "There must never be defeat again." This battle-cry was his sole programme of peace, and it was as a ruthless god of vengeance that he opposed not only the Germans, but the weak prince of peace from America. Taking the silent peoples out of the latter's hand, he made himself their spokesman and the utterance of their confused and evil inspirations. Wilson had ceased to be the mighty world-ruler who had been foretold us; a second ruler stood by his side and tried to rise above him. A nightmare struggle commenced between the old and the new leader, between waning reason and waxing greed.

The issue of the struggle could not be doubtful. The Allied nations, deeply stirred by their own experience and guided with skilful energy by their Governments, practically ratified the secret treaties after the event. No doubt there were many who felt that the moment had arrived for laying the historic foundations of permanent peace; but they were outnumbered by those who felt that an historic and possibly unique moment had occurred to lay the foundations of national power on the ruins of an arch enemy. No doubt it was relevant to ask when a League of Nations should be founded, if not now? But it seemed even more strictly relevant to ask when, if not now, strategic frontiers, economic advantages, colonial territories, predominance by land and sea, sensational grandeur and resounding fame were to be obtained? And forthwith all rushed to obtain the advantage of the moment, which not only seemed more attractive and, at the moment, more intelligible, but apparently did greater justice to past sacrifices; and there were many who honestly believed that after so much suffering they had to be unjust to the enemy to be just to themselves, that after so many sacrifices avarice was an act of intelligent retaliation, and that lasting peace could be secured, not by reconciliation, but only by dictation. The result was a treaty of peace which had no room for a League of Nations.

Was this possible, and could a peace without a League be the result of Wilsonian propaganda and a Wilsonian war? The enemy countries had been deeply affected by his idea of the League; could it be that there was no room for it in its country of origin? As neutral and belligerent Wilson had preached without ceasing that certain definite terms of peace were the essential condition of a League; now, day after day, these condition were being sacrificed and the plan of an organization of this kind was left aside as though it were superfluous or at best unimportant. The Messiah of the League soon had to recognize that he was unable to create the real content of a League, although he was compelled to outline its organization and to place it by the side of the Peace Treaty. As the inter-Allied struggles for a new reality became more acid, so the necessity grew for him to keep alive his dreams, and as his first Thirteen Points were swept away, the need grew more desperate to take refuge with the Fourteenth Point; this much was due to his self-respect, to the nation which he had led into war, and also to the enemy whom he had enticed into peace. He struggled with Clemenceau for this last remnant of the League ideology, and the latter, while despising the fancies of

THE WAR VICTIM 75

the obstinate American, allowed the prophet from beyond the ocean to ride his hobby-horse only because he needed his consent to the territorial, military and financial conditions of peace. Wilson received the League Covenant and had to promise that he would allow the League to be destroyed. In the end the prophet, who had always insisted upon the identity of Peace Treaty and League Covenant, had to be thankful that a Covenant was created simultaneously with the treaties of peace and was, indeed, placed at their head, while he was also permitted with English support to eliminate some of the worst barbarities from the treaties. Thus Wilson's fortune perforce became also his misfortune: the dwarfed realization of the League in many respects facilitated the plans of his fellow victors, and in certain cases allowed them to recoup themselves for desires they had had to forgo by alternative combinations, as well as to obtain security for their acquisitions; while the vanquished, despite their severe disappointment, obtained in some instances an alleviation of their worst injuries, and a ray of hope in darkness otherwise complete.

In these circumstances it did not take long to perfect a League Covenant in a world completely indifferent to the League. The Peace Conference was guided by Clemenceau; President Wilson was allowed to be chairman of a League of Nations Committee which Clemenceau permitted Léon Bourgeois, the old apostle of republican solidarity, to attend. While Clemenceau's emissary was allowed to express harmless and indefinite approval of the League on behalf of France, the political debates of the Conference deliberately sabotaged the League. The programme of the Committee was drawn up by the Conference itself on the 25th of January, the future League being described as an organ of international co-operation, and its task as the assurance of treaty obligations and the creation of means to prevent war. Its organs were to be an international conference, meeting at regular intervals, and a standing organization, a secretariat, which was to pursue the business of the League in the period between conferences.

This constituted the foundation of the League. At the meeting, which was not attended by delegates of either the vanquished Powers or of any neutrals (who in the interval had drawn up some excellent suggestions), Wilson spoke and the world had a last opportunity to believe in a League. Once again the President recalled the admirable principles which had been present to the mind of the neutral American Chief. With eloquent words he made a kind of appeal to his own conscience as against his opponents at the Conference; he claimed that it was an obligation of honour to make good the declarations with which he had led the Americans into war; he repeated that they had gone forth like Crusaders not to win a war, but to ensure the triumph of a cause, and, appealing to his own past, he exclaimed: "Like them, I am going on a Crusade."

The Crusade began. The vanquished and the neutrals having been excluded, the League of Nations Committee was constituted, in spite of the protests of the minor Allies, in such a way that the five great Powers were assured of the decisive influence in the foundation of the League. Each of the great Powers was represented by two delegates; the United States by Wilson and Colonel House, the British Empire by Lord Robert Cecil and General Smuts, France by Léon Bourgeois and Larnaude, Italy by Orlando and Scialoja, and Japan by Baron Makino and Viscount Chinda. Of the remaining Allies, Belgium, Brazil, China, Portugal and Serbia received one seat each; later on Greece, Poland, Roumania and Czechoslovakia joined them. The Crusade on behalf of the League was conducted almost exclusively by the Governments who were carrying on, next door, in the Conference proper, their campaign of rapine for the extension of their territories and the oppression of alien races.

The first draft was completed by the Committee within a few days. President Wilson had brought numerous documents and memoranda on the League with him on the *George Washington*, although few of these plans were due to his own inspiration. We know that his first suggestion was indebted to the outline provided by the League to Enforce Peace before which he delivered his first League of Nations speech. His further plans, however, were based upon a draft which had been worked out by an official Committee under the chairmanship of Lord Phillimore on the 20th of March 1918, which had been partly under the influence of American and English pacifists, so that in a certain sense Herder's utterance on the Abbé St. Pierre's dreams, quoted by Ter Meulen, is correct: "Pious wishes of this kind do not fly into the moon, but remain on earth, and became manifested in fact when their time is ripe." The so-called Phillimore Plan formed the basis of a draft completed on the 16th of July 1918 by Wilson's friend, Colonel House, on the former's instructions, as well as of four further drafts, the work of Wilson and his collaborators, the first of which was completed before his journey to Europe, while the other three were worked out in Paris. A plan produced by General Smuts, another produced by Lord Robert Cecil, and a third by the British Government, completed the material at the disposition of the Committee. Wilson's so-called Third Plan and the last-mentioned British plan formed the basis of a new text which was produced by the American jurist, David Hunter Miller, and the British jurist, Cecil Hurst, in collaboration. This text was destined to be the foundation of the confused and unmethodical deliberations of the Committee on which Miller himself has given us valuable information in his famous work *The Drafting of the Covenant*. By the 14th of February 1919 Wilson was in a position to submit the completed plan to the third plenary meeting of the Paris Conference. In this decisive hour his language was less eloquent than at the initial meeting. His speech touched upon the details of the plan, praised the unanimity of the delegates, gave instructions for its future application, and failed to reach the heights which he had attained a few weeks ago. He was disquieted by the opposition in his own country, and found it necessary to cross the ocean and to expend a mass of eloquence to woo the soul of his compatriots. Having returned, he found himself compelled by domestic hostility to introduce into the Pact the mysterious and insincere passage on the Monroe Doctrine, as well as the possibility of leaving the League. Thus dangerous elements of weakness were implanted in his work at two decisive points. In the eleventh hour the smaller victorious Powers and the neutrals were admitted to the Conference and were allowed to introduce a few alterations which, if of no great importance in point of fact, were valuable psychologically and artistically. Eventually the League Covenant was adopted by the majority of States at the fifth plenary meeting, on the 28th of April 1919. When it was presented to the remaining world at the Hôtel Trianon at Versailles, this fundamental law of nations had become an indissoluble part and first chapter of the Peace Treaty, as Wilson had wished it, and also because in fact the other Allies could be induced to accept the League only by this commingling of League and Peace Treaty.

Behind their barbed wire, and caught between the hatred of a hostile nation and the growing despair of a distant homeland which was still suffering under the blockade, still awaiting the liberation of its imprisoned sons, and was now crushed to the ground by the draconic conditions of peace, the German delegation, which had been called to Versailles to sign and not to debate, commenced their unwearying war of notes. Although weighed down by heavy cares for the territorial, economic, financial and military preservation of the country and for its dignity and honour, the Germans did not forget the League. The German League of Nations expert, a member of the Peace delegation, was the same Professor Schücking who had placed such hopes in the work of The Hague and at the outbreak of war had been hampered so cruelly in the pursuit of his Crusade on behalf of international law by the authorities of his own country. Shortly before leaving for Versailles the Government instructed him to prepare an official draft for a Covenant in collaboration with Dr. Simons, the chief of the Judicial Department and future Foreign Minister, Dr. Gauss, and a number of officials of the economic section of the Foreign Office. The

THE WAR VICTIM 79

plan was soon drafted and Schücking reported on it at a meeting of the Reich Cabinet. Its foundations were to be looked for in Schücking's former studies. The Covenant of the German Professor of International Law and his colleagues comprehended the vast subject almost exhaustively, and was drafted more liberally than any of the preliminary plans which had been placed before the Paris League of Nations Committee; on the other hand, it constituted not so much a suitable instrument for an international treaty, as an index for a treatise on the League. Its fundamental idea was that the function of the League must be to embody an international democracy; it set up the principle of equality among all States, declined to grant the Great Powers any privileges, and sought to set out by the side of the Conference of Government representatives (the Assembly of States) a genuine parliament of nations to which delegates were to be sent by the several national parliaments; an idea which had been discussed behind the scenes at Paris, but which had been regarded as hopeless and which accordingly had not found a place in any of the drafts. (Wilson paid it the flimsiest of tributes by advocating a liberal composition of the Government delegations to the Parliament of Governments when delivering his explanatory speech on the Covenant.) This fruitful idea had been put forward by Schücking with the greatest eloquence in his report to the Republican Cabinet; the Government, however, despite all the eloquent speeches delivered in Germany on the League now that it was too late, continued to drift in a sea of confusing and perplexing problems which inevitably appeared more important. There is a legend that Scheidemann, the fifth German statesman after Bethmann Hollweg, Michaelis, Hertling, and Max von Baden, who had to deal with the problem of a League of Nations peace, and the first who had to deal with it in the period of its practical and tragic realization, interrupted the professorial exposition and referred the matter to a sub-committee—exactly as his opponents did in Paris. A sub-committee accepted the draft with a minimum of delay, and without submitting it to the General Cabinet hurried to Versailles accompanied by the blessings of all those who were anxious to see the disastrous end of the war leading into a better future. The German pacifist, Dr. Hans Wehberg, wrote an enthusiastic introduction to the German draft when it was published in a popular edition: "Almost every point of the draft reveals complete reliance on a policy of justice. In the Paris draft there is a definite contradiction between the introduction and the various articles. The Paris draft desires to see in the League not only a preventative against war, but also a means for bringing about international cooperation; but the methods recommended for this end are inadequate. The Paris draft implies the danger that the old principles of the States will continue to exist and even to be strengthened in the League, while the German draft suggests the sole way which can be of advantage to the peoples. In spite of the discouraging experiences of the last months we will not give up hope that the German suggestions will be adopted in their main points with the amendments here suggested, so that Wilson's great plan may culminate in the alliance of nations which has been hoped for during the centuries."

But the German aspirations could no longer be fulfilled; their draft and the remarkable commentary on the Paris plans which it contained was neglected, and the application for the immediate admission of Germany to the League met with a haughty and chilling refusal. "The Allied and Associated Powers," Clemenceau replied, with the approval of Wilson, who attempted to hide an uneasy conscience behind a cold and hostile attitude towards the Germans, "are not in a position to comply with this request. . . . In view of the present feeling among the nations it is impossible to expect the free peoples of the world to join forthwith on a basis of equality with those who have been the cause of so much injury. If this step were undertaken prematurely it would hamper instead of promoting the process of reconciliation which every one desires. The Allied and Associated Powers believe that if the German people proves by its actions that it intends to fulfil the conditions of peace, if it desists from the policy of aggression and alienation which led up to the war, and if it becomes a people by whose side it is possible to live in neighbourly comradeship, the memory of the past years will soon vanish and it will soon be possible to complete the League by the admission of Germany."

Protests were in vain. The League which had been designed to embrace the world and to realize the dreaming of mankind was destined to remain the work of the victors. German, Austrian, Bulgarian and Hungarian interests were eliminated, and the ideas of scholars like Schücking and Lammasch, however good and valuable, found no place in the new doctrine. The work of embodying the dead letter in reality, of constructing the League and its organs, and of creating and filling the chief positions was to be reserved for the victors, with the result that the vanquished, forced to their knees by an ultimatum, found themselves unable to distinguish between Covenant and Treaty. The National Assembly at Weimar accepted everything under protest, and on the 28th of June 1919 the German plenipotentiaries, Müller and Bell, with impotent rage signed the Pact together with all the other enforced conditions in the Hall of Mirrors at Versailles, which Clemenceau had decorated with the tragic figures of unhappy victims of the war who were here exhibited before the conquered. Wilson solemnly attended; he did not perceive at this moment that of all Clemenceau's guests the most unhappy war victim was his own League, a pale skeleton staring upon the Peace Ceremony with vacant eyes.

Peace by Treaty had been concluded; officially the war had been concluded. It had been concluded like every other war —the Treaty and not the League was to assure the peace, and the League was to assure nothing but the peace. The Allied Powers and the German Empire with its Allies had not waged war to realize a League of Nations, and even Wilson had done so with ambiguous feelings once he had joined the Allies.

Yet a League could arise only if it were the object of unremitting, clear and jealous aims. For centuries mankind had known that it could not be created by the cool deliberation of diplomats at their desks: it had always been understood that it required the terrific object lesson of a war before it could be realized. But it had also been thought of as the principal result of a war, summing up all the war experiences, and not as its by-product. In no circumstances could a League be allowed to be anything but a work of reason; and at the end of the Great War this was impossible. The only hope remaining was that the post-war period might speedily atone for the sins of the peace.

On the 10th of January 1920, the necessary ratifications having been effected, the Covenant came in force with the rest of the Treaty as a monument of the victory of one group and of the other's humiliation. On the 16th of January the supreme organ of the new League of Nations, which had been designed to make an end to the last of wars, met at Paris under the chairmanship of Léon Bourgeois. One of the belligerent parties was excluded, and thus the League deprived itself of a grand spectacle of reconciliation which might have won for it the confidence of the world and given its feeble body the first breath of a soul. The Allies with difficulty thinly disguised as a world institution the community of interests subsisting between them, by admitting the collaboration of a gallicized Spaniard; in fact they were amongst themselves once more. They were undisturbed in peace as they had been in war, and with much talk and plotting began to make use of the new instrument to consolidate their conquests and the new positions they had acquired.

Germany was not the only country absent on this day of mingled greatness and pettiness. America too was missing; the father of the peace was absent from the council table. Where was Wilson? Let us carefully scrutinize his weary and tormented countenance: for fate had severed him from his work and we shall not see him again. He had led his nation into war, but it declined to be led into his peace. In the new League the two nations were missing which he had addressed with such power, solemnity and calculating skill, while he held the glittering Points in his hand. What a defeat and what a vengeance! Wearily and without success he wandered through America in order to win back his forces. He had triumphantly caused it to be embodied in the Pact that the first meeting of the League Assembly and the first meeting of the Council should be summoned by the President of the United States. He assembled the Council, but meeting after meeting took place without him; and when the hour of the first League meeting approached, he was compelled to assemble it and to take no share in its deliberations. His defeat was the greatest in the war, and of all the war victims his injuries were greatest. He lost his office, he collapsed, and within a few years of his great triumph he died. His name was destined to be mentioned rarely in the League Assemblies, and rarely to inspire their deliberations. Dressed in mourning and motionless, his widow sat in the front row of the diplomats' box, and gazed on the alien commotion before her.

Meanwhile what of Clemenceau, the conqueror of Wilson and of the League? The French nation, marching at the head of the world, allowed unbridled power to the man who embodied its needs and feelings at the end of the war. He had led them to the intoxication of victory from the depths of despair; but at the moment when his work had been done and the nation was ready to breathe freely within its frontiers, it did not allow the leader of the war to reach supreme power in peace. As America deserted Wilson, France deserted Clemenceau with an equanimity which even his German enemies felt to be ingratitude. But it did not help the world that France was weary of the domestic tyranny which she had needed and had reluctantly borne before the enemy. Outside she allowed the barbarous law to continue; outside, the Treaty and the Pact were to rule for years with inexorable harshness as the embodiment of tyranny, and years must elapse before Clemenceau's opponent, Aristide Briand, could cautiously proceed to complement the physical by moral sanctions. Fear was destined to remain, and wherever we look we shall meet the countenance of fear. In the midst of peace it will crouch behind the seats of the French League delegates, and will ensure the domination of dead Clemenceau over dead Wilson.

What has become of the German champions of the League? Matthias Erzberger, who, in the last moment, had associated the voice of Germany with the debate on the League of Nations, had signed the Armistice conditions, and had finally advocated the acceptance of the Peace Treaty before the National Assembly at Weimar, fell the victim of nationalist assassins. What of Professor Schücking, who had been rejected together with his excellent plan? He looked for consolation in study, and together with Dr. Wehberg, the pacifist advocate of his plan, wrote the first important legal commentary on the enemies' Pact, a good, a thorough, and a German work, which no ultimatum could mar.

CHAPTER VI

PAPER

THE League of Nations has come into life; it has begun to exist, if only on paper. And this paper trembles in our hands while we are being carried through the European landscape, somewhere near Paris, somewhere near the Rhine, or in Northern Italy or any other regions whose names belong to the history of this paper. We look through the window; and we look back again at our paper. It is written in English and French, and there are as many translations as there are languages spoken by diplomats, although not nearly as many as there are of the Bible, or of Andersen's *Fairy Tales*. The title of the paper is impressive; in English, in accordance with Wilson's wish, it bears the pious name of "Covenant," in French it bears the sonorous name of "Pacte," and in German the plain, yet solemn, description of "Satzung." But in every language it has another name which is its true description: "First Chapter of the Treaty of Versailles," "First Chapter of the Treaty of Trianon," "First Chapter of the Treaty of St. Germain," and for a time, while the Turks were willing to put up with it, "First Chapter of the Treaty of Sèvres."

It is perhaps the fault of the second unhappy description if the pious Covenant, the sonorous "Pacte," and the solemn "Satzung" afford little suggestion of piety, resonance and solemnity, and perhaps not so much of the title as of the mental attitude underlying the title. We have not forgotten with how much enthusiasm the idea was proclaimed which the paper attempts to realize. Our venerable prophets indulged in resounding speeches and splendid verbiage, and Professor Wilson himself became a poet and discovered images to fire our imagination and devised arguments to intoxicate the understanding; and yet the paper which represents the culminating point of all the centuries of declamation and enthusiasm is boring with all the dullness of mediocrity. The elements of poetry contained in some of the drafts which preceded it are absorbed in the brief Preamble, and even the Preamble lacks the mainspring of enthusiasm; despite some impressive sentences, it does not reach a higher level than that of a professorial dignity. Behind it we can see the uplifted finger of the mentor of mankind, giving good advice to the nations; but no note from the heart is heard. The law of the new Covenant contains no major harmony. The twenty-six articles which follow the literary effort of the Preamble—twice as many as the superstitious President had originally demanded—are the embodiment of red tape, and their style is no more exciting than that of official notices as we find them in railway trains or underground stations. We are informed in bureaucratic language of the executive departments to be formed, their powers and procedure; but their novelty, their significance and their deeper meaning is not touched upon; they remain dead; and the whole performance is obscured by a mass of dispassionate details such as we find in the rules of every corporate body, governing elections, resignations, expulsions and subscriptions. It never occurred to the authors of the new law that, if it was to live, it must be read by the nations as well as by solicitors and judges.

Was it impossible to find a language appealing to the heart and filling the imagination? The skilful politicians who had prepared and sanctioned the paper were surely not inhibited from feeling and calling up enthusiasm and from infusing into their paragraphs some of the emotion with which they had been so lavish in the explanatory speeches preceding and following the paper. Alas, the paper, even if they had taken somewhat more trouble, could not have turned out much better than it was; for it was not the work of the nations, but of diplomats and politicians who deliberately refrained and had to refrain from proclaiming thought or evoking feelings which could take the form of generous words. The renunciation of lofty principles precluded a brilliant formulation. If the equality of nations, great and small alike, had been recognized and proclaimed, the Covenant would automatically have run in a more impressive rhythm. If the world had been informed that the foundation of the League meant the reconciliation of enemies lately locked in deadly grapple, and if the axiom had been formulated that in future there must be neither conquerors nor conquered, a piece of splendid prose would have resulted, worthy of a place in any anthology. If the Peace Conference had resolved on the immediate disarmament of all States, this single point would have given life and grandeur to the entire text. If a new spirit had been infused into the hearts of men, a document would have resulted without any conscious artifice which, like the Declaration of the Rights of Man of the great Revolution, would have penetrated the consciousness of nations, and would have constituted a more effective propaganda for the League of Nations than the flood of *communiqués* and pamphlets which Wilson's pale heritors release over a bored and indifferent world in order to make good or seem to make good the omissions of Paris.

Let us look through the Covenant; not with any ulterior thought or in order to obtain an advantage for ourselves while placing the adversary at a disadvantage, nor in any learned endeavour to obtain a legal definition or legal knowledge, but simply and eagerly in order to find the peace. Our search is, then, a threefold one; we look for an attitude of mind to create a feeling of peace among the nations, an organization to ensure peace between them, and a method to prevent a breach of a peace: the principles, the apparatus and the programme of the League. In the final version of the Paris Covenant we find these three spheres impinging on one another, no attempt being made to distinguish between them by appropriate headings or arrangement. The fundamental part is mainly to be found in the Preamble. A breath-taking sentence informs us that the high contracting Powers—to wit the Governments—between whom the Treaties of Versailles, Trianon, St. Germain and Neuilly had been concluded—the victors of the Great War and with them the vanquished, accept the Covenant of the League of Nations—i.e. as far as the conquered were concerned, are compelled to accept it. The Covenant is accepted in order to develop international co-operation and to complete international peace and security (or to guarantee them, according to the French version, which was drawn up from the English text without any final check of the original, but which nevertheless has the same authority as the English original). The completion and guarantees are further enumerated in the Preamble. "By the acceptance of obligations not to resort to war" ("certain obligations" in the French version), "by the prescription of open, just and honourable relations between nations," "by the firm establishment of the understandings of international law as the actual rule of conduct among Governments, and by the maintenance of justice and a scrupulous respect for all treaty obligations in the dealings of organized peoples with one another." A clumsy sentence, illustrated only by two clear ideas—the acceptance of an obligation not to go to war, and the demand for open relations between the peoples; and even these ideas are dimmed by the reference to the Peace Treaty.

But no sooner have we left behind the introduction and the programme contained in it than we enter upon the Articles and Memorandum, and with them on recollections of war and victory. Who are the members of the League? The victors, or as Article 1 blushingly puts it, "those of the signatories which are named in the annex of this Covenant," i.e. the Powers signatory to the Peace Treaties with the exception of the defeated, who are compelled on the one hand to join in the foundation of the League, but on the other are compulsorily excluded. Further, among these original States members we find not only the British Empire, but also the different Dominions belonging to the Empire. The remaining members are a number of neutrals or, as Article 1 expresses it, in a renewed access of modesty: "such of those other States named in the Annex as shall accede without reservation to this Covenant."

Among these States we look in vain for Russia, the former

Ally of the Entente, and for the States newly formed along the Russian frontiers with the exception of Poland, which has found a place in the list of victors; nor do we find States like Mexico, which are unacceptable to certain Great Powers for reasons of policy. Thus the League enters upon its functions with two groups of League members, the original, i.e. the victors, and the invited ones, i.e. the majority of neutrals. Apart from these we observe the group of the excluded States, i.e. the suspect, the vanquished and the doubtful, who may be admitted if they are States, dominions or self-governing colonies and if their admission is agreed to by two-thirds of the members—i.e. by the victors, without whom no two-thirds majority is possible. Further, the excluded States must fulfil a number of conditions which were not demanded of the original and invited members: they are required to offer effective guarantees of their sincere intention to conform to their international obligations and to the rules to be drawn up by the League relatively to naval, military and air forces and armaments.

Such are the fundamental conditions on which the League was raised: they import the war into the peace and divide the new world between victors and vanquished. We shall, indeed, find the authors of the League indignantly denying that their work is merely a monument of victory, whenever the Germans, returning disappointed from Versailles, pursue it with hostile suspicions; and we shall find the enbarrassed neutrals sharing this indignation and refuting the charges of the disappointed victims by referring to the extension of the League of Victors by the admission of neutrals. In spite of all denials, Article 1 remains engraved upon the base of the monument of peace; and even when the day comes on which the vanquished join the League and official propagandists extol its growing universality, the Covenant will continue to be a reminder that some were at home in the League from the beginning, while others had to knock at the door and pass a preliminary examination. Each copy of the Covenant will have to contain this explanation as a supplement to the official explanatory literature for the benefit of German, Austrian and Hungarian students and scholars—and surprise will be expressed that no enthusiasm for the League is felt in those regions.

Article 1 had expressly begun by declaring that the League was not built on a basis of universality; at the end it modestly points out that it does not adopt the principle of permanent duration either. Every member can withdraw from the League at two years' notice, provided that up to this point it has fulfilled its international obligations and those arising from the Covenant. In this way a return to the lawless, pre-war state is left open; for what is to happen if three, four or five members, if the majority, or if all, give notice and withdraw? There is no answer to this question: Article 1 provides us with Articles of Association but not with the lasting community of nations. The Covenant is pregnant with dissolution and destruction, and the League is designed to be neither completely universal nor lasting. To whose advantage is this restriction? Is it an aid to the League and to its effectiveness? The Powers which founded the League reserve to themselves the right to control its composition and duration. On the day on which France and England write a brief note conforming with the last paragraph of Article 1, the slender mould of the old ideal will be broken in a thousand pieces, however ardently the other nations of the world may desire the League to preserve the peace.

However, whatever the duration of the League, there is in existence a will for united action: What is to be its form and expression?

This will is implemented in Articles 2 to 7.

Article 2 declares that the League of Nations acts within the framework of the Covenant by means of an Assembly and a Council, assisted by a Standing Secretariat; by means of an Assembly or Corporation of Nations as the first and less poetic version of the Paris League of Nations Committee had called it. As we read the word "assembly" we feel that after our painful wanderings through the war-time atmosphere of

Article 1, we have met the first fine and noble idea; we feel that it is inspired by the promises which occupied the very centre of every plan for the organization of a League from the beginning. It is the essential word of the Covenant, the word which marks its real inception, and might have succeeded in giving a soul to a misshapen body; for it brings us that famous Council, Congress, Assembly of States or universal Parliament which had been the dream of enthusiasts through the centuries. According to the provisions of Article 3, the Assembly is to meet at regular intervals as well as for special occasions; each member State is to be represented by three delegates, having one vote between them, and the meeting is to be empowered to deal with all questions touching the sphere of activity of the League or the peace of the world. Naturally the Assembly can be considered perfect only if the League becomes really comprehensive and the Assembly itself ceases to be merely a continuation of the Paris Peace Conference with the addition of a number of neutrals. It is the moral core of the League and it may become identical with the League itself. But already the Council stands by its side and above it—a body of which Wilson's first drafts knew nothing, which was added to the Covenant in Paris, and which introduced a fundamental change in the entire structure of the League; for the Council—the Executive Council, as it was called in the first draft—is the real executive organ of the League and is destined to remain so in practice.

What is the meaning of the League Council? Is it a committee of the Assembly, elected by and responsible to it, an organ of the Assembly, and consequently an organ of the community of States? Its spiritual origin does not lie in the idea of the solidarity of nations, but in an alien and hostile idea— the destructive notion of a concert of Great Powers. Its home is not the world of the League, but the old world of the policy of might, and its roots do not lie in the depths of the League; it has been grafted on to the League, and since it concentrates within itself the powers of the League it becomes identical with it. It is not so much an organ of the League as an organ to check and counteract it, whose innermost meaning it had always been to substitute the harmonious co-operation of all States for the hegemony of a few. It is the most important constitutional organ of the new community of States, and as such it introduces into international law the concept that greater might is greater right; and through it a state of affairs sanctioned by history, but not by justice and ethics, is made the foundation of the new order. It had originally been the intention of the Allied Great Powers to make the Council their exclusive domain, having the United States, France, Great Britain, Italy and Japan for sole members. One of the authors of this plan, with all its implicit hostility to the essence of the League, was none other than Lord Robert Cecil, whose ambition it had been at the time of the League Assembly to play the part of democratic apostle of the League rallying the minor Powers around himself. His plan of the 14th of January 1919 provided for a Conference having two organs, the one corresponding to the Assembly and meeting at four-yearly intervals, and the other meeting yearly but consisting only of the Allied Great Powers and of such other Powers as the former should recognize as Great Powers. It was due to the obstinate resistance of the minor States members rather than to Wilson's forgotten formula of the equality of great and small Powers that a number of non-permanent members of the Council were admitted by the side of the permanent members, i.e. the victorious Great Powers. Article 4 of the Covenant declares: "The Council shall consist of Representatives of the Principal Allied and Associated Powers"—thus introducing into the law of the community of nations two terms surviving from the war, viz. "principal Allied and Associated Powers"—"together with Representatives of four other members of the League" to be selected by the Assembly from time to time. It had originally been intended that the predominance of the permanent members of the Council over the non-permanent members was to be part of the Constitution. But, although this principle was eventually broken down by the withdrawal of the United States and by the gradual increase of non-permanent members, it was the case in 1919 that the Allied Great Powers, sure in their control of the minor non-permanent Powers, most of which belonged to the victorious group, also controlled the entire Council. Even in later years they could continue to rule securely; for they exercised permanently a control which was granted to the others only provisionally. According to Article 4 the composition of the Council depended on their good will, since permanent and non-permanent seats in the Council could be created only by unanimous resolution of its members simultaneously with a majority resolution of the Assembly.

Theoretically an influx of elected members in numbers not envisaged by the founders might have altered the nature of the Council and with it the nature of the League; and indeed the election of non-permanent members of the Council was for a time the most important sovereign act of the Assembly, which in this manner cautiously penetrated within the structure of the Council and brought about a slight interrelation between these two organs, with the result that the Assembly was enabled to exercise some influence on the resolutions of the Council. Further, Article 4 permitted all members of the League to join the Council table and to enjoy the rights of a member of the Council for all debates on questions touching their interests; and by virtue of this provision the enormous predominance of the Great Powers might have been slightly modified. But it was soon to appear that those who possessed the reality of power within an organization, not by virtue of its Covenant but because they also possessed power outside, need fear no infringement of their predominance. This lasting predominance which, in violation of one of Wilson's chief principles, was assured to the Great Powers, was the more important because the competence of the Council overrode that of the Assembly. If the Council had been intended to act as a retarding element urging prudence and recalling the actual historical distribution of power, in other words, if it had had the competence which certain constitutions allow to the Upper as against the Lower Chamber, this kind of bicameral system might have had a certain meaning, because in that case the States enjoying the reality of power would have been placing their superiority temporarily at the disposal of the community. In fact, however, the most important Articles of the Covenant, and numerous Articles in the various Peace Treaties, surrender the entire executive within the League to the Council. The Council controls the entire organization; the essential means for the composition of international conflicts lie within its hand. In the name of the League it wields practically the entire executive power for the sake of which the League was founded or with which it was later entrusted from without. And thus, if in spite of every disappointment the League eventually penetrates to the masses it continues to mask a number of Great Powers admitting the smaller Powers to their consultations in turn, and not so much controlled as sanctioned by numerous congresses of which they are members themselves and which they dazzle with their prestige. Thus the Great Powers actually increased the power which they possessed before the war; for they now had the right of interfering regularly in a mass of international questions which formerly they could not have dealt with so openly and methodically. Operating under the name of the League, on League responsibility, and employing League machinery, they are enabled to take steps which they would have found it less expedient or easy to take with their own machinery, in their own name and on their own responsibility. Instead of weakening them, the foundation of the League corroborates their power and gives it a legal title which affords a welcome disguise to this power. If we consider Articles 2 and 4 alone we might think that the Council and the Assembly were organs of equal competence; and if we look into the debates of the Paris League Committee, we find that the possibility of the later development of the various competences and their interrelation was to be left to future development. Article 3 provided that the Assembly was to deal with all questions falling within the sphere of activity of the League or touching world peace, and Article 4 defined the powers of the Council in similar terms. But such restraint is of little avail when the remaining Articles of the Covenant and the provisions of the Peace Treaties co-operate to transfer the bulk of League activities to the Council and to provide that future development shall merely confirm the *status quo*. Externally this distribution of power was to manifest itself in the fact that the Assembly meets only once annually, although it has the right to meet much more frequently, and that it held only one extraordinary session in the course of twelve years; while the Council meets four times annually, besides meeting for numerous extraordinary deliberations. By the end of 1931 the Assembly had met thirteen and the Council sixty-five times.

Indeed the question might be raised whether it sufficed to create the organs of a League and to allow them a definite competence, in order to assure a united and organized activity of the various Governments. The meaning and extent of this co-operation must depend upon the capacity of the new organs to pass resolutions, and the degree of this capacity must depend on whether the idea of international deliberation actually passes into the consciousness of Governments. It is only in this way that the League can fulfil its essential function of reflecting with increasing accuracy the will of an organized community of States. Hence the extreme importance of Article 5 of the Covenant, which lays down the force, the speed and the rhythm of the League's activity: "Except where otherwise expressly provided in this Covenant or by the Terms of the present Treaty" (i.e. the Peace Treaty) "decisions at any meeting of the Assembly or of the Council shall require the agreement of all the members of the League present at the meeting." Thus, except for points of order which Article 5 does not touch, since otherwise the organs of the League would be paralysed, the principle of unanimity is placed at the forefront of the new League; a principle whose nature and application was to provide unending material for the labours of international jurists and diplomats. It clearly and audibly announces that the League is no super-State, that it does not infringe upon the sovereignty of individual States, and that each member possseses a right of veto. As a result the League can become an abnormally slow and clumsy piece of machinery destined to produce uninspiring and disappointing compromises. In the first instance it might seem that this principle is intended to preserve the independence of the minor States; in practice it will soon be seen that it constitutes a dangerous threat to their influence, which the existence of the Council had sufficiently compromised. The right of veto could be exercised more easily by a major than by a minor Power, since the latter could not but be far more sensitive to pressure from the majority. Further, its paralysing force is felt most frequently in the Assembly with its numerous members, so that here, where they might constitute a majority, the minor States are rendered powerless; they are thus precluded from contributing to the passing of the majority resolutions and thereby augmenting their own power and that of the Assembly relatively to the Council. The exceptions to the proviso of unanimity hardly alter the relation between Assembly and Council, or major and minor Powers. The Assembly is at a certain advantage in that unanimity is not required for the admission of new members of the League and for the election of non-permanent members of the Council; but this greater degree of flexibility is rendered nugatory in the other important cases where a majority of the Assembly can be cancelled by a veto within the Council. Again, many of the exceptions to the principle of unanimity within the Council provided for in the Peace Treaties are designed simply to favour the victorious Powers by safeguarding their interests against the veto of one of the members of the Council. Conversely, the same Peace Treaties expressly provide for unanimity where the victorious Powers exercise the right of veto, e.g. in decisions on an *Anschluss* between Austria and Germany. Thus any single victorious Power can exercise a control over this act of self-determination, and the relevant articles of the Treaty of Versailles and St. Germain are rendered valueless, although of course they retain their theoretical significance and permit Germans and Austrians to exercise diplomatic and other propaganda in favour of this principle.

If we had nothing more than this Council and this Assembly, the League activities would consist of conferences with decent intervals between—choral dances at the edge of politics passing across the stage to disappear again behind the wings. A certain unity must be provided, and accordingly Article 2 follows the example of many older plans and provides a standing Secretariat by the side of Council and Assembly. Article 6 proceeds to explain that a Secretary-General appointed by the Council is to be at the head of this Secretariat and that he is to appoint other officials with the sanction of the Council. The standing Secretariat is our second great discovery in our wanderings through the Paris documents; it provides the new policy with a standing organ, a domicile for the League and an embodiment for the idea of the League; an international head office whose mere existence can gradually impress this idea upon the consciousness of the nations. The Secretariat links together the meetings of the League, which in the first period were widely isolated in time and space. It obviates the impression of disconnected Congresses being formed, and comprehends them into an idea. Although the Council with its permanent Great Powers bears the responsibility, the Secretariat is identified with the League for the outer world. It is the Secretariat, far more than the annual Assembly and the nomadic Council, which necessitates a permanent seat—which almost every prophet of the League had realized to be an indispensable preliminary to the realization of the League.

To the disgust of the French, who shared the Belgian wish to settle at Brussels, Wilson selected, for the seat of the League, Geneva, a town appealing to his Calvinistic instincts, the Council, however, being permitted to move its domicile at any time. A permanent seat was an incalculable advantage in any case, and the particular seat chosen was a further success; and indeed Geneva, which Article 7 introduces into the Covenant of the League—"The Seat of the League is established at Geneva"—is the third great word of the Covenant. At the moment of its foundation Geneva was almost as Belgian as Brussels and almost more French than Paris; nevertheless it was a Swiss town which could do justice to its high task, and in fostering the idea of the League could leave behind its own warlike convulsions and resume a tradition more truly international than the origin of the League itself, and one which, in spite of the complications of the four years of war, it had attempted to carry on by means of the Red Cross and the international organization for the care of prisoners of war. Geneva, with its francophile atmosphere, allowed the League, with its Parisian inspiration, to become acclimatized; and, on the other hand, it might be hoped that at Geneva the warlike memories of the League's foundation might be forgotten more rapidly than in Paris or Brussels. The word Geneva is thus the first international word of the Covenant, and it is also the first word containing a reality. A city emerges from the paper—a city we all know, a city on a lake with waves, and with a living population. We are drawing nearer to our goal.

CHAPTER VII

THOU SHALT NOT . . .

WE have reached the goal; we have a Council, an Assembly and a Secretariat; it is time to begin our labours.

It might be thought that the ill-constructed machinery of the new League must be inadequate to its functions. But a beginning must be made, and everything depends on our task. Once this is properly apprehended and courageously formulated, the machinery will sooner or later adapt itself to it.

For a number of years we have known the fundamental problem from which all other problems must be derived. It has been proclaimed a hundred times in every language; and it is called the foundation of lasting peace. It is called the abolition of murder in international relations; and for this reason the call to down arms is not the foolish hobby of a few enthusiasts, but the clear and natural battle-cry of all fighters in the cause of peace. The Hague Conferences had failed; but the idea of disarmament, though often stifled, had never been killed, and it had found a place in all the peace discussions of the war. Wilson had solemnly embodied it in the fourth of his Fourteen Points: there could be no lasting state of peace without the abolition of standing armies, and the armed forces of every country must be reduced to the minimum demanded by internal security. Such had been the universally recurrent formulation of the demand for disarmament. Although a few jurists or statesmen might believe that disarmament was possible without international organization, yet even in the age of big armies nobody thought it possible that such an organization would not contribute to abolish the permanent preparedness for war: armaments and the League were alternatives, and the advocates of the one must be the opponents of the other. The League was an improvement on armaments, just as armaments were an inferior substitute for the League. A League was impossible if the possession of physical power placed one group of nations above the others, and in this sense disarmament does not imply a diminution of the power of individual States, but a harmony between the Powers at the disposal of all States. The League is a community of Powers.

We have a Council, an Assembly and a Secretariat; and now all these organs are waiting for the arms to be laid down on their tables. It is true that the Preamble was cautious in its prohibition of mass murder, and that it remained dumb on disarmament. The Covenant, on the other hand, having devoted Articles 1 to 7 to the organs of the League, boldly tackles the problem of disarmament in the following articles. Surely here there is cause for hope. True, it is somewhat surprising that there is so little room for the expectation and experience of centuries, that the innumerable plans and pamphlets of thinkers, the resolutions and minutes of congresses and societies, are compressed in two articles of thirty lines; but of course each line will be the more lucid, and each word the more weighty. Two articles and thirty lines—no vessel of clay, but a cup of pure gold filled with pure wine. We are full of hopes as we take up the paper.

Before we begin to read, let us close our eyes for a moment and attempt to forecast those weighty articles. The problem cannot be a very difficult one. Let us consider. The League of Nations is being founded, and two articles treat of disarmament. Surely they cannot announce anything other than Wilson's fourth point, and to declare that, with the day of incorporation of the League, the reduction of armaments of all members comes into force. Next must follow the details—rules for the reduction of armaments in the various countries, methods so that the reduction shall be rapid, guarantees to ensure its duration and to prevent evasions of the new law. And if the two articles, with their thirty lines, should not suffice for this important work, we are sure to find an annexe containing the practical realization of the general principles. In any case, as soon as we have read the last line of the two articles, we shall know that arms are no longer the *ultima ratio*, that a new era has commenced, that the door has been shut upon the past, and that from now onwards we shall live in a League of Nations.

We open our eyes and begin to read. Article 8 begins as follows: "The members of the League recognize that the maintenance of peace requires the reduction of national armaments to the lowest point consistent with national safety and the enforcement by common action of international obligations." They merely "recognize," then; still, no doubt the next paragraph will contain stronger terms; for "recognition" can only be the prelude to more exact provisions. But the text also contains the words "lowest point," and this has a better sound. First, however, let us see what minimum is meant. It is the minimum compatible with national security and the fulfilment of international obligations by united action. What is national security? Here our suspicions commence. Recollections begin to arise. Why "national" security? Wilson's fourth point had spoken of internal or domestic security, by which he had meant to convey that disarmaments were to remain only to the extent necessary to preserve order at home. Internal security had also been the expression used in Wilson's last Paris draft, and it had only been at the last moment that the word "national" was substituted for the word "internal" in the deliberations of the League of Nations Committee of the Paris Conference. Only a word had been changed, but it had sufficed to change fundamentally the idea of disarmament. A formula consecrated by tradition and international commitments had undergone a tiny alteration; but the alteration recuscitated a world which men's hopes had already doomed. This alteration permits the way to disarmament to be barred, and provides an incontrovertible argument against every attempt at a rapid and thorough realization of the theoretical recognition of the idea of disarmament as enunciated in Article 8. This alteration followed on embittered struggles which dealt with the interpretation of that concept of national security which had been cunningly smuggled into the Covenant and with the principle of disarmament itself. Twist and turn the paper as we like, the fact is one which we must admit: the tender "recognition" does not lead up to vigorous rules for disarmament; on the contrary, Articles 8 and 9 themselves are only the introduction to disarmament in the distant future.

This suspicion will be confirmed by every sentence. On the future realization of the principle of disarmament the next paragraph of Article 8 merely promises that "the Council, taking account of the geographical situation and circumstances of each State, shall formulate plans for such reduction for the consideration and action of the several Governments. Such plans shall be subject to reconsideration and revision at least every ten years" (the French text here adds "if necessary"); and "after these plans shall have been adopted by the several Governments the limits of armaments therein fixed shall not be exceeded without the concurrence of the Council." That is all. After "national security" we have "geographical situation," and after that particular "circumstances," and after that "revision by the several Governments"—petty and harmful words which can be used to obstruct any attempt at realizing the idea of disarmament and which were selected in order that they might provide such an obstacle. And in the following lines of Article 8 the dangers for peace inherent in every armament industry and in every vested interest concerned in the preparation and outbreak of war are dealt with in ambiguous terms. True, we are told that such an industry is open to grave objections; but the Article confines itself to providing that "the Council shall advise how the evil effects attendant upon such manufacture can be prevented, due regard being had to the necessities of those members of the League which are not able to manufacture the munitions and implements of war necessary for their safety." What gentle language! There is here no prohibition and no binding measure to bring about a prohibition. What tender care for the manufacturers of munitions and arms in the victorious States! Clearly their exports to the minor and newly formed States among the Allies are not to be interfered with.

It has by now become obvious that the League in its present form means no radical step towards disarmament. But perhaps we may hope that we shall proceed without delay towards a limited limitation. Unfortunately the League was not based upon the accomplished fact of a programme of disarmament: perhaps the necessary work will be undertaken once the Covenant is in force. The Council is supposed to be working out plans for the reduction of armaments; but we are not told when it does so, and with what time limit. What is to happen if the League delays in working out the plans? What will be done when, if ever, the plans are prepared? Will the Council, with all its privileges, or will the Assembly, which after all is competent on questions of peace, bring forward these plans in order that they may be voted on? By no means. The Council simply prepares the plans in order that they may be revised and resolved upon by the various Governments. By the Governments? Yes—by each several Government. And are these sovereign Governments bound in any way? They "recognize," but they accept no obligation. The expression "the members of the League bind themselves" so freely used elsewhere in the Covenant, is carefully avoided in Article 8, where it ought to stand at the head. The only obligation is accepted by the Council, namely, that of not bothering the Governments with any settlement of the disarmament question until they have revised these plans and resolved on them; but no word tells us when they will do this, nor does a single word prescribe effective measures against the admitted danger which armaments imply for peace in the interval—in the interval between the moment when Article 8 comes into force and preparation of the Council plans is completed, in the interval between this completion and the revision, and again in that between the revision and the Government decision. Plainly there is no hurry. Unfortunately much can happen in this unlimited period. Or is there hope that the League, whose mere existence might constitute a moral obligation to reduce armaments, may vanish in the course of these undefined periods? Only a single sentence deals with the idea that something must be done in the way of disarmament in the course of the indefinite period, and this is the only sentence creating any kind of undertaking. "The members of the League undertake to interchange full and frank information as to the scale of their armaments, their military, naval and air programmes and the condition of such of their industries as are adaptable to warlike purposes." By these provisions the principle of open diplomacy is rightly applied to this, the most dangerous of all international relations—the relation between the soldiers, guns and battleships of the various countries. But we shall soon see that this provision merely leads up to the production of a military year book, a stout book of reference, excellently printed and bound, with figures provided by the various Governments, by the League Secretariat, where it can be bought for twenty-five Swiss francs. Year after year the *Handbook* will show that the remaining provisos of Article 8 have remained a dead letter, and that armaments are being increased without cease or restriction, and while perusing the book we may smile bitterly at the thought that this open and complete exchange of information between the Governments is being supplemented by their less open but even more complete secret service organization.

Such is Article 8, the article of unanswered questions. Will the four lines of Article 9 which now follow afford us light, proclaim a clear determination or point a way? The beginning is full of promise: "A permanent Commission shall be constituted"—and for a moment we hope that this is the beginning of an attempt to answer the decisive question of the authority to prepare and control disarmament. But Article 9 does not raise such exorbitant claims. The permanent Commission is formed "to advise the Council on the execution of the provisions of Articles 1 and 8 and on military, naval and air questions generally." This sole authority for disarmament provided in the Covenant is to be merely the technical assistant of the Council when dealing with the indefinite programme outlined by the previous article, and is to tender advice to the Assembly when dealing with the exceptional conditions of Article 1 when admitting new members. It could play a beneficent part if it were given suitable members—champions of disarmament and representatives of the masses.

Soon, however, we shall rediscover it changed into a purely military cabal, to which those of the Great Powers who oppose disarmament delegate their most reliable generals and admirals. It is easy to imagine the advice emanating from such a source. We may well ask why Articles 8 and 9 remained so modest. Was disarmament an unknown field? Was it desired to gather material and study methods before making a confident beginning? Were the authors of the League too diffident to attempt the new task which they unselfishly left to a later generation? Must it be left to posterity to garner up the wisdom necessary for the practical fulfilment of the fourth of Wilson's Fourteen Points? Let us look a few pages ahead, not closing our eyes this time, but carefully scrutinizing the section which constitutes Part V of the total work of which the Covenant is Part I. This scrutiny is necessary and even essential; for in this final section all the wisdom, experience and methods which we missed at the beginning are outlined with a clear mind and a certain hand. Here no pressing tasks are left to posterity by inarticulate embarrassment or blushing diffidence: here the meaning and methods of disarmament are laid down, not in two articles and thirty lines, but in fifty-four articles covering twenty pages. A great European State, until recently the greatest military power in the world, and possessing a population exceeding that of France by twenty millions, is informed that it must be content with a professional army of 100,000 men without reserves, with no heavy guns, no tanks, no modern fortresses, no anti-aircraft artillery, with only six armoured vessels, six small cruisers, twelve destroyers, and twelve small torpedo boats; and that it must accept in its own territory, and behind its most important frontier, a demilitarized zone without troops, fortresses or barracks. Its existing armaments are ruthlessly destroyed within a minimum period. A rigorous system of supervision immediately entering into force and exercised, first by the neighbouring States, and later by the League, is to ensure that this drastic disarmament is drastically maintained. In order to bring about this disarmament no plans devised by the Council and no investigation by the Government are requisite. The "national security" of the country, and the part it will play in any joint action in order to carry through its international obligations, is neglected equally with its geographical position and with any special circumstances. No provision is made for revision of these terms at the end of ten years and no allowances are made for the needs of its armaments industry or its purchases of material of war. For once the League has refrained from anxious thought on the criteria and methods of disarmament as applied to this country: with the completion of the Covenant all these disarmament regulations are also complete. Who can fully grasp these comprehensive and thorough regulations constituting as they do a ruthless and deliberate realization of the principle of disarmament as applied to the sixty millions of Germans who, possessing no natural frontiers, live in the heart of Europe surrounded by France, Poland and Czechoslovakia, and separated from England only by the narrow seas?

Germany is compelled to adopt a system of disarmament which should be an example for every other Great Power; and similarly the regulations applied to Austria, Hungary and Bulgaria, analogous in method and execution, might furnish a useful example for the minor Powers. A hundred thousand men for Germany would mean roughly eighty thousand men for France instead of her present peace army of 650,000 men and the war establishment of 4,500,000 men with which her system of conscription provides her. The necessary experience is provided in black and white, printed and bound; wisdom is ready on the shelf; the method has been carefully drawn up and rigidly applied; and it has been drawn up and applied by the same Powers which are members of the Council, and as such are required in Article 8 to prepare general plans of disarmament. Well may we ask why Articles 8 and 9 are so diffident.

No doubt it is hoped soon to copy these examples; for we note that all the complete and detailed provisions of disarmament laid down in the fifty-four articles of Part V of the Treaty of Versailles are prefaced by an important and solemn passage. "In order to render possible the initiation of a general limitation of the armaments of all nations, Germany undertakes strictly to observe the naval, military and air clauses which follow." This is a clear and unambiguous sentence; as Professor Jean Rey explains in his excellent commentary on the Covenant, it "expressly provides that the disarmament imposed upon certain Powers is merely to be the preliminary for a general disarmament." For the proviso clearly shows that "even if, according to Article 8, the States members are not in a position of equality, yet there was no doubt in the minds of the authors as to the temporary character of this inequality." Certain it is that the solemn conversations with President Wilson on the subject of the Fourteen Points give the Germans an indisputable right to insist upon equal disarmament for all States. Further, the German delegation at Versailles on the 29th of May 1919 agreed to the draconic disarmament regulations of the Treaty only after having declared that Germany must forthwith be admitted to the League as an equal partner and that German disarmament "must be the beginning of a general restriction of armaments of all nations and that, within two years of the conclusion of peace, the other States, in accordance with Article 8 of the Allied League Draft, begin to restrict their armaments and abolish conscription." In their ultimatum of the 16th of June the Allies themselves insisted upon recalling the provisions of Article 8, upon announcing impending negotiations on a general plan of disarmament and on emphasizing the fact that their terms on German armaments not only intended to prevent Germany from resuming her warlike and aggressive policy, but also constituted a first step towards general restriction and limitation of armaments; the Powers in question would attempt to realize this restriction as being one of the best methods for the prevention of wars; its realization would be one of the first duties of the League. What is the meaning of all this? If the victors began by compulsorily disarming Germany and her Allies, they were themselves resolved to proceed to a general restriction and limitation of armaments. Such sentiments found a ready echo; only—why did not the Powers commence? For what were they waiting? Let us hear their explanation. They find themselves obliged to declare that the recent vast growth of armaments in the States of Europe lay at the door of Germany. Because Germany increased her armaments her neighbours had to do the same, under pain of being the powerless victims of German aggression. This is a mere assertion, but it is one which, like so many others, they had the power to fling at the enemy who was powerless to reply, in the note accompanying their ultimatum. The following is their conclusion: "It is therefore right, as it is necessary, that the process of limitation of armaments should begin with the nation which has been responsible for their expansion. It is not until the aggressor has led the way that the attacked can safely afford to follow suit. Germany must consent unconditionally to disarm in advance of the Allied and Associated Powers."

The insolence and cynicism of such language was the intelligible result of the brutality and sense of tragedy characterizing the relation between victors and vanquished at the end of the war; but it becomes unintelligible if we turn from the end of the war to the beginning of the League. We now witness the cleavage in the question of disarmament; we find that it has become the compulsory disarmament of a few countries enforced by a coalition of other countries; and we find a later disarmament on the part of the latter being announced which, however, is to be undertaken only as the result of lengthy joint debates within the League. Surely this is not the most practical method for a "general" disarmament; and surely, in any case, if the work of disarmament is to be carried through in two stages—which is all that the victorious Powers undertake—it will be best to hasten as much as possible and to perfect the one kind of disarmament by entering upon the other. The arbitrary condition for this undertaking—namely that the aggressor is to lead the way in order that the victims of his aggression might safely follow—will soon be an undeniable fact; indeed, it is a fact already, for Foch's armistice conditions destroyed the German power of resistance so thoroughly that on the 11th of November Wilson could triumphantly exclaim that Germany was no longer in a position to fight. It would seem accordingly that there is only one explanation for the modesty and diffidence of Articles 8 and 9, namely that general disarmament is to be something different from German disarmament, the disarmament of the latter being merely temporary. On the day of general disarmament Part V of the Treaty of Versailles will be cancelled, and German armaments will be subjected to a new regulation in accordance with the plans which the Council will meanwhile have perfected in accordance with Article 8 of the Covenant. . . . Or are we to assume that the Preamble of Part V of the Treaty and the Allied assurances of the 16th of June are worth no more than Wilson's Fourteen Points, and that the victors' intention is not only to effect disarmament in two stages, but to sabotage the whole idea of disarmament—if indeed they seriously contemplate it at all? Are so many ruses of war to be followed by a ruse of peace? Yet surely if a Power is not only the author of a treaty of peace, but also of a covenant indissolubly connected with it, it is impossible for the methods outlined in Part V not automatically to become the methods of Part I, or to devise methods based on Part I which do not automatically replace the methods of Part V. And if the Allies aim at sharp practice, how can the League connive at them? Its duty is to make good without delay the chronological discrepancy in the work of disarmament, and to prevent the task entrusted to it from being sabotaged; any other policy would be suicidal.

The position might be considered paradoxical; and indeed the foundation of the League and the peace imposed at Versailles were themselves paradoxical. A vast group of Powers, comprising France, Great Britain, Italy, Poland, Czechoslovakia, etc., is attempting to secure its power, which it deliberately confuses with its security, on the disarmament of the neighbouring States: such is the meaning of Part V without the Preamble, and this is a negation of the idea of the League, whose function it is to make a community of armaments the foundation of security. However, the very name of the League constitutes an obligation; and consequently this same group, having arrogated this name to itself, is obliged unwillingly to admit the principle of general disarmament and to announce indefinite measures for the future. The Preamble of Part V and the declaration of the Allies preceding the signature of the Treaty constitute an attempt to hide this contradiction. However, the paradoxical position turns into a position of emergency from which there is no escape: the spirits of Part V knock urgently at the door of Part I. If a League is to be formed the door must open and an identity be established between the disarmament regulations of the Treaty and the disarmament promises of the Covenant. And the great struggle which gradually commences between the champions of this identity and those who deny its urgency or necessity is destined to become more than a struggle for the regulation of the relations between victors and vanquished or the observation and interpretation of given promises and obligations; the realization of the League itself is at stake. Until this struggle has ended with a clear victory of the principle of the League over the principle of force, the Paris Cabal, even after the admission of the vanquished, remains the policeman of the victors; it is the protector of the strong and a threat to the powerless. The divine commandment "Thou shalt not *kill*" becomes the cunning and human order "*Thou* shalt not kill," or "Thou shalt not kill *me*."

"Thou shalt not kill" is the great commandment of the

community of nations, and for this reason all those who hate the lust to kill voice the call to down arms. Those who carry arms are, according to them, more prone to murder than those without; they are without peace and restlessly obey the dim urge to power. But do men and nations kill only because they bear arms? And why do men and nations kill? An attempt to unite them in a peaceful society must not content itself with taking the knife from their hand; it must eradicate the greed which grows into a lust to kill and is ready to snatch at the first weapon to hand. "Thou shalt not kill" is not enough, and "Down arms" is not enough; those who seek peace must stifle the covetousness which causes one nation to look enviously at the next. And accordingly the next commandment of the Covenant must be, "Thou shalt not covet they neighbour's house, Thou shalt not covet thy neighbour's wife, nor his manservant, nor his maidservant, not his ox, nor his ass, nor anything that is thy neighbour's." It is for this reason that all the earlier plans for a League placed a respect for territorial possessions and the independence of neighbouring States by the side of, if not before, the abolition of armaments as a condition of lasting peace. For the same reason the draft handed by the German peace delegation at Versailles to the enemy demanded the reciprocal guarantee of territorial possessions by members; and for the same reason President Wilson had placed the prohibition of covetousness at the head of his plans, although Lansing, his Secretary of State, wisely foreseeing the opposition which might arise at home, had controverted him. Every appeal against covetousness, however, had proceeded from the assumption that those who must not steal must not be at the mercy of thieves, and that covetousness must not be confused with the justifiable desire to recover stolen property; and nobody had emphasized more strongly than Wilson that the League must be based upon a just peace, leaving behind it no bitterness, and that consequently a territorial status must be brought about deserving the guarantee of the community.

Indeed in many circles it was considered self-evident that

any guarantee of the territorial status implied the possibility of a territorial adjustment. When Palier de Saint-Germain published his *New Essay on a Plan for Everlasting Peace* (1788), he had urged the Powers to conclude a sincere, irrevocable and enduring League for the mutual guarantee of their possessions, territories, states and rights; but he had also added that this guarantee must be without prejudice to any just claims which might arise at a later time. When Colonel House, at the President's request, drafted the League Plan of the 16th of July 1918 he excepted from the guarantee such territorial changes as might be rendered necessary in future through alterations in the existing racial conditions and desires under the right of self-determination, and should be considered necessary for the well-being of the nations in question by three-quarters of the members, all territorial changes to be accompanied by equitable compensation and due account being taken of the superior importance of world peace over all questions of frontiers. The first two of the so-called Wilsonian Drafts elaborated these considerations, and pointed out that territorial changes might be necessitated by changes in social and political relations as well as by alterations in ethnical conditions and desires. They also went on to state that the visible interests as well as the welfare of the nations in question, to whom any changes must be acceptable, were to be treated as a ground for revision. In the third draft (of the 20th of January 1919) Wilson confined the obligation to guarantee territorial integrity to external attacks, his object being to except internal revolutions. In the course of the Paris negotiations Wilson finally surrendered the principle of revision. The Anglo-American Draft, worked out by Miller and Lord Robert Cecil (27th of January 1919) became the basis of negotiations. In this Draft independence and inviolability were guaranteed and even "protected"; but for the binding demand for revision a mere recommendation was substituted and, although the idea of the right to self-determination was preserved, the important proviso of a three-quarters majority was dropped. Wilson himself destroyed these important reservations in his fourth Draft, that of the 2nd of February 1919. The passage dealing with the guarantee confines itself to demanding that the Powers must respect and protect from external aggression the political independence and inviolability of States members. This is all that Wilson considers it necessary to say: a stroke of the pen expunges all the additions which have hitherto been considered essential. The existing frontiers are confirmed, and the States members called upon to protect them; and this demand is not weakened by any mention of change or of the right of self-determination. In this way the preservation of the *status quo* is embodied in Article 10 and becomes one of the foundations of the Covenant in its final form. Only a feeble reflection of the watered-down annexe to the Cecil-Miller Draft recurs elsewhere within the Covenant, viz. in Article 19, and there it is expressly detached from Article 10 and is formulated as follows: "The Assembly may from time to time advise the reconsideration by members of the League of treaties which have become inapplicable and the consideration of international conditions whose continuance might endanger the peace of the world." The Assembly is vaguely permitted to advise; but no mention is made of the occasions for such advice, e.g. right of self-determination, ethnical, social and political changes, or the welfare of nations; no mention is made of any three-quarters majority, and the request is no longer made compulsory.

A long and dangerous road leads from the mere respect of territorial possessions guarded by the elaborate safety device of revision, to the final version of Article 10, which, deprived of every guarantee of peace, uncompromisingly demands the active protection of existing frontiers through all the States members, the only possibility of a peaceful organic development of territorial conditions being confined to the recommendations of Article 19. The whole world is in a kind of paralysis, and in such a world the League strives to guarantee peace not by permitting a peaceful development to take place, but by ensuring that the paralysis shall continue. Here any resistance to a peaceful solution of the paralysis is not opposed as a breach of the peace; on the contrary, those who cannot endure the paralysis because of its unfairness are so opposed. The rigid hostility which was the author of Article 10 and whose icy breath chills all the subsequent regulations of the Covenant must surely appear ominous even in a world possessing the blessings of an Armistice: what of the world of the Peace Treaties of Versailles, Saint-Germain, Trianon and Neuilly? Here these regulations constitute yet another advantage to the victor, another compulsion for the vanquished, and another danger for peace. A principle necessary in itself in any peace organization is abused by the victorious Powers in order to cause the territorial acquisitions won by war and ultimatum to be guaranteed not only by their Allies, their first colleagues within the League, but also by the neutrals, who were invited to join it, and finally by the vanquished, who inevitably joined at a later date. The whole world is asked to protect their frontiers. Whatever Holland may think of the frontier of Eupen-Malmedy, she is called upon to preserve it for Belgium. Germany is asked to champion the Italian domination in the German Tyrol against Austria, and Hungary, itself mutilated by the Treaty of Peace, to protect the corridor against her old German Allies for the benefit of Poland. Only an inhabitant of Mars, ignorant of all the documents relating to the Great War with the exception of the Covenant, could see in Article 10 a working foundation for an international peace organization; and we, who are inhabitants of this world which was ravaged by the war, and not healed by the peace, who have not forgotten why the last war became inevitable and who will never forget that, contrary to Wilson's principles, new millions live within frontiers and under conditions which they tacitly repudiate—we cannot believe in the virtue of Article 10, nor in a League of Nations based upon this article.

More clearly and insultingly than any ultimatum of the victorious Powers this article reveals the monstrous discrepancy between the requirements of a true League of Nations and the system on which the League organization of 1919 is constructed. In the Treaty of Versailles and the other treaties, the founders of the League sounded a note of brusque demand; having filled their pockets, they unctuously declared in the neighbouring Covenant: Thou shalt not covet. Once again the emphasis rests upon the "Thou," a false emphasis is introduced into a correct sentence, and a fatal printer's error into the most important printed document in the world: a deadly germ is introduced into the new work at its inception.

CHAPTER VIII

THE SIEVE

WHERE are we? The landscape which we watch unrolling by our windows is not a pleasant one. The powerful nations confirm their power with the assistance of the organs of the community of nations. Relying on Foch's armistice conditions, and not on Wilson's points, the armed Powers watch over their possessions, and for better security, instead of introducing order into the world, ask the world to guarantee them their possessions. Theirs is the kingdom, the power and the glory.

And yet no other hand than theirs can give us the fulfilment of their sacred promises; having organized an ephemeral victory, they are now called upon to lay the foundations of a lasting peace. From the cloudy plains in which they allow our disappointment to roam, they suddenly seek to distract our attention to the shining summits which had been the object of our immemorial longing, and build an ideal city high in the clouds.

The new law of peace is laid down in the seven articles from Article 11 to Article 17. With a certain solemnity Article 11 proclaims the fundamental idea that "any war or threat of war, whether immediately affecting any members of the League or not, is . . . a matter of concern to the whole League." Could the new spirit be expressed more clearly and bindingly? The article further demands that "the League shall take any action that may be deemed wise and effectual to safeguard the peace of the nations." Could the new obligation be expressed more simply and definitely? It may be asked how the League is to formulate its "interest" in every war and threat of war. According to the Covenant the Council and the Assembly are the two bodies responsible for questions touching world peace; will this problem be left to a separate committee of the Council and

THE SIEVE 117

the Assembly? It would be natural to leave it to the Secretariat to observe events in the outside world, to watch the clouds on the horizon from its lofty point of vantage with the keen eyes of international conscience, and to ring the alarm and sound the tocsin. Light is thrown on the question by Article 11. "In case any such emergency should arise, the Secretary-General shall on the request of any member of the League forthwith summon a meeting of the Council." The Secretary-General! No doubt he will summon the Council in compliance with his duties as the highest permanent official of the League by virtue of the mandate which the League has given him, and of the scrupulous observations which he and his staff, carefully trained for such an eventuality, have made. Not so. The Council is summoned on the request of any member of the League. The second paragraph of the article declares further that it is "the friendly right of each member of the League to bring to the attention of the Assembly or of the Council any circumstance whatever affecting international relations which threatens to disturb international peace or its good understanding between nations upon which peace depends." And on this occasion not a word is said to indicate that the Secretary-General must immediately assemble the Council. We are disappointed. The beginning had been brilliant; the continuation is mediocre. Our first survey of the new order has revealed a wide and deep abyss. We see that the Covenant provides for no independent alarm apparatus which begins to function as soon as international relations become dangerous or there is a threat or actual outbreak of war. It would seem that the Secretary-General is simply a messenger without initiative of his own: the initiative for a convocation of the Council is left to any member State which, if it thinks fit, can request the Secretary-General to assemble the Council in order to deliberate on the threatening danger. The League does not formally charge the Council and Assembly with the duty of dealing with any disturbance of international relations, a function which might be automatically exercised by some special body; what the League requires is simply the demand or the friendly right of individual member States. The world peace is not watched over by any impartial and objective authority, independent of Cabinets and superior to political and diplomatic machinations. Such an authority would be the veritable centre of the League; but in fact no exact and incorruptible seismograph has been erected for the benefit of the nations, an apparatus which would function independently of diplomatic wishes. Instead, when there is danger of war, some Foreign Office, having carefully considered its own interest, must begin to function before the League can function in its turn; the storm can break without the alarm being sounded at Geneva. Such methods would not be tolerated in a sovereign State, a town, or for that matter in a village; but the streets of the nations are patrolled by no constable of peace to disperse riotous assemblies, to handcuff the footpad lurking in the dark, and to warn and protect the peaceful citizen. Instead, the victim of aggression himself, or else some good-natured, phlegmatic, not too selfish and not too lazy passer-by has to proceed to the distant police station and awaken the station sergeant so that the latter may take the necessary steps in order to bring about the requisite measures. Such is the purport of Article 11, the first, clearest and most important in the peace system of the League.

We proceed to Articles 12 to 17 of the Covenant, and enter upon a maze of paragraphs. At first sight all is confusion here; there is no single principle unequivocally defining the objects of the League as far as the preservation and restoration of peace is concerned, or laying down clear directions for the behaviour of the League organs and the individual members of the League. There is here a tiresome overlapping of rules, with repetitions and complexities which it is impossible to read through without a superhuman effort and which most readers skip with a sigh. At a first glance it is impossible to see the object of our journey.

According to Article 12, when a dispute arises between

members of the League which might lead to a conflict, it must be submitted either to arbitration and investigation by the Council or (a proviso added after the formation of the Permanent International Court) to judicial methods. The verdict of the arbitrators or the judicial verdict is to be reached within a reasonable period, and the report to be drawn up by the Council within a maximum of six months of the day on which it dealt with the dispute. What next? The members of the League agree in no case to resort to war until three months after the award of the arbitrators or the judicial decision or the report by the Council. This is not much, but it is a new and important provision, because time is gained and there is a slender, a very slender, hope that premature mobilizations may be prevented.

Article 13 binds members of the League to submit disputes "which cannot be satisfactorily settled by diplomacy . . . to arbitration or judicial settlement," if they recognize that the disputes admit such a solution or such methods. Thus the disputing Powers are allowed to decide whether to appeal to authority, a liberty which is only partly restricted by the enumeration of certain disputes generally admitting of arbitration or judicial settlement. Such disputes comprise interpretations of the Covenant, all questions of international law, all facts which would amount to an infringement of an international obligation, and the extent and nature of reparations appropriate for such an infringement. What follows once arbitration has been completed or a decision arrived at? The members undertake to carry out in full good faith any award or decision that may be rendered and that they will not resort to war against a member of the League which complies therewith. In the event of non-compliance the Council suggests steps to be taken to ensure compliance. It is a matter for congratulation that members of the League are to refrain from making war on States of good will: but what of recalcitrant States? The Council suggests "steps."

Next to Article 11 it is Article 15 which deals most thoroughly with the pacificatory functions of the League. The latter article asks what is to be done if a dispute which might lead to war is not (in compliance with Article 13) submitted to arbitration or judicial procedure. The reply is that in this case the dispute must forthwith be submitted to the Council. By whom? Again by one of the parties which informed the Secretary-General, who, in his turn, arranges for a preliminary investigation and requires the disputants to submit material; this material can be published. What are the methods for settling the dispute itself? "The Council shall endeavour to effect a settlement." If the Council—whether by persuasion, compromise or intimidation—is successful, all is well; but what if its endeavours are fruitless? The first step then is to shed much ink, to publish a report on the dispute, and to submit suggestions for its composition. Either a unanimous or a majority resolution is possible, and besides each member of the League has the right to publish a separate report outlining its attitude. If a unanimous resolution is reached (the disputants not being included), the obligation arises for all members, as is explained with the utmost lucidity, not to make war upon any party complying with the resolution. If a unanimous resolution is not reached, however, the provisions are distinctly obscure: "the members of the League reserve to themselves the right to take such action as they shall consider necessary for the maintenance of right and justice." Finally, if on the motion of one of the parties the Council recognizes that the dispute is the sole concern of this party it is the Council's duty to refrain from interfering. There is not much ground for hope in the fact that, as we read further down, the Council or one of the disputants can carry the disputes enumerated in Article 15 before the Assembly; for the Council is assured of predominance by the proviso that a resolution can only be reached by the unanimous vote of all members of the Council not concerned in the dispute, beside a mere majority vote of the Assembly.

Finally, Article 16 informs us of the sanctions to be applied by the League for disregard of its rules for the regulation of disputes. The beginning of the article is effective: "Should any member of the League resort to war in disregard of its covenants under Articles 12, 13 or 15, it shall *ipso facto* be deemed to have committed an act of war against all other members of the League." For a moment we hope that here we find the power of the nations united to ensure peace. Perhaps we are right; at the same time it is by no means established who decides whether an act of war has actually been committed. Further, the acts of war which cause the machinery of the League to function against the aggressor have been selected with a great deal of care; and finally we discover that the machinery itself is exceedingly complicated. The cases in which a part—only a part—of the organized world must act are few and simple. In these instances the members must forthwith break off all trade and financial relations with the guilty member and "resort to the prohibition of all intercourse between their nationals and the nationals of the covenant-breaking State and the prevention of all financial, commercial or personal intercourse between the nationals of the covenant-breaking State and the nationals of any other State, whether a member of the League or not." But it is worth asking which members can successfully take such steps and exert pressure upon the others. Clearly it is only the Great Powers with their vast economic and financial machinery and their control of the seas. It is true that the economic and financial measures, successful as they proved during the last war, when employed by the founders of the League, are not to be the only ones, for the Council is further required "to recommend to the several Governments concerned what effective military, naval or air forces the members of the League shall severally contribute to the armed forces to be used to protect the covenants of the League." Who is to "recommend"? Clearly the Council: and in the Council the great and powerful nations are predominant. Whose armies will form the predominant part of the League forces? Clearly those of the great and powerful members of the Council which dominate the new world as they did the old. It is the actual distribution of power by virtue of which the members of the Council are made the protectors of peace, and it is this which gives the meaning to the further provision of Article 16, in which the members of the League promise mutual support and guarantees against loss in the execution of economic and financial sanctions as well as against any special steps taken by the offending State against one of themselves; further, they "will take the necessary steps to afford passage through their territory to the forces of any members of the League which are co-operating to protect the covenants of the League." At the end of these regulations, with their alternation of cautious obscurity and brutal frankness, we are informed that any member guilty of non-compliance with any obligation contained in the Covenant can be expelled by the Council. Once again it is the Council that plays the decisive part.

When these regulations for the preservation of peace among the nations were devised the authors excluded a number of important States from their community. Nevertheless Article 17 claims the right of applying the new machinery in cases of dispute between a member and a non-member, the latter being required to recognize the obligations applying to member States with some modifications to be determined by the Council. If he refuses and makes war on a member the provisions of Article 16 must be applied—i.e. the economic, financial and military sanctions. A similar demand can be made by the Council even if neither disputant is a member of the League: only in this instance the wording of the Covenant does not imply any obligation upon the League to take part or to interfere in the war between these States. In such a case it is obviously no longer the League's business to preserve the peace; and if the two non-members refuse to recognize the provisions of the Covenant for the regulation of disputes, "the Council may take such measures and make such recommendations as will prevent hostilities and will result in the settlement of the dispute," but we are not informed what measures are to be taken and what the Council will do with its suggestions. Such are the traffic regulations posted by the League in the squares and streets of international life. Will they contribute to international calm? A little, because people will say that they are better than nothing. Will they rouse enthusiasm? We think not. The Preamble itself had been content with declaring that the members of the League undertook obligations—not the obligation—not to resort to war. We now perceive that none of the articles constituting the peace machinery contains an unequivocal prohibition of war, and that none stigmatizes war as a crime. Such a declaration was reserved to certain later utterances of organs of the League which, however, found no place in the Covenant. Nowhere is war outlawed; the attempt to do so was reserved to the Kellogg Pact, which having been concluded years later and outside the League, weary attempts were made to harmonize it with the Covenant. Nowhere do we find an unequivocal obligation laid upon the League to prevent every breach of the peace, and, the attempt having failed, to re-establish peace. The only prohibition relates to war not preceded by any attempted mediation, and although this proviso is important and capable of further development, there is nothing to say that once the attempts at mediation have failed, war may not be carried on under certain conditions and after a certain period.

A scrutiny of Articles 12 to 17 will not lead to the discovery of lasting peace; it will only lead to the recognition of the difficulties attending the merest provisional preservation of the peace in the League such as it is. Ambiguous signposts point to the narrow paths leading to various mediating authorities, thence of various decisions, and thence again to various possibilities of peace—or even of war. Once the complicated machinery has begun to work, the question of peace or war can remain in suspense for months, poisoning the air. If a small and feeble State seizes a favourable opportunity to revolt against oppression and injustice, it will find itself surrounded by a thousand barbed wires; its feet will be hampered, and finally, tied hand and foot, it will be dragged before the multiple authorities who will present it with a peace worse than war. A strong and powerful State can cut through all obstacles at a blow or, if it prefers, can win a peaceful victory by virtue of the Council procedure, where its influence continues to predominate even if it is precluded from voting, and where its friends and allies, the partners of its fortunes, are assembled. These devices may postpone war or facilitate reflection which will prevent the worst; but they will never produce a real state of peace. If the methods of the Covenant succeed in preventing an outbreak of war the destructive effect of war will be prevented; but no condition of real peace will be created because there is no method for eradicating the potential causes of a war. At best a temporary calm preceding a fresh storm and fresh attempts at mediation can be brought about. If finally one of the belligerents succeeds in placing himself in the right by the methods of the peace procedure, and a permitted war thereupon breaks out, the methods of the League will have been satisfied, but its real purpose will be unfulfilled; nor can there be any guarantee that the war will remain localized as soon as various Powers win back the freedom of action guaranteed to them. Such an adventure contains infinite possibilities of destruction; once the first shot has been fired and the first frontier skirmish has taken place, the whole structure of the League may begin to shake. The consequences cannot be foreseen; and though the relevant articles of the Covenant have evidently been applied—witness the ensuing battle, murder and sudden death—the remaining articles will soon be void. And what of a League war with its hideous sanctions, its hunger blockade—the mildest of the measures enumerated in the Covenant—and with its collective military action? The League had been permitted to follow the last war only at the cost of tireless labour and painful concessions on the part of President Wilson. Can it seriously be believed that after the last shot of the League War has been fired, we should find the League its former neat and orderly self? Soon after the Covenant was drawn up the German international jurists Schücking and Wehberg had written: "Theoretically the Covenant of the League merely introduces the distinction between a permitted and an unpermitted war." We may add that practically it merely distinguishes between wars acceptable and wars unacceptable to the founders of the League. Wars are divided by them into two classes—those which they wish, and those which they do not wish to wage; wars which are expedient and which are waged under the guise of sanctions against breakers of the peace, and wars which might prove expedient to others, and therefore must be prevented by the League. In those cases where the system can really be applied impartially to prevent war and to re-establish peace it can hardly be more than the red cross of politics, a juridical, military and scientific apparatus to minimize the risks and consequences of war. Accordingly the nations will soon perceive that such a system cannot produce any law on which they can securely rely, and their Governments will exploit this discovery in order to embody conflicting national interests more effectively within the machinery of peace. The day will come on which the officials of all countries begin their wanderings in the desert in order to reach the promised land of peace sanctions. Some will advance behind the pillar of fire of the sanctions of Article 16, and others behind the Ark of the Covenant of Article 11: their task will be to let the fine sands of the vast desert in which they wander run through the giant sieve of the six Covenant articles whose holes they try to fill in vain: and behind them the robust and keen-eyed General Staffs will be found advancing on horseback, always ready to assist the zealous seekers with their own peculiar methods of securing the peace.

Since Articles 11 to 17 do not wholeheartedly condemn war, they are also debarred from explaining at any point why war should be condemned. This is their worst sin of omission, for here the Covenant renounces its capital task. It extends international law, but not international morals. It does not create the will to peace, evokes no horror or detestation of war, and does not uproot war from our minds, our hearts, and our inherited customs. Nowhere does the Covenant seize upon our imagination, in no single passage the meaning of war is mentioned; it is forgotten that it signifies barbarism and misery for nations and individuals, that it is written in men's blood shed by men, and that it is collective as well as individual murder. In Articles 11 to 17 of the Covenant war is mentioned as calmly and inevitably as in a military textbook, and it is only in the single Article 11 that a modest mention is made of peace.

But the Covenant has yet a greater defect: it forbids us to rejoice in the peace. Of what use is the best machinery unless it contains an apparatus to ensure that peace shall be accompanied by justice? Of what use are the most eloquent declamations against war so long as the detestation of war can still be neutralized and overcome by the detestation of a greater injustice? When the peoples pronounce the word of peace they would like to declaim it with a full voice so that its name may resound far and wide; but when they turn to the Covenant they become confused and diffident, for when they say peace the different nations do not mean the same thing. They will look at each other with suspicion whenever the occasion arises for the new apparatus to function; the victors will tremble for the peace which is identical with their victory; in the guarantees of peace they will see only guarantees of their own security, and whenever they see some inevitable and universal rule they will look about for other guarantees more favourable to their own requirements. The conquered on their part will struggle against the thought that the peace which they desire and need more than the others is too strong to be broken by the puny means at their disposal. They will resent the thought that it is to perpetuate a detested state of defeat, and consequently they will find a secret interest in undermining the structure of the peace. The nations watch over the peace as embodied by their

Pact with an insincere and unclean mind; the ones inspired by restless obstinacy and blind insistence, the others full of revolt and dangerous mute hopes. They stand on opposite sides of a painted wall, thin and full of holes, trying to spy out each other's secrets. From its first hour the new League is poisoned by a lie; this is the innate sin whose burden it must bear.

In the midst of the pretentious verbiage of the articles laying down the peace we find the brief Article 14. Perhaps this embodies the best promise of the Covenant. Certainly it contains the greatest effort of the Covenant, for it mentions the Permanent International Court which had been implied in almost every previous League plan and demanded by the pacifist organizations active before the Great War. The Hague Conference had not succeeded in leading to its foundation; and although the German, Austrian and Hungarian suggestions for a League brought forward in the course of the Peace Conference had rightly seen in it the most important problem attending the foundation of the League, Wilson would completely have forgotten it without his great countryman Elihu Root. Although Article 14 does not actually create the Court, it provides for the drafting of its rules by the Council; these rules to be presented to the members of the League. After the Court has been embodied its competence is to extend to all international disputes submitted to it by the parties concerned. It is further to be empowered to give an opinion on questions submitted by the Council or the Assembly. On the other hand, no provision is made to compel recognition of the new authority —an omission characteristic of the imperfections of the peace system erected by the Covenant. The various States will recognize the Court at their own free will within time limits set by themselves and with limitations laid down by themselves. The structure of the Hague will resemble that of Geneva to the extent that the first thing to be erected will be an impressive front, behind which international anarchy can continue to flourish. Nevertheless it has the chance of becoming one of the few realities among the illusions of the League, for it can exert the moral impulse which will enforce a continuation of the building. The hopes of the Covenant are centred in it, and it alone may purge the sins of the Covenant.

Articles 1 to 7 of the Covenant provided an inadequate organization of the League; Articles 8 and 9 dealt inadequately with the question of disarmament, so essential for a state of peace; Article 10 settled the fundamental question of the political independence and territorial integrity of the member States in a manner injurious to a permanent peace, and Articles 11 to 17 had provided all too modest adumbrations of a procedure for the preservation of the peace. The Covenant now returns to its beginnings, and in Articles 18, 19 and 20 discusses some of the fundamental problems touching the coexistence of nations within a League. Article 18 contains the attempt to realize the principle of open diplomacy—a principle expressed in the Preamble and consistently proclaimed by Wilson in all his manifestos. "Every treaty or international engagement entered into hereafter by any member of the League shall be forthwith registered with the Secretariat and shall as soon as possible be published by it. No such treaty or international engagement shall be binding until so registered." An important proviso which, if conscientiously observed, may grow to be of the utmost significance. But will unregistered treaties cease to be concluded and considered binding by the parties thereto merely because the Covenant declares unregistered treaties not to be binding? And further, is secret diplomacy necessarily identical with a diplomacy of secret treaties? Does the Preamble dissipate the ancient obscurity which is part of the traditional technique of international diplomatic relations? Every Government can keep the community of nations and even its own people in the dark with respect to its foreign relations: after all, these are not exclusively laid down in treaties. Our chief question, however, is this: does the registration and publication of treaties suffice unless a universal rule governs the contents and tendencies of the treaties themselves? Fortunately Article 20 attempts to allay our suspicions.

"The members of the League severally agree that this Covenant is accepted as abrogating all obligations or understandings *inter se* which are inconsistent with the terms thereof, and solemnly undertake that they will not hereafter enter into any engagements inconsistent with the terms thereof. In case any member of the League shall, before becoming a member of the League, have undertaken any obligation inconsistent with the terms of this Covenant, it shall be the duty of such member to take immediate steps to procure its release from such obligations." Our hopes rise once again; for this article not only provides us with an important continuation of Article 18, but also constitutes a grave appeal to the various Governments to observe the obligations of the spirit of the Covenant in the conduct of foreign policy. Yet here again, even more than in Article 18, we miss any interpretation to make impossible, or at any rate more difficult, an evasion of the article; nothing is said of an enforcement of the new rule or of sanctions in the event of its transgression: we have to trust the sense of duty of the member States and also of the organs of the League—the Council, the Assembly or the Secretariat, who have to administer Articles 18 and 20. A constitution is imperfect without individual legislation, and similarly the Covenant has to be completed in its applications by the newly appointed international organs. Unless the first years of the League witness the development, improvement and practical application of Articles 18 and 20, we can infer that the methods they were meant to overcome will and perhaps must continue to predominate because the other provisions of the Covenant foster them.

And indeed the very next article is designed to damp the expectations aroused by Article 20. If the one prohibits the conclusion of treaties not complying with the provisions of the Covenant, the other hastens to add that "nothing in this Covenant shall be deemed to affect the validity of international engagements, such as treaties of arbitration or regional understandings like the Monroe Doctrine, for securing the maintenance of peace." What is the meaning of this strange proviso? We know that Wilson had attempted to ensure for the United States an exceptional position within the League by means of a formal declaration in favour of that somewhat mysterious and ill-defined principle the Monroe Doctrine, being driven to this step by the pressure of public opinion and fear of the Senate, although the latter's ire was not placated by this dangerous concession. For a long time France resisted such a weakening of the Covenant, for she saw in it a weakening of the United States' obligations with regard to the territorial settlement of Europe: in other words, a weakening of Article 10, to which indeed the American objections had originally been intended to apply. But the question was a vital one for Wilson, and on this occasion he succeeded in having his way. The reference to the Monroe Doctrine was, however, worded so indefinitely that instead of weakening Article 10 it weakened Article 20 and acted to restrict the prohibition of special treaties incompatible with the Covenant; and in this sense it is exploited by its former enemies.

Between the mingled promises and disappointments of the articles which are designed to furnish the rules for the treaty policy of the members of the League, and which simultaneously turn the fundamental questions of the League into a loose commentary on the Covenant, we find Article 19. This article, which seeks to provide a desolate world with the vague hope of an improvement at some date, constitutes the atrophied remnant of Article 19. Its proper place was with Article 10, but it has been separated from it. It might have found a place near Articles 11 to 17, but it was not given a place in this group of articles. It has been assigned a place and formulation far away from the fundamental articles of the Covenant, where it is impossible to see in it one of the Covenant's great utterances. Nevertheless it exists, and even a small utterance may some day be pronounced in a great voice. As yet it does not contribute to undo the ugly structure of the League, for it does not bind its beneficiaries; but already it is beginning to undo the ugly state of mind which created and ruled this world, for it allows its victims to complain and to discuss the preservation of the peace from political and ethical as well as from legal points of view. It cannot confirm the League save with the connivance of the victorious Powers; but, as it stands, it may suffice to break it unless the Powers learn reason and acquire courage.

CHAPTER IX

"A SACRED TRUST OF CIVILIZATION"

WE have reached the last stage. Five more articles and the Covenant will have revealed its secrets. Yet much remains to be done and to be ordered: only five articles more to perfect the structure of the world!

Let us lean back for a moment, while the Covenant crackles in our hands. Let us assume that Articles 1 to 21 have proved satisfactory: let us dream that the spirit of peace rules over the nations of the civilized world. They have organized their lives on the principle of equality. They have delimited their possessions equitably, and they have submitted themselves to judicial bodies and agreed to abide by their decisions. Would this suffice to ensure world peace? Would it mean that the ancient idea of domination by one nation over another has been surrendered? Surely the League would still be in its beginnings; it would still be a Christian republic, a European concert, and a Western community of cultures, so long as the vast majority of mankind formerly described as heathen and now as uncivilized remains excluded from the circle of international solidarity. The world of Article 21 confines itself to the free and autonomous countries, while the oppressed and exploited, the peoples not yet developed or not yet capable of development, which were "colonized" or "protected" by the Great Powers in the course of history, remain outside the pale of the League.

They have no place among the signatories nor among the invited States nor among those nations which may be admitted later with a two-thirds majority, nor yet among those which Article 17 attempts to embrace. Unknown and unnamed, humble slaves by the side of the world citizens, they follow in the train of the recognized members of the world Trust.

Yet surely a comprehensive League must throw light upon

"A SACRED TRUST OF CIVILIZATION" 133

the relationship between civilized and uncivilized nations, a relationship which in reality is that between conquerors and conquered. Is it possible to introduce a lasting order into the relation between the nations of Western civilization (even if those non-Western nations are included who have had the skill to exploit the armoury of the West) so long as their relations to other races remain unsettled? Surely these latter races are a source of dangers which an international order should obviate. So long as their rights are not clearly established an excuse exists for the continuance of the concept of domination —for the retention of fire-arms which might go off among the dominant nations. Can there be arbitration between French and Spaniards if the debate between them and the Moroccans is settled by the arbitrament of machine guns and aerial bombs?

Admittedly the Great War could not solve the vast problem of the co-existence of dominant and subject races. Admittedly the better version of the League which Wilson had dreamt of would not have afforded a satisfactory solution. But though the League of Nations could not become a League of Races, and though the relation between the two worlds of ruling and subject races was governed by the principle of might inevitably associated with colonial policy, yet the least that the League could do would have been to devise a colonial policy of its own. The colonizing activities of the different Governments have only two grounds: brazen self-interest, and the ethical argument that peace is being assured to the uncivilized parts of the world and a guardianship exercised over races not yet of age. It was the duty of the League to give international force to the only valid ground and to replace the dubious national sense of responsibility by an actual international responsibility.

If the task was a limited one perhaps it was all the easier to fulfil. For those who did not wish to tackle the problem in all its complexity the urgent questions of the day which were amenable to international treatment had long been awaiting settlement. By 1919 every newspaper reader knew that colonial policy had become as great a danger for peace as the race in armaments. A great proportion of previous wars had been due to colonial rivalry, and the Great War itself might be traced back to the acquisition of Libya by Italy. Before and during the war every newspaper reader knew that colonial questions are invariably economic questions of primary importance, and that the problems of the supply of raw materials, of the disposal of surplus populations, and of the open door in colonies and protectorates are international problems of primary importance. For years it had been recognized that the protection of colonial populations against national and private exploitation, their ethical, economic and intellectual advancement, and the increase of their political rights, was an international problem.

Would the Wilsonian Covenant provide a minimum programme of colonial activities under the aegis of the League? When the American President proclaimed his Fourteen Points he contented himself with allowing his fifth point to demand "a free, open-minded and absolutely impartial adjustment of all colonial claims, based upon a strict observance of the principle that in determining all such questions of sovereignty the interests of the population concerned must have equal weight with the equitable claims of the Government whose title is to be determined." This was a colourless and twisted formula, due rather to the embarrassment caused by the colonial problem to the prophet of the League and of Allied victory than to a clear-sighted recognition of the necessity of basing colonial policy upon international solidarity.

For a moment it might appear as though Article 22, the longest in the Covenant, with its nine paragraphs, was intended to lead up to better things. It states that certain principles are to be applied to certain colonies and regions, "which are inhabited by peoples not yet able to stand by themselves under the strenuous conditions of the modern world." It adds that the "well-being and development of such peoples form a sacred trust of civilization and that securities for the performance of this trust should be embodied in this Covenant."

Such a sensible assertion of international responsibility for the less developed races, together with the well-formulated idea of the guardianship of the League, might well meet with our approval. Unfortunately the article is headed by the dry remark that the principles in question are to be applied "to those colonies and territories which as a consequence of the late war have ceased to be under the sovereignty of the States which formerly governed them." Thus it is not every colonial region and not all the peoples that hitherto were unable to exercise self-government, but only a few who were taken from their former rulers, that are to become the beneficiaries of the sacred trust of civilization. From the point of view of the League such a procedure is meaningless.

Here is yet another regrettable instance of the fundamental idea of an international organization being cleft in two. But perhaps we may hope at least that the principles applied to the arbitrarily selected colonies will be compatible with the idea of a true League, and that there will be a League colonial policy whose partial application might some day become universal. Our question is answered in paragraph 2 of Article 22. "The best method of giving practical effect to this principle is that the tutelage of such peoples should be entrusted to advanced nations who by reason of their resources, their experience or their geographical position can best undertake their responsibility, and who are willing to accept it, and that this tutelage should be exercised by them as Mandatories on behalf of the League."

Let us reflect for a moment. Paragraph 1 of Article 22 gave us a general principle; a sacred trust of civilization is to be applied to a certain limited number of colonies. Paragraph 2 informs us that these districts are to be administered not by the League, but by a number of Powers acting in its name and particularly suited for their task. This solution is peculiar and indeed almost unintelligible; it has a forced air, is based upon no universal principle, and, without special explanation, its suitability is not apparent.

Let us begin by asking which are the regions to which the Covenant presents this special system of administration, which are the Governments whose sovereignty over these regions has suddenly ceased to exist and which are the Governments called upon to succeed them. Was the need for improvement and reform so crying in these colonies that in common humanity a new system was demanded? Were the displaced Governments strikingly unfit for the work of colonial administration? Are the Governments replacing them peculiarly apt, so that the mandates could be handed to them and not directly to the League? These are necessary questions, but we look in vain for the necessary answer in the subsequent paragraphs of Article 22. We find only a few vague words and phrases dealing with certain communities previously appertaining to the Ottoman Empire, with Central Africa, South-West Africa, and certain islands in the Australian Pacific, and although these allow us to form some vague notions about the regions in question and their former overlords we are told nothing about the new administrations or given any hint to enable us to grasp the scope and significance of the problem. In vain we search the pages of the Covenant for enlightenment; and since we are not given any general principle based on the idea of the League of Nations, we can understand the new system only in the light of certain political facts. Once again we have to make use of the Treaty of Versailles, whose first part is the Covenant, and to interpret its connection with the Covenant in the light of our knowledge of events during the war and the so-called Peace Conference.

We now discover some remarkable facts which throw a light upon the vague phrases of Article 22 with its scattered references to certain geographical data. During the Great War the Ottoman Empire and the German Colonies had been partitioned in a number of secret Pacts among the Allies, and Wilson seized upon the idea of a League Mandate system in order to prevent the annexation of the former Turkish and German possessions outside Europe while at the same time removing them from the control of their former owners. This idea was imported into the various League plans by General Smuts, who, however, wished to see it applied also to Russian, Austrian and Turkish territories. Wilson's idea had never been to institute a system of League Mandates for all colonies or countries with backward populations; the problem as he envisaged it was to organize a joint control of the League of Nations over the non-European remnants of the conquered States. Was this solution more just or more moral than the blunt policy of annexation which it tried to prevent? We may perhaps say that the Allied solution was more honest than that of the President, although in this particular instance he defended his solution heroically because he was under the illusion that it was inspired by League of Nations principles. In the upshot Wilson won a formal victory, as on so many other occasions, while the reality of victory went to the Allies. An open annexation was prevented and a kind of Mandate system arranged for the former Turkish and German possessions outside Europe; but the Mandate was given to those Powers which had already assured themselves of the control over the German and Turkish possessions by conquest or by secret treaties. The result of this annexationist deal is Article 22, with its *a posteriori* pretence that it is the outcome of the discussions on the tasks of the League. The truth is that the language was the language of the League, but the partition the partition among the Allies. The Germans were given the Treaty of Versailles to take or leave.

Not a word is said about the fate of the colonies they surrender. What is the fate in detail of these overseas dominions, on which so much care and industry and heroic defence had been expended? In Part I of the Treaty of Versailles, Article 22, under the general heading of League of Nations, they can read the answer: in the interests of a sacred trust of civilization these possessions are to be administered in the name of the League by certain developed nations whose names are not given. Which are the nations in question? The same Powers to which the possessions had to be surrendered by virtue of Article 119. The victims of Allied rapacity find their stolen property which the Allies had taken from them at the end of the Treaty, at the beginning of the Covenant, disguised as the League Mandates of the "advanced nations." The treatment of Turkey was similar. Paragraphs 1 and 2 of Articles 22 are a foolish and impudent trick to empty the pockets of Peter and fill those of Paul to the accompaniment of solemn music. During this performance the League plays the part of juggler's assistant. The conquered regions are administered in its name, the Allies allowed to divide the spoils at their pleasure, and the solemn protests of the victims meet with a nonchalant shrug of the shoulders.

Having lent its good name to this deception the League did not find it necessary to strain at gnats. In the following paragraphs Article 22 coolly and unblushingly justifies with principles alleged to be of general application the various forms chosen by the Allies, with an eye to their own interests and to existing possibilities, for the annexation of German and Turkish possessions. "The character of the Mandate," it benevolently explains, "must differ according to the state of the development of the people, the geographical situation of the territory, its economic conditions and other circumstances." Hereupon a number of groups are invented, which later will bear the names of A, B and C Mandates in the unimaginative language of official League of Nations bureaucracy. The A Mandates turn out upon examination to be Turkish provinces which are admitted to possess a certain national existence, and which are to be administered with the advice and assistance of a mandatory State until they are ripe for independence. These are Palestine, which stands under a British Mandate, and in accordance with a war-time promise is to provide a national home for the Jews; the Iraq, or Mesopotamia, which is attached to the British Empire by a treaty with the King, and whose mandatory character is a pure fiction, and Syria and the Lebanon, which are treated as French Mandates. The B

"A SACRED TRUST OF CIVILIZATION" 139

Mandates are made up of the majority of the German Colonies in Africa. Cameroon and Togo are divided between France and Britain, and German East Africa is handed to Britain under the name of Tanganyika, though a part of this colony is passed on to Belgium later as the result of negotiations under the name of Ruanda-Urundi. The remaining German colonies in Africa are degraded to the rank of C Mandates. German South-West Africa is handed to the South African Union, German Samoa to New Zealand, Nauru to the British Empire in general, and the other German possessions in the Pacific south of the Equator, including German New Guinea, to Australia; the Northern islands are handed to Japan. The distinction between B and C Mandates, both of which contain certain provisions for the welfare and protection of the natives, consists in the fact that category B provides for certain restrictions in the sovereign rights of the Mandatory Power by prohibiting fortifications, the erection of military strong points, and the military training of natives except for defensive purposes and by recognizing the economic equality for all member States of the League, whereas the C Mandates simply "can be best administered under the laws of the Mandatory as integral portions of its territory. . . ."

But since the League is compelled somehow to manifest its alleged guardianship over the colonial nations, Article 22 assigns to it a number of tasks. The Council, as the Covenant cynically puts it, shall explicitly define "the degree of authority, control, or administration to be exercised by the Mandatory . . . if not previously agreed upon by the members of the League."

This, however, was not necessary, since the Allied and Associated Powers had previously, albeit not without difficulties, drawn up the rules for the exercise of mandates, which the Council sanctioned with a few slight alterations. The Council further has to scrutinize the annual reports handed in by the Mandatory Powers and is required to form a permanent committee for this purpose which assists the

Council in all questions relating to the exercise of mandates. This exhausts the colonial programme of the League. With the exception of a distant hope of future independence for the A regions, of certain regulations for the protection of natives in the ex-German colonies directed against traffic in slaves, arms and alcohol and ensuring liberty of conscience and religious freedom, and with the further exception of Article 23, which mentions the obligation of a just treatment of natives among various general duties of the League, the colonial regulations of the Covenant are drafted with an eye to the sole interests of the policy of conquest and expansion of a few Great Powers. Instead of setting up a law of universal application for colonial policy the League Covenant undertakes the work of providing a cloak for the colonial arrangements of a minority of victor States. At a later date these States agreed to certain restrictions of their sovereignty, which the League merely registered and supervised. In so doing it was not attempting to initiate a new colonial policy, but merely facilitating matters for the Great Powers who were unable in the face of President Wilson's resistance to prosecute an undisguised policy of annexation. The disarmament of Germany had been described in the Treaty as a preliminary to a general reduction of armaments; and although the Covenant was sufficiently diffident in the formulation of its own rules for disarmament, and began from a state of complete inequality, it did at least contain the promise of general disarmament, and left it open to the member States to insist upon its ultimate achievement. But in the colonial question the League is degraded to be the accomplice of one or two Governments, and no attempt is made to pretend that the advantages given to some at the expense of others imply any general problem for the future. Article 22 deals neither with the colonial problem nor with any problem interesting the League. It simply lays upon it a task which lies outside its general sphere, contributes nothing to the accomplishment and preservation of a state of peace, in no way promotes international co-operation, and in fact is utterly unrelated to the League's fundamental idea—that of an international organization. The whole article, which was drawn up by the Council of Ten during the Peace Conference, and was only then grafted on to the Covenant, is altogether out of place in this document.

Misplaced though it is, however, it is firmly embedded in the Covenant of organized mankind. The permanent mandate commission develops from it, compelling the Council and permitting the Assembly regularly to interfere in a problem which does not concern and indeed conflicts with the fundamental idea of the League. It occupies the very centre of the Covenant and it cannot be overlooked. It occupies more space than the articles which lay down the development of the League, than the article dealing with the revision of inapplicable treaties, than the rules for open diplomacy and the regulations for general disarmament. Its removal would mean a change in the Peace Treaty as well as in the Covenant. Many articles of the Covenant could be improved without far-reaching alterations. Others might some day obtain a more beneficent force by virtue of the progressive development of international co-operation; but Article 22, which remains even after the entry of Germany into the League as a standing insult to the nations, can neither be improved nor rendered beneficent. It is a monument of the defeat on one side and of the victory on the other: it is the hideous memorial to the ugly hypocrisy of which all concerned, including the great President, were guilty in their dealings with the fundamental law of the nations. We can close our eyes for a while to the fact that it does not even attempt to solve the colonial problem. We can endure the fact that it deepens the cleavage between conquerors and conquered, so long as every other event reminds us of this cleavage; but the cynicism with which it scorns the fundamental principle of the League will always be unendurable. Official and semi-official propagandists of the Geneva arrangements will skilfully attempt to explain away the historical irritant which makes these articles intelligible; newspaper readers, students, diplomats and League officials hastily skip the vague sentences and they are not even conscious of the monstrous nature of these words; but even those who are indifferent to the colonial policy of the League or to the return of the German Colonies must be impressed by the malignity of these articles and must impugn them if they have any sense of international decency, honesty and trust. It is not the article and its provisions which are at stake, but a language and the spirit of a language. The fight against such a language and such a spirit in international dealings is the real fight on behalf of the League. It is here that we find the sacred trust of civilization of our time.

CHAPTER X

THE PRISON HOUSE

WE continue our journey. Whither does our journey lead? When watching the muddy waters of colonial imperialism we observed the cunning interplay between the Covenant and the Treaty, since when we have been following the mazes of the latter. From now onwards we discover the name of the League in many different places; we find new tasks assigned to it, bringing new rights and duties. The Covenant ignores them; but the Covenant is nothing and the Treaty everything. It is the latter which selects the problems and designates organs, rules and methods, while the Covenant is mute and in principle ignores them. The Treaty becomes the real home of the League; it entices us away from Wilson's garden and leads us further and further into Clemenceau's gloomy retreat.

We are now faced by a new League, with new functions and a new appearance. The League of the Covenant was unprepossessing; but, though the composition of its organs was such as to place the functions of the League at the disposal of the authors of the Treaty, and although its general functions were formulated so as to leave the masters of the world outside and above the League a means of existing based on their own might, yet at least an attempt was made to preserve the fiction that even its most preposterous provisions were supposed to serve or to prepare the weal of all nations, and it was only the insanity of the article dealing with the Mandate system which revealed the rude servant of the strong against the weak. But now that we leave the Covenant and proceed to the neighbouring treaties, the only aspect revealed to us is that of a grinning servility unrelieved by any nobler trait. The Covenant no longer dreams of standing on its own feet. It knows only the authority of its masters, forgets every creative thought, contents itself with an empty name, and is ready, aye ready, for every compromise; for compromises between the victors disputing the spoils of victory as well as for compromises between the pre-Armistice promises and the post-Armistice treachery.

Let us examine the various treaties. We find first of all Article 34 of the Treaty of Versailles, which deprives Germany of all rights and claims upon the district of Eupen and Malmedy in favour of Belgium, while the latter seizes the region and is instructed to stage the farce of a plebiscite within the course of six months.

"The results of this public expression of opinion will be communicated by the Belgian Government to the League of Nations, and Belgium undertakes to accept the decision of the League."

What has happened? Did the inhabitants of Eupen and Malmedy wish to leave Germany? Have they appealed to the incipient League by virtue of the right of self-determination preached by President Wilson? Far from it. Their only desire is to remain part of Germany. The Allies simply tear these frontier districts from Germany and give them to Belgium without consulting the population. Meanwhile, in order to deceive the world and to preserve appearances, a hint is given to the League to hold itself in readiness for an alibi. The League hastens to comply.

Pursuing our studies, we reach Article 80 of the Treaty, which provides that Germany strictly recognizes the independence of Austria within the frontiers laid down by treaty as between Austria and the Allied and Associated Powers and admits that this independence cannot be infringed save with the consent of the League Council. Once again what has happened? Is Austria afraid of being absorbed by Germany? Has she turned for help to the new League? Far from it: Austria has solemnly resolved upon *Anschluss*; it is the Allies who, in violation of the right of self-determination, again and again proclaimed by President Wilson, have prohibited the *Anschluss*. The League is appealed to only to preserve appearances. The Council's sanction is made an essential prerequisite.

THE PRISON HOUSE 145

What does this mean, and what is the Council? The Council, among others, represents France, Italy, and Belgium; its resolutions must be unanimous, which means that France, Italy, and Belgium make the resolutions, which in turn means that the League is appealed to in order to cloak the prohibition of an *Anschluss*, which prohibition of course conflicts with the right of self-determination. A nod, and the League hastens to render its services.

Nor is this procedure unique. Articles 45 to 50 of the Treaty of Versailles, with an exhaustive annexe of forty paragraphs, transmute important parts of the Prussian and Bavarian industrial region with their purely German population into the so-called Saar district. The administration is taken out of the hands of Germany, the coal-mines are handed over to France, and the whole district is briefly embodied in the French customs system. Meanwhile the League is appointed trustee to govern the country through a commission of five members (one of these being a Frenchman, another a native of the Saar district, while the remaining three must be natives of other countries) without any real system of popular representation, while it is provided that fifteen years later a plebiscite under League of Nations supervision is to decide whether the population is to belong to France or Germany, or to continue under League of Nations administration. The League thus assumes a heavy responsibility involving a mass of work and care. What has happened in reality? Is the population of Saarbrücken, Saarlouis, Neunkirchen, St. Ingbert and Dillingen anxious to leave Germany? Is it turning to the new and indeed as yet inchoate League for help and governance? By no means; for although Article 46 refers among other things to the rights and welfare of the population, this is yet another instance where a population is placed under a new administration and threatened with a foreign domination in defiance of Wilson's doctrine of self-determination and against its will. Why does the League participate in such high-handed action? The Treaty of Versailles seeks to justify it by the necessity of indemnifying

France for the destruction of the Northern mines by handing over the Saar coal and ensuring its exploitation. The history of the Peace Conference shows us, however, that this alleged question of reparations is in fact a purely territorial question, and that France wished to annex this district in order to obtain besides Alsace Lorraine an easy point for debouching into the Rhineland. Indeed the French generals attempted to change this district into an independent State under French protectorate during the actual course of the negotiations, and under the very eyes of Wilson, who gradually grew angry. The provisional Saar arrangement with the plebiscite after fifteen years was a concession to the President and also gave the French an opportunity of annexing the district at a later period, when a plebiscite at the time of the conclusion of peace would have meant a decisive defeat. It was hoped in Paris that within the fifteen years the economic and administrative pressure of France in the Saar district itself, its encirclement by French troops in Lorraine and the Rhineland, and the irregular French occupation, would succeed in breaking the resistance of the population, inspire them with French sentiments, and result in a plebiscite favourable to France. If in spite of everything these hopes were disappointed, there still remained the chance of making it a buffer State under a League administration actually controlled by France. In order to realize this plan, the League was needed; France beckoned to the League and outlined its peculiar tasks. Nor was it for the League to reason why. It hastened to comply, and at its very first meeting began to assume its twofold role as prescribed by the policy of Versailles: for France that of a prefect, for the Saar district that of an autocrat.

More and more the League becomes useful and indispensable. In Article 100 of the Treaty of Versailles Germany is compelled to renounce in favour of the Allied and Associated Main Powers all rights and claims on a carefully defined region, comprising the city of Danzig and part of its surroundings. In Article 102 the Allied and Associated Powers resolve

THE PRISON HOUSE 147

to constitute the city of Danzig and the district designated in Article 100 as a Free City to be placed under the protection of the League. The next article describes the system of this protection. The constitution of the Free City is drafted, in collaboration with a High Commissioner of the League, by representatives of the Free City, duly appointed, and is placed under the trusteeship of the League. Further, the High Commissioner, who is domiciled at Danzig, is charged with deciding in the first instance on all disputes arising between Poland and the Free City with regard to the Treaty or the complementary agreements and arrangements. Article 104 provides that the Allied and Associated Main Powers arrange a treaty between Poland and the Free City by which the latter is to be placed within the Polish customs system, while Poland is assured of the use of the Port of Danzig, of a number of traffic privileges, of the conduct of foreign affairs and of certain other prerogatives. The Treaty was concluded in November 1920; what is its meaning? Had the population of Danzig, good and loyal Prussians and Germans as they were, experienced a sudden desire to relinquish their home-land in order to become a Polish harbour, a sovereign dwarf State without an independent foreign policy and under the protection of a League which itself had hardly begun to function and in any case was the tool of the Allied Powers? Not so; it was in spite of violent and desperate protests and in defiance of Wilson's principle of self-determination that the population of Danzig was cut off from Germany. Why? Was this the only way to give Poland access to the sea, which, although Wilson himself demanded it in this instance, had been closed to Austria and Hungary and which even Czechoslovakia did not possess? The German counter-proposals made at Versailles contained, after the blind precipitancy of the German war aims, a mass of belated but reasonable formulae for a compromise, among them a far-reaching solution for the present question which would have ensured for Poland all the economic advantages and the benefit of a free port without violating the integrity of Germany, of

Danzig or of Wilson's principles. Poland, however, required the annexation of Danzig in the same way as France required that of the Saar basin; the new Treaty, which in the eyes of the Allies was a concession to Wilson, was intended simultaneously to afford the Poles an opportunity for the future realization of plans which had failed for the moment. The Treaty gave and the League guaranteed them a number of privileges and means of exerting pressure in the economic and political, or at any rate the foreign sphere, and it was hoped that these would bear fruit in the future. Once again the Conference beckons the League, which in turn hastens to obey and dispatches its High Commissioner into the new State, where the League, destined to fail for years in exerting a practical influence upon its own members, proceeds to play at governing and protecting in the same way as at Saarbrücken. The League is a lackey and nothing but a lackey, however eagerly the attempt is made to give it the role of benefactor here or in its colonial activity. An attempt will even be made to persuade us that it is rendering imperishable services to the cause of peace—in Western Europe between Germany and France and in the East between Germany and Poland; where it is in fact controlling and supervising the remnants of the territorial arrangements of the Treaty of Versailles we shall be told that it is the epoch-making example of a new political co-operation, creating new forms of international life in disregard of ancient national prejudices and embodying prophetic hopes of the ages. Only—we look in vain among the Allied Powers for any counterpart for this innovation. Within their sphere of domination the ancient national prejudices have remained; and indeed the French took the opportunity offered by the Peace Conference in order to abolish customs restrictions in the frontier district before the very gates of the future home of the League; before the war French national pride had remained unperturbed by them: now they had become intolerable to French susceptibilities. The new forms were invented solely for the conquered; and these were forms not of economic and political co-operation, but new forms of violation of the right of self-determination with the assistance of the League. Belated attempts to harmonize these political devices with the spirit of the League fail to afford any moral justification: they are the work of the Treaty and belong solely to the world and spirit of the Treaty.

We are far from having exhausted the instances where the articles and paragraphs of the League are servile instruments for the regulation of a few remaining difficulties left over from the Peace Conference. If we would know one of the most important of its new functions, which the Covenant ignores, although it is destined constantly to affect the future operation of the Covenant, we must continue our pilgrimage through the gloomy regions of the peace treaties. We come to the treaties concluded between the chief Allied and Associated Powers on the one hand, and Poland (28th of June 1919), Roumania (9th of December 1919), Jugoslavia and Czechoslovakia (10th of September 1919) and Greece (10th of August 1920), as well as to those concluded between the victorious States and the minor defeated States. If we read Article 12 of the Treaty between the chief Powers and Poland, whose provisions are repeated in the other treaties, we suddenly meet with the name of the League again. We read that "the stipulations in the foregoing articles, so far as they affect persons belonging to racial, religious or linguistic minorities, constitute obligations of international concern and shall be placed under the guarantee of the League of Nations. They shall not be modified without the assent of a majority of the Council of the League of Nations. The United States, the British Empire, France, Italy and Japan hereby agree not to withhold their assent from any modification in these articles which is in due form assented to by a majority of the Council of the League of Nations.

"Poland agrees that any member of the Council of the League of Nations shall have the right to bring to the attention of the Council any infraction, or any danger of infraction, of any of these obligations, and that the Council may thereupon take such action and give such direction as it may deem proper and effective in the circumstances."

Differences of opinion between Poland and a member of the Council with regard to these provisions are to be held a dispute of an international character under Article 14 of the Covenant and can be submitted to the International Court, from whose decision there is no appeal—an unexpected and pleasant innovation. In these and analogous provisions of the treaties we find the League playing the noble part of guarantor and protector of minority rights, a subject never touched upon by the Covenant. Is the League at pains to rehabilitate itself?

Let us read the provisions of the preceding article which the League is here supporting. They assure the minorities of equal rights with other citizens (which goes without saying), guarantee the free use of their language on all private and public occasions (which does not prevent the Government from making the majority language the official language), allow minorities to establish charitable, religious and social institutions as well as schools of their own at their own expense, and engage the Government to make arrangements for the teaching of the mother tongue of minorities wherever the latter are living in large numbers, which, however, does not prevent it from considering the majority language as compulsory and from providing majority schools in pure minority districts, which we shall soon find exerting strong moral and material pressure on the population; and finally they provide that minorities shall have their fair share of public monies devoted to educational, religious and charitable establishments. The principle, in short, is to allow the local civilization to flourish by the side of the State civilization. These meagre obligations which the Council is asked to safeguard are inviolable, as it solemnly declared in its meeting of 22nd of October 1920, and lay upon it the obligation of assuring itself of their continued observation. So far so good; have we at length discovered a task of the League, however modest, of really universal application? Have we harvested some tangible result for the realm of the Covenant after our wanderings in the realm of the treaties?

Once again we ask what has happened? What are the minorities which are to be protected? Let us reflect for a moment on the conditions necessary for the continued existence of any League. Briefly summed up, Wilson's principles mean that the various States can be united into a League capable of guaranteeing a continued existence of the members States only if these various States are of such a nature that their populations are willing to belong to them. This much being granted, what kind of minorities shall we find in such States, and what kind of protection will they require? Surely the new League is, as it was in Napoleon's dreams, the fulfilment of all national desires, and consequently minorities and the need to protect them can exist within the sphere of the League only where the most rigorous application of the right of self-determination did not succeed in bringing about perfect identity between State frontiers and ethnical frontiers, or where a religious or cultural community had to remain isolated in the midst of a population of which it shared the nationality but not the religion and culture. For groups of this kind which were fated to be minorities—for these *natural* minorities, as we are tempted to call them—groups which have been accustomed for centuries to live in the midst of a different majority and which hitherto have been protected only by national regulations or inadequate treaties, the League of Nations could provide a safeguard, provided always that Wilson's principles were applied in their entirety. With this proviso such majorities could be given full liberty to remain as loyal to themselves as to the State to which they must necessarily continue to belong, and if there remained a residue of intellectual maladjustment, the mere existence of the League would suffice to remove it. If the League consisted of States which had eliminated the most dangerous internal animosities by recognizing and carrying through the principle of self-determination, one of the gravest causes of war would be removed, and simultaneously the minorities would be freed of the danger of murderous conflict with kindred peoples. The result would be a proportional growth of affection for the kindred race and of loyalty towards the majority. In a League thus constituted and inspired the protection of minorities is simply the last practical refinement of an order based upon the right of self-determination, and such was the League which Wilson had promised us.

Is this kind of protection for minorities contained in the documents in which we have suddenly discovered the name of the League? We examine the contracting Powers, count the treaties, glance at the map and at the records of the Peace Conference, and come to the conclusion that the minorities here dealt with are not the irreducible remnant within an order based on self-determination, or so-called natural minorities, but large parts of entire populations, millions of people, mostly living along the frontiers, who had never required protection, and until yesterday had been living with their own people and within their own State, from which they were severed by force and in defiance of their right of self-determination at the very moment when this same right was put into operation to the fullest extent among the victorious Powers. They were made minorities artificially in the same way in which a poisoner will *make an angel*. The minority rights allowed to them are the cynical substitute for the right of self-determination of which they are deprived, and the safeguards taken over by the League are the cynical substitute for the fundamental law of its existence of which the League was deprived at its foundation.

And if we repeat the process, and make a fresh scrutiny to treaties, signatures, records and maps, we shall discover another curious characteristic of the new protection afforded to minorities. It does not exhaust the case to say that Poland received a present of Germans and Ukrainians, Czechoslovakia of Germans and Magyars, Roumania of Magyars and Jugoslavia of Germans. Surely Germans were also annexed to Belgium, to France and to Italy in defiance of the right of self-determination, and in part admittedly on purely strategic grounds. Are there any treaties to protect these minorities—treaties between the chief Allied and Associated Powers and France, Belgium or Italy? We look for them in vain. These are artificial minorities which were forcibly detached from their own countries when the League was founded, and which nevertheless were deprived of the minimum rights of minorities and of the League of Nations safeguard. Similarly there are a number of States which were not among the vanquished containing unprotected pre-war minorities whose existence is forgotten. What does this mean? How can the minority system of the League be confined to an arbitrary group of minorities?

How can Article 12 of the treaties between the main Powers and Poland and Roumania guarantee respect for the rights of minorities if the Powers signing these treaties and causing them to be safeguarded by the Council not only violate the right of self-determination, but even repudiate, as far as they are concerned, its feeble substitute, the protection of minorities? Italy is a member of the Council, and as such is required to uphold the League safeguards for the Germans in Poland and for the Hungarians in Roumania; but is she likely to do so while the Germans and Slavs within her own frontiers are refused minority rights, and the State can decline majestically to be accountable to any authority at any time or place? We knew that the League admitted no right of self-determination: is it also to refuse protection to minorities? All that we find is protection of minorities in a few countries, safeguarded by inter-State treaties such as have been in existence for centuries, with the sole difference that in place of the Powers concerned the League is appealed to for certain definite functions, though it is not permitted to fulfil any general function in its capacity as League. Once again the League is merely a servant. Whose servant? The friendly servant of minorities? No: for in that case it would try to serve all minorities. Is it the servant of the victors? No: for Poland, Roumania, Jugoslavia and Czechoslovakia resent the protection and safeguards which restrict their sovereignty and make unceasing attempts to set them aside. Nevertheless the League is their servant— the servant of their own interests, to which they are blinded by the first intoxication of autonomy or enhanced power, but which are properly appreciated by their powerful patrons. Clemenceau, the President of the Peace Conference, explains the matter in his famous letter to the Polish Prime Minister, Paderewski. He expressly points out that an ancient practice makes it customary to lay down certain principles of government when States are newly founded or expand, and proceeds to draw the attention of his protégé to his accretions in territory and alien population: "These populations," so he urges upon his recalcitrant beneficiaries, "will be the more ready to accept their new status if they are assured of protection." It is this argument which contains the origin and meaning of the restricted minority protection, far more than the *démarches* and petitions of certain minorities, claims of the defeated Governments, or the insistence of Wilson and General Smuts, who sought in vain to embody safeguards in the Covenant. The League enters upon its function of protector of minorities, not as the friend of deracinated or oppressed populations, oppressed and deracinated by the Allies themselves, nor as the opponent of the majority nations, whom the Allied Powers themselves had created and enriched, but as the friend of the majority Governments and as the protector of the new order, exposed to special dangers in certain countries. The power of the State is not as firmly secured in the east and south-east as in such countries as France and Italy; and it is here that the protector and guarantor of the rights of minorities protects and guarantees the peace treaties which destroy the right of self-determination of a part of mankind and *pro tanto* stand on an insecure foundation. And the same fear of anarchy in the new world leads it to apply these safeguards, not only to the minor conquered States (who have naturally been deprived of practically all their natural minorities) but also, in later treaties or diplomatic manifestos, to other minorities in the Balkans, the new Baltic States, Memel and Upper Silesia, while simultaneously the Great Powers are exempted from any application of the safeguards to their own territories.

A pretty state of international morals, a pretty world and a pretty League may be expected to result from such deception and duplicity. Is it a consolation to hear that at least part of the world has been improved, that the demands of morals have been satisfied at least in part, and that the League has done good in some places and at certain periods of its existence? Such a consolation inevitably calls to mind the enormous price which the League demands for the partial and limited protection it affords. The "artificial" minorities, which in truth are no minorities but whole peoples betrayed and sold, must pay for the feeble ministrations of the League by acting as though they were, that is, by becoming "natural" minorities; they are asked to barter the birthright of self-determination against the mess of pottage of minority protection. On no account are they permitted to become irridentists. The Poles had preserved their will to become a nation through the centuries despite the shameful partition of their country; the Czechs, inspired by the same urge, had revolted against Habsburg authority; and such movements had been permitted, had been praised as the pattern of heroism and steadfastness, and had been gloriously rewarded; but what had been permitted to Poles and Czechs was forbidden to the minorities enjoying League protection. They are forbidden to resist or to hope: in Poland and Roumania, in Jugoslavia, Czechoslovakia and in Italy they must go through their military service and act as loyal citizens. Their life is one long sacrifice, both in the intellectual and the material sphere, a perpetual struggle which their children inherit; and not only that: they have continually to defend themselves against the assimilative desires of the new rulers in order to preserve at least their "cultural" peculiarities. How can such a struggle be accompanied by the required loyalty? With the day in which the League minority protection comes into force, a terrible cleavage arises in the everyday life of each individual, and we shall soon find that the compromises poisoning the national mind are uglier lies than all the other compromises. It is possible that the hideous tragedies which to this day continue to be acted in every country with a minority will give way some time at least to the appearance of national harmony. It is possible that the theories devised *ad hoc* by the sponsors of the minority system will some day bring a philosophic balm to the wounds inflicted by arbitrary force. Yet however much it is urged that nations and State are not identical, that culture is the attribute of the citizen, and that the nations should form a non-political union not co-extensive with State frontiers, the fact will remain that the condition of the minorities will be resignation founded on impotence enforced by a superior power. Even the fortunate minorities who will be described as realizing the ideal of a model application of minority protection will simply be a group of helpless and defenceless men, and their continued existence will be a bitter accusation against a League which has been deprived of its own essential principles. True, the League protects and safeguards; but the beneficiaries of these activities are a few special treaties and, since it knows nothing of the right of self-determination, it can never satisfy the minority nations. What it safeguards and protects is the new order, and since this new order is based upon no universal, ethical rule, it will fail to forge a link between the nations. It is no bridge between the minorities and their masters, nor yet between the old and the new owners of the surrendered populations; what it protects and safeguards is a group of interests; peace it does not protect or safeguard.

No—it is no rich harvest that the League has reaped for the Covenant by its excursion into the neighbouring treaties. Once again it had been beckoned to, and once again it had hastened to obey. What can be the result of such adventures? The League is simply the uniformed turn-key before the dungeon of oppressed populations; the populations of the Saar, of Danzig and of Austria, and, above all, the "minori-

THE PRISON HOUSE

ties." It looks after the security of the community of States, and since this security demands it, it ensures a certain minimum of care for the prisoners lest they break their chains in sheer desperation. Often during our Geneva promenade we see the sorrow-worn faces behind the barred windows. If the passers-by perceive this grief and sorrow, they reflect that the unhappy prisoners are criminals and conspirators who unfortunately had to be deprived of their liberty in the interest of society; the prisoners will no doubt become accustomed to their position, will enjoy better treatment if their behaviour is satisfactory, and in any case are in a happier position than those nameless ones who disappeared in the subterranean oubliettes of history since the date of the great catastrophe. The passers-by are half reassured and turn to go; they have forgotten the unhappiest victim of all—the jailer himself. Never had the President of the United States dreamt that such mediocrity would be his fate. He who, in the Covenant and the promises preceding the Covenant, had undertaken the highest tasks of justice and humanity had to content himself with the part of warder in the prison erected by the real rulers. As he passes along the cells where the minorities lie in chains, he rattles his keys, hands them their jug of water and their portion of bread, puts on an important air, and feels a momentary pride in his office. He forgets that he himself lives in prison, is himself the victim of the iron law which binds his charges, and that he too is deprived of sun and air and cannot become free until the bonds of the prisoners are broken.

CHAPTER XI

BETWEEN THE RHINE AND THE KIEL CANAL

OUR path still leads us through the Treaty; but though the Covenant has been left far behind, we almost experience a longing to breathe again the thin air of its uninspired articles. We shall never believe in the Messianic destiny of the League unless it is given a more generous outline; its appearance rather is that of the *golem* of the Allies. It turns a hostile countenance upon us and threatens and terrifies us wherever we look. With the adoption of the Mandate system it has given its blessing to the destruction of the German overseas empire. On the Western frontier of a betrayed Germany it watches over the Saar, and on the demilitarized zone along the Rhine it prepares to take over the inheritance of the inter-allied military control. On the Eastern frontier it guards the banks of the Vistula against every endeavour to unite the disrupted empire. Along the Baltic coast, the frontiers of Poland and the Baltic States, along all the frontiers of Central Europe and down to the Balkans, it stands guard over the enforced settlements of 1919. In the south it stands sentry by the Alps, and has laid its heavy hand on Austria. Wherever there is a gap in the wall surrounding the subjected nation it fills the breach; we find its Protean face in every treaty of the time, and everywhere it is on the side of might. Never does it look into the future. With myopic eyes enclosed in blinkers it is compelled to wander in a chaos which it is permitted to cleanse but not to order. Fain would we be back in the thin but purer air of the Covenant and its uninspired articles.

And yet we find its name in the very midst of the treaties. In the Treaty of Versailles, between Part XII, which opens the Kiel Canal to the battleships of the entire world, and Part XIV, which throws open the left back of the Rhine to enemy occupation, we suddenly meet the League in Part XIII—Wilson's lucky and unlucky number; and its appearance is almost transfigured. It discards the iron rigour of the oppressor and, more clearly than in the Covenant, displays the features of a benefactor of mankind. Its task now is not to serve one country at the expense of another, or artificially to cover the defects of an arbitrary territorial order; it is a task worthy of itself and one which will benefit the community and the cause of lasting peace. Between the regulations for the Kiel Canal and the occupation for the Rhineland, there is a long chapter headed "Labour," in which, surrounded on either side by the most cruel and foolish demands of the victorious Powers, the fundamental law of social peace is laid down.

We have here a second Covenant. It begins with a plain, impressive preamble written with far more grace and style than the Preamble of the Covenant, and proclaiming with much greater clarity and vigour the League's aim of establishing world peace, whence it is concluded that such a peace can be built only on a foundation of social justice.

It is pointed out that the conditions of labour mean injustice, misery and privations for large numbers, whence a degree of discontent endangering the peace and harmony of the world. Hence it is necessary to improve these conditions of labour and to effect this improvement by international measures, since retrogression in one country hinders progress in another. Consequently the high contracting Powers, inspired by a sense of justice, humanity and the desire to secure the lasting peace of the world, form a body which is called the International Labour Organization, a body independent by the side of the League, but having identical members. It is given an assembly of its own in the shape of a General Conference, a Secretariat in the shape of an International Labour Office, and a Council in the shape of the Administrative Council of the Labour Office. An external connection with the League is brought about by providing that the Labour Office is to be domiciled at the domicile of the League, that it is to be an integral part of the organization of the League, that its budget is to form part of the League budget, that the Council and Secretary-General of the League are to effect a certain liaison, and that all appeals to the International Court in labour questions must pass through the League.

What a surprising discovery this is in our wanderings through the Treaty; and also what a welcome old friend. Many former champions of a League had demanded an international regulation of labour conditions, and even the Holy Alliance had dealt with the proposal to form a Labour Commission at Aix-la-Chapelle. Many experiments had been made in this direction; among them at the International Berlin Conference convened by Germany in 1890, which followed similar plans made by the Swiss Government in the previous year; at the private International League for the Protection of Labour, formed in Paris in 1900, which had an office at Basle; and at the various Berne conferences and the labour conventions adopted by them. However, it was not until the war rent the world and simultaneously gave a stimulus to all plans for international co-operation, that the demand for a League of Nations in the social sphere really came to life. The Allied Trades Union Congresses followed by the labour organizations of the neutral countries and the Central Powers demanded with growing insistence that the Peace Treaty must protect the labouring classes of all countries from the effects of international capitalist competition, and assure them of certain minimum moral and material safeguards in the political and economic sphere. As early as the 25th of January 1919 a special commission was formed during the Paris Peace Conference to deal with international labour legislation, a procedure analogous to that pursued with regard to League questions, the chairman being Samuel Gompers, the leader of the American Federation of Labour, while trade union leaders and Socialists like van der Velde of Belgium, Barnes of England, Jouhaux of France and Cabrini of Italy were members. An international Labour code was completed in less than two months. It fell short of the dreams and wishes of the trade unions; for it failed to provide binding obligations for any State, while the difficulties of erecting a super-State were even greater in its sphere than in that of the political preservation of peace. Gradually, however, it produced an enormous apparatus leading to world-wide official activities which often have a more lively and effective air than the labours of the neighbouring League.

Why had the International Labour Organization cut itself loose at the Paris Conference? Why was it not placed on the same level with other labour organizations which grew out of the Covenant later, and why was it not put under the all-embracing roof of the League of Nations? It was not due to the ambitions of the leaders of the Second International that a sphere which, after all, is no more than one among many spheres of international co-operation was given a magnificent domicile of its own from the first moment. The more powerful reason for this urge towards independence and expansion lay in the peculiar tasks, preoccupations and fears which faced the world rulers towards the end of the war. The vision before them was far from being that of a harmonious creation, a kind of heaven-wide dome overvaulting an orderly world. They were chiefly tormented by two dangerous problems; and the dreams of a higher organization which were in the air towards the end of the war were intended to be exploited in the interests of their solution and not of the pure realization of an ideal. The Covenant was put at the head of the Peace Treaties in order to allay political cares, to guarantee a new territorial order, and to secure the new distribution of power; the Labour code, however far-reaching were the ideals of the trade unions, was cast for the part of ensuring the existing social order. The victorious Powers were afraid of two enemies; first the conquered nations, headed by the German Empire, which had been scotched but not killed and which might rise again and break the new order; the second Bolshevism, Wilson's growing bugbear, with its gospel of social world revolution. The methods of the campaign were adapted to the forces of the enemy. The authors of the League were convinced that an iron rule with a tribunal and police forces of its own was a more efficacious weapon in the hands of the victors to subdue the former enemy than an equitable composition, immediate peaceful co-operation and the grant of a minimum of justice and magnanimity; and they were equally convinced that the second enemy, whose strongholds were spread over the entire world, whose ambushes were in every country and which might launch attacks from a hundred points in Red Russia and the conquered or newly formed States in their condition of social and political upheaval, was far too dangerous to be mastered by the simple methods of domination applied to the first. It was the social enemy who was considered the more dangerous, and consequently a second League, whose fortunes were dissociated from the doubtful prospects of the other League, was formed, to be the arena of the struggle with this foe. This fear also led to a certain recognition of the forces of the modern world when dealing with the Labour Office, while they were disregarded with the League. The League is governed by the Covenant, it is a political institution and Governments only are admitted; the peoples are excluded. The Labour Office is a social institution and has a place for representatives of employers and labour by the side of Government representatives. Each country dispatches two Government representatives, one employer and one representative of Labour, to the "Conference"; and the composition of the Administrative Council of the Labour Office and of the various committees which do the practical work ensures representation to each of these groups. As in the League Council so in the Administrative Council, the predominant position of the Great Powers is recognized; but the Great Powers are not the same in both bodies. The concept of an industrial Great Power was formed, and this concept was not necessarily identical with that of a military Great Power. The decisive step, however, was taken at the beginning, when the conquered States were granted admission to the labour organization. The first Labour Conference at Washington—before the ratification of the Peace Treaty, the entering into force of the Covenant, and the official existence of the League—was pleased and gratified to admit Germany and Austria, although they were not allowed to become members of the League. By excluding Germany from the political League a dangerous enemy was to be made harmless during the difficult transition period, and the new work was to be completed and consolidated without its co-operation; but it was fully realized that in the social League, where it was the spirit of revolution and not Germany which was the enemy, every collaborator was worth having.

Was it mere caprice to allow the representatives of the productive forces to function in the same deliberating body with the representatives of State authority, and thus to allow them the appearance of equality? Perhaps; and certainly this idea does not become more logical by giving a majority to the votes of the several Governments; for in fact it is impossible to determine the balance of forces. In any case the founders of the Labour Office went as far as they had to go, and devised a formula of satisfactory appearance. The first task was to form organs in which the most important social problems—hours of work, unemployment, accidents, old age, illness, protection of women and children, working conditions, labour law, displacement of labour, etc.—could be discussed by all concerned and studied scientifically. In this way the first objective was reached; for the time being an international safeguard was provided for the threatened capitalistic order, tempered by an "Article 19" which, since in this instance it was unequivocal and had not been docked of its force, was of respectable appearance and, in some instances, of actual efficacy. In this as in the other League, the last thing thought of was any improvement of the world; the plan was not to solve the social question or to bring about revolutionary changes in property and labour, but a safety-valve was opened of adequate elegance and efficiency to obviate the most pressing danger. The world is presented with the spectacle of a vast parliament meeting first once a year, and later more frequently, in which the debate is not between the nations but between the classes—and in which the civil power can sometimes control decisions more vigorously and independently than at home. While the countries oppose each other in the political League next door, the Labour Office shows us the labour of all the member States arrayed against their employers, sometimes against the several Governments, and sometimes combined in curious compromises. Under the brilliant management of the director of the International Labour Office, Albert Thomas, a French Socialist and former Minister of Munitions, whose adroitness was equalled by his enthusiasm, friendly as well as hostile words were exchanged and international agreements —the supreme object of these disputes—on social problems of the day were neatly set down in black and white to be ratified —or not ratified—at a later date. Whatever their fate, these agreements left the international struggle between representatives of Governments, capital and labour, to come before the various Legislatures whose function it is to adapt them to the international principles and thus to crown the work. The method is impressive, skilful and efficient, and it is to the advantage of all concerned. The Governments have a means of controlling events; capital is provided with a safety-valve for its employees, combined with a powerful international organization; and labour, although well aware of the conservative nature of the whole institution, is provided with a new and powerful instrument for carrying on its campaign at home and abroad; its international solidarity is recognized and it enjoys the advantage of not being compelled to make a revolution until it has the wish or the ability.

With all its advantages and faults, with its honesty and speciousness, the International Labour Organization takes us back from our wanderings through the world of peace treaties among which, curiously enough, it has a place, back to the world of the Covenant. This is its proper sphere, whence the article dealing with the mandates—a real and dangerous stranger within the Covenant—had exiled us. We now find Article 23 following Article 22 smoothly and without transition, and as though there were not an abyss between the two. And yet the latter deals with the mandates, while the former at long last and in the eleventh hour briefly sums up some of the real tasks of the League in the sphere of international co-operation. The connection between the League and the International Labour Organization is established at the beginning of the article, which demands that members of the League shall "endeavour to secure and maintain fair and humane conditions of labour for men, women and children, both in their own countries and in all countries to which their industrial and commercial relations extend." For this purpose—and this is the sole reference to the labour organization—it is provided that the necessary international organization is to be formed and maintained. Within the structure of the League the tasks of the member States are few. They are bound to treat the natives of the colonial districts equitably, generally to supervise the agreements on White Slave Traffic and the traffic in opium and other dangerous drugs, to supervise the traffic in arms and munitions in those countries where such supervision is essential in the common interest, and to secure and preserve the freedom of communications and transit and the fair treatment of the trade of all member States, it being expressly added that the interests of the regions devastated during the Great War must be specially considered. Finally they are required to bring about international measures for the prevention and cure of diseases. These requirements are not formulated exactly or convincingly. The obligations on the member States and the instructions addressed to the League are enunciated in vague terms and covered by a general proviso in favour of existing or future treaties. Article 23 is merely a brief and modest sample taken from the vast field of international co-operation, and is far from exhausting the human pre-occupations and cares which the League might attack in international collaboration in order to promote solidarity and hence international peace. Many important tasks of such a collaboration are simply disregarded by the authors of the League; other problems arbitrarily selected which were introduced into the Covenant during the Paris negotiations through the activity of interested bodies—e.g. the opium and White Slave Traffic—have little if any connection with the aims of a League whose chief object is peace. Other questions did not require the foundation of a League in order to become the objects of international care. They had been dealt with for years at international conferences, and had found permanent homes in bureaux and commissions formed as a result of international agreements. Feebly and clumsily, hampered by vested interests but inspired by the desire to extend its own narrow foundations easily, if artificially, the League now stretches out covetous hands after these problems.

Article 24 provides that, with the concurrence of the States concerned, international bureaux and commissions of this kind will be placed under its jurisdiction; in other cases, too—e.g. the regulation of international questions by general agreements in cases where no international bureaux nor commissions exist—it promises support; while finally in Article 25 the members promise to promote and support the national voluntary Red Cross organizations. But such an arrangement does not provide a brighter outlook for the world programme of international collaboration, for it fails to provide any centre whence the various activities could radiate. It does not proclaim a central idea, systematically subordinating the diverse endeavours to the one goal of peace, in the same way in which the preamble of the Labour code endeavours to proclaim a central idea for its own limited sphere. We can feel the embarrassment and indifference with which the authors of the League proceed to organize international collaboration; the important political business has been completed, and the remaining work is done hurriedly, unmethodically and ungraciously. But precisely because their self-interest allowed the central task of the League to atrophy, so that a healthy development of international debate on the vital questions of the nations was restricted *ab initio*, the secondary discussions, hitherto merely outlined sketchily, will expand with double vigour. Nevertheless we continue to ask whether they constitute a sufficient motive force to lead the League out of the world of the treaties and into the realm of its proper tasks. Or shall we find that while the mustard seed of the opium and White Slave Traffic provisions grows into a mighty tree overshadowing all else, the chilly silence which broods over the remaining parts of the Covenant grows all the more disquieting?

Article 23, Article 24, Article 25 pass under our eyes, and the last page of the Covenant is reached. The previous page had contained a feeble and embarrassed suggestion which compressed the idea of peaceful international co-operation within three brief articles. Does this complete the organization of the world? Have we returned to the Covenant from our long exile only to leave it again so soon, and this time for ever? Much has remained unsaid and there is much that we could wish to hear. Yet only one article remains before we shall have reached our goal.

CHAPTER XII

THE LAST WORD

THE last article! We draw our breath with expectant awe. Once again we are waiting for a great word, for a last and a first word of promise, for a vista of progress and improvement. Here surely there is a unique opportunity to repair much harm in a few lines, and to set down untold wealth in a few words. It is the last note that determines the fate of the Covenant; and surely in its last passage the Covenant will profess its real belief to the peoples assembled at the Peace Conference no less than to the exiles listening in the distance. It will utter words of confession and of consolation; it will admit that under the necessities and confusions of the end of war a torso has been created, the result of inevitable selfishness, of pardonable fear, of human despondency, and of diplomatic scepticism. The moment of its creation was one unpropitious for the creation of any noble or generous work, and we know that our work can in no sense fulfil your wishes and your dreams. All we could give you was a beginning: you must take it as we offer it—as a promise and as an earnest for the future. An hour will come when we shall cancel the hate-inspired articles which are still infected with the poison gas of the war, when we shall reconstruct the mutilated articles in the finer shape of their original inspiration, and when we shall crown our labours by solemnly embodying the unborn articles which will give the world a new countenance.

Have no fear; we will not hold the law in our hand perpetually or for our sole advantage; the future is to belong to all. We were the authors of the work; you are the beneficiaries, and it is for you that we are waiting. We made the beginning; it is yours to perfect.

Is this the inspiration of the concluding article? Does it throw open the gates to a world of new freedom? Its words are curt and imperious: "Amendments to this Covenant will take effect when ratified by the members of the League whose Representatives comprise the Council and by a majority of the members of the League whose Representatives comprise the Assembly. No such amendments shall bind any member of the League which signifies its dissent therefrom, but in that case it shall cease to be a member of the League." Is that all? That is all. The door is closed and the iron bolts are shot.

Apparently, then, any change requires the consent of all the members of the Council, including as permanent members the Allied founders, Great Britain, France, Italy and Japan. Without their consent not an iota of the Covenant can be altered. We, they say, have made the Covenant in the shape in which we needed it, and it shall remain our instrument. True, Germany will one day become a permanent member, and thus possess the permanent right of veto. But will that help her? The States which, with equal skill and selfishness, compounded the treaties with the Covenant and the Covenant with the treaties, have reserved their authors' rights for all time. They can reject every improvement devised by others, and continue to rule in complete disregard of all the other member States. On the other hand, if any alteration is made with their sanction which does not suit another State not represented in the Council, and hence unable to enforce its temporary or permanent veto right, such State "ceases to be a member". It ceases to be a member. At the end of the last article, as at the end of the first, we are informed that the League need be neither universal nor permanent. Dissatisfied States can and must go. The only gate which stands at the end of the Covenant is one which does not lead up, but out. This is the Covenant's last word.

Yet is it indeed the last word? It is not for the obstinate complacency of Article 26 to utter this last word, and indeed the Covenant's last word must be of the same kind as all its other words. It is the last word of a diplomatic document whose first words established a severance between the conquerors and the conquered, between those who gave and those who obeyed orders. But is it the last word of the League? Is it the last word of the last war document? And what is this document to us? It is not the living gospel word, nor the stone table of the law descending from the mountain of divine inspiration; it is a flimsy first page in the Allied ledger. The strong light which it radiates spreads from the shining armour of the victors; but itself is no more than paper. The authors of the Covenant, their Allies and friends, continue to smile: "The work of selfishness can be preserved by selfishness, confirmed by prudence and maintained by indifference and cowardice. Thus what was paper becomes steel." Perhaps—but whether it is of steel or of paper, the Covenant is neither more nor less strong than the peoples will have it. The last word never rests with paper or steel; it is the living peoples who have the last word.

But here our slower companions on the voyage to Geneva utter a word of caution. Halt! beware of blind idealism; beware of mystical demagogy; when turning the pages and reading the words of the Covenant, beware of haste and of bitter feelings. Why is the last word so evil, and why is the first so much to be condemned? If a League was to be created at the end of the war, who was to create it other than those who had the power; and if the League was to be powerful, could it have any other foundation than their own power? Could the Powers be expected, while prudently basing the new order on their inevitable preponderance, to leave their work at the mercy of the precipitance of less responsible member States? Without permanent members of the Council the League would have been ignoring realities and there would have been no guarantees for its continued existence. Could the Powers who proclaimed themselves permanent members of the executive permit a simple Assembly majority some day to upset their great and necessary prerogative? If the authors of the League were led by careful deliberation to adopt the principle of unanimity for the resolutions of the Council and the Assembly in other cases, as well as of the superiority of the Council over the Assembly, surely they could not be asked to leave the most important of all resolutions—those relating to changes and innovations in the structure of the League—to the decision of others than themselves. Surely it was a sufficient advance and blessing that the principle of change within the Covenant was admitted at all during the Paris deliberations. The day would come when Germany, despite her present weakness, would have a seat among the mighty, would share their right of veto, and would profit more by the injustices of the Covenant than by its just points. Have patience, and you will find the conquered sucking honey from the poorest flowers. Why condemn Article 19, in which the claims for revision of the treaties are regulated? It is in the interests of Germany and of Hungary to see it as efficient, as comprehensive, and as effective as possible, since they themselves will some day appeal to it. Do not too loudly condemn the insincerity with which Article 8 advocates disarmament: it is in your interest to erect it into something grand and strong before the public eye. And above all, be just; if you admit that at the time of its creation this document could not be better than it was, do not forget that it is also better than all its predecessors. You are shocked by the interpenetration of Covenant and Treaty; but would you prefer the naked Treaty without the raiment of the Covenant? True, not every minority enjoys the privilege of special rights; still, a large number of minorities are protected; an authority is provided before which they can complain, and there is a place where any Government, and particularly that of the country where they form a majority, can raise a voice to plead for them. Surely this is infinitely better than the dead letter of the old Berlin treaties. Surely Danzig, with its League of Nations Commissioner, is more German than under a Polish governor. You are indignant because war has not been eradicated root and branch: but has it ever been assailed more dangerously than in Articles 11 to 17? The methods of mediation and the principle of compulsory mediation may be slow and difficult, but they would have made the Great War impossible. You dislike the language of the Covenant; but was there anything behind the lyrical fervour of the Holy Alliance, outpourings which did not contain the shadow of an organization nor the faintest suggestion that war might be prevented? Do not speak of the prophets; the appeals to Crucé, to Kant, and to Victor Hugo are a weariness; had a single Government placed its signature beneath their dreams or phantasies? The present document, as any rate, is binding upon its signatories, and these are the majority of all the Governments in the world. When the Great Powers merged their interests with those of the community the latter's claims inevitably received less attention than in the Utopias of thinkers. But a promise, however modest, backed by the power of France and the might of the British Empire is more valuable and, in all its aridity, more eloquent than the most romantic vision of a French poet or a German professor. Before the League there was nothing; the League offers us something that had never existed before. Never before had the major and minor Powers of the world been united in a body resembling the League. Never had they possessed permanent organs, common methods of procedure, common laws and common tasks, all of them admitting of improvement and development. The Covenant is one of the greatest and most effective creations of history, and its imperfections will be removed by time; only the normal course of events must not be hurried. Have patience; at the end of the journey salvation awaits us.

We hear the familiar voices. How often have we heard their siren note? They are seductive in their appeal to our cunning or our sloth, and it would be pleasant and restful to listen to their message. They are not always false; but rarely do they tell the whole truth, and the partial truth which they contain and which is summed up in such slogans as "Better than nothing," and "More than before," may grow into a powerful reality if suddenly the Covenant were to be endangered, and the Powers who signed it should wish to tear it up again, leaving nothing in its place. But what are we to do with the temptations which are designed to appeal to the despondence of the vanquished and aim at converting the natural critic of an inadequate piece of work into a clandestine beneficiary? Surely such cunning despondency must soon turn against the practitioners of such despondent cunning. The vanquished will receive their full rights only through a just Covenant; but they will be foolish piously to put up with all its wrongs for the sake of the few devious subterfuges which it offers them if they are sufficiently skilful and persistent. In any case our main fear remains—a fear which future events will frequently justify—that the victors will make the vanquished the partners of their guilt so that the latter will become oblivious of the League, like the former, under the pressure of their immediate tasks.

After all, the ultimate aim of all these enticements is to deprive us of the hope and with it of the desire for a better League. If they say better than nothing, they are trying to persuade us, in comformity with the French proverb, that the better is the enemy of the good; yet conversely the good is also the enemy of the better. Of what use are the praises of a progress that has been completed? It is a long way from the wooden raft to an ocean liner, and in the interval impressive passages will have been made in various sailing-vessels. As for ourselves—what is it that we look for in the Covenant and in those of its chapters which are scattered among the neighbouring treaties? Need we concern ourselves with the coming century, or with the children who are now going to school? What is at stake is peace, but not the peace of the future world or of the future heaven; it is the peace of to-day and of tomorrow that is at stake. Here there is no room for waiting or for experiments; to rely upon the normal progress of human affairs would be wrong. If we allow the distance between the present day and the day of the conclusion of peace to grow too considerable, if we allow ourselves to slumber or to rely on vague promises, the moment of salvation will be lost irrevocably, or at least for a long period, and the cause of a just and enduring peace too will be lost. In any case—why wait, and for what? Are our minds too dull to elaborate with sufficient speed and thoroughness the idea of the immediate necessity of a lasting peace? Must we wait until our brains have grown more subtle, and our knowledge more profound? Knowledge of a dazzling clarity has long been available; the idea of a League was completed in all its details centuries ago. Must we expend long and patient labour before the technique of peace can be devised? Every statesman, every diplomat, every jurist and every parliamentarian has it at his finger-tips in the same way in which every general staff and Minister for War possesses the technique of hostilities. What is missing is the will to the League. The Covenant would be a great advance on every document previously signed by statesmen but for the existence of the Versailles Treaty; but even in a less chaotic world it would be no more than an advance. Its disastrous inadequacy is not due to the fact that its authors and their contemporaries were too foolish or clumsy to produce a better pact: if that were all, we would have to wait until they had grown more intelligent and more adroit. The fact is that we know that they did not want a better pact, and that their not inconsiderable intelligence and indisputable skill were employed to make it as bad as possible. Deliberately they allowed it to fall short of the requisites—the practical requisites—of peace, and the only reason was a will to power more powerful than the will to peace. We all appreciate why they did not desire peace, and why they halted at the very beginning of their road; speaking historically, we can even pardon their hesitation. But equally we cannot approve their hesitation; it would be folly to interpret their weakness or cowardice as a benefaction or as a unique method for producing a better League. If we would advance at all, we must overcome the voluntary as well as the involuntary paralysis of the will, however intelligible in view of the unhappy circumstances the latter may be. The diplomats may be interested in praising an advance which caused them to shudder at first, when their tradition had no place for it, and to which they are reconciled only because it quickly adapted itself to this tradition; the jurists, the professors of the abstract science, may praise it because honestly they know how little existed before the League, and the jurists of the applied art may zealously praise it because they require it professionally. But does it contain anything to provoke the admiration of the nations? Their urgent need does not require any advance in the investigation of a problem; what they need and what they have always needed is a solution; and always while they were waiting, war came and destroyed them. If once the nations begin to praise the progress made by diplomats and jurists they will be lost; for then what was progress yesterday will be stagnation to-day, and retrogression to-morrow. Accordingly the Covenant, with its various branches in the peace treaties, with its injustice and hypocrisy, its omissions, its false assumptions, and its impossible promises, cannot satisfy an earnest well-wisher of the League; and if the soothing words of propagandists should ever compel their admiration, the Covenant will gradually become inoperative, to be torn to shreds in the next war. The champions of the League must remain dissatisfied, turbulent and sleepless if the statesmen who make history, and the jurists who write and interpret the necessary papers, are to be roused from their deadly satisfaction in their work and from their murderous complacency at facts sanctioned by history; for only so will they proceed on the great and urgent journey which is to lead us back to the better Wilson and to the predecessors from whom he drew, consciously or unconsciously, the force which later deserted him. They must enter upon the last journey to that promised land which Wilson had clearly seen and proclaimed from the mountain-top before he lost his way in the desert and gave to us forged tables of the Law. If the advantage or disadvantage of various countries, the improvement of diplomatic procedure, or the new theories of professors alone were at stake, we all would have time, patience and superior calm; but in fact it is the cause of the nations, as Napoleon said, which is at stake, and there is no more urgent cause in the world. The question is not whether the document is better than any previous document; what we require is the best possible document. We demand the true tables of the Law which we all but held, only to lose them again. A journey to Geneva can have one meaning only: to bring back the tables and to set them up in the city of the League.

Meanwhile we have to deal with the Covenant, such as it is, with its twenty-six mediocre articles and the numerous relevant articles of the treaties. With all its defects, this paper is now to be called into life: to work, then! An office in London, a Secretary-General (a diplomat and an Englishman, prudently designated in an annexe of the Covenant), a handful of officials who collect their friends and acquaintances, British and French, and, during the first weeks, while there were hopes that their country might join the fold, Americans, a number of tried allied and neutral friends of the war period—between them these form the nucleus of an inter-Allied Civil Service, a sheltered bureaucracy ambitious to become the priests of the new religion. There follows the Paris period, and a domicile in the Senate building; next a nomadic period, during which a few ministers and diplomats, the reserve team of the Supreme Council of the end of 1919, desirous now of becoming a Council of the League, and hence the controlling executive organ of the new foundation, tour different towns all over the world. Eventually a fleet of furniture vans is seen discharging the London typewriters and filing cabinets before an hotel of the Quai du Mont Blanc. A few official *communiqués* are turned out for the benefit of the world Press and in opposition to the Wolff Bureau. A few French and English shorthand typists are discovered, with pretty faces and dazzling silk stockings, full of zeal and good will, who introduce a brighter atmosphere into the city of Calvin and of the tourist industry. Such are the preliminaries; now to work. Will the paper turn into something living? Under the hands of the diplomats of the Supreme Council, the civil servants and the pretty English and French girls—an allied world, partly still involved in the war-time atmosphere, but partly beginning to look forward to a more cheerful time, a world which multiplies, forms departments, and begins to elaborate a hierarchy of its own—paper begins to beget paper. From the Geneva typewriters, duplicating machines and presses, vast rolls, endless ribbons, whole avalanches and blizzards of paper go leaping, rolling and sweeping over the country. Simultaneously the outlines of the League structure detach themselves from the paper articles of the Covenant and achieve three dimensions. Organs, committees and offices are formed, no longer consisting of letters, but of human beings, who, first figuring merely on lists, soon appear in their natural dimensions, standing on legs of their own, smoking a pipe or a cigarette as their choice dictates, and sitting round tables where small shields proclaim the name of a country—the country which is theirs and which they represent. The organs create new organs, new lists and new tables, and eventually the biggest hall, with the largest number of tables in Geneva, is hired and furnished. Forthwith hundreds of people sit behind the shields which bear the name of forty-five and later of fifty-five different countries. Thus a cell is formed, and out of the cell a world on the edge of the world.

Meanwhile the tears and groans of reality remain outside. Soldiers cross the frontiers to begin new wars, or else march around their barracks, pre-war automata newly wound up. Trade unions and captains of industry occupy their respective fortresses and launch attacks upon each other. Bandits of every class roam over the unquiet world. Thrones are won and lost. Money swells into a vast and empty mist whence a new mintage falls into new pockets. Vast industrial undertakings flourish by the side of vast famine. Black, brown and red shirts fight in the streets and shoot from lorries; a shrill jazz music whose top notes sear the mind fills the towns of every continent, and is heard alike in palaces and slums. Gramophone records which we call newspapers register the idle noise. The concert begins with Poincaré, Briand, Stresemann and Mussolini, unless it happens to begin with Carpentier and Schmeling; the repertoire includes Josephine Baker, Eckener, Thomas Mann, Lindbergh and Charlie Chaplin, the fantastic wireless programme of every civilization and the fortune-tellers' advertisements of every suburb. Now and then the name of Geneva passes through contemporary consciousness, or the shadow of some League of Nations secretary emerges only to be swallowed up in the mad fandango of real actualities and even more celebrated celebrities. Meanwhile at the edge of the world the attempt at a new world is being built up, of paper and wood.

Who can escape the magic which emanates from every existent entity? Something has begun to exist, and the persuading, seductive and proselytizing voices begin to sound more urgently. Who dares assert that the organization acting and developing in a hundred new directions is not the true League? Surely at any rate the similarity is remarkable. Is there anything else that is more similar to the League? Is there no League in existence as yet? Perhaps; and yet we have a Council, an annual Assembly, an International Court, a Labour Office, and a Permanent International Secretariat, to say nothing of the growing confusion of bodies like permanent commissions and temporary commissions which grow and expand, some of which had not existed before, while others had existed under a different name. All of these now form one body. These various arrangements are admittedly restricted in their functions. No doubt they were not composed without after-thought; it must be granted that they do not exclusively serve the common cause; we know that they are the servants of one cause rather than of the other. And yet in many cases, even if not in the most important, they are the only institutions which will always be at the disposal of all. With all their faults, they have one vast merit—they exist. They are so many houses and huts, cells, and temporary structures, scattered, unequal, sometimes hardly supporting each other, and often separated by wide empty spaces. They are hardly protected from incursions from without, but at any rate they exist. Above them all, rightly or wrongly, waves the flag of the League, and there is nothing else on earth to bear this name. The great name is peculiar to these institutions, and if they draw splendour from it, they give in exchange a reality to the name.

It is this name which confuses and hampers us and which yet entices and seduces. It is a finer name than all that it denotes; at the same time it beautifies everything that hides beneath it. It adds nobility to every expression in which it occurs. League Council: the origin and composition of this Council is soon forgotten and perhaps was never known; but the word League suggests a world of confidence to our consciousness. League Assembly; League Secretariat; League Delegate; League official and League expert—they may be shadows or skeletons, but they achieve merit through this name. They may not deserve it, but they give it a countenance: they may even harm it, yet they cause its name to be pronounced in the most distant regions of the world. It is the name which confuses and which captivates us; it cannot be pronounced without tenderness, or listened to without hope; gradually even the most recalcitrant are gathered under its charm. The Germans and Hungarians, who have every reason to resent the Paris device, hear the name; they know that it is a tool in the hands of enemies—the instrument of their degradation, designed to perpetuate their misfortune; and yet they are charmed and join in the chorus. And even before the hard-headed politicians who continue to fulminate against the institution with its secret and open faults settle down within the League—for they are at home everywhere, and their policy makes use of every instrument—the idealists are drawn by the flag which floats above those buildings.

Confused and at heart ashamed, they wander through the unfamiliar rooms, slinking along the walls and shaking their heads, finally to look up for consolation to the flag above. It is a strange gathering which surrounds that lofty symbol, and in its heart calculating profiteers rub shoulders with ardent zealots.

For now, beside the other conflicts, the greatest and most protracted conflict of all is about to break out—the conflict which, in fact, is a continuation of the secular conflict about the League. Here the opponents are not the conquerors and conquered of the late war, and it is not the maintenance or revision of the Treaty, but the League itself which is at stake. This conflict is latent behind every conversation, every document, and every thought relating to Geneva, and often enough it will rage within a single person; it is the conflict of those who would like indissolubly to identify the name of the League with the present distribution of international arrangements and gradually to deprive it of every other aim and object until all are compelled to make use of the goods which it purveys, the name of the League becoming simply a trade mark; and those, on the other hand, who agree reluctantly to allow the plan devised at Paris to usurp that great name and who agree to lend their help only because they hope that the name, instead of falling to the level of the institutions which it covers, will give them a kind of magic inspiration and raise them to its own level. They hope that it will become a programme with a more urgent appeal than that of the Paris programme, a banner which will not be dragged in the rear, but which will stream in the van, and which is not given but only lent to its present beneficiary. The present arrangements may collapse some day; if they do, the flag must not be buried under their ruins, but must be kept clean until the day comes when it can be hoisted over the real League.

We shall discover this conflict at the core of all the other conflicts which will meet us in the city of the nations. It has been haunting the last part of our journey and has thrust into the background all other cares and desires, while we, impatient and excited, stand at the window and read the names of the last stations.

CHAPTER XIII

THE STAR OF THE SALÈVE

OUR journey has come to an end—a journey through the dreams of peace and the reality of war, the wisdom of plans and the folly of treaties; it has been a long journey of much promise and little performance. The iron caravans rush to their goal through smiling valleys and over gloomy ravines. Even in this last hour how different are the feelings inspired by this journey!

From opposite sides the French and the Germans are approaching the city of promise. Hours ago the latter left their frontiers behind them and turned their looks towards a new horizon. Looking up from their dreary documents and their confused cares, they have glanced at German-speaking Basel, itself almost a part of Germany, have looked with interest at the mixed races of Delsberg and Biel, and have passed along the foothills of the French Jura, with its great and its little, its silent and its melancholy lakes. They have circled around Lausanne, with its hills, and French air, and southern gaiety. Already hours have been spent in the land of Swiss peace and Swiss internationalism; their mind has been filled with images belonging to a more serene and happy world, a world miles distant from their German prejudices and cares. The preparation for a new and greater experience is complete; the personal element and the elements of home have been purged away; their minds are open and prepared to accept with thanksgiving everything that is strange and new.

The famous tunnel of Chexbres is entered; they leave it and enter into dazzling light. Before them, and finer than Hodler could paint it, they see the expanse of the Lake of Geneva, radiant and caressing and romantic to the first glance, serene in its distance and its calm, lofty in its surrounding mountains; the scale of its colours forming one harmony of gentleness and tenderness, of peace and reconciliation, soothing every mental conflict, and enhancing every lofty thought. This is no lake; it is a great, a gracious, a philosophic dream. Past the wheels of their train move the cultivated vineyards clustering round the neat churches and formed into a pattern by white paths and white walls. Their green merges into the pale, smooth, half-waking, half-sleeping, the smiling blue of the wide surface of the lake, to merge on the other bank with the blue-green swelling hills, the blue-white Alps and the dazzling white crests of Savoy, to mingle with the light blue of a wide and flawless sky. Every outline is plain and restful and saved from hardness by a fine, semi-transparent film of mist; the shimmering air is a shimmering light, equably and softly spread by an invisible shade. The journey is a magic journey through peace, visible, perfect and convincing.

And, if we enter this peace in the evening, we experience an equal bliss. The blue above and below is deeper, and yet it is gentle and seductive and full of light. The green and white edging has disappeared, but the blue is spangled with gleams of gold. The thousand lights which are scattered at our feet over the land, which frame the lake and flash and pass over its surface, ascend the mountains on the far side, first in small groups, then, in the higher regions, scattered, until finally, after an empty space of blue, they are spilled over the whole sky. These and the blue which at this time does not draw life from light and air, but itself radiates air and light, are the same peaceful bliss and the same blissful peace in the radiance of the night as in the radiance of the day. Nowhere do day and night resemble each other as here, where nature is not appreciated by the eyes, but is absorbed by the senses of the heart and the understanding. Drenched in harmony we approach the goal awaiting us, hidden as yet behind the windings of the lake and the vast dome of a hill, in a distance which descends from the splendours of the mountain into the gentle, quiet and friendly calm of the plains. We enter into a paradise, and around us wave the blue ribbons and veils of a most peaceful nature.

THE STAR OF THE SALÈVE 183

Very different is the last course of the French. Beneath their wheels the turbulent green waters of the Rhône provide a wild, overpowering and romantic spectacle. The cliffs press upon the railway and tower into the sky. All that they see and breathe, and all that inspires them, until the last moment, is their own country and the glory thereof. Only a short day or night lies between Paris and the moment at which they cross the frontier and, seeing before them a peaceful valley, pass along their own river and so into the town. The advertisements are French, as they were at home, and the people walking in the streets under the railway viaducts have a French appearance: between departure and arrival there is no experience and no new vision. If it suits their convenience they can enter the sleeping-car in Paris in the evening and in the morning leave it in the station of a provincial holiday town which might well be French. The invisible frontier is passed unnoticed, and the League—their League—awaits them without any previous vision of Switzerland or lake, without transition and without surprise, at their very threshold, as the natural continuation of their country—a suburb of Paris.

But whatever their provenance, and whatever the course of their journey, the participants have arrived; the product of diverse experiences, diverse images and diverse histories, the debate between the nations is about to commence.

The journey is at an end. The prophecies and theories, the attempts and failures, the search for an ideal, the bargaining for advantages, the anger, the disappointment, the satisfaction, the points and articles, the tormenting reflections, and the crackling paper read through a hundred times, have been left behind. Before us is an actual town; a town of stone and asphalt, with houses and tables and chairs around. Work is to be done; problems are waiting to be attacked and solved. The question is not whether there is a League, whence it comes, what are its aims, whether it is the right or the wrong League and whether it is an experiment, a fraud, a fulfilment or a promise. The town has been reached where the debates are to take place; the League, whether it exists or not, has its town, a town with houses, tables and chairs.

The trains have stopped. The waiting throng moves along the platforms, first slowly, then more hastily, finally in confusion; it separates, it joins again, it flings itself upon the doors of the coaches. Everywhere there are compatriots looking for compatriots, eager, respectful, friendly and in a kind of holiday mood. Hats are raised and hands stretched out; greetings are acknowledged; we leave the train, and the reality of firm ground is beneath our feet. Is the reality good or is it bad? At any rate it is solid ground—it is Geneva. The Consuls-General, the Consuls, the Vice-Consuls and heads of departments, the delegates permanently accredited to the League, and the League officials hasten to present their official smiles. Representatives of societies are drawn up; with them a few students, a girl and a bouquet; likewise a photographer and a plain-clothes man whom everybody knows as well as the Consuls and the bouquet. Gravely the delegates leave their coaches; and now, on the dark and narrow platform, the foreign ministers and statesmen of the greater part of the world are collected; the historic figures move between scaffoldings and porters, taxis and trunks. The governors of the world are collected in this station.

We cast our eye over the mighty ones of the Great Powers. There is about them at once something touching and amusing. All are somewhat excited, as people are excited after a long journey not quite without meaning and importance; they experience that degree of satisfaction and excitement which people do experience on meeting families and friends at the station. As they hurry along they raise their voices, look for a witticism or an epigram, succeed in provoking laughter, and noisily join in. The flashlight is busy; everywhere there is hurry and confusion. But the confusion of this station is different from that to be witnessed at any other time or place. There is a mixture of holiday feeling and of the satisfaction felt at the commencement of term. The circles surrounding the ministers and delegates and their friends, as they descend the platform, grow more dense and lively; there is a confusion of gestures, simple and pompous, hearty and submissive. At the edge of the groups young women stand on their toes to see the great men. The ordinary traveller makes his way past these obstructions and while looking for a taxi or wondering what has become of his wife or cousin, angrily turns his head and shrugs his shoulders at this unique class of travellers who advance at ease in line abreast, who stop amidst the throng every now and then, who seem to enjoy the inhospitable station and actually to feel at home in it.

The fact is that they do feel at home in it; not so much because they are surrounded and protected by throngs of their compatriots, as because, while they walk along the platform, the long silence of separated nations gradually begins to yield. Already each of them begins to sense the new world, which is that of the others as well as his own, which in a way belongs to all, and which each of them entered not for his sake, but for that of the others. A minister stands surrounded by a crowd of countrymen, exchanging handshakes and deep in good-natured conversation. But with a sudden flash, his attention is drawn away and turns from the surrounding circle, for a colleague from another country has crossed his field of vision. Salutations and conventional words of greeting are exchanged; hands wave. Through the wall of compatriots a hand is stretched to the other, and almost a conversation had begun. Soon, however, he is claimed by his own people; for to-day he is theirs. And yet he has already felt that this salutation was the important and the expected element in his arrival. He and his colleague are counterparts. To-morrow they will speak and work and dispute, side by side or in opposite teams; for the moment each drifts towards the exit as part of a national group, but as they move they still feel and sense the existence of the other. Solidarity? Not that, nor anything like that; rather a feeling as between colleagues; not otherwise deputies belonging to different parties might salute each other when meeting at the station. Community of nations? Not that, nor anything like it; but there is a professional community among people designated to be the spokesmen of their nations; and here, on this station, they belong to each other even if their nations are not so bound. The nations cannot yet speak to each other; but individual men can converse together from among these groups. The Geneva conversation has begun.

Meanwhile the cars have been reached. The Consuls-General and Vice-Consuls, the permanent delegates and secretaries, the journalists, the girl who has got rid of her bouquet, the heads of departments and the plain-clothes man, salute the honoured guests whose cars proceed to roll impressively down the wide rue du Mont Blanc. With its lofty French dwelling-houses, the solid insurance offices and travel agencies and the solemn rigidity of the post-office, it is like the entrance to a powerful and busy capital. At the other end the landing-stages, the steamers and the lake are waiting in shining confusion. Before us the pont du Mont Blanc stretches with its elaborate lanterns; on the left, the widening corner of the lake, with its quays and parks, and its dark, still water, where the wild ducks sleep, the gulls scream and the swans float; on the right, where the lake grows narrow before it turns into the Rhône which here begins its journey to France, we see the little triangular island with its dark trees, and the Rousseau monument which, hardly a stone's throw away, reflectively watches the arrivals. Here all is calm and clear radiance; a deep and harmonious silence despite the cars which would like to produce a metropolitan impression. On every side there are flags and streamers. The foreign arrivals feel flattered and smile; they do not know that the flags above the hotel where they are to live were hoisted for their benefit and that the colourful display in the streets is made for the benefit of a musketry competition, a cantonal gymnastic display or an automobile exhibition. It does not mean, and its greeting is not addressed to, the outer world; it merely denotes the twenty-two Swiss cantons, and that is why the bull's head of Uri is displayed, and the crozier of Basle, and hence the

Vaudois motto: "Fatherland and Freedom." The new arrivals are at liberty to feel that Switzerland too is a fatherland, and perhaps the nationalistic display oppresses the stranger who had already been prepared to embrace the world.

High above the dark city a light has flashed and sends down its beams. Is it the star which these wise men have followed? In all probability it is not their star but the light of that lean hotel, the objective of Geneva excursionists, on top of the Salève, on whose broad, bare back the secretaries, male and female, will go clambering next Sunday, while their chiefs with their ladies will proceed in gorgeous cars to Annecy, Evian, or possibly to Thoiry, where they will lunch copiously and with enthusiasm and where, if they have a taste for such things, they can inspect the Stresemann-Briand relics which are preserved here and bear witness to the journalistic marvels of this promised land between Alps and Jura.

The car stops. A curious crowd gathers before the hotel. They raise their hats politely, and even a few cheers are heard. Those old friends the manager and the porter do obeisance in the hall. From the cocktail bar an old acquaintance, the gramophone—it has been improved since last time—is heard; and above all this splendour the national flag flutters, which was left behind a few days or hours ago, and which we now meet again. Each delegation has its hotel or its suite, with offices, waiting-rooms and coding staff; within a few minutes a miniature Quai d'Orsay, Foreign Office, Wilhelmstrasse and Consulta is arranged. The arrivals have dressed and have begun to dine. Peace can commence.

Meanwhile a scattered rearguard moves down the rue du Mont Blanc: international pacifists, national petitioners from oppressed regions; people who have carried their faith or their necessity together with their meagre luggage by third class through the world until they arrived at Geneva. They wait for the dangerous cars to pass, blink at the coloured flags which now seem to wave in their honour over the deserted streets, and finally find their way into the cheap hotels around the station, whence they proceed to send their first picture-postcard home, or to address their hundredth petition to the League.

BOOK II
THE HOTEL

CHAPTER XIV

HOTTOP'S PALACE

THE garden of the Hôtel National with its tasteful arrangement of magnolia trees stretches as far as the quay; somewhat unexpectedly it is presided over by the chocolate-coloured statue of a negro girl, who lifts towards the sky a lamp which is never lit, where she stands in the middle of the lawn; a pretty but an unintelligent creature. A white stone balustrade stretches in front of the young negress and forms the boundary of the hotel garden. On its lake side we find a sober marble tablet inscribed: "To the memory of Woodrow Wilson, President of the United States, Founder of the League of Nations."

Can it be, we ask, that this historic figure once lived in this magnificent building? No, but they tell us he does inhabit it now....

Let us examine the hotel with the tablet commemorating the American President.

In its last pre-war edition Baedeker told us of this agreeable and first-class hotel that it contained 230 beds with rooms from 4 to 12 francs; breakfast 2 francs, luncheon 4.50 francs, and dinner 6 francs; full pension 14 francs. Other contemporary documents and oral tradition inform us that the hotel was built in 1873-4, and was opened on the 4th of July 1875, the day of American independence, and that, from its first day, just like the old Hôtel d'Angleterre, it housed a number of extraordinarily high-class and famous people with their retinue: Countess Mathilde von Trani, born a Bavarian Duchess, and sister to Empress Elizabeth of Austria, Prince George of Greece, the Grand Duchess of Mecklenburg-Schwerin, the Duchess of Devonshire, the Arch-Duchess Gisela of Austria, the Maharajah of Karputhala, the Khedive Abbas Hilmi of Egypt, the Duke of the Abbruzzi, the German Secretary of State, Kiderlen-Wächter, the Serbian Minister

Patchitch, the American Ambassador Herrik, the newspaper magnate Hearst, and three very famous ladies—Princess Chimay, the prima donna Mary Garden, and the tragedienne Eleanora Duse. The famous morganatic marriage between the Duke of Croy and Miss Leishman was celebrated in the rooms of this hotel. It was here that the American Consul used to give his receptions on Independence Day, and all the Americans took their cocktails in the bar before they went to Evian. When the work of reconstruction began all over the world at the end of the Great War it had been intended to renovate this hotel too; it was closed on the 3rd of November 1919 in order to instal eighty-two new bathrooms, running water in all rooms, an extensive loggia on the fourth floor, and a noble hall on the ground floor—in short, to modernize the whole building; and the capable manager, Herr Hottop—like the amiable writer Rodolphe Töpffer, a Genevese of German extraction—had hoped to carry these labours to a successful conclusion in June 1920. The execution of this plan was, alas, delayed, by a number of strikes, like many another piece of European reconstruction, and the re-opening celebrations had to be postponed until the 15th of August 1920. But now history interfered with the affairs of the hotel. Shortly before the opening day, so eagerly awaited by numerous important visitors, Article 6 of the Covenant was fulfilled: it had been found that the League could not be prevented from settling in Geneva, and the Secretary-General, Sir Eric Drummond, bought the building for 5,500,000 Swiss francs. The new baths were removed and the permanent Secretariat of the League, as provided in the Covenant, began to domicile itself in the lofty entrance hall, the wide corridors, the dining-room, the smoking-room, the ladies' drawing-room, the bar and all the tasteful bedrooms; from cellar to attic all was League. Sir Eric's plain and comfortable office furniture was placed in the big, sunny, corner room on the first floor, from whose windows Francis Joseph's sister-in-law had admired the view over the lake: and who had a better right to it than he? For even if a special Annexe to the Covenant had not designated him as the first official of the new organization, and if he had driven up to the hotel at the end of the quay in his private capacity and with a single suitcase, Herr Hottop would have led the descendant of the royal blood of Scotland to the room reserved for princes. Herr Hottop himself—no less a person than the manager? Alas, once he had handed over the management of his house to Sir Eric, Hottop himself became an international League official; he was put in charge of the building, and after preparing so many choice luncheons for queens, princesses and American heiresses, he was allowed to arrange cheap staff lunches for the benefit of the shorthand-typists among the unbeautiful radiator pipes of the basement. The commissionaires, familiar for years with the splendours of the cosmopolitan world, with its brilliant heights and obscure depths, became League of Nations commissionaires. Even the fine, big, and ageing dog, whom years ago a noble but insolvent guest had left behind as a pledge, entered the service of the newly organized world; and for many years before he died the most peaceful of deaths he would lie on the steps of the entrance hall on the hotel carpet, the faithful guardian of domestic security, growling at night and somewhat upset by the fact that the inmates came in the morning and left at night under the new regime; for like manager, commissionaires and dog, the hotel carpet had been taken over by the League. With indelible lettering on durable material it glows on the threshold of the Secretariat, unadorned by symbolic escutcheons or banners, and without any motto proclaiming a solemn or lofty function; and the only salutation for the throng ing nations is the name of hotel proprietors swept away in the convulsions of history.

And now we are wiping our feet on the familiar mat; we enter the hall. Behind us at the entrance the taxis and the big cars of the delegations, with the little fluttering national flags near the driver's seat, jostle each other in the narrow forecourt, where the garage foreman of the League, Herr Schwalbe, with his staff of commissionaires, is attempting to introduce a first order into the international chaos. Black morning coats, of tight or of confortable cut, surmounting the classical black and white of official trousers, well tailored summer lounge suits, and between them a few ladies' light confections, hurry up the steps and sweep us with them into the big white hall with its simple decorations which, as yet gloomy and unilluminated by the modest candelabra, lies empty and bare before us. Gradually, however, it becomes more lively and soon international greetings sound in cheerful confusion.

For a moment we are at a loss in this ante-chamber of a new world. In front of us and separated from the hall which formerly stretched as far as the garden by a wall of glass and wood, and contiguous with the hotel terrace, whence a leisurely flight of steps sweeps between slender pillars down to the little garden by the lake, we find the old debating hall of the Council. With its blue carpets, white panelling and heavy red curtains, it presents us with the colours of France whose mountains we can see through its windows. From its doors two wide corridors lead to the offices of the League. On the left we find the old drawing-rooms and libraries, now converted into committee rooms, and the old dining-room in front of which a vast and bare structure consisting entirely of glass windows extends over the lower levels of the garden and nearly up to the lake. This is the new hall of the Council and former dining-room veranda which, after an energetic speech of Stresemann's—one of the few international successes scored by Germany at Geneva—was increased to twice its former size with much money and little taste. From every side lake and mountains, hills, sky, green waving branches, peace, graciousness and a distant dreamy magic send their influence through the walls of the glass coffin of peace. By its side a vast modern unadorned cube with a glass front has been erected, the gift of the city of Geneva and the domicile of the Disarmament Conference. On the right a corridor leads from the entrance hall past big, clumsy telephone boxes and shabby hotel sofas to the telegraph office and the Press room, the *ci-devant* American Cocktail Bar. At the entrance, at the foot of the gorgeous double staircase—we shall meet this staircase recurrently at dramatic moments, like the momentous stairs affected by certain stage-producers—we find Herr Hottop's old reception-room, whence he continues to rule discreet and invisible. By its side is a new reception-room for the new masters—the presidents of the various League Conferences and Committees. This room is adorned with a quaint picture showing naïve peace allegories—an upturned helmet and pretty little birds twittering around it; while on the other side we find, devoid of all allegory, the branch of the English bank whose function it is to pay the salaries and effect the other financial transactions of the League. A few steps further the old-fashioned lift floats into the heights above slowly and methodically. It has room for seven persons only, and consequently a chattering queue of delegates, secretaries, globe-trotters demanding tickets of admission, officials, typists, pacifists, petitioners and journalists permanently besieges it. At its whitewashed shaft the five-storeyed world of the Secretariat begins.

Cautiously and with hesitations the lift begins to raise us, suddenly stopping because at the first floor we are joined by a girl with a white apron and a full tea-tray and at the second by a messenger with a heap of documents and letters—the brief companions of our important journey of discovery. Meanwhile, we have an opportunity to read on its walls the first international instructions with which the permanent Secretariat presents us: "Officials are reminded," so one of these notifications, over the striking signature of the Italian Assistant Secretary-General, the Head of Staff, Marchese Paulucci di Calboli Barone, Mussolini's former Chef de Cabinet, informs us, "that lighted cigar or cigarette ends must not be thrown out of the windows because they might set fire to the curtains on the lower floors."—"Dogs are not allowed," so we are told in another regulation signed by the same high official, "to be brought into the offices without special permission."—"The mixed bathing arrangements at the Villa See-Perle are open to all officials at a fee of five francs." By the side of this notice a list of the new tender English novels purchased for the staff library inspires feelings of sweet sorrow, while we are somewhat surprised to find by its side an invitation to the Armistice celebration of the British Legion. Do we feel annoyed; had we expected our pilgrimage to be greeted by quotations from the Covenant? Patience—with the slow motion of our lift our souls are destined to rise from the depths of the hall below to the higher regions of international cooperation.

And indeed no sooner have we left the lift than the click and rattle of international collaboration descends on us from every floor. Here the typewriter rules; and the various private League of Nations Unions which are looking for symbolic arms should place a typewriter in the centre of a shining sun to make up the world flag of which they dream. Where formerly chambermaids and waiters glided down the soft corridor carpets, shorthand typists, pointed pencil and notebook in hand, now hurry in and out of the rooms, where weighty and unintelligible words hail down upon their amiable and polyglot brains. Messengers bowed under a heavy load of documents come and go with dignified speed. Along the wall which formerly presented us with the impressive and soothing void common to the corridor walls of all hotels, where the only sign of life behind the doors consists in neat and shining shoes or strong and energetic boots, vast filing cabinets are piled; some of them plain like wardrobes in servants' rooms; others are modern structures in green steel. All are full of papers, piles of papers, masses of papers, which are turned out behind these walls, reach to the very ceilings of the bathrooms, fill the air with a musty smell, overflow into the offices, crowd the corridors, tumble down the lift and stairs into the halls and saloons, and flow in avalanches over the habitable globe.

For behind all these doors grave men are walking up and down or sit behind desks of a size commensurate with their rank and lighted by ugly little lamps which formerly stood by the side of the beds in the bedrooms, provide a bad light, and prematurely spoil people's eyesight. They brood fixedly or else they are dictating. They dictate official notices which migrate from one office to the next, they dictate marginal notes to the papers which the messengers fling on their desk every moment; they dictate personal and official reports, national and international letters, translations, invitations asking Governments to attend conferences and sessions of committees, memoranda and enquiries. They prescribe the conversation of the nations and they write it down; they try to awaken the spirit with dead letters and to freeze the spirit into dead letters. At the beginning there was paper—and then there was paper again. But these human registering and propaganda machines do not only affect the nations at a distance and in the dark; already they are physically attached to the world debate. They have hardly dictated ten lines before they begin to shout down the telephone, and before them, on the shabby velvet and silk of the easy chairs in the stuffy hotel rooms, visitors sit from every quarter of the world—the small permanent Geneva delegates, the big delegates from abroad, colleagues, secretaries, experts, inquisitive League of Nations tourists, journalists and other officials of the House. In every room representatives of all the nations may from time to time be found gathered together, urging, insistent, discussing big and little contemporary events, persuading themselves that they and their opposites are the symbols of a country and of a complete idea; and words like "Germany," "France," "Siam," "Abyssinia," "Cuba," and "New Zealand," roll over the desks like so many billiard-balls. "Japan cannot . . ." "Surely England must . . ." "The Uruguayan view is . . ." It is a grand Noah's ark. They chat and discuss, full of their own importance; the world around them sinks away, and they think that they are the world.

And, inflated like their own papers, they themselves overflow into the corridors. Officials can be seen standing in corners by the side of the filing cabinets, papers in hand, playing at international conversations with other officials and with international guests. On their hasty passage from office to office they lean over balustrades and whisper or call out to each other. Eventually, talking and gesticulating, they drift down the stairs into the halls and corridors and their dialogues are merged in the vast rumour of talk which covers the entire city. They dictate, they talk, they translate, they duplicate, and talk and talk again, without respite and without end. The nations are gathered in converse.

They are gathered together, and yet they are separated. Where one Frenchman is, there you will find another, and close by there is a fourth, a tenth, a twelfth. Where there is an Englishman, there is England. They form groups and cliques, and even where they do not care for each other—and when do countrymen abroad care for each other?—they cleave together like limpets. Wherever we look, English and French are gathered together; they have the best rooms, turn out and read the most important papers, and with their numbers, their rank and their languages, which they have imposed upon the entire House as the official and standard languages, they command every conversation and every piece of work. The only ones who are left to themselves are the representatives of the minor nations, unless they follow the Dutch example, enter the Tower of Babel in force betimes, and obstinately defend their position. A melancholy Hungarian sits lonely in the international throng, and just because he is lonely he produces an international impression. What else can he do? But even the isolated ones are not without the company of their nationals; after all, there are such things as telephones, letters, delegations in Geneva and legations at Berne. In his report to the Council on the foundation of the new bureaucracy, Lord Balfour had pointed out that, once they had been appointed members of the Secretariat, officials ceased to be the servants of their country and for the time being became the exclusive servants of the League, their functions being not national, but international; and a similar view is expressed in later reports and in the definitive regulations governing their appointment. They are appointed by the Secretary-General and are under his sole control; and the official documents reiterate that they must render no services to their home Government, unless such services are also at the disposal of every other Government. The Russian ex-princess, Lithuanian by the unkindness of fate and League official by its favour, is required to mete out equal treatment to the Lithuanian Foreign Minister and disturber of the peace, Voldemaras, the irrepressible plebeian with the short and scrubby hair, who scandalized Geneva for years, and to his pale, fundamentally timid but artificially blood-thirsty Polish colleague, Zalesky. Will this prevent her from rendering assistance to the Lithuanian *enfant terrible* in all his political escapades, however great her internal reluctance? The Councillor of Legation from the Wilhelmstrasse, whose career has hitherto been that of a German civil servant, and who is firmly resolved to continue as such at an early date, must show the same loyalty to the Quai d'Orsay as he does to the head of the League of Nations Department in Berlin. But is he more likely to discuss important questions of the Saar or of disarmament with the former or with the latter? The French head of a department must give the same services to the German as to the French Foreign Office; but this will not prevent him from taking the train to Paris four times a month and whispering all the secrets of the Secretariat to his principals in Paris. Surprise would be caused in Geneva if he were to take the train to Berlin with equal frequency, and the French Embassy in the German capital would be extremely astonished if his first and last visit were not paid there. Thus the internationalism of the League officials as formulated by Lord Balfour and the League regulations would seem to be a sham. Fortunately everything is explained by the one word liaison. Is this word meant to denote the necessary nexus between Germans and French, Roumanians and Hungarians, Italians and Jugoslavians? Far from it. It means that, in the interest of the Secretariat, the Lithuanian officials establish liaison with Lithuania, the Germans with Germany and the French with France. If the Secretary-General, who theoretically has ceased to be British, goes to London before every important meeting, and the Italian, who has ceased to be Italian although he wears the Fascist badge in his buttonhole, goes to Rome, this is supposed to be liaison. Where does it begin, where does it end, and what cause does it serve?

Yet one day critical rumours arose. A crisis broke out, supported by former officials, the delegates of the minor States and the Press, and it was felt that the time had come to clarify and strengthen the international spirit. The world had called for a reform of the Secretariat; an international spirit must be created and safeguarded. What was the result? It was resolved to condemn young men, fresh from the University, to League labour for life; men without other experiences than those which they would collect in a long bureaucratic career, and without other political opinions than those which would be demanded of them. They will spend their lives in Geneva, with graduated salaries, compensations, a pension system, and with children to be born to them by wives whom they will meet at Geneva; no other influence will act upon them than that of the Secretariat, which is their little world. Certain friends of the League are pleased; others doubtfully shake their heads. Once the international man has been bred, such as the Covenant now in force for some years demands him, will the surrounding world be such that he reflects it as modern officials indisputably reflect the modern world? Will the world above him be such that he can obey it without becoming the servant of a few dominant foreign Powers, instead of serving his country, or a harmonious community of States? The world above him are the high officials whom he assists, and to assist them will now be his exclusive task; a body of functionaries who will be enabled to pursue their own national policies unhampered by any national policy among their subordinates, and even assisted by their internationalism. Indisputably, if the lower ranks are freed from bonds—thin telephone wires which in fact are heavy chains—forming the link between their international fiction and a nationalistic reality, it will be equally necessary to detach the highest officials from the bonds which, up to this day, have been the chief reason for their selection and official activity. If we go through the corridors of the hotel we can see here and there zealous reformers gliding into the less important offices, vacuum-cleaner in hand, to visit these industrious officials of the rank of Head of Department where they sit and draw up private memoranda for their Governments with innocent cunning. Here the reformers try to suck nationalistic rubbish out of their documents and their heads and to fill their souls with pure devotion to the international law. But when they reach the solemn rooms of the highest officials the reformers take good care not to enter. They walk past on tiptoe, lay their fingers to their lips and whisper *hush*. They would not like to interrupt; for the unofficial ambassadors of the Powers who rule within as the highest officials of the international community are occupied on important labours; behind their sound-proof doors they are deciphering the secret instructions of their Governments which have reached them by the latest couriers; or else they are dictating to their trusty secretaries, male or female, sworn officials, as it were, who have to take down the secret diplomatic report which is expected at home as confidently as the diplomatic reports from the Embassy. Were they to show this report to their international colleagues who are ensconced in their several rooms behind their respective sound-proof doors it would assuredly be a kind of treason. But we need not fear that such a horrid thought will occur to them; they know their duty and the reformers with the vacuum-cleaner pass by, full of respect.

And we, who follow them, arm ourselves with patience and approve. If the officials are not international they are no worse than the League. If the domestic arrangements of the hotel are wrong, they are no worse than the Covenant. If the servants of the new work are predominantly British and French, the work which they serve is itself French and British. Better to let them be as they are, what they are—French, British, Japanese and Italians—and to look in their hearts; the nature of their work must contribute something beyond the contribution of nationality. They have been at work in Geneva for twelve years. If six hundred men of the most diverse nationalities work together in one house for years, and the house is entitled to appropriate the name of League of Nations, they must be something more than Belgians, Chilians, and Dutchmen. Surely the grave, eager men who invite us to their rooms and there buttonhole us are something more than the appendage of the home authorities who dispatch them; and indeed a glance suffices to assure us that they are before everything appendages of the papers which fill their lives and experts for one of the departments of the House. Surely this is reassuring; here surely we have a first stage in the metamorphosis of nationalism into internationalism. Only the question is whether the League derives more benefit from their expertness than from their nationalism. If we look at them we soon conclude that they might display equal industry in any other office in the world, and devote equal zeal to the study of trade statistics or serums. They themselves complain often enough that they are hardly aware of the League; nor will their conversation throw much light upon it. Yet we may be sure that they are none the less efficient officials; they may even be among the best. Their work may not have much to do with the main purpose of the League; at the same time Article 23 of the Covenant requires experts and furnishes them with their *raison d'être*. The work they turn out is conscientious and efficient, and their minds are equally impervious to the fine ideals and the evil reality of the League. Those who are not engaged for life leave the House as they had entered it—highly efficient experts in a limited sphere of which they know something, in which they have improved their knowledge, and in which—this is the reason why most of them leave—they would like to become even more expert. While they are members of the institution, let us recognize their merits and salute them kindly when we meet.

Are we likely to approach more closely to the League by the aid of those impressive persons who seem born brothers of the experts but infuse a greater deliberation into their conversation? They are an attractive body, an extremely attractive body, and we would like to call them the monks of the League of Nations. They did not come to Geneva to exploit their expert knowledge, but to withdraw quietly and for a maximum period from the noise of a world of which they are afraid, although perhaps they never knew it; and thus they retire into the cells of Hottop's monastery whose casements open on the blue mist of the magic lake, there to worship in pious silence, to write memoranda in the spirit in which the Acts were composed and peruse the breviaries of their documents. They are by no means blind dreamers or enthusiasts; real monks too are rarely guilty of that weakness. Honourably and with a full sense of responsibility they fulfil the prescribed ritual, and trust in appointed authority. Many of them are good men; but they do not contribute much to give an inner emotion or driving force to the new institution—and without these an unresponsive and hostile world is not easily set in motion. Nevertheless, provided their numbers remain restricted, and they are assigned a retarding role such as the hurrying League machinery demands, they may play a valuable part; and, as we look into their closets, we will not grudge them a tribute of friendly recognition.

But alas, too many of the inmates of the international hotel whom we meet in the course of our journey are neither experts nor philosophers, but simply bureaucrats, *ronds-de-cuir*, as the glorious French expression has it, which names the official after the leather seat on which he spends so much time. They are not attached to their country, their papers, or even their own souls; what matters is their salary. They arrive punctually, they sit punctually and they go punctually, they draw their salaries punctually and they go on leave punctually. They might come, work and go like this in any other office in the world, and they would be equally alien in any other office. But they are equally indispensable; the gravity with which they surround themselves when checking accounts or counting chairs in the debating halls may seem out of place in the central institution of the new world; and yet we cannot but greet them with a smile. Unfortunately their spirit penetrates into the scene of more important labours; as a rule they are all that the outer world perceives, and thus its belief in a new work associated with a thousand sorrows and hopes is shaken rather than confirmed. And yet they could not be other than they are. Let us salute them albeit with restraint, and let us pass; and above all let us beware of confusing them with the next group with which they are only too ready to confuse themselves: the diplomats.

It is these latter who are the typical League of Nations officials; and these, the products of the last few years, constitute a real danger for the hotel. Not all of them are the products of legations or foreign offices; but all would like either to enter these institutions or look as though they had entered. For them the League which, as they say in the speeches, has risen out of the last groans of dying soldiers and the tears of orphans, is a purely social affair. The most significant aspect of the dream of mankind is the fact that it provides them with a diplomatic passport drawn up by their Governments, with a first-class ticket provided by the Secretariat treasurer for official journeys, the receptions at the delegations, and with the *entré* to the harmless *salons* instituted at Geneva by a few ladies of high society. They have well-cared-for hands and well-cared-for brains, play bridge, and give luncheons or dinners. When you see them standing in a drawing-room or sitting at a banquet next to councillors and secretaries of legation, you can hardly tell who belongs to the delegation and who to the League Secretariat. They are interchangeable and, in fact, are daily interchanged; they are entirely satisfied with the world as it is, if not with their position in the world, and progress for them means promotion. They work efficiently and intelligently, and in the normal course of events have a certain career before them; after the next war we shall find them among the ranks of their countrymen at the Peace Conference or, with luck, in a higher position in the ensuing League. Without exception they are pleasant and good-mannered; almost without exception they are intelligent; with few exceptions, they are industrious. They are even international, with the internationalism of all diplomats, hotels, jazz bands and wars. Let us salute them, but without excessive emotion, for they will always be with us; somehow, somewhere, we shall find them again, holding higher positions but otherwise unchanged.

They have politely accompanied us to the door and bowed us out with that combination of elegance and correctness which is so essential for a career. But what is the lively and altogether undiplomatic uproar which greets us in the adjoining rooms? Here there is no professional, monastic, bureaucratic or aristocratic routine, or calm, or elegance: here all is fire and excitement; eyes flash and hands gesticulate. We have discovered the most interesting group of all, the busybodies. These are the real driving force within the League. They are the electric current which makes the wheels go round; the war is not yet over for them, and in their hearts the sacred flame of the civilian eager to do his duty like the soldiers, were it only in some civil function or behind the lines, is burning still. Before all the other groups they have the one advantage that they never rest; they are always fighting for a cause, good, bad or indifferent, and have a mission in which they believe even if its object is not above criticism. They have come into contact with professional diplomats in the course of their work only during the war or the peace conferences, and consequently these semi-diplomats have not yet acquired the cool scepticism and the distinguished calm which invariably accompanies the professional diplomat in his unhurried progress through war and peace. They are plagued by an unceasing urge to do their duty whatever it may be, to deserve the high salaries of which they are half ashamed, to achieve tangible results and to render tangible services. In the works of peace they see the logical continuation of the works of war, and are happy only if something has happened, a plan is being devised or carried through, and confusion is being rendered less, or more, confounded. Once they have left the office they suffer boredom. Nothing would please them better than to be awakened several times a night by the telephone and to be dispatched to look after some international problem. Their eyes begin to sparkle if some miniature conflict breaks out where the League might play a part; for now they are at work to bring about League interference or alternatively—if such is the wish of the chiefs—to prevent it. Something must be done; to report all quiet on any front is anathema. At the same time they are far from being inefficient; they are probably the best servants of the League, combining devotion to their countries or Governments with devotion to their international activities and their international field of activity, convinced that their countries' most vital interests are centred in the League and that the League must be the scene of every endeavour. By focussing the national interest upon Geneva they set Geneva in motion and make it a hive of industry. Most of them are genuinely in love with the League as they see it, i.e. coloured with their national colours and vibrating with their own enthusiasm. They wish something to happen because they cannot wish their sphere of activity to grow narrower. They are ready to sacrifice a certain percentage of themselves, to grow beyond themselves and to advance a few yards beyond their nationalistic standpoint. At the same time they constitute a considerable danger for the whole structure; the rhythm of their feverish activity is perverse, and the basic note of their complicated chords is false. So far they are the most active and fervent workers in the League; but they will never provide it with that honest and simple-minded foundation from which alone it can grow into the heavens.

All these functionaries, whether playing the parts of monks, experts, bureaucrats, diplomats or busybodies, are fundamentally loyal to their work as they understand it. They may not be the apostles of international fraternity, but at any rate they achieve a kind of decent professional solidarity. Naturally the twilight of the new profession is the natural sphere of numbers of gifted adventurers, who display very considerable talents in exploiting their national and international position in the struggle, in advancing at Geneva on the strength of their alleged position at home, and at home by virtue of their alleged position at Geneva, and, by means of sham knowledge, sham performance and sham connections, carving a far from sham career. The majority, however, are straightforward, efficient and intelligent, in exactly the same degree as their colleagues in the Civil Service at home. However, the name of League official is greater than they and their office, which is backed by no driving or consuming force. After all, what do they see in the League? For one it is a filing cabinet, for the other the town of Geneva, for a third the national delegation and ministry, for a fourth an immediate superior. Are river navigation and railway transport the essence of the League? Is the annual report of the Mandatory Powers the League? Is the meaning of the League exhausted in influential relations to the *chef de cabinet* at the Quai d'Orsay or a party leader at Westminster? They sit in their different corners, do their work, wander around the corridors, or whisper down the telephone, and few there are in the highest positions who can comprehend the totality of the work; and even this totality is restricted by reservations and by the policy of the several Powers. Even those officials who would like to have a comprehensive vision of the whole work must not allow their looks to range too far. A director of the disarmament department must not go beyond the bureaucratic execution of the programmes set up by the Council and the Disarmament Commission; an official of the minorities section must blind himself to the fact that the Tyrolese in Italy possess minority rights as well as the Hungarians in Roumania and the Ukrainians in Poland. And what official could venture to show recalcitrance to his own Government should it pursue a policy hostile to the League? Worst of all, officials are not allowed to dream; the world is full of people desiring a better, a more efficient and a more generous League, but there is no room for such idealists within the walls of the League Secretariat. It is their fate to subject themselves to the strict law of a timid concentration upon a few tasks sanctioned internationally. They are the only living beings who can be compelled to admit that whatever is, is right and to defend the incomplete against progress. They sit under the tree of League of Nations knowledge, but they are not allowed to use their knowledge to perfect existing institutions. They are the prisoners of an incomplete work which it is their function to preserve, with the result that nowadays there is hardly a place where the ultimate aims of the League are mentioned more rarely than the Secretariat. This is the reason why a wave of semi-hysterical relief passes through the building on the Quai Wilson, if somewhere, however modestly and gently, blood is shed; for now the moment has come to appeal to Article 11, and it is permissible to think, write and speak of peace. In the greater world people smile or laugh at the excitement which is caused at Geneva by insignificant international disputes; they do not know or understand what passes in the big or little rooms of Hottop's Palace. Really, the free citizens of the free nations ought not to laugh, smile or mock: they are allowed from morning till night, at breakfast, lunch, tea, or any other occasion, to speak, proclaim or sing the word of peace. At Geneva the word must not be pronounced until an actual event has happened which, after engaging the attention of the necessary authorities, has found its way into their documents and has become the fit subject for the application of the Covenant and for a telegram drawn up by one of the Secretary-General's most efficient diplomats and signed by the President of the Council. It is for this reason that the poor wretches are seized with sudden bliss; it is for this reason that they smile happily and whisper: "Peace."

One beam from the distant sun which warms all mankind save them has fallen on them at last.

Are there no League of Nations officials in Hottop's hotel? Not yet; but among the various nationalities, the various monks, experts and busybodies, and even among the bureaucrats and diplomats there are some whose secret ambition it is to become League officials. Some entered the League buildings inspired by this desire at a time when participation in this experiment was something of a venture; others during the post-Locarno period, when it seemed that the last war was over and the origins of the League would soon be forgotten. Many, alas, have since left the House, disappointed and finally resolved to fight the battles of the League on a more suitable ground; but those who have remained behind and have acquired a sense of their real function desperately resist submersion in the unpleasant mixture of nationalistic aggression and international bureaucracy which is turned out in Hottop's Palace. It is these who have earned our affection and our thanks. We must not describe them or mention them by name; to designate might be to harm them, and we must not hamper their struggle: they are our hope, and they are the future.

CHAPTER XV

COUNTESS TRANI'S ROOM

It is among the six hundred officials who write, dictate, talk, form cliques, play at Noah's ark and liaison day after day and are concentrated on their country, their profession or their dreams, that we must look for the new League and its future. Its activity is dissipated over the world, divided between Council and Assembly, Conferences and Committee, and labelled with the great and little name of diplomats and statesmen; and it is here, where all its work commences and whither it returns, that we must look for its traces. To discover the new world we pass through the wide corridors and through offices big and little, open the capacious filing cabinets and inspect the pretentious and more modest desks.

The new proprietors of the Hôtel National have strictly adhered to the hierarchy devised by Herr Hottop. The first floor, and the wide shining parquet of the vast ante-room where messengers float with serious air, receives us with its traditional quiet distinction. Here, in the spacious rooms reserved for royalty, with their wide windows looking over the shining lake, is the domicile of the Secretary-General and his staff. It is here that our investigations must commence.

In one of the ante-chambers of the Secretary-General's room, a strangely uncomfortable and disorderly apartment, we are received by the Secretary, who is also the cousin of Sir Eric; a slender, distinguished figure with pale and yet youthful features wearing a smile at once diplomatic and girlishly diffident under hair unexpectedly white. Despite her modest rank she is more important in this house than the highest officials; she is called the "Tiger" with mixed familiarity and fear; and at the courts and embassies whither she accompanies the Chief on his journeys she is received like an ambassador.

COUNTESS TRANI'S ROOM

Noiselessly the door to the room of the Countess of Trani opens, noiselessly the Secretary has vanished.

The big room whose lofty windows are draped with semi-transparent white curtains is filled with a dim milky light. Before us there is a long conference table with a dozen chairs standing mutely around it. In the very furthest corner, behind a small simple orderly desk, between the pipes of a dreary radiator and the shade of a melancholy reading-lamp, we discover, a figure almost indistinguishable at first, the master of the House. He points to a leather easy chair by his table, and while slowly and with hesitations the conversation commences we observe the man, the one high official in the world whose sole function it is to think from morning till evening for eight hours a day of nothing but the League.

A remarkable man; not very striking at first, and on second thoughts a little awe-inspiring. He should be short and is tall; his hair should be grey and is fair; his appearance attractive although the features are irregular; intellectually attractive but without warmth, and almost startling by a curious mixture of external diffidence almost amounting to shyness and of internal self-confidence almost amounting to pride. He is a Scot, and more sensitive, more nervous, more complicated and more European than Continental prejudice would expect. We know that he plays golf every Saturday afternoon, when his conscience allows it, like all his countrymen, and that he goes trout-fishing on his holidays.

His game of golf is his greatest pride, and there is nothing he takes more earnestly than his fishing; he observes the same method and economy with his ideas as with his revenues, although there is no shortage of either. For the moment he takes charge of the conversation; casting down his eyes, and, now and then, scribbling a brief memorandum on a scrap of paper furtively and almost as though he meant to keep it secret; rarely he leans back to give us an attentive look, and soon lowers his head again, remaining motionless for a time. He speaks with caution and prudence but not without a certain vividness; he rigorously defines his subject and yet is not afraid of little excursions into fundamentals. While he does not carry us along, he is never jejune and sometimes interesting. Although he is rarely convincing he absorbs our attention, stimulates and confuses us; nobody is likely to leave his room with the same assurance with which he entered.

The longer we listen and observe, the more interesting and attractive does he become. We are soon aware that he possesses a lively and well-oiled thinking machine which operates with perfect exactness and noiseless accuracy, although not always without internal friction and pains for its owner; for this pious Roman Catholic, as he is by choice, has not cast off a Protestant conscience. The machinery is checked and the brake applied with the will to self-restraint natural to a trained official. We feel that his intellectual effort is most valuable where it is as lonely as that of a philosopher or a poet. He prefers himself as partner for his dialogues, although in company he is agreeable and ready to hear opinions even if he has no intention of availing himself of them. His marginal notes on the work of his colleagues have a completeness and a finish which would allow them to be printed without alteration. His replies to aggressive or offensive diplomatic notes are masterpieces of prudence, adaptability, and sometimes of firmness. Not many can boast to have outwitted him, and we may be sure that the few who succeeded had to pay dear for their success. His adaptability, his pliability, is almost feminine—or Latin; but he is also capable of an altogether Nordic obstinacy. He does not scorn diplomatic cunning if he feels sure that it has a moral foundation; even when it would be easy to defeat an enemy he does not launch a direct attack, for he is not anxious to obtain the appearance so long as he has the reality of success. He gives way with the politest of smiles until his adversary surrenders to the illusion that his diplomatic opponent agrees with him, becomes excited, blunders and eventually is entangled in one of the numerous nets suspended in the House. Once he is caught in the snare or has run his head into a wall,

Sir Eric puts on a shy and embarrassed smile, plunges his hands into his trouser pockets, looks and possibly for a moment is unhappy, perhaps even murmurs an apology, but knows, although he does not show it, that he is the winner. Indeed, he is almost always smiling, a somewhat clumsy, a somehow elementary smile, strangely underlined by his protruding lower lip; he smiles at the Council table and smiles when, without looking right or left, he moves through the building of which he is master. The effect is all the more convincing and almost threatening when he ceases to smile. If a word is heard in the Council or in a Committee Meeting which runs counter to his convictions, or seems to imply a threat to the orderly labours of which he is the warden, when a conflict which he is resolved at all costs to avoid seems imminent, his features become severe, reserved and vexed, sometimes irritable and nervous, and sometimes remarkably fierce. Whenever this happens everyone, down into the obscurest corners of the room, feels that something in the vast machinery is out of order. In such cases the angry expression worn by the Secretary-General is a danger signal, producing the same effect as when the engines suddenly stop in a steamer. Not until his brow clears, and his hands, ceasing to play nervously with the papers in front of him, lie quietly on the table, can we rest assured that we can move full speed ahead.

We scrutinize the high official, the only one in the world whose profession it is to think of the League for eight hours a day. What, in the play and opinion of his time, is the position of this man, who belongs partly to past history and partly to the history of the future? Everyone respects him; everyone recognizes his merits to the full. The members of the Council, the Assembly, and the various foreign offices, honour in him one of the most capable, if not the most capable contemporary diplomat. They respect his devotion to duty no less than the superior intelligence with which he has created and maintained the diplomatic machine installed at Geneva. They praise his high sense of duty, his delicate tact, and the unique skill with which he unravels tangled situations and circumvents threatening obstacles. They readily see in him their master. His subordinates experience a kind of cool and shy respect. Do they feel affection for him? They probably do not know whether he feels any affection for them. As for the public, on those rare occasions when it concerns itself with him, it hesitates. Is it aware of him? Clearly it does not know whether he is aware of the public. It reads his name in the paper and sees his picture, with its somewhat diffident smile, by the side of the great ones of the world; but it does not understand him, and generally underestimates his actual and very considerable achievements. But though it is unfair, a correct sentiment stands behind the wrong judgment; it is felt that this man, who ought to be a sensation, is nothing of the sort.

We look at him once more. No, he is certainly not a sensation. On the other hand, he is the perfect Secretary-General; the Secretary-General of the League Council, i.e. of a body of practical politicians, the Secretary-General of the League Assembly, i.e. of a body of speakers, and the Secretary-General of organs looking to him for technical assistance and diplomatic arbitration. But is this eternal role of Secretary the only one which he ought to play? Is he not the one official in the world whose privilege it is to think for eight hours a day and even for a few hours a night of the League, the one permanent and conspicuous leader of the League, the guardian and champion of the ancient idea now realized, if only provisionally? He is equipped before all the world with the power to preach a sweeping crusade; but it does not appear probable that this man, with all his intelligence and sensibility, has grasped that part of his task which concerns the future. Clearly his strict view of the literal meaning of his office, a view so entirely consonant with his reluctance to come into the limelight, does not allow him to give the League, besides an organization, advice or mediating services, or a soul. Wherever possible he has remained in the background, avoided doctrines wherever he could, refused to interfere personally in the happenings of the day, or out of these happenings to mould a future plan. He was not anxious to train disciples for the future completion of a work hardly yet begun.

In Countess Trani's room there is a big conference table. On the ground floor there are vast halls with any number of chairs. But never yet has it occurred to the Secretary-General to assemble his subordinates to celebrate any event—a New Year's reception, or the tenth anniversary of the League, or has he taken any other occasion to encourage them, to inspire them with the feeling that they are the servants of a great cause, to raise them to himself, and to train them for their common mission. He sits in his lonely tower with his secretaries. From time to time a colleague, an assistant, or a head of a department, is summoned. Each week he presides at the general discussion devoted to current questions. He receives the foreign permanent representatives, who leave the offices of their delegations in the town and call with all the pomp and circumstance of accredited ambassadors, rehearse their protests and requests, intrigue for their subordinates and confidants to obtain League positions, and fight for some petty advantage of their country within the world-embracing system. To the discussions with these persons he brings superior intelligence and industry; but he never shows himself among his own people: most of his colleagues do not know him and have never exchanged a word with him. Thus it is hardly to be wondered at if even the well-disposed among his officials have difficulty in feeling that they have any mission, and if the tie with the British authorities seems to be stronger than that which binds him to the international office to which he belongs and which alone he ought to serve. International arrangements and methods of collaboration are certainly destined to benefit by the activity of this admirable Secretary-General; but no arrangement or method has been invented to keep the great international problem permanently before the eyes of the officials, and to awaken them to the higher meaning of their activity. Every week, almost, hordes of students and teachers and members of all kinds of societies appear at the Secretariat. Excellent lectures are delivered to them on the general task and activity of the League; only the League officials have to go without lectures of this kind. They alone are never raised above the pettiness of every day. Yet the League is not advanced if Sir Eric has made of the Secretariat a technically admirable instrument, unless he succeeded simultaneously in inspiring the idealism which ought to be the characteristic of this Ministry, distinguishing it from every other Ministry and making it the ethical centre of the world: here was something above the limited programme contained in the Covenant and the diplomatic position of the Governments. Sir Eric has, of course, a perfect answer which completely discharges him as an official: the League is simply an inter-governmental institution, a method of collaboration between Governments on certain fields which have nothing to do with the general idea of, or a general enthusiasm for, the League. The only task assigned to the Secretariat is to perform the auxiliary function demanded by the Council and Assembly, Committees and Conferences for their Agenda, to observe silence and to refrain from dreaming. If the Secretary-General were to gather his staff around him, showing them the ideal of the League in its grand outlines, still more if he were to appeal to the delegates and to champion the cause of the community before these representatives of national individualism, it might easily happen that one of the Governments would call out indignantly: "Stop! What are you doing? Are you the Secretary-General of the future League? Did we appoint you to develop an idea which we deliberately did not wish to realize? Not so fast: it is your function to serve the institution known as League of Nations, however small and inadequate it may be, for we wanted it such. You should be the last to be deceived by the label which we gave to our work." Such might be the language of the Secretary-General's employers; and they would be right. Yet surely it would have been a great thing if Sir Eric Drummond had risked such an historic rebuke and had dared to be in the wrong. The world would have listened, and the League itself might have effected its first great advance.

Where are we? Are we in the League? No! We are in the Secretariat, in the ante-chamber of the Council, of the Assembly, of the Conferences and of the Committees; in the secret archives of the Paris foundation, in the coding office of a radically unchanged if improved diplomatic language; between the levers and switches of a vast administrative mechanism. We are in the instrument-room of a sea-captain who follows his course, makes the harbours prescribed, and has to take care that the passengers and goods advised are conveyed to and discharged at their destinations. He rules the ship and everything contained in its iron flanks; and as he pursues his way on the wide ocean, surrounded only by sea and sky, it might be thought that the ship was the world and the captain its king. But we know better; we know that the real world is hidden behind the mists on the horizon. We know that it is not he who sets the course, but the great shipping companies. Admittedly there are captains who, although dependent upon the owners who equip their vessels, follow their own path on the seas. But the Secretary-General of the League was not appointed, and his career has not trained him, to pursue such an adventurous course. It is not for him to discover a sea-route to India or to find the North Pole. It is not the bold adventurer's urge to increase the slender heritage of man and to bring new visions before those who remain at home which can fill the mind of this skilled diplomat and official. He is not a pioneer but a most experienced and prudent officer, who commands the international giant liner with skill and dignity and will some day hand it over with dignity and skill in order to receive his well-earned reward in the shape of a post in the Home Fleet. And yet—for after all the League cannot exist without a miracle—is it not possible that shortly before the day on which our captain is due to exchange his international for a national post, he might rise above his function, remain at his post with an inspired and purified deliberation, change the course and use his experience and authority to commence a new and bolder voyage? . . .

We look at the man, the one high dignitary in the world who is allowed to think of the League day and night. Is he aware of his favoured position and of his tragic fate? Does he know that he must be the great historic figure of our time, and that the picture of himself and of the new work as it will appear in our grandsons' school-books depends upon himself as much as upon external circumstances?—Sir Eric suddenly rises— just slightly embarrassed, with just the least awkwardness— compelling us to rise, and now slowly walks past the simple orderly desk, passes us and almost imperceptibly drifts towards the door. On his way he halts at two important points where he intends to settle the real question which matter and on which hitherto he has hardly touched. He stops first at the big Conference table where he suddenly becomes alive, and then a few steps further at the chimney-piece against which he leans, half dreamily, and half amused, to conclude the conversation exactly as he had intended at the beginning. He has slowly manœuvred us to the door and dismisses us with an air that is almost embarrassed and only just falls short of warmth. The audience is concluded. We salute the pale, slender, intelligent assistant; and now we are outside on the quiet and shining parquet. Meanwhile we may be sure that Sir Eric slowly returns to his desk, where he remains standing reflectively for a few minutes, his hands in his pockets. Suddenly he sits down and a lucid, brilliant and elegant summary of the conversation, ripe for a White Book or for a footnote of History, appears under his hands which have suddenly been galvanized into activity.

But perhaps we shall find the League in the neighbouring room, the light and elegant apartment belonging to the French Deputy Secretary-General, with its fine antique reading-lamp and the carefully preserved and tastefully framed engravings. The French Deputy Secretary-General is neither more nor less than the Deputy on behalf of France; the Covenant, which provides for a permanent Secretariat and in its Annexe designates by name the first Secretary-General, makes no mention of such an appointment as that of a Deputy Secretary-General, still less of a Frenchman as its holder. But France and Britain share the world between them. The International Labour Office was put in charge of a Frenchman, assisted by an Englishman; the League proper was put in charge of a man of British nationality assisted by a Frenchman. Why this system of assistants? Was the Secretary-General intended to manipulate with caution and skill the diplomatic instrument known as the League, while the assisting Frenchman was to embody and cherish the general human idea which bears the same name? We all would have appreciated such an assistant, nor would it have mattered if he was a Frenchman. The first captain is bound by a thousand ties, must never give rein to fancy and is bound by a time-table; and we would have welcomed with open arms a vice-captain—not because of his different nationality but because of his different function— whose duty it would be to look through a telescope of his own, to pluck the other's sleeve, point into the distance and whisper: "Why not leave the standard route and investigate this unknown island or try that shorter course? Why not devise a new time-table to lead us securely to our destination?" Such a vice-captain would have been welcome indeed: but such were not the instructions of the Deputy. The case was not that a human being had been detailed to assist an official, or a visionary the diplomat: a Frenchman had been detailed to assist the Briton, his telescope is a French glass trained on the same objective as the British. And if he takes his colleague by the sleeve, it is not to point to a new horizon, but to explain that French as well as British harbours should be visited. Of course he must not explain openly that he is in the League only as a Frenchman, nor must he throw additional emphasis upon the British role of his colleague by insisting upon his own French role; and accordingly a special field is assigned to him, not in the world of thought, but in the world of administration.

The Secretariat is divided into departments. The Secretary-General, while controlling the whole establishment, has also reserved for himself the supreme control of certain departments, viz. the so-called administration or minorities department, and the departments for mandates, social questions, disarmament, justice and information. Meanwhile the Deputy Secretary-General is in supreme control of the so-called Technical organization, viz. the economic and finance department, and the health and communications department. The sole purpose of this arbitrary and superfluous arrangement is to provide a background to explain the Anglo-French aspect of the supreme control. We must admit that the present Deputy, Monsieur Arenol, takes his function seriously and does his best, bringing all the dignity of an ambassador and the intelligent, yet phlegmatic zeal of a skilled official and expert to the maintenance of the French position by the side of his British chief, and to the pursuit of his special tasks as an expert. He even believes in the international mission of the administrative building, although for him, as for every Frenchman, the meaning of internationalism is to secure a good international position for France. Personally extremely agreeable and the soul of honour, he is, personally, as far from any visionary quality as his British colleague. One day he will quietly exchange his high international office for an important post in the Paris banking world, and it will be all in his favour if, having been a true Frenchman in Geneva, he can surround himself in Paris with a faint halo of internationalism.

Below the bridge where the Frenchman and the Briton are studying their charts, we find three disappointed subordinate officers. England and France having divided the control of the world between them, the members of other Great Powers deserve at least a consolation title, and accordingly an Italian, a Japanese, and since Germany's admission, a German Under-Secretary-General remind us that the League was not built up on the principle of the equality of the member States, and that the so-called Great Powers had permanent seats in the Council reserved unto them. One day the other Powers did revolt against the principle which reserved these posts to the Great Powers and demanded a democratic distribution of posts within the Secretariat. By a coincidence the three Great Powers simultaneously complained that their representatives enjoyed only the appearance of supreme control and that, far from being Secretaries-General, they were simply directors of departments without any right to interfere with the functions of the British Secretary-General and his French Deputy. Meanwhile certain of these inferior Secretaries-General were engaged in fierce dispute to discover which of them occupied the lowest rank in their inferior category. In his own opinion the highest position was that of Marquese Paulucci di Calboli Barone, a little man, of considerable intelligence, who had succeeded as the result of much skill and obstinacy in remaining true to his old profession as he had pursued it while Chef de Cabinet to Mussolini. Somewhat lower is the rank of Herr Albert Dufour-Feronce, a worthy Leipzig merchant who had grown up in London and who had been carried into diplomacy at the end of the war. His function now is to wear an amiable smile on his French Huguenot features, while translating his German vexation into perfect English. The lowest rank is that of the Japanese Under-Secretary-General, Mr. Sugimura, a giant of a man, who has retained the lofty eloquence of the fluent French which he acquired in his previous activity as national delegate to numerous League conferences, an eloquence which the French and the Secretariat lost years ago, and a rhetorical idealism which no European ventures to essay. Perhaps for these reasons he was long looked upon as the rising sun of the Geneva world bureaucracy. True, the Marquese Paulucci di Calboli Barone is superior to his colleagues by but an infinitesimal degree, but we can never forget this degree, for his colleagues never forget it. The German Under-Secretary-General is director of the department of so-called intellectual collaboration and of the international bureaux, the Japanese is Under-Secretary

General and director of the political department. The Italian, on the other hand, is Under-Secretary-General *tout court* and not director as well, which is more, and not, as one would be inclined to believe, less. He is Under-Secretary-General and is in charge of internal administration with a number of higher and lower assistants; and he is in charge of it in the same way as the French Deputy is in charge of the technical organs. This is not much, and in fact not enough for the Italian, though it is a little more than the German and the Japanese can show.

All the foolish quarrels within the house of peace are remnants of the late war and will clearly require another war to remove them. Meanwhile, they have led to irritating internal revolutions, and allow us little hope that we shall find a purer form of League in the rooms of the Italian, the German and the Japanese Under-Secretary-General than in those of the French and the British chief. At the same time there is some consolation in the fact that the lesser officials have only one title, and a definite sphere of activity unconnected with their nationality. "Internal administration," "intellectual collaboration" and "politics": here there is a powerful climax and a reality; and if these departments are not so much the scene of national representation as of international work, it is here that we shall discover the League. Our journey, our paper programme and the first hotel impressions are left behind and the work can commence.

True, the gorgeous and resplendent chamber allotted to the Italian Under-Secretary-General, with its far too richly inlaid table, will provide us with the show, but not with the meaning of work. His sphere is vast, comprising every floor of the house, the garrets, and the various private houses leased on the other side of the rue des Pâquis, and connected with the main building by a wooden "Bridge of Sighs," whose owner is supposed to be one of the ablest translators in the Secretariat. The sphere of the ruler of this domain is entirely concrete, and embraces a number of well-paid, superior officials, and besides these the small and industrious multitude of clerks, bookkeepers, checkers, stationery supervisors, stenographers, translators, correctors, draughtsmen, scribes, posting clerks, typists, telephonists, post officials, nurses male and female, porters, messengers, chauffeurs, commissionaires, charwomen and cleaners. It is the sphere of the modest but indispensable helpers, beginning with the trained, intelligent and multilingual translators of the conferences to the local staff taken over together with Herr Hottop's hotel. It is the sphere of the three thousand chairs which stand downstairs in the committee rooms, the two council halls, and the Assembly buildings, which are hither and thither moved in various combinations, some being destined for ordinary delegates, without arm-rests, and with simple leather seats, while those for the presidents are softer, more dignified and have a more comfortable form. It is the realm of the simple, uniform, square brown tables, which are placed together to form vast configurations, of the innumerable blotting-pads and ink-wells, the neat white piles of notepaper, the carefully sharpened red pencils waiting patiently at their post parallel to the paper, of the ash-trays, the water-bottles, and the shining glasses. The noisy "pool," too, belongs to this realm, the vast room with its multitude of typewriters on which the texts which grow into the air below from the rows of tables and chairs are written down, with its duplicating machines, which vomit hundreds of copies of drafts and shorthand notes, and with the miniature trolleys in which these are wheeled into the meeting halls and the posting department. All these more or less perfect instruments with the men and women attending on them form the sphere of the Italian official: more than half of the international servants of the new work belong to this vast, noisy and restless department. It is they who create the bustle, the movement and the external show of League activity which foreigners admire. But are they the League? It is easy to imagine that one day Hottop's hotel should change its function once more, and become—why not?—the domicile of an institution for the prevention of

League ideals. All these chairs and tables, blotters and pencils, spittoons and typewriters and all the worthy persons who serve these objects might well be retained.

Neither the ash-trays nor the cashiers will notice any change, and when cries of "Long live war!" are heard in the debating halls, the interpreters will rise as obediently as heretofore and repeat, with quiet zeal, "Vive la guerre!" If we walk through the halls, rooms, garrets, and annexes, controlled by the Under-Secretary-General, where he sits behind his highly ornamented desk, if we look into his private room, the room of his treasurer, who administers the League budget of thirty-five million Swiss francs, the vast, admirably managed publishing department, the department for the control of material, the stenographers' room, the editing department, the archives, the "analytic index," and the library, we cannot but do justice to the vast organizing labour involved. We shall rejoice to note that the cause of peace, now that so many experienced civil servants with war experiences are at its disposal, need not lack efficient bureaucratic support any more than the cause of war. But such work is not the League; chairs, pencils and documents are not the League, and we must continue our search in this labyrinth in order to find the men who sit on these chairs, the hands which wield those pencils, and the minds and hearts whence the divine inspiring spark crosses over to the never-ceasing flow of documents. Fortunately, intellectual collaboration is the sphere of a German Under-Secretary-General, and politics that of the Japanese. These are words with a meaning: to work!

CHAPTER XVI

LAUGHTER

WE go but a few steps further, past a few more doors of this impressive first floor. And yet great is the change. We leave the department which rules the chairs with the thin leather covering on which the nations sit, and we reach the department which rules the harmony of intellects. We cannot but envy the Under-Secretary-General and director of the department for international intellectual co-operation and international bureaux. However much the amiable Herr Dufour is annoyed by his slight inferiority to the Under-Secretary-General of the internal administration, the work he does behind his modest desk is infinitely above that of his colleague. "International intellectual co-operation!" We hold our breath while we move along the carpets of the silent corridors. Have we reached our goal at last? Is not international intellectual co-operation the League itself? Far from the shock of arms of a forgotten barbarism, and far from the calculating subtleties of an outworn diplomacy belonging to a lower form of intellect, it is our privilege to witness the co-operation of the moral forces of united mankind, our duty to watch the intellectual leaders of the nations. It is a solemn thought.

While taking a look around the offices of the department, we recollect that we are entering upon virgin soil on which the founders of the League had originally declined to tread. The idea of a republic of scholars and artists who, by tradition, stand above national frontiers clasping hands across a war-tormented world is an old and solemn one; but the founders of the League eliminated it from the Covenant during the Paris deliberations, despite ingenious suggestions from Belgian quarters. They had found a place for hypocritical methods of administering annexed colonies, and for anti-opium measures, and this was to be the total task of organized mankind: the signpost which stood by the road to peace never indicated an intellectual or a cultural goal. The draft plan submitted by the conquered barbarians at Versailles had found a place for the cultural mission of the League; in its quality of international community of labour it was to undertake the task of serving the intellectual as well as the material advance of mankind. But this valuable suggestion together with all the other contributions humbly tendered by the Germans to the masters of the world were thrust aside by Clemenceau's grey-gloved fist.

Did this idea possess such a compelling force that it inevitably recurred at the first meeting of the League Assembly as provided by the Versailles Treaty? The ancient Belgian pacifist and senator, Lafontaine; moved the adoption of international intellectual co-operation as part of the programme at Geneva, and the second Assembly (1921) adopted this motion after perusing a report produced by old Léon Bourgeois, Wilson's senile successor. Hereupon an international commission for intellectual co-operation was formed which soon gave birth to numerous subordinate committees. In the different countries so-called committees for international intellectual co-operation were formed, a special section for international intellectual co-operation was created in the Secretariat, and after many justifiable hesitations and rather unsuccessful precautions the apparently magnanimous but actually interested French offer was accepted, by which an institution for intellectual co-operation domiciled at Paris was to exist as a practical instrument side by side with the new machinery. This institute, of course, became the French cathedral of the new international religion.

By whatever means, however, the intellectual co-operation of the nations had now found a place within the League; an organization with manifold ramifications, having for its first President the French philosopher Henri Bergson, a restless, elegant figure, with high trembling voice, well-turned periods and delicate movements, half an eighteenth-century marquis, and half a Sociétaire de la Comédie Française. By his side we note the impressive figures of other intellectual masters of the age: Albert Einstein, with white, bushy hair, dark moustache and the observant child's eyes, the gentle scholar who joined the undertaking uninvited, and made a noisy exit only to re-enter almost unobserved; Madame Curie, the assistant and widow of the discoverer of radium, with grey, somewhat dishevelled hair and kindly, intelligent eyes, a woman of mixed Franco-Polish extraction; the mathematician, Painlevé, whom we also occasionally find presiding over the Board of the new Parisian Institute, as well as in the Cabinet where he is Minister for War, stout, bourgeois, and rather dreamy; and the tall, lean figure of Professor Gilbert Murray, Bergson's first successor at the head of the organization. In the sub-committees we find the great names of the French literary historian, Thibaudet, of Galsworthy, of Paul Valéry, member of the French Academy, of the German musician, Weingartner, and the German writer, Thomas Mann, to say nothing of innumerable professors, curators and librarians from all countries. They sit around the long tables, seriously and reflectively debate, and are not averse from allowing themselves to be photographed on the terraces of the historic buildings in Geneva or elsewhere which are the scenes of their deliberations. Not without emotion do we contemplate the pictures which we are proudly shown in the course of our pilgrimage through the first floor of Hottop's Palace; for these photographs call up a grandiose vision—a vision of a true future Council of the nations; a creative idea reaching back far into the history of the idea of a League of Nations. We forget the banality of the allied cabal whose ministers shook the League out of the embroidered sleeves of their diplomatic uniforms, and we return to the origin of the idea—to the succession of thinkers who are its true begetters. We salute the intellectual leaders of the age, and warm at the thought that soon we shall meet them; for surely—else why have they been summoned hither?—they will complete the work of the poets in a higher reality after its interruption by crude diplomatic materialism. Already we can imagine their hands about to grasp the laurels of success; and indeed, unike the prophets of old, they no longer stand in a world of hopeless chaos. No longer, like the Abbé de Saint Pierre, need they fix the realization of their dream at two centuries hence; the two centuries have passed. The thinkers of to-day are the contemporaries of an attempt at practical organization; they need not dream of the house of the nations; the house is ready and there is a mansion prepared for them which they themselves are allowed to perfect. For every dead philosopher, dead scholar, and dead poet of the past centuries a living counterpart is busy upon the living work. Here surely there is ground for hope and consolation. True, the old philosophers' League plan had penetrated to the politicians in 1919; but in their hands, whose only object it was to comprehend and organize a loose collaboration of cabinets and bureaucrats, it had shrunk to pitiful dimensions. Had they recognized two years after the completion of their incomplete work that they had forgotten the ideal while busy with patching up the Peace Treaty? Had they been inspired by repentance and good will? For now the call went to the students, poets, artists, philosophers and teachers: all who were inspired by an idea or a sense of humanity received their call: the call to help, to give a soul to the skeleton of the Paris Conference. At length the famous secret article for everlasting peace, the second annexe in Kant's great outline of a League of Nations, came into force: "the maxims of philosophers on the conditions rendering peace possible should be consulted by the States armed for war." Such was the saying of the Königsberg sage, which implies the idea and the programme of a committee for international intellectual co-operation. "It is neither to be hoped nor wished that kings should become philosophers or philosophers kings: the control of power inevitably biases the free judgment of reason. But if both would understand their business, it is essential that kings or sovereign peoples should neither banish nor silence the complaints of philosophers but allow them free speech."

Will they be allowed free speech, and will they be listened to when they come to deal with the Covenant? It is their knowledge which is to devise a more rational rule for the coexistence of the nations; it is their imagination which is to point new ways to reconcile differences and to overcome prejudices; it is their intellect which is to replace written or spoken notes by the exchange of ideas. François de la Harpe concluded his famous peace essay which, in 1767, received the prize of the Académie, with the words: "You, whose right and talent it is to speak to mankind, great writers and eloquent philosophers, it is your task to plead for the peoples before their rulers in the interests of both." "Writers are the legislators of the human race," Crown Prince Frederick of Prussia wrote to Voltaire. "Their works are at home in every part of the globe, and once they are known among mankind they spread ideas which exert a controlling influence upon other ideas."

The hour has come; and from every part of the world they hasten to Geneva: men and women, philosophers, poets, musicians and professors, enlightened minds, seeing eyes, warm hearts and sensitive hands. Their multitude is vast, and with them they bring the knowledge and dreams of our days, the laws of heaven and earth, the machines and the rhythms, the retorts and the cathedrals. Their throng floods the hall—but, will they penetrate into the Assembly? Shall we find them occupying an honoured post among the various delegations which they adorn by their wit and intellect? Have they an equal seat at the Council? Are they summoned to the committees of disarmament and security which they could provide with such admirable maxims? The army of students and artists obeys the call of Geneva and advances in impressive ranks from every city of the world, eager to set to work, to lift its voice, to be heard and to unlock closed doors. No period was richer in problems, in needs, and in riddles than ours. We have here the intellectual *élite*, ready to help the League; the splendour of the thought whose rough-cut shape it conceals was great enough to draw the eager masses from their laboratories, their studies, their lecture-rooms and their libraries. Hundreds of magi hasten to the manger where a new mankind is to be born.

They stand before the doors.

Through the windows, each time they are opened by the commissionaires, and through the doors of the Assembly Hall, the loud babel of League representatives can be heard. The Columbian delegate and Minister at Paris is speaking: "Gentlemen," he is saying, "it is the peace of the world, and the well-being of mankind, which is at stake"; the Prime Minister or the head of a department in the Foreign Office of the Republic of Esthonia replies. Five hundred diplomats are sitting, standing, chattering and voting in the huge hall; the intellectual leaders of mankind are waiting at the doors.—Through the windows of the Council room, and through the door whenever it is opened, the voices of the diplomats can be heard. The Foreign Minister of the Republic of Poland, a former official of the Dual Monarchy of Austria-Hungary, earnestly proclaims: "Gentlemen, the peace of the world demands . . ." The scholars and artists stand thronging at the doors, their heads full of ideas and their hearts full of hopes. Through the doors and windows of the big committee rooms the voices of ministers and experts can be heard. The intellectual leaders wait at the door. "Excuse me," the commissionaire tells them, "not this way, please. Kindly walk across the corridor. First left, then right. This way, gentlemen." A hospitable door opens and shows the way into an empty room with empty tables, empty chairs and blank paper. "Kindly take your seats. This room is reserved for you. You will not be disturbed. The other rooms? I am sorry, gentlemen. This one is the Assembly, the other one is the Council, the third one is the Committee of Security. This room is your place, gentlemen: the Committee for International Intellectual Co-operation; you may commence." The intellectuals enter, they sit down and take possession of their realm, unlimited as yet. Other doors open into other empty rooms with empty tables and chairs. "Kindly take your seats.

These are the sub-committees." Committees, sub-committees? Are the intellectuals to be submitted to organization? Yet, after all, why not? They will come to an agreement, set up rules and suggestions, fit the parts together into a whole and then—for surely that is their destination; surely the intellectual caste having been nothing is to become everything—one of their number will enter the big halls adjacent in the name of all, where the temporary rulers of the League are at work and reach their unaided decisions, will mount the platform and will say: "Gentlemen, the cause of world peace demands . . ."

Not so fast. The programme drawn up by Council and Assembly is ready on the table, and the sub-committees, among which the army of students, philosophers, poets and thinkers is divided, bear the following names: Inter-University Relations, Science and Bibliography, Art and Literature, Copyright, Instruction on League of Nations Aims and Exchange of Teachers. The labour of years will be devoted to grave questions like the following: Is an international auxiliary language to be adopted? The answer given by the intellectual committee is in the negative. Are experts to be induced to publish dangerous inventions relating to chemical warfare? The intellectuals decide, after long deliberations, that it does not concern them. Should steps be taken against the system of the *numerus clausus*? Beyond our competence, although free admission to the universities is desirable in itself. Should an international university congress be convoked? Should an international political university be formed? Shall we organize the pooling of archives and of archaeological studies? Is scientific terminology to be standardized? Shall we resolve on the protection of beauty spots, on the publication of scientific works, on the creation of an international meteorological office? Shall we organize international relationships? Resolutions upon resolutions are adopted, are passed on to the Paris Institute, and are forgotten. At the same time certain charities for intellectual workers in impoverished countries are organized, and financial support is given to private individuals and State organizations. An international librarians' union is founded, to facilitate the exchange of books among libraries and to found an international museums' office to assist in the exchange of works of art and to organize exhibitions; and indeed an exhibition of plaster casts of well-known works of art is organized under League auspices. An international committee for folk art is formed, whose function it is to study folk-dancing and folk-songs, and to draft an agreement on scientific patents. Investigations are instituted on the recognition of university diplomas, and resolutions are passed recommending the translation of literary masterpieces. Strange specimen lists of the best works of the different countries are drawn up. At Rome, a cinepedagogic institute is founded and financed by the Italian Government, which, like the French, is anxious to conciliate a part of the intellectuals of the world. An unsuccessful attempt is made to introduce systematic instruction on the League in different countries; a mediocre propaganda pamphlet on the Geneva Institute is published for the benefit of teachers and ministers of education. An educational periodical is founded which, together with the cinema periodical and the curators' organ, extends the scope of the League's literary activities without enriching it; and experiments are made—an attempt not destined to go beyond theoretical discussions—in the co-ordination of institutions for the scientific study of international relations.

Years are spent in session at Geneva and numberless other towns: competent Secretariat officials produce and explain agenda, and are listened to impatiently; and on no occasion are all these able men permitted to go beyond the mediocre sphere of bureaucratic organization, or to push aside the amateurish accumulation of material dealing with the unessentials of intellectual life, unconnected with the League, and requiring no League; subjects which were dealt with years ago more seriously, more successfully and with stronger regard for the idea of peace on international lines. Before the war there were Carnegie foundations and Nobel foundations, international museums, an international peace institute, a "conciliation internationale," a central office of international institutions, an international students' league, an American peace school league, a students' union of cosmopolitan clubs, an international bureau of teachers' associations: but no attention had ever been paid to them comparable to that devoted to the main and sub-committees for intellectual co-operation at the League. Before the war there were scientific congresses; there was an exchange of professors, teachers and scholars; French assistants were employed at German schools and German assistants at French schools, and every university had foreign lecturers; there was a bureau for intellectual property; there were scientific organizations for such things as seismology, oceanography and medical problems; libraries, like those of Paris, London, Rome and Vienna loyally exchanged books; there were international exhibitions, and national exhibitions abroad; peace societies with numberless branches, and the interparliamentary union, devoted themselves to the task of intellectual *rapprochement*; socialistic and religious bodies did their best to promote a spirit of understanding, and in these individual undertakings the leadership lay with the intellectuals much more definitely than in the Paris or Geneva Institutes, where bureaucrats and agents were the real rulers, and men and women whose names and offices were famous in the most diverse intellectual spheres were set to work on narrow amateurish exercises in the "technique of co-ordination" practised by the officials. And but for the fact that the department for international intellectual co-operation had the distinction of belonging to an Under-Secretary-General and of possessing premises on the first floor of Hottop's hotel, our journey of exploration through the Secretariat would have carried us to other spheres of activity—perhaps to the communications organization—first. If it had done so we would have been saved many illusions and disappointments, for we would then have realized that the stereotyped "technique" of international co-operation as turned out by the Secretariat—

with its international organization, its committee, sub-committees, expert committee and secretarial staff provided by the relative department of the League Secretariat—had been unthinkingly applied in the very sphere of thought. For years scaffoldings were erected into the void until the day came when even the authors of this foolish and ambitious work realized that the growth of the scaffolding only made more embarrassingly apparent the surrounding void against whose background its geometric tracery was exhibited.

What followed now was inevitable. A Commission was appointed to reorganize the work of intellectual co-operation, and its preliminary work forced the International Commission, despite all its diplomatic reticence and tact, to condemn the work effected hitherto, a condemnation all the more crushing because partly at least it was tacit. The Commission admitted that the mistake might have been made at the beginning of constructing a framework too wide, rigid and complicated, which afterwards was filled artificially. This led to a multiplication of authorities leading in turn to complications and retardations, eventually producing more paper than any other tangible result. It was not of much avail that this discovery led to a simplification of the mechanism. The sub-committees were reduced in number and a reconstruction of the Paris Institute was resolved upon and partly carried through.—If the framework grew narrower, the enclosed void also would gape less widely; but it still remained a void. The discovery that more paper than any other result had been produced did not help so long as the root of the evil was left untouched; and this root consisted in the fact that Kant's "secret article" had not been realized and had never been intended to be realized. In its programme of reforms the intellectual committee had declared that its aim must be to interest the educated world in the League and hence to produce a frame of mind among the nations favourable to mutual understanding and to a peaceful solution of conflicts. In other words, the intellectuals were to give their approval to the League as it was and to be exploited for propaganda purposes. Certainly this meant a reliance upon the intellectuals; but it also meant that they were not to play a creative part. They were not to stimulate, improve or advance the League: and they were to serve it as an immutable institution. They were not allowed any real influence; they were meant simply to lend their names; but at the same time it was necessary to keep them employed and to give them a task outside the proper sphere of the League. Accordingly, to keep them busy, plaster casts of museum statues were made and folk-dances studied in order to produce a "frame of mind." The intellectuals, harnessed now to the League, were given work and in some instances their vanity was satisfied; but the intellectual current which had created and for years had given vital force to the idea of the League was eliminated. The driving force of the intellectual leaders was not wanted, and in order to render it harmless they were employed on insignificant subsidiary activities which if they became too ridiculous could be reorganized. The international intellectual co-operation of the League comes to mean the surrender of any intellectual collaboration in and elaboration of the League itself. Kant had foreseen this development in the commentary to the "secret article." He knew that philosophy would ever be the handmaid of force, and only asked whether she would walk before her mistress with a torch, or behind her carrying her train.

And so we witness the humiliating spectacle of the philosophers as train-bearers to the League. For years the League has been profaning the idea of intellectual co-operation, and in so doing has destroyed for years to come the unique opportunity of utilizing the noblest forces for its ideal. And yet, as we walk through Herr Dufour's department, as we listen to the debates of the committees, the sub-committees or of the Paris Institute, and hear the lyrical panegyrics pouring from the lips of Helene Vacarescu of Roumania or of a few lyrical South Americans, our mouths begin to twitch. In spite of our annoyance we begin to smile and then to laugh. As we hurry through the next department with our handkerchief pressed to our mouth, the commissionaires look askance, while the intellectual officials raise their eyebrows, and all the good people in Hottop's hotel manifest disapproval. And yet we may be sure that Henri Bergson, who escaped from the office of President of the Committee some years ago, would have understood and approved our amusement. Many years ago, before the Committee ever existed, his elegant work on *Laughter* provided us with absolution in advance. In it the professor recalled the definitions of the comic given by Spencer and Kant. According to the former, laughter is the result of an effort suddenly meeting with a void, according to the latter an expectation suddenly dissolving in nothing. According to Bergson the essence of the comic consists in the application of mechanism to nature, or in the grafting of a mechanism on something living. "In order that a ceremony shall have a comic effect," he explains, "it suffices for our attention to be concentrated on its ceremonious elements; all we have to do is, as the philosophers call it, to neglect the matter and to think only on the form." He adds: "There is no need to labour this point. Everyone knows how easily the pleasure we take in the comic vents itself in social ceremonies having fixed forms. . . . Every form and every formula is a ready-made frame for the comic."

Let us depart from the ready-made frame of intellectual co-operation, and let us re-assume a serious mien; for we have now reached the department of the third Under-Secretary-General, the director of the political department. Let us leave the regions of empty tables and chairs, and of full but unemployed brains, and enter the sphere of contemporary political activity. Here is the power and the glory for whose benefit the physical chairs and the metaphysical brains exist.

CHAPTER XVII

MR. SUGIMURA'S MAP

As we enter the room of the Under-Secretary-General and director of the political department it is not so much the icy sheen of Mont Blanc that strikes us, seen through the wide-open window, nor the sunny smile on Mr. Sugimura's vast Buddha face that warms our heart. What fascinates us is a vast map which dominates the entire room. We cannot tear our eyes from this colossal reproduction of the world, and we feel as though the wall which it covers were a vast window opening upon the entire world and the manifold life of the nations.

"My field is the world" was the inscription placed by Ballin over the gorgeous Hamburg-America building on the banks of the Alster. Are we to assume that the welcoming smile of the Japanese director before his triumphant map carries the same message? It is in the offices of the bulky and amiable Mr. Sugimura that we hope to find Article 1 of the Covenant which defines the sphere of the League and the important question of its extension; Articles 3 and 4, which declare the Assembly and the Council as competent for all questions relating to world peace; and Articles 11 to 17, which seek by different roads to preserve or reconstruct it—in short, the organization and the methods of international foreign peace. Since the retirement of the first director of the department, the French Professor Mantoux, it has been Mr. Sugimura's function to prepare, record and carry out the political labours of the Council and the Assembly; so that we can quite understand why he hung the world in his room, and now stands by its side smiling his Japanese smile; polite, thorough and slightly theatrical. And for this reason we feel a certain excitement as we stand before the big white surface. We hope for a dazzling vision and a profound harmony which will teach us the fate of the world transformed by war and by peace.

But, while we carefully consider it and examine it in all its details we soon find that it remains quiet and cool, silent and senseless. The five continents lie side by side, smooth and dull; within them, dull and smooth, the big and the little countries. The mountain ranges are placed in the correct position and the rivers flow into their appropriate seas. The north is at the top and the south at the bottom, the east is on the right and, appropriately enough, the west is on the left; Mr. Sugimura's map is a correct map, but not an eloquent one. It gives itself airs, but it tells us no more than the maps in every other office and in every classroom—those banal pictures of the world behind which we never sense the souls of the manifold nations, the murmur of the blue seas, or the raging of gales above white glaciers. Why is the map so mute, empty and void? Mr. Sugimura's map begins to have a sinister look: it has a secret which it refuses to reveal. Has the League completed its work, and is the map no more than a flag of victory? Has the League not yet begun its work and is the map an empty frame that has to be filled in? Is the League dead, and is the map simply its tombstone? We must uncover its secret and call to life the experience which it implies.

When was it born? Whether it is a common political map or whether it is the unique and fulfilling map of the League, its birthday is the 10th of January 1920, the day on which the Treaty of Versailles gave new frontiers to the nations and the Covenant tried to give them a new mentality. On what does it live? Originally the generous principle of universality was meant to inspire it; but we saw above that it had to content itself with the meagre nourishment of Article 1, which originally admitted only the victorious Powers, and afterwards only the majority of neutral States, to the new era, leaving the fate of all other countries to special conditions and the resolution of the League Assembly. Thus the League Map of the 10th of January 1920 was in reality the map of the victors—which admittedly included Liberia and Haiti, but on the other hand no longer included the one real victor, President Wilson's native country. Even when the first Assembly met in the winter of 1920, with its twenty-nine "victorious" original members—excluding Educaor and the Hejaz, which had failed to ratify the peace treaties—and with its fourteen invited neutrals, it was still equally far from true neutrality and from true universality. It might perhaps be hoped that it would begin to grow and change its appearance now; nearly a year had passed since the Covenant came into force and two years since the conclusion of hostilities. The Assembly no longer met in Paris or in Versailles, but at the headquarters of the League at Geneva, far from those hotbeds of hate and fear, of insolence and pride, which had caused the number of members to be so foolishly restricted. At last the League could forget its gloomy origins and attempt to realize the idea of universality.

And now two liberal-minded neutrals leave the ruck of minor Powers and present their urgent suggestions to the victorious nations. Argentina brings forward a number of wise and beneficent suggestions for the democratization of the League, among them the important proposal to substitute for the narrow provisions of Article 1 a declaration to the effect that every recognized State is a member of the community of nations unless it makes an express declaration to the contrary. But the founding nations preserve a strict control of their imperfect work, and at their suggestion the Assembly refuses to discuss the proposal, which eventually is handed over to the tender mercies of a commission; the first generous attempt to extend the composition of the League ends with a sensational restriction. Led by the Foreign Minister, Pueyrredon, the Argentine delegation leaves the Assembly; and although no formal resignation takes place, it is never seen again. Now, however, Switzerland begins to act. She had not definitely joined the League until her neutrality had been confirmed and a plebiscite, held chiefly under the impression that Germany would soon be admitted, had confirmed the resolve of the Government. Thus the President and Foreign Minister of the Federation, Herr Motta, was fulfilling a national as well as an international duty when he deplored, in memorable and generous words, the absence of the United States, of Germany and of Russia in the new League, and pointed out that it must prove a failure within a few years unless the principle of universality was actually realized. But no sooner had he pronounced the name of Germany—a name which was in every decent person's mind at this first meeting and which was cautiously hinted at in the speech of the British Labour delegate, Barnes, and that of the South African, Blankenberg—than the French delegate, Viviani, who had been Prime Minister at the outbreak of war, arose, a pale and rage-distorted visage. Raising in the air a hand trembling with fury, he interrupted the Swiss President with loud and imperious voice, demanding leave to speak; and when Motta had brought his bold and statesmanlike speech to a conclusion hastily mounted the tribune and hurled insults into the hall. He insulted absent Germany by exclaiming: "It would be an immoral spectacle for history and for the world, which might disgust it even more than the sanguinary years which it has witnessed, if a State were to be admitted which does not fulfil its obligations"; and he insulted the neutrals, the only members whose presence could produce the illusion of a League of Nations in this assembly of victors, by flinging in Motta's face the impudent and malicious words: "If the nations which roused themselves to the work of vengeance and liberation had not been victorious, you, gentlemen, would not be here to assist our work of reclaiming humanity and justice." The Assembly burst into frantic applause, the galleries joined in, and Lord Robert Cecil, who was present in those days in South African disguise, hastened to express his admiration to Monsieur Viviani. The spirit of Versailles was still abroad.

Thereafter the map of the League was destined to extend slowly and inadequately; for it was dominated by Article 1, from which special rules for the admission of new members in the form of a questionnaire with special conditions for the conquered nations were derived. After long deliberations in committee and sub-committee, Costa Rica was admitted, which, although belonging to the victorious group, had not signed the Treaty of Versailles and was punished for this recalcitrance by having the new regulations applied; Luxemburg, which, although neutral, had received no invitation and, further, had to withdraw her application for re-confirmation of her neutrality before admission; and, after certain difficulties, Albania and Finland. On the other hand, Lithuania, Latvia and Esthonia were asked to wait a year; Liechtenstein, San Marino and Monaco were refused on the ground that they were too small, and hence incapable of fulfilling their League obligations, and the Ukraine, Armenia, Azerbaijan and Georgia were rejected because they, for their part, were all too much in need of League assistance and might for this reason constitute a danger. Soon these death-bed candidates vanished from the number of independent nations; and the same fate overtook Montenegro, which was soon swallowed by its allies the Serbs, and whose protest did not interest the League. Two vanquished States, however, were admitted, mutilated Austria and diminished Bulgaria; and, if they had been admitted with tact and hospitality, the League would not merely have acquired two new members, but morally would have acquired half the world. But the committee in which their fate was discussed was, in fact, a tribunal. Viviani's wishes were fulfilled. The deciding judges were also the victors of these States; Austria was treated, like a repentant sinner, with a proud and insulting charity; she was held not to be responsible for the sins of the old monarchy because she had gone to every length to win the approval of the rulers and because, as the Czechoslovakian Foreign Minister, Benes, boldly announced to the Assembly, she implied a minimum risk and could not give rise to any dissensions within the League. There was also the wish to detach her from Germany. Meanwhile third-degree methods were applied to Bulgaria; confessions, manifestations of repentance, apologies and promises, continued to be extorted; severe rebukes on her behaviour during the war were administered, the ex-King was insulted, the objects stolen during the campaign drawn up in lists and reproofs given because the "war criminals" had not yet been punished. The Bulgarian representatives were compelled to express the strongest disapproval of their country's war policy, to beg recognition for having deposed their King, to furnish proofs that all war-time politicians had been eliminated from the Government, and to apologize for the regrettable retention of a few officials from that period. In order to enter the League they had to submit to humiliations infinitely greater than those implied in the Serbian ultimatum of the old Dual Monarchy; and even so, no generosity was shown. Although they grew more humble and even pointed to the fact that their present Prime Minister had opposed the war, the fact was not placed to their credit, because, as was reproachfully pointed out, the said official had disapproved of war merely because he was a Socialist. In the end the poor wretches were ready to promise anything; and even so, pressure had to be brought to bear by Britain and a good report furnished by Marshal Foch, the League authority for the disarmament clauses of Article 1, before the neighbouring victor States gave a grudging assent to the admission of Bulgaria, unblushingly pointing out that it was better to have the enemy of yesterday among them in order to supervise him the more securely. France alone opposed the admission of Bulgaria to the end, and in committee as well as in the Assembly Monsieur Viviani resolutely refused to vote. Why was he more Serbian than Jugoslavia, and more Greek than the Greeks? Bulgaria in itself did not interest him; but behind her he saw the shadow of Germany, and here all weakness was misplaced.

The first Assembly had taken good care that the universalism of certain zealots remained under the control of the gloomy dispensation provided by Article 1, so that the second Assembly (1921) was in a position to reject the Argentine proposal on the ground that, while the idea of universality inspiring the proposal was deserving of sympathy in principle, it did not do justice to present-day world conditions. The Assembly con-

MR. SUGIMURA'S MAP

fined itself to admitting the three Baltic States which had been waiting since the previous year, and to informing the Hungarians who had applied for admission that their application was hopeless, and that they would do well to move for its postponement. It was not until the third Assembly met in 1922 that Hungary was admitted to the forecourt of the League. Even this admission was the result of wearisome negotiations; her loyalty and disarmament were thoroughly investigated, and an inter-allied military commission at Versailles was requested first to furnish a certificate. The Hungarian representative, Count Banffy, was compelled solemnly to promise adherence to all treaty obligations, and the Czechoslovakian representative, Osusky, was permitted to declare in open session that this promise also applied to the prohibited return of the Habsburgs. Two more members were admitted in 1923. Ireland, which hitherto had belonged to the League merely as a component of the British Empire, was admitted as an independent State, now that she had achieved dominion status, while Abyssinia joined the League, for which Germany was not yet considered ripe, because, although her explanations on the slave traffic were inadequate, and her constitutional position unsatisfactory, she enjoyed French protection and introduction. For 1924 we have to note the adhesion of San Domingo and the resignation of Costa Rica, which quietly left without mentioning the true explanation, which consisted in the amount of the subscription and the promptness with which it was demanded. 1925 passed without a single candidate knocking at the gates of the League; but in the following year a sensational change took place on the League map. A German delegation solemnly entered the Assembly Hall and a German representative took his seat on the Council. Have we reached our goal? After Lithuania and Bulgaria, after San Domingo and Abyssinia, Germany had become a member of the League. However, her entry was accompanied by upheavals and convulsions—Spain and Brazil withdrew, the map shook and trembled as though in a gale, and for a moment it seemed as though it would be torn to tatters.

The movement for the admission of Germany started from the victorious Powers who had excluded their enemy in 1919. It had never been intended permanently to eliminate Germany; at the same time her immediate presence was considered inexpedient. The new world constructed without her was to be organized and settled, so that when Germany joined later she would take her place in it without being able to effect any sensible change. Accordingly, under French leadership, every attempt made to admit Germany on principles of justice or universality was systematically opposed. For this reason a condition was created in which the date and manner of the admission of Germany was wholly controlled by France. At the same time it was feared that Germany would elude them altogether some day, and refuse to join, and accordingly hints were made occasionally—e.g. like those made during a second assembly by Lord Balfour on behalf of Britain, and by Noblemaire on behalf of France—in which a later admission was adumbrated in general and inconclusive terms. A skilful but frequently insincere propaganda emanating from the Secretariat was placed at the disposal of this policy. Among the neutrals public opinion was stirred up against the immediate entry of Germany, while within Germany sympathies were roused for the League and the suggestion spread that the exclusion of Germany was not so much due to the fault of the Allies as to that of the German Government. Following the outline of policy laid down in Paris, the French agents at Geneva were busy everywhere representing the German claim for a permanent seat in the Council as excessive and running counter to the democratic spirit of the League, in short as a manifestation of "pan-Germanism," while simultaneously all German circles open to them were hypocritically assured that the unconditional and trustful entry of Germany would soon be rewarded by the Assembly, which would grant a non-permanent seat. The aim of these intrigues is clear. While preventing world public opinion from supporting the entry of Germany, it was desired to prepare German public opinion against the day when France should think it expedient for Germany to join. This public opinion would then exert pressure on the Government, would make real or feigned resistance more difficult and above all would render it impossible to make conditions before joining the League. The French availed themselves of the fact that in Germany no less than elsewhere there were wide sections who, despite every disappointment, confused the actuality of Geneva with the ideal League, and that in Germany sympathies with the League were a matter for the Left, and antipathy for the Right. Gradually a position arose making a free decision very difficult for the German Government. It was an inestimable advantage that the German Minister in Berne, Dr. Adolf Müller, himself a Social Democrat, was in a position to observe events in Geneva at close quarters and to use the whole weight of his admitted diplomatic skill to oppose all propaganda directed towards a premature, inadequately prepared and unconditional entry into the League; and that President Ebert, likewise a Social Democrat, readily listened to the advice of his distinguished colleague and had sufficient insight into the difficulties of the problem to oppose precipitate optimists with all the skill and reserve at his disposal. In this way an intermediate position was maintained and Germany was preserved from succumbing to the first attempt when the Allies should think fit to resume the debate which had been broken off at Versailles.

It was in 1924 that this conversation was resumed. But if the cessation had not taken place under the inspiration of the League, the resumption was equally far from such an inspiration. The question had not changed since 1919, and it was still the political relation between the Allies and Germany that was at stake. Since the Armistice this relation had resembled a continuation of the war by means of methods hardly differing from open hostilities, and containing ultimatums, economic, mental and military oppression, the support of the Separatist movement in the Rhineland, the occupation of places on the right bank of the Rhine in defiance of the Treaty, and the

French and Belgian invasion of the Ruhr district. Meanwhile, seeing her first attempts to reach an understanding with the Western Powers fail, Germany had successively looked towards Russia and towards passive resistance for salvation, turning finally towards the so-called Western orientation suggested and patronized by Britain. Thus the French and German policies found their first point of contact on lines suggested by Britain, leading from the German surrender on the Ruhr to the London reparations agreement. The next point of agreement was to be found on a line leading from London to Geneva. It was suggested to Britain by France that it would be well to have the former enemy within the League in order there to supervise him—the same argument with which the Little Entente had greeted Bulgaria at Geneva. Simultaneously the Germans were assured that Geneva offered them a unique opportunity to emerge from their isolation and, with British assistance, to settle their post-war problems. The Parisian considerations met with an echo in Berlin. Before the London Conference took place Mr. MacDonald proclaimed through the Press the keynote of the impending discussions, to which the Foreign Minister Stresemann and the Chancellor Marx replied in Reichstag and Press, announcing a general readiness to join combined with the serious formulation of German hesitations and conditions. In September 1924 MacDonald submitted the question to the Assembly—openly but undiplomatically pointing out that the League could give the world security only if dangerous or so-called dangerous States, as well as those endangered, were its members, and concluding with the blunt assertion that Germany could no longer remain outside the League. With tragic impressiveness he insisted that the League could not afford to leave Germany outside, and that no debate on disarmament, the conditions of peace, security or the protection of small nations was possible with this threatening empty chair in their midst. He clearly hinted that he would like to see the question of Germany's entry settled in the course of the session.

The French Prime Minister, Herriot, the one great hope of all friends of the League next to MacDonald, was not in so great a hurry. Employing a mixture of sentimental eloquence and dry impudence not uncommon with French speakers, he insisted that France entertained no hostile feelings and had fought only against German militarism and its detestable principle of "necessity knows no law." According to him, France did not desire German unhappiness and was ready to receive proofs of German reconciliation. Incidentally he recalled the obligation contained in Articles 1, 8 and 9, relating chiefly to disarmament, and declared—an obvious reference to certain Germany demands—that the League knew neither exception nor privileges and that respect of treaties and obligations was its common law.

It might hardly be expected that Germany would address an application during the session after so chilly an "invitation." But the Government was besieged on every side. In the general confusion German observers, both official and unofficial, and international mediators, both serious and otherwise, continued to pullulate in the corridors of Hottop's. The French propagandists redoubled their efforts; the Press was full of polemics and sensational reports; and while the Assembly was carrying two strange but grandiose undertakings to an end—the Protocol which was to confirm the world of 1919 and the "plan of investigation" which was definitely to ensure the one-sided disarmament of Germany—new deliberations and *pourparlers* were commenced between Berlin and London. For the moment Germany refrained from applying at Geneva; but before the end of the session, on the 23rd of September, the Government decided to take steps towards entry, and on the 29th a memorandum was addressed to the several Council Powers in which an attempt was made to clear up the question of its conditions. These consisted in a permanent seat on the Council, in proportional representation in the League Secretariat and other League organs, and in "active participation" in the colonial mandate system. Further, Germany wished to be exempted from the sanctions of Article 16, i.e. to be assured that she would not be compelled to undertake any measures against her Russian ally, and further declined to accept "moral charges," a condition which was a discrete attempt to fulfil promises to the German public that the Government would rebut the charge of war-guilt. In their replies the Council Powers confined themselves to sanctioning the permanent Council seat and the proportional participation in the League organs; and when the Berlin Government addressed a memorandum directly to the League Secretariat (12th of December) in which the attempt was made to obtain a concession with regard to Article 16, the Council declined to entertain any conditions in respect to this dangerous Article, although its reply on the 14th of March 1926 expresses a desire for German collaboration. For Germany, however, this question had gradually become the core of the whole problem of entry; by the majority it was identified with the problem of retaining the western orientation without giving up the eastern orientation, and it seemed that an impasse had been reached. Meanwhile the debate on the entry of Germany initiated by Britain had come to be a part, and not even the most important part of the debate, likewise initiated by Britain, on the conclusion of a pact of security between the chief former enemies. Before the reply of the Council had been received a note from the Berlin Government (9th of February 1925) had opened this new phase in German-Anglo-French relations. It was in the course of these separate negotiations that the question of the entry of Germany was settled: the French reply described German participation in the League as an essential condition for the realization of the German plan, and Berlin replied by professing readiness to join while simultaneously reiterating the previous demand and more particularly the provisos with regard to Article 16 and by recalling the promise of general disarmament as implied in the Preamble of Part V of the Treaty of Versailles. The difficulties which until recently had stood in the way of entry suddenly seemed less serious. If the pact bargain designed to regulate post-war relations in the West were to be concluded, the League bargain, which suddenly appeared much less important since it was merely complementary to the pact question, would hardly come to nothing. And indeed, when the new treaties were concluded at Locarno which were designed among other things to reaffirm the frontiers of Alsace-Lorraine, and thus to reassure France, and to protect Germany from fresh invasions, it was provided that they should not come into force until Germany joined the League, while simultaneously a harmless interpretation of Article 16, meant chiefly for German home consumption and for the benefit of the Russian Government, was drafted. The entry into the League is merely the last and by no means the most sensational formality in the Locarno policy.

But even now we have not reached the goal. The League map, already apparently nearing completion, suddenly begins to shake in every quarter. Admission to the League had ceased to be a grave and fundamental matter for the League, and had become a matter of political bargaining between the Great Powers; but besides this bargain a number of other bargains between the Great Powers were subject to negotiation, and a collision between these bargains might lead to the most serious complications. Some of the Powers who had solemnly promised Germany a permanent seat in the Council had secretly promised permanent membership to Spain and Brazil, who, since the foundation of the League, had enjoyed non-permanent seats subject to annual confirmation; and even Poland, who had hitherto failed in her attempts to obtain a League seat, had been encouraged to hope for a seat in the Council. The Great Powers who really controlled the League were firmly resolved not to allow their own position in the Council to be weakened, and consequently would have liked to diminish Germany's future position as a Great Power by increasing the number of permanent seats and by visibly placing her on a level with Poland. Such a perfidious attitude called forth the utmost indignation in Germany; and indeed any change within the Council would have amounted to a breach of faith. The neutrals, too, were frightened at the ruthless exploitation of the undemocratic Council by the Great Powers. The prospect of the promotion of Germany did not only shake Eastern and South-Western Europe, but also South America, and soon spread through Asia, where China and Persia applied for permanent seats. The organization of the League was strained to breaking-point. Meanwhile Germany hoped to overcome the crisis by rapid action. On the 10th of February 1926 the Foreign Minister, Dr. Stresemann, caused the Consul-General, Herr Aschmann, to hand in the German application to the Secretary-General, a document bearing the dignified title of "Motion of Admission" and briefly recapitulating the exchange of notes with their well-known demands and their scanty replies. In order to expedite the entry into force of the Locarno treaties an extraordinary Assembly for the admission of Germany was convoked for the 8th of March. The Chancellor, Luther, the Foreign Minister, Stresemann, the Secretary of State, von Schubert, and numerous worthy bureaucrats and diplomats were in session at the Hôtel Métropole, where they negotiated feverishly with the representatives of the other Locarno Powers. The Assembly met and rapidly sanctioned the application in Committee; and now the unanimous Council resolution on the creation of a seat for Germany was anxiously awaited. The resolution, however, hung fire. All the latent passions within the Council came to light, and self-sacrificing (or possibly diplomatic) offers by the Swedes and the Czechoslovakians to resign their non-permanent seats and thus to provide a place for Poland were rejected by Germany and could not in any case have led to a practical result because they did not obviate the chief danger, which consisted in the Brazilian veto. Brazil insisted upon a permanent seat, although this State, which had joined in the foundation of the supreme organ of the League, was in possession only of a non-permanent seat; as an alternative she threatened to vote against Germany. Meanwhile the Assembly

MR. SUGIMURA'S MAP 251

and with it the world was waiting. The suspense lasted a fortnight. When the Assembly met for its final session, the Germans, in full dress, and with the text of their inaugural speech in their pockets, were rushing restlessly about their hotel, still hoping that the Brazilian representative, Mello Franco, would receive telegraphic permission at the last moment to waive his extortionate demands and that they would be called into the Assembly by telephone. Meanwhile Mello Franco, with twitching and yellow face, was standing on the platform and shrilly declaring that his Government's instructions were irrevocable and definitive. The grotesque adventure had ended. Sir Austen Chamberlain and Briand, afraid for the security of the work of Locarno, sent an embarrassed message to the absent German delegates and declared Germany to be "morally" admitted, while a manifesto of the Locarno Powers attempted solemnly to affirm the will to co-operation. But Germany had not been elected, and the Assembly dispersed, disturbed and unsuccessful. In anticipation of the ordinary Autumn session, a special Commission attempted to remove the difficulty by increasing the non-permanent seats from six to nine and by increasing their duration from one year to three years; meanwhile three semi-permanent seats (i.e. admitting of re-election) and intended for Spain, Brazil and Poland, were devised. But Poland alone accepted the solution; Spain and Brazil were too deeply touched in their pride and announced their resignation. With Brazil's disappearance the Brazilian veto ceased to be operative and the course was clear for Germany. On the 9th of September 1926 Stresemann appeared at the head of his delegation, this time after Council and Assembly had voted the admission of Germany. On the following day he entered the hall of the Assembly, and Briand, in order to make it quite clear which Power ruled the League and which Power admitted Germany, solemnly welcomed him. The moment seemed to be a solemn one: but have we really reached our goal? Has Wilson's error been rectified and Clemenceau's malevolence made good? Is unity entering upon a destructive world and is the inter-allied society approximating to a League? Looking at the map of the world on the 10th of September 1926, and finding the great Central European State definitely a part of an attempt at a League of Nations, whose frontiers have ceased to threaten along the North Sea, the Rhine, the Alps and the Sudetic Mountains, we might be tempted for a moment to forget the bitter memory of all the great and evil days and years of the war and the peace. For a moment the prophets of old are by our side. But while their shining figures disperse the shadows of Wilson, Hertling and Clemenceau, we soon begin to feel that figures like those of Briand, Chamberlain and Stresemann will equally be dimmed by their radiance.

What were the errors to be rectified, and what has, in fact, been rectified? The first error was Wilson's blunder, which allowed a pseudo-League to be erected by a few victorious Powers. Next came the malignant dispensation of Versailles which rejected Germany's request for immediate admission to the inadequate League. Wilson's fault continued to live after him, and Clemenceau's guilt could have been cancelled only by the first Assembly. The later admission, six years after the entry into force of the Covenant, was merely part of the Versailles programme. The Germans had to struggle before even this was granted in decent form, and in the course of this struggle the whole perverted world of the League threatened to collapse; and thus they failed to observe that on the 10th of September 1926 they were obediently fulfilling the movements prescribed by the Versailles mechanism on the 10th of January 1920, and imagined that their entry into the League crowned their own successful struggles and meant the liberation from the fetters of Versailles. They overlooked the fact that the League of the others was by no means their League, that years must pass before the creation of a true League, and that very different efforts and gestures would be required to reach this goal. For the moment, the idea of the better League did not oppress them any more than the other Powers. They had fought for their permanent Council seat at Geneva, for a share in the various League organs, and for liberty of action in the event of a conflict between the League and Russia. At home they had given as reason for their resolve the necessity of championing certain German interests, e.g. that of the population of the Saar and other minorities, and the principle of equal armaments. Even the idea of participating in the Mandate System was considered.

But in fact Germany belongs to the League no more than before and no more than the others. She had really belonged to it once only—at the time when Max von Baden tried to console Germany with a noble ideal. To-day they have reached the same point as French, British and Italians. Geneva is to be the scene of their policy, or at least of part of their policy, as with the other Powers; but they forget that they are without the means and talents at the disposal of their former enemies, that they are unlikely ever to be in the position to exploit the League like the others, and that the difficult and probably vain attempt to find a comfortable home in the League in its present inadequate shape will carry them further away from the true League, which alone can help them. Their only hope, and one which a man of Stresemann's intelligence, courage and temperament might have fulfilled, was that the Germans might fulfil the immediate task of the moment, might then cease to enjoy the naïve pleasure of comparing the struggle of their own impotence with the omnipotence of the others, and might finally commence a bold and generous campaign for a better League. In fact, however, we shall watch them struggling hopelessly and in most cases vainly with the German questions at Geneva. Even the evacuation of the Rhineland, which normally should have been the preliminary to their entry, is brought about only as the result of a slow and weary struggle, and even so is granted only as a *quid pro quo*. Stresemann collapsed even before the completion of his immediate tasks, exhausted by the everlasting alternation of effort and disappointment; well-meaning experts or diplomatic intriguers took his place at Geneva, people who might possibly have a better appreciation of the immediate utility of the League in its present status but certainly had no eyes to see the future value of a better League, and even these were soon overcome by the mass of problems and difficulties; and so even this last hope soon vanished into nothing.

Once more we look at Mr. Sugimura's world map. The League has accepted Germany, but it has not thereby become a League of Nations; the name of Germany is on the map, but the map has not become any the more impressive. Although Spain returns before the expiration of the term of her withdrawal and is rewarded with a semi-permanent seat on the Council, Brazil continues to sulk and the Argentine does not return again. Russia and the United States are more firmly resolved than ever not to join. 1927, 1928, 1929 and 1930 pass without a single candidate; at last, in 1931, Mexico joins. This country declines to become a formal candidate or to undergo the preliminaries to admission, and suddenly the Assembly forgets its former strictness, forgets Article 1, the questionnaire, the committee and the sub-committee which had been intended to be a "tribunal," defies its own Covenant and its own rules, and accepts Mexico with a solemn resolution in which it regrets the error committed when she was not invited at the foundation of the League. Nor need we be surprised at this procedure; Germany had been caught, and the stringent rules invented in 1920 in order to intimidate and keep her at a distance until her presence was needed had now become superfluous. The only peculiar point in the magnanimous procedure reserved for Mexico consists in the fact that Germany, which had to submit to a preliminary examination, however superficial, even after the Locarno agreement —we remember that Herriot demanded no exceptions and no privileges—now takes her place among the magnanimous Powers inviting Mexico and apologizing for a wrong in which Germany had no share, and of which she, far more than Mexico, had originally been the victim. The sudden magnanimity of the League, however, is of little avail, even though it leads to the appearance of the name of Mexico on the League map. Perhaps Iraq and Syria will cease to be mandated territories subject to Britain and France under the League, and perhaps Britain and France will become member States veritably subordinate to the League; perhaps; but only the publicity artists of the League can pretend that the map of the world becomes the map of the League by changes such as these.

Let us examine these propaganda artists at work in the fourth floor of Hottop's. In order to provide an appealing version of the League they take fine white maps where the continents, the big Powers and the little countries are shown lying plainly and smoothly side by side; and they paint every State entered in the member list of the League with the hopeful blue of the star-spangled banner which, since Wilson's crusade and the Paris Peace Conference, has become the semi-official colour of the League. By now almost the entire world is blue, and only a few white patches break in upon the celestial hue. The whole of Europe is blue, save for the tiny Turkish and the vast Russian part; the whole of Asia is blue except for the Turkish and Russian territories, Hejaz, Afghanistan and some other minor States; the whole of Australia and the entire Continent of Africa are blue, and even in the dual Continent of America the only disturbing white is that belonging to the United States and some of the Ibero-American republics. Finally our skilled draftsmen present us with a fair, round disc placed in a corner of their propaganda maps; the disc is all blue with a tiny white sector, and we are asked to infer that the vast majority of the population of the world belongs to the League. We are presented with the work of their industry and complacently told: "The world is my field . . ."

If we would call to life the mute and empty map in Mr. Sugimura's room, may we take things equally easily, or must we not rather operate with more numerous shades, and mingle our blues with greater care as soon as we take to brush and palette? Let us begin with Europe. Certainly Europe is in part identical with the League; but we also know that the League is essentially the Council, and that the Council is essentially a group consisting of the permanent members and of those which, like Poland and Spain, are continually re-elected or which, like the Little Entente, are regularly permitted to have a joint representative possessing one of the non-permanent seats. Accordingly we can allot a deep and glowing blue to France, Britain and Italy, possibly to Germany, and to the Little Entente, Spain and Poland; the rest of Europe will have to remain white, or at best will receive the lightest of light blues. Next comes America. The United States and the South American republics which have resigned will be white; the remaining Latin-American republics can be granted no more than light blue, despite the fact that a permanent arrangement among the Assembly members invariably gives three of them a non-permanent Council seat; the fact is that their position in the Council is merely decorative, and that they exert no proportional influence at Geneva. A faint and almost invisible light blue will be granted to the Dominion of Canada; for although it spreads impressively on the propaganda maps across the width of the Continent, and for a time enjoyed the privilege of Council membership, it is merely a member of the British Commonwealth whose individual components are never allowed to mention disputes arising between themselves at Geneva. Next we come to Australia. Here again, as also in New Zealand, we find the colours of the British Empire. If we turn towards Asia we cannot but grant a deep blue to Japan with her permanent seat on the Council. China, on the other hand, despite her four million square miles and her four hundred million inhabitants, will at best be marked in light blue. All the square miles in China give a colour only to the propaganda maps, but not to the League; all the Chinese inhabitants serve merely to swell the population disc and do not add life to the League. The faint pretence of membership contributed by the vast bulk of China gives to the League an artificial prestige; but simultaneously the country has to struggle in vain for a measure of respect within it, and even after its exertions have been rewarded by a non-permanent seat on the Council, it is unable to exert a greater influence on the Geneva debates than any one of the three Latin-American Council Powers. If ever in her disappointment she were to leave the League, it would involve no change in the Geneva procedure; the only difference would be that the propaganda maps of the Secretariat would openly display the white desert which has been in existence for years, and that the almost complete circle of the population disc would shrink into a melancholy crescent. It would seem then that the vast Republic of China must not be granted the true blue of the League, and that amiable members like Persia and Siam, whose activity at Geneva is generally confined to the declamation of lofty sentiments, cast in a flowery Oriental style, before the empty benches of the Assembly, cannot claim more than a faint blue. Accordingly the whole continent does not seem to offer much room for the League painters. India, although it is entered as an independent member in the list of the Secretariat, cannot even lay claim to the consolation colours of the other dominions. Exploited and occupied by Britain, and in revolt against her oppressors, she is not allowed to carry her vital questions before the Geneva tribunal; in fact she is a member of the League even less than Soviet Russia, who, on the rare occasions when she does participate in the Geneva debates, represents her own interests, and not those of Britain. Indo-China must also remain white, for it is merely a part of the French colonial empire; its name never appears in the Geneva lists, and is never pronounced at the League debates. Nor can we grant the League colours to the huge continent of Africa. We may grant the dominion pale blue to the Union of South Africa, we may accord it, though with hesitation, to the empire of Abyssinia, since we are too polite to refuse it to those other dusky members, Haiti and Liberia; but Egypt, and the huge expanse of the European protectorates, colonies and mandated territories must remain white.

Can Mr. Sugimura still believe, while looking at his map, that the world is his field? If the colours have been correctly applied the secret will soon be solved: the League is Europe, without Russia and Turkey; and Europe to-day means France, Britain and Italy with their friends and Allies, with whom Germany and the medium and minor Powers are associated for certain general questions. The League also is Japan; it is Japan's European *pied-à-terre* where she can take the temperature of the rest of the world. The rest of the map is coloured merely by League atmosphere and propaganda, and we may almost fear that we have been infected by the excessive simplification of colours employed in Hottop's Palace. Is it really necessary to be so lavish of the Wilsonian blue, and would it not be more straightforward to follow the universal practice and to give each country its own colour—the colour of its real and everyday life, which it discards only in order to wear the League uniform on holidays and for festive reunions? Let France and her colonies appear in red, Great Britain and the Dominions in green, Italy in yellow, Germany in violet, and every country in a colour of its own on Mr. Sugimura's map. All that he need do is to draw a dark blue line surrounding the various colours of the permanent European Council Powers, the Little Entente and Poland, with a loop embracing Japan. A second light blue line could be drawn around the whole of Europe without Turkey and Russia, and finally the names of certain non-European member States might be underlined in blue. Indeed we may go further and draw a firm line in the French colours around France and her Allies, another one in the Italian colours around Italy and her adherents, and finally (in honour of the obligations implied in the Kellogg Pact) we might draw a third dotted line in the American colours around the entire map, excluding only a few Latin-American States. We could then entitle the whole coloured picture: "Political Map of Europe and its relations to the rest of the world," adding, in smaller lettering, "taking into consideration diverse treaty obligations and facts such as the existence of a League organization." Having done this we shall have fulfilled our task and shall have changed the pretty picture in the political department into an instrument which can be usefully employed by Mr. Sugimura and his subordinates. At the same time the map will have lost its mystery; foreign visitors and guests can converse with it; only—so we now recognize—it had a more calming, a more truly League-of-Nations effect so long as it was mute and void, for now that we look at the vast continents and States and contrast them with the thin and frail lines surrounding them and bearing the Wilsonian colours, we begin to suspect that they will break like pack-thread as soon as the vast and coloured mass begins to draw breath and stretch its limbs —unless, of course, the unwearying endeavours of the League, unless the unwearying labours of Mr. Sugimura . . .

Mr. Sugimura stands smiling by the side of his map, calmly smiling his Japanese smile; polite, thorough and slightly theatrical.

CHAPTER XVIII

COLOURS AT THE FRONT

SUDDENLY Mr. Sugimura ceases to smile. He looks at us gravely, leaves his huge map, walks heavily over to his desk, and smiles once more as he points to a slim copy of the League Covenant.

We are asked to admit that the map of the League is not coloured solely by Articles 1 and 2, which determine its extent and its organization: its second and more important vital principle is derived from the methods for the preservation and restoration of the peace contained in Articles 3 and 4, and 11 to 17. Assuredly it was so from the beginning; and even before they have to be applied in practice, their immanent virtue suffices to unite the scattered nations in the consciousness of their common task, and individually to ennoble them. The new rights and duties created by these articles must compel the Council to cease to be the instrument of a few Great Powers and to make these Powers the instrument of the Council. It will cause the non-permanent Council Powers elected by the Assembly, first four, then six, and eventually nine in number, not to behave like petty supers, condemned by narrow national interests to follow in the train of the Great Powers or to observe a cautious indifference, and instead to become conscious of their rank and to rise above their old personality; and even the other member States outside the Council who are concerned in the preservation of the peace, individually by virtue of Article 11 and collectively (as soon as they have constituted themselves as the Assembly) by virtue of certain other articles, have now ceased to be indifferent spectators on the confines of the League world. Beside their narrow individual existence they lead an international life which gives them a higher responsibility. Accordingly we need not be troubled because the Dominions are not really independent members, because

India is merely a decorative mummy, because China is merely an item in the Geneva propaganda apparatus, and because entire continents are non-existent for international co-operation and the Great Powers decline to have anything to do with it. The regenerative force of the new rights and duties can do without the immediate co-operation of all the nations, and it suffices if ten of them are willing to recognize Article 11. It does not so much matter that the League is to be co-extensive with the world; what does matter is that the League is to have a field of its own within the world: carefully cultivated it must gradually bear fruit.

We look away from Mr. Sugimura's Covenant and back to the map on the wall. Is there room for hope? Certainly it would suffice for the creation of a first real League field that a restricted number of nations, whether strong or weak, should acquire a sense of their new dignity and wear it in the face of the world. We must admit that the weak may even be ready—and because they are weak, must be ready—to acknowledge the superior virtues of the law of peace. It is even possible, although more difficult, for them to demand the application of this law to other States. There must also be numerous instances where the stronger Powers are willing to consider the setting in motion of the peace apparatus against other nations. But, if the pacifying virtues of the Covenant are to change the rigours of the map, the stronger Powers must above all be ready themselves to submit to the law. Even the narrowest field for the League can exist only if all members are ready to take a seat among the judges and equally to appear before them and accept their verdict. What secret virtue is there in the Covenant to induce, to compel the strong to disregard the temptation and even compulsion implicit in their greater power? The faults deliberately introduced by them into the Covenant prevent its merits from developing in the fruitful manner anticipated. We said that ten States would suffice to keep intact the idea of the League; but it is essential first that these ten Powers should be ready in the two ways described above. If they divide into two camps—the camp of those who have the power to apply the peace apparatus and also to disregard it, and of those who must acknowledge every power, both the old power appealing to force alone and the new, which appeals to the League apparatus—then the Covenant does not amend the map at any point of its vast extent. It merely complicates and falsifies it, rendering it useless for all purposes of improvement and development.

It is not the organization and not the method employed by Mr. Sugimara that will alter the map. We must ask first whether the will to the League continues to exist, or has begun once again to exist? This is the only question we address to those mysterious continents: the will to the League alone can correct the picture of the world as painted in the League offices. If this will is still alive and has reawakened the nations and Governments, it will seize upon the incomplete Covenant and call forth the virtues dormant beside its faults. In that case it may rely for a time upon the Versailles dispensation, relying on it with a kind of easy irony, not incompatible with a silent and lasting resolve to spread its wings and leave it behind; for its home is the old dream of the League, which led past every entanglement, to the confusions of the Covenant, and will lead from the Covenant to the true League. Does this will continue to live, or does it live again? That is the only question. . . .

Mr. Sugimura smiles his Japanese smile, shrugs his shoulders and points with just a little hesitation, a little embarrassment between his Covenant and his map to the full-charged filing cabinets, with a gesture to indicate that the answer will be found in them. . . . And indeed experiences have been gathered there for twelve years; for twelve years a policy has been pursued not unmindful of such obligations as those implied in the existence of the League organization—twelve years filled with the most tragic confusion of all times, with the unforgotten agonies of the war, and the torturing fear of an even more evil future. Assuredly during such a period the will to the League, if existing at all, must have manifested itself and grown in strength a hundredfold. Assuredly if it had ceased to exist, a hundred opportunities must have occurred to awaken it. The League was the child of opportunity; events emerging out of the gloom of time bring it nearer. They create a longing for League mediation; they forge the compulsion for League solutions. Wherever the old sentiment of force arises and is opposed by the sentiment of justice, wherever a dispute breaks out and the demand for a peaceful solution is heard, there the League is being born. Pale blue lines do not alter the multicoloured map of the world; but, in the same way in which once we outlined the war fronts with coloured national flags, so we will now plant the blue flag of the prophet at each point conquered by the forces of peace and justice. We will not plant them in the hopeless capitals of the old States and of the new sham organization, nor in the bureaucratic experimental station for timid methods to bring about a timid peace as practised at Geneva; but in all scattered, humble, brave and terrible places, whose names we hardly knew yesterday and which have suddenly grown notorious through some relapse into barbarism or some victory of international understanding, those honest blue flags shall be planted. Where these flags are found, isolated at first, but soon in denser clusters, they outline the front of a triumphant thought; their blue sheen strengthens the pallor of the thin lines on the map and gradually outshines the crude international colouring. The stream of events flows towards us and brings with it the stages of the League, and as they come nearer we, with our flags, await them.

The time is ripe and the ground is ready to receive the blessings of a saving thought. On the day after the conclusion of peace Germany was a country, subjected through the instrumentality of the League idea, and cast out from this same organization. On the bitter soil of this country which knows no power, no friends and no hope other than the hope for justice and international solidarity there will be ample opportunity for great and moving occasions for League activity. But, alas, already the names of Saar and Danzig find a place on paper but not on the map, and already the papers which deal with Germany's most dangerous frontier problems are transferred from the political to the administrative department. The complaints of the German populations of the Saar and Danzig, whose national rights have been disregarded, and the bitter yet submissive notes of protest addressed by the Reich to Geneva, do not belong to the sphere of the clauses designed to preserve or reconstruct the peace, and vanish in the internal politics of Hottop's Hotel. For a moment it seems as though the Belgo-German frontier would be the scene of League activity; for here the Versailles Treaty hands over the question of the State to which Eupen-Malmedy shall belong to the League itself, and the plebiscite, according to the solemn assurance of the victors, is carried out under League auspices. The Council, however, allows the plebiscite—an open vote— to be sabotaged, and shows no surprise when, of 63,000 inhabitants, only 271 can make use of this meaningless right of self-determination. Not for a moment is this plebiscite regarded as an international matter, but merely as a prearranged bargain between the League and Belgium. The Belgian suzerainty over the district is confirmed without check, and when the German Government rightly demands that this monstrous malpractice shall be examined by the Assembly, an equally competent body, it is curtly informed that the Council does not wish to revert to the affair. Thus Dr. Bernhard von Bülow, a gifted young German diplomat, is perfectly right in saying, in his *Versailler Völkerbund*, that excellent critical work on the new institution, that the Council simply made itself an instrument of a hostile League and "missed the opportunity of acquiring what hitherto it had been lacking, the power of a moral right." The Belgian colours float over the first scene of a League dispute along the German frontiers. . . .

Soon a new problem approaches from the tragic danger zone of Eastern Europe; and this time the question facing the new organization and its methods is indisputably within the competence of the League. The Treaty of Versailles had provided for a plebiscite in Upper Silesia, the whole of which district had been claimed by Poland during the Paris Conference; a two-thirds majority for Germany resulted, and accordingly Upper Silesia should have remained part of Germany. France, however, as the advocate of Poland, clamoured for partition in the Supreme Council of the Allies, while Britain hesitated, being reluctant to take the open responsibility for new misdeeds in the spirit of Versailles. Suddenly it was remembered that there was such a thing as a League, and in August 1921 the Supreme Council appealed to sub-section 2 of Article 11, which draws the attention of the League to any act endangering international relations, peace and understanding between the nations, and requested the League Council to draft recommendations for a settlement of the frontier. Here, if ever, there was an opportunity for the League to dissipate the sultry atmosphere in the East. For once it was the Covenant and not the Treaty of Versailles which controlled the activities of the League; and, by virtue of Article 11, the League had the right and the duty to treat the problem of Upper Silesia as part of its general work. What view did the Council take of its duties? The Council was composed of the Powers represented at the Conference of Ambassadors, their Allies and the gallicized Spanish Ambassador in Paris, and it treated the matter, not as an international or as a German-Polish question, but as an inter-allied commission. No German representatives were heard or consulted; only despairing petitioners from the threatened regions wandered through the corridors of the Secretariat, a plucky official from Berlin of the name of Mayer, secretly and without hope, studied the map of Upper Silesia in the fourth floor of the Hôtel des Bergues, and a few German journalists, deeply shaken, would rush along the quai du Mont-Blanc to the post office, thence to send tragic telegrams to their ostracized country. The result produced on the 12th of October 1921 was in conformity with French and Polish wishes; the Council's recommendation cut country and people in two, and when it was found that even the Poles did not desire the mutilated industrial and political body to bleed to death, a temporary economic solution and regulations for the protection of minorities were substituted which had to be settled in a special German-Polish agreement. The Japanese President of the Council, Ishii, celebrated this solution as an act of justice. The act of justice was communicated to the Germans by the Supreme Council in the form of an ultimatum, their protests were disregarded, and the disclaimer pronounced by the Chancellor Wirth in the Committee for Foreign Affairs was equally disregarded with the disclaimer pronounced by the former Minister, Schiffer, the German representative in the subsequent technical German-Polish negotiations at Geneva. The Polish white eagle on red background floats above the German town, which the maps in the political department now show as standing east of the frontier drawn at Geneva.

The propagandists at Hottop's inform us that the time is not yet ripe. During the years immediately following the war the League cannot be expected to see the world with other eyes than its founders', or to act differently than the Conference of Ambassadors. However, four years after the coming into force of the Covenant, Eastern Germany once more becomes the object of the Geneva activities. This time it is Memel that is to test the will of the League. Once more the Council assembles by virtue of Article 11, and once more it treats the problem not as an international one subsisting between Allies and Germany, or Lithuania and Germany, but as one submitted solely by the Allies. In Article 99 of the Treaty of Versailles Germany was deprived of the Memel district, and nothing was said about the future of the German population and the German territory; after Lithuania had invaded the district its possession had been confirmed under certain conditions assuring its autonomy within the State of Lithuania, and when Lithuania rejected some of these conditions the German population turned to the Council for help in this difficulty (25th of September 1923). Once more the Council made itself a tool in the hands of the victors, and, disregarding its pacifying mission, which made it its duty either to reject the function imposed on it, or else to go further and to examine and solve the problem in its entirety, confirmed the Allied decision in its main outline. The yellow, green and red of Lithuania were hoisted by it over the German territory of Memel, and the Council was satisfied that it had served the ideal of the League by supervising certain problems of communication, the protection of minorities and the rights of autonomy. Another opportunity to build up the League had been missed in the East.

Meanwhile the greatest opportunity of all was missed in the West, and missed so thoroughly that no references to it can be found in the maps of the political department and no syllable in the *communiqués* of Hottop's mentions it. On the 11th of January 1923, three years after the Covenant came into force, with its Article 10, Article 11 and so many other pleasing articles, France invaded the Ruhr district—ostensibly in order to enforce the payment of reparations and actually in order to accelerate the dissolution and disintegration of the country. The most dangerous dispute since August 1914 had arisen, and if it was not given the name of war the omission was due only to the fact that the invaded country had been prevented by the disarmament provisions of Versailles from firing a shot at the invading troops. The French claimed that the dispute was not an international one, and that they were merely exercising the rights laid down by treaty; but the rest of the world knew that violence was being done not only to Germany and justice, but also to the truth, and that this monstrous excuse, creating a war zone in the heart of Europe and in defiance of the League, clamoured for the application of Article 11 more loudly and urgently than any of the numerous cases where the Allies made use of this Article. But the world remained silent. Germany could not set the League in motion and Britain preferred other diplomatic measures in order gradually to entice France from her exalted military self-sufficiency. The other members of the League did not dare to destroy the new instrument, which they recognized as being the prerogative of the Great Powers, by turning it against its masters prematurely, and confined themselves to timid hints. Germany was prevented from making an appeal and was obliged to fight for her "territorial integrity and political independence," as Article 10 has it, and, as Article 11 has it, to protect herself, without assistance from the League, against "any threat of war" and "every circumstance whatever which threatens to disturb internal peace and the good understanding between nations." The blue, white and red tricolour waved undisturbed on German soil, and the only blue which could be entered in the map of the political department for the Ruhr would be the horizon blue of the invading French troops. No sooner, however, had a preliminary settlement of the reparations question been reached in London, partly by passive resistance and capitulation, partly by the tacit support of Britain and partly by German diplomacy, and no sooner had peace been reached at Locarno, than harmonious songs of praise were intoned in Council and Assembly, commending the beneficent work of the League principles. When Germany went through the solemn paradox of rewarding the icy silence of the League by joining its organization, the delegates and officials who would have witnessed her destruction unmoved broke into enthusiastic applause; and the friends of the ideal League scattered throughout the world joined in with even greater sincerity. The day on which Stresemann entered the debating hall in Geneva might surely prove as important as the day on which President Wilson entered the banqueting hall of the League to Enforce Peace: at last the forces of the idea of solidarity were liberated and the Covenant might develop its modest virtues. Five years, however, passed, five years full of exhausting struggles by Germany against the League which continued its one-sided supervision of German disarmament, against the League which favoured the French on the Saar, the Poles in Danzig and all the minor victorious Powers in their oppression of minorities, five years during which the reparations negotiation and the gradual evacuation of the Rhineland had to be forced on outside the League. And then suddenly the problems of the German south-eastern frontier are suddenly brought before the Council—like the problem of the western frontier years ago. In the spring of 1931 Germany and Austria, whose political union had been prohibited by the treaties of Versailles and Saint-Germain save with the sanction of the Council, resolved to form a non-political Customs Union open to other States and leaving the two States completely independent. Forthwith the plan was opposed by France and Czechoslovakia as a threat to European equilibrium, a danger to peace and an infringement of the peace treaties, and of the so-called Austrian Protocol produced by the Council in 1922, by which Austria, then on the verge of financial collapse, had been granted international financial assistance and had simultaneously been obliged once again to undertake to preserve her "independence." The Council, which had not been disturbed by the Ruhr invasion, was now called upon to investigate the question whether the Customs Union plan was compatible with the Treaty of Saint-Germain and with the Austrian Protocols. A new Austrian League Committee assisted it, the Hague Court was appealed to and the plan was described by a majority of one as incompatible with the Protocol, although not with the Peace Treaty. But France and her friends were not interested in legal experts, and before asking their views had made it clear that they would recognize them only if they supported the French thesis; and before learning them were resolved on their own initiative to crush the newly awakened German desires to pursue a more active foreign policy. Shortly before a verdict was reached at The Hague the Austrians, tied down once more to the Protocols, and next the Germans, were forced to surrender. On Mr. Sugimura's map the blue, white and red of France and the white, red and blue of Czechoslovakia are waving along the Austro-German frontier. Five years after the day on which Stresemann had hoped that a new era in League politics was beginning his unfortunate successor at Geneva,

Dr. Curtius, the Foreign Minister, had to submit to the most humiliating German defeat since the end of the war, and to agree that the clever author of the *Versailler Völkerbund*—he had meanwhile become League delegate and Permanent Secretary in the Foreign Office—was still right in his vigorous terminology, and that the League continued to be an instrument of a League of enemies.

Meanwhile the propagandists of Hottop's Hotel busily point east and west, north and south on the world map. The convulsions which continue to torment Germany to the present day and which partly are caused by Germany herself are no criterion of the League's growth. The treaties of the early period cannot yet be disregarded, and outside the unhappy complex of German problems the League is marching from success to success. On the ruins of the Empire of the Czars, where new States with indistinct or without any frontiers were formed, sometimes without capitals or a native language and hardly ever possessing a definite popular will, quiet and order are created in certain important instances. Particular fervour is displayed by the apologists when dealing with the Aaland dispute, that model instance of the new methods, when as early as the first year of the League's existence, Articles 4, 11, 15 and 17 of the Covenant were applied, and useful methods of procedure were developed. The preliminary legal questions were examined by a committee of jurists, the dispute by a political committee, and local investigations were made. Already the apologists hand us the little blue flags for us to plant on these symbolic isles. First, however, let us look at the facts. The islands, together with Finland, had been ceded by Sweden to Russia in 1809, and when the war ended the inhabitants wanted separation not only from Russia, like the Finns, but also from Finland, in order to return to Sweden. A dispute broke out between Sweden and Finland, and when Britain appealed to the Council by virtue of Article 11, Sweden demanded a plebiscite of the islands, while Finland maintained that the League was not competent for this alleged internal affair. The Council affirmed its competence, but did not provide a plebiscite. The white colours of Finland, with their blue cross, were set up for good on the islands because, in the opinion of the investigating committee, the detachment of any region from a sovereign State was such a radical step that it should be taken only in the last resort. From this discovery, which unfortunately had not been applied to Memel, Eupen-Malmedy and Upper Silesia, it followed that the lauded League activity confined itself to providing a treaty between the disputants guaranteeing the political and cultural autonomy of the islands within the Finnish State, and an international agreement providing measures for demilitarization. The blue flag is not likely, after all, to fly so soon along the borders of the old Russian Empire. It gives a wide berth to Eastern Carelia, whose autonomous rights as laid down by treaty Finland would like the League to preserve, and nobody dreams of setting up the blue flag at Enzeli on the Caspian Sea against whose bombardments by Soviet Russia Persia protests before the Council. Not a single occasion arises where we see it shining above the dizzy confusion of the blood-red Soviet banners and the red-white eagle flags whose conflict ebbs and flows on the Polish frontiers. For, while the incipient League diplomacy, League bureaucracy and League expertise elaborates its methods in the Aaland case, war rages between Poland and Russia, and no one appeals or wishes to appeal to the League. The Polish commander, Marshal Pilsudski, was later able to write in his astonishing book *The Year 1920* that the issue of the struggle settled for a certain time the fate of millions of human beings, and that the nerves of the civilized world were thrilled; but in the League Assembly then in session and in the Council, Poland's powerful allies predominated, who supported their allies financially, economically and martially; and those bodies had sound nerves and did not move. Only when the time had come to save Poland from new enemies, Wilson's banner was waved energetically, albeit in a limited sphere. And now we witness **the strange** tragedy which, under the name of Vilna, moves across the League's revolving stage.

The first act begins with the Peace Conference. No definite frontier was drawn between Poland and Russia; the only line of demarcation was the so-called Curzon line. In the spring of 1919 Poland crossed this line and occupied the Vilna territory, which, however, was later evacuated; and in July 1920 the Russo-Lithuanian Treaty was signed at Moscow restoring to the Lithuanians their ancient capital of Vilna. In September 1920, just before the meeting of the first League Assembly, Poland, fearing Lithuanian intervention, appealed to the Council, which hastily staged a reconciliation between Poland and Lithuania—represented by the grand pianist Paderewski, and the little professor Voldemaras—confirmed the original Curzon line which assigned Vilna to Lithuania, and caused it to be watched by a military commission. But no sooner had Poland's military position been improved by French support than the Polish General, Zeligovski, crossed the line of demarcation, ostensibly without instruction from Warsaw, occupied the city of Vilna, and proclaimed the independence of the territory. The second act begins. Lithuania appealed to the Council against this *coup*. The Council remained inactive, arranged a so-called neutral zone not interfering with the Polish occupation, and thought for a moment of a plebiscite. Finding itself unable to induce the Poles to withdraw Zeligovski's troops, it dropped the plan with a sigh of relief as soon as Switzerland refused to allow the supervising troops necessary for a plebiscite to pass through her neutral territory. In fact, the members of the Council were in no position to take League measures against their friends the Poles. What reply were the Belgians to give if the Polish representatives were to ask quietly about the Eupen-Malmedy plebiscite, and how were the French or Italians to answer if they enquired why there had never been a plebiscite in Alsace-Lorraine and the Tyrol? Accordingly the Council preferred to save its face in the immediate negotiations between the aggressor and his victims. The ingenious Belgian

Minister, Hymans, who conducted the negotiations, put his trust in a political plan of a wider scope than any League mediation, by which Poland was to be guided away from the road of brutal conquest to the gentler methods of peaceful penetration, not merely of the territory in question, but of the whole of Lithuania. According to this plan the Vilna district was to continue to belong to Lithuania, but was to form a separate canton within a Lithuanian federation consisting of two cantons; Polish was to be recognized besides Lithuanian as the State language, and Lithuania was to be united to Poland through a common body for foreign policy, a military treaty and a system of economic and transport agreements. But Poland had a firm grip of Vilna and hoped that Lithuania would become hers without Hymans' device; accordingly she feigned to accept this plan as the basis of negotiation, but suddenly changed her mind when Hymans complied with her request for a plebiscite of the Vilna population. Lithuania, which had originally adopted the plan, now demanded the restoration of the *status quo*. After a vain attempt by Hymans to produce harmony by a revision of his plans, the Council, in September 1921, passed on the whole affair to the Assembly then in session. The latter body addressed an appeal to the feelings of wisdom and brotherly recollections of the two countries. Poland replied to this kind gesture by arranging, through the so-called provisional committee of the Vilna Government, for pro-Polish elections within the territory illegally occupied, by recalling Zeligovski, and by allowing his troops to remain. Would the Council act? Once more it bowed before accomplished facts, declared (13th of January 1922) that the rejection of its latest recommendations by the two Governments put an end to its mediation, withdrew its military commission, and substituted a provisional line of demarcation for the neutral zone, which left Vilna to Poland, but was not intended to touch territorial questions because, as the Council solemnly declared, it could recognize no solution of a dispute brought before the League if reached outside the scope of its own recommendations or without the concurrence of the parties concerned. Lithuania rejected this decision; Poland, of course, accepted it. In September 1923 the dispute came before the Assembly again, which passed it back to the Council, which, in turn, sanctioned the setting up of the two administrations within the neutral zone. This meant the sanctioning of the Poland conquest; the third act began. Finding the Lithuanian protests somewhat too violent, the Council became energetic; but its energy was directed against Lithuania. Article 15 was brought forward, Article 16 was appealed to, and the threat was uttered that if Lithuania had recourse to war she would be looked upon as a State committing an act of war against all members of the League. Indignantly Lithuania pointed out that this new resolution contradicted the former and insisted on the question being referred to the Permanent Court. Five days later a reply was received, not, however, from the League but from the Paris Ambassadors' Conference, which now fixed the "Polish Eastern frontier" on the application of Poland and in conformity with Article 87 of the Treaty of Versailles. This frontier was simply the provisional line of demarcation which the Council had laid down with the express proviso that it was to be subject to territorial arrangements. When Lithuania appealed to the Council urging it not to recognize the decision of the Ambassadors' Conference, the former body declared the incident closed, and allowed the Polish colours to wave triumphantly over the ancient capital of Lithuania.

The fourth part of the tragedy now begins. Lithuania and the League had both been defeated, and both had to find some means of preserving appearances. Lithuania had recourse to a hedgehog policy, a policy symbolized physically and intellectually by the prickly aggressiveness of her speaker, Voldemaras; she refused to recognize the frontier and the existence of a state of peace, and inundated Geneva with complaints of Polish aggression. The League meanwhile was anxious to hush up the case by superficially ameliorating Polish-

Lithuanian relations, and thanks to the skilful mediation of the Dutch Minister, Beelaerts von Blokland, and thanks to a proviso hinting at Vilna, it succeeded in inducing Lithuania to enter into negotiations for the restoration of normal relations. Eventually, one night in December 1927—outside, Geneva was celebrating its patriotic carnival, the Escalade—a meeting of reconciliation was celebrated attended by the solemn figures of the Council members in evening dress and full of good food, strictly supervised, from the first row of the spectators' gallery, by Marshal Pilsudski. Already at the next meeting von Blockland had to report failure. New Lithuanian complaints came thick and fast. But the League had an uneasy conscience and reacted angrily. Solemn Sir Austen, who saw in the Council a mixture between an English club and the Greek Olympus, met the impudent eloquence of the Lithuanian hedgehog with particular brusqueness. Yet do what they would, the world rulers could not hush up the affair. In September 1928 they found it on the table again and sought a way out of the embarrassment by dropping the case itself and confining themselves to a modest secondary problem.

Conflicts between Bulgaria and her victorious neighbours introduced the League into the familiar dangers of the Balkan world. Here it acquired little glory. We find it acting the part of obedient assistant to the Conference of Ambassadors in the weary struggles between Albania and Jugoslavia, and Greece and the Great Powers about the frontiers recognized in principle in 1913 and altered by the Allies in favour of Jugoslavia only because, as the Council solemnly declared, the Ambassadors' Conference thought it best in the interests of peace and security to leave the strategic points in the possession of the stronger, more responsible and more advanced Power. These and similar manifestos were not calculated to confirm a belief in a non-partisan authority capable of preserving the peace—a belief nowhere more desirable than in the Balkans. When the Albanians were compelled to submit to the Council, their representative bitterly declared that his country had had unpleasant experiences in the past; and when the Greeks were compelled later to give in on the same question, their spokesman did not omit pointedly to recall Lafontaine's fable of the plague-stricken animals: the verdict is black or white according to the plaintiff's richness or poverty. It is not so easy to plant the blue flags in the region between Lake Constance and the Black Sea.

And yet the inglorious confusions of the Albanian dispute provided the League with a striking occasion to acquire strength and world-wide prestige. Accompanied by the Council's blessings, a commission of the Ambassadors' Conference was occupied on fixing the frontiers of Albania when, by a deplorable mischance, the Italian members were murdered on Greek territory (27th of August 1923) by unknown assassins. Certainly a regrettable incident, but not a political event necessarily involving an international conflict. Numerous ways were open to Italy to reach a rapid and satisfactory solution; but this permanent member of the Council, whose function it was to support peaceful and conciliatory methods of negotiation, unhesitatingly selected the very method which, in the opinion of the founders of the League, had led to the Great War. An ultimatum was addressed to the Greek Government in terms as severe as those of the Austrian ultimatum to Serbia in July 1914; and although the Greek Government met the Italian demands at least as readily as, nine years ago, the Serbian Government had met those of Austria, the Greek island of Corfu was bombarded by the Italian fleet four days after the assassination (31st of August 1923) and, two days after the ultimatum had been presented, occupied as a military pledge. On the following day Greece appealed to the Council for assistance under Articles 12 and 15 of the Covenant, and simultaneously the Conference of Ambassadors addressed a note to Greece demanding an investigation into the assassination and claiming the right to fix the compensation payable to Italy. The League was face to face with what was practically, and in principle, the most important and exciting of disputes. A permanent Council Power, one of the founder States and

COLOURS AT THE FRONT 277

one of the great military Powers of the world, had invaded the territory of another member, a joint founder but a small and weak Power. Would the Council have the courage to compel Italy to evacuate the occupied Greek territory, and only then to decide the respective claims for compensations or any other just reparations? Or would the League strike its colours when faced by force? A number of moving and impressive meetings took place, and wise and sometimes even eloquent words were heard from the British representative, Lord Robert Cecil, who was convincing and even seemed convinced when he coldly reminded the Italian, Salandra, of the provisions of the Covenant. But, although the Swedish, Belgian and Uruguayan representatives supported Cecil, Italy continued to dispute the Council's competence and insisted that the Ambassadors' Conference alone was competent. Thus the Greek appeal relating to the Italian occupation of Corfu was not once debated officially; the Council confined itself to diplomatic suggestions for the Ambassadors' Conference to facilitate the solution of the question of the indemnity to be paid by Greece, and was prevented by Italian objections even to these suggestions from publishing them as a formal manifesto; the suggestions were brought to the notice of the Paris body merely as part of its minutes. No League colours could be hoisted over Corfu, and during all the embarrassed Council procedure the green, white and red of Italy was allowed to fly above the island with impunity. The case ended without the Council having reached any conclusion, the Ambassadors' Conference simply communicating to the Greeks the decision on the indemnities to be paid. The decision agreed partly with the Italian demands and partly with the Council's own suggestions, and the Council expressed its satisfaction at finding that the documents handed over to the Conference had rendered good services. Greece having accepted the terms and having deposited the indemnity in a bank, the Conference further declared that the Italian Government would evacuate Corfu, on the conclusion of its Greek investigation, on the 27th of

December, but would reserve the right to claim restoration of the costs of occupation before the International Court. The case was concluded; but in fact all that had been settled was the Greek-Italian dispute on the indemnity payable by Greece. The only case which mattered was not settled, namely the Italian invasion of Greek territory, and the use of armed force by one member State against another, with its open infringement of the Covenant. It was not until later, and, as was expressly stated, independently of the Corfu incident, that a committee of jurists whose findings were accepted by the Council declared that in principle the Council was competent if appealed to under Article 15, although measures not intended as acts of war were excepted.

The Albanian dispute with Jugoslavia and Greece had occupied the League since March 1921. The Greek-Italian conflict lasted from October to November 1923. Is it due to the influence of the building where we are staying if, like its permanent inmates, we all but overlooked another conflict, despite the fact that, between March 1921 and October 1922, it was of even more vital interest to the Greeks than the two other cases? This conflict, now forgotten at Hottop's, was the Turco-Greek war, which, unregarded by the League and unhampered by its organs, changed the map of the world, cost countless human lives and caused incalculable suffering in Asia Minor and in the Balkans.

When war broke out the Great Powers who were permanent members of the Council proclaimed, not the necessity of League interference, but their own neutrality, care being taken to stress the freedom of private trade, in other words freedom to traffic in arms, a liberty of which full use was made. The Council itself remained inactive, and even the Assembly, which met twice in the course of the war, disregarded Article 3 and refrained from interfering. In vain the Belgian delegate and pacifist Lafontaine lamented during the session of 1921 that Greece and Turkey were massacring each other, and that a world armed to the teeth lacked the courage to interfere. The Persian Emir, Zoka Ed Dowleh, solemnly expressed his astonishment that "despite the existence of a League the Council has done practically nothing to put an end to this war, which might easily involve the rest of the world." The Greek delegate, Monsieur Frangulis, whose country was at the moment engaged in a victorious offensive, was allowed to mount the platform of the Parliament of Peace and boldly plead for the war as a "work of liberation and pacification." The Assembly of 1921 expressed its regret that the League took no part in the endeavours to put an end to this unhappy conflict: this was the period during which the Greeks were doing badly. Lord Robert Cecil, at the time South African delegate, expressed his regret before the 1921 Assembly; but Lord Balfour, as the representative of Britain, upheld the view that it was not the function of the League to wind up the Great War and perpetuate the conditions of peace, and that consequently it could not interfere in the Greco-Turkish conflict, since this conflict was but a concluding phase of the Great War. Even when Nansen succeeded in bringing the case before the political committee of the Assembly, the British representative, Lord Fisher, expressly opposed any League interference in negotiations actually initiated by the Great Powers, and the Assembly had to remain satisfied with the meagre resolution in which the hope was expressed that the Council, without interfering in the negotiations under consideration, would take appropriate measures in view of the stage reached by the negotiations in order to comply with the pacificatory wishes of the Assembly. Naturally the League neither interfered nor took any appropriate steps, and the preliminary peace between Greece and Turkey, as well as the definitive peace in which all the European Powers interested in the Near East participated, was brought about without League assistance. Indeed this was the first occasion on which the Great Powers permitted one of their treaties dating from the Great War, a document inevitably composed under the aegis of the Covenant, to be overset, and the Covenant itself to be eliminated from the new treaty. At the same time it was thought expedient to follow the precedent of the Paris Peace Conference and to use the Lausanne Conference in order to provide a sop for the League in the shape of certain regulations as to the application of the treaty; sufficiently meagre sops calculated for a sufficiently modest appetite. Simultaneously the juicy Mossul affair was provided—the problem of fixing the frontier between Turkey and the British mandated territory of Iraq, a problem which had proved insoluble at Lausanne, and which the League Council was intended to solve should immediate Anglo-Turkish negotiations prove fruitless.

We may wonder whether the Powers who employ the League at will, eliminating it from questions of war and peace and appealing to it to solve their difficulties according to their convenience, were aware of the enormous responsibility which they were placing upon it. If they set the League in motion unnecessarily in order to draw the frontier line between a minor Power and a vast empire, they must be equally resolved to allow it to function impartially, unless they desired it to lose the last remnant of credit. At first it seemed as though a serious investigation would be made and as though the British case was not very prosperous. But the Empire, with its permanent Council seat, was well aware that time, its power, and the political pressure which it could exert on the Council members and the diplomatic compensations in the European sphere which she was able to offer to overcome the reluctance of France, whose interests bound the latter country to Turkey, must lead to ultimate success. It calmly watched the League's conscience, the Swedish representative, Branting, exhausting himself in his labours on the Mossul question.

It waited while the committee of three laboriously compiled an exhaustive body of facts, drew up at Brussels one of the famous "preliminary" lines of demarcation intended to prevent military movements, and finally allowed yet another committee to proceed to Asia in order to investigate locally the possibility of drawing a frontier line. But the result of all this industry, businesslike though it seemed, was no cause of misgivings for Britain. Instead of bringing one complete suggestion before the Council the committee produced a whole list of suggestions. The territory might remain undivided; if the Council preferred to partition it a certain frontier was suggested and the wish was expressed that the unpartitioned territory should be attached to Iraq provided that the entire country, with this addition, was to continue for twenty-five years under the mandate of the League and that the minority rights of the Kurds were to be safeguarded. Alternatively, and if these conditions were not fulfilled, the disputed territory was to remain under Turkish control. Clearly the final solution would lie with Britain, so long as no definitive ruling of the committee in favour of Turkey was provided, and as soon as the conditions for adjudging Mossul to Iraq were clearly set forth. Realizing this danger the Turks lost all confidence in the Council, declined to recognize it as arbiter, and were willing only to accept its mediation, since in that case their own vote would count in any resolution taken by the Council. When the Permanent International Court upheld the competence of the Council for purposes of arbitration, Turkey protestingly withdrew all her previous concessions and angrily reaffirmed her claims on Mossul. The case, however, was already decided. After renewed attempts at mediation and renewed investigations, a solemn meeting of the Council took place (16th of December 1925) at which the line of demarcation was raised to the status of permanent frontiers—as in the Polish-Lithuanian dispute—and Britain was required to conclude the treaties demanded with the enlarged Iraq. Turkey remained aloof; force had conquered. The Union Jack waved over Mossul, Turkey could not afford to remain in isolation, and within six months was compelled to conclude renewed associations with Britain by the Treaty of Angora, which recognized the new frontier with some minor alterations. No spectacle is more pleasant to the peace society at Geneva than that of a maltreated State finally submitting with a good grace; it eases everybody's conscience. When Britain informed that exalted body of the Angora agreement, the Italian representative, Scialoja, that wise and venerable sceptic, could declare with a smile that fresh proofs had been furnished of the value of League mediation in international disputes.

While the Council was engaged in winding up the difficult disputes remaining from the Turco-Balkan war, in which its own role had been passive, fresh firing had broken out in the Balkans. On the 19th of October 1925 a Greek sentry was killed on Bulgarian territory. Two days later Greek troops crossed the frontier—no doubt they had learnt the lesson of Corfu. There was skirmishing in the course of which forty-eight Bulgars were killed or wounded. Alarmed, the Bulgars appealed by telegram to the Secretary-General under Articles 10 and 11, who, after informing the President, the French Foreign Minister, Briand, called an Extraordinary Meeting of the Council for the 26th of October to meet at Paris. Briand himself addressed a solemn telegram to both parties, reminding them that Article 12 forbade them to have recourse to war, and requested them to give instructions without delay to prevent fresh military operations from taking place while the Council was engaged in dealing with the dispute and to ensure that the troops of the respective Governments be withdrawn immediately behind their frontiers. Admiration mingled with surprise was universally felt. How much greater was the Council's energy when Greece attacked Bulgaria than when Italy attacked Greece; how much graver was a Balkan frontier conflict than a Greco-Turkish war. But the energy and the gravity of the League continued, and with them the world's admiration. At the same time Greece adopted a remarkably reasonable attitude, immediately accepting the mediation of the League Council. Thus the President was in a position to reiterate the League's authority as soon as the session commenced, and to decree—previous requests not having met with full success—that within twenty-four hours he must be informed that the troops had received unconditional orders to withdraw behind their frontiers and within sixty hours that this order had been complied with. The troops were further to be informed that any reopening of hostilities would lead to the severest sanctions. The Council further was in a position to supervise the withdrawal of the troops through the French, British and Italian military attachés; for Greece was helpless and, therefore, ready to concur; and once the immediate danger of war had been removed, the Council was in a position to appoint a special committee to investigate the causes of the frontier incident. It was enabled to appoint yet another committee to draw up a definitive report, to sanction this report on the 14th of December 1926, to order Greece to pay compensation to Bulgaria, to certify that she had acted without malicious intent and to recommend both countries to reorganize military conditions along their frontiers. The Council was omnipotent, and the world could exclaim with enthusiasm that the League had become a reality at last. For years to come Briand could make the violins in his voice plead before the Chamber, the Assembly, before his electors and at every kind of banquet, recounting the solemn moment when his brief telegram prevented a great war. At last the political department was enabled to plant the blue flag on its map; and soon the League jurists summarized the methods applied in this petty frontier dispute, and formulated binding rules intended to guide the League in its pacifying endeavours. Meanwhile the propagandists at Hottop's compiled pamphlets and books praising the enormous difference between the new methods of the League and those of 1914. Now, so we are told again and again, Article 12 of the Covenant binds both parties not to have recourse to war. An organization is provided to remind them of their obligation; this organization begins to act, distinguishes the immediate cause of the conflict from its deeper causes, and appoints experts to solve the problem of the cessation of activities and other experts to settle the dispute itself. The apologists rashly forget even the most recent past—the Ruhr invasion, the Russo-Polish and the Greco-Turkish wars, the Corfu incident, the Vilna affair, and all the other cases where the League failed to act, where aggressor States refused to comply, or where the Council sided with the aggressors. They forget that there have always been wars or conflicts whose outbreak the Powers wished to prevent—just as there are wars which they do not wish to prevent. They forget that the Secretariat library contains Fried's brilliant *Handbuch der Friedensbewegung*, which enumerates some eighteen wars which never broke out for the years 1904–1910 alone. And above all, these hasty propagandists do not consider the future which may give the lie to their prospectus. Their only concern is to exploit their cheap successes in order to refute a conscientious criticism of the defects of the organization and of its lack of spirit, and thus to prevent any real progress.

These cheap successes raised an appetite for a second helping of cheap successes. The propagandists' desires were now directed towards a particularly dangerous quarter, dangerous not for peace, but for their private interests. For some time they had been afraid of losing their ornamental branch on the other side of the Atlantic, and if, hitherto, Geneva had carefully refrained from interference in the United States sphere of influence, such reticence was merely a transatlantic act of homage equivalent to that shown in the old world to the Ambassadors' Conference. Thus the United States were permitted to bombard and occupy Nicaragua, a fellow member of the League, unhindered. After useless endeavours the League allowed Bolivia and Peru, who had wished to invoke Article 19 against Chili, to settle their affairs outside its competence. During a frontier conflict between Panama and Costa Rica it confined itself to the modest part of super. But once Brazil had withdrawn and all efforts to induce Argentina to return had failed, the growing Secessionist movement of other Latin-American States began to threaten the budget as well as the credit of the League; and the Secretariat, where so many intelligent Latin-Americans were planning and plotting and a not inconsiderable number of French coquetted with traditional vivacity with the Latin Content, considered that the time had come to manifest League activity in the new world. A serious conflict was not in existence, nor would it have proved attractive. No individual State had appealed under any one article of the Pact. It was now that certain professional League enthusiasts, who during the Ruhr invasion had never dreamt of allowing themselves to be influenced by the Press, became wildly excited during the Council meeting at Lugano in December 1928—Briand was President—when they read in the papers that on the 9th of December a fort had been captured in the Gran Chaco, the wild district between Bolivia and Paraguay, that it had been recaptured, that the Bolivian Government had handed the Paraguayan Chargé d'Affaires his passports, and that military preparations were in progress on either side of the frontier. These enthusiastic newspaper readers induced the Secretary-General to take a serious view of the case; and after preliminary soundings had been made by the United States, Briand was induced to repeat his performance of 1925 and to send pacificatory telegrams to the two Governments. The precaution was observed, however, of requesting them to apply methods consistent with their international obligations and appearing most suitable in the given circumstances. This caution was observed for the benefit of the United States and the Pan-American peace machinery. The first result of this *beau geste* was to provoke a voluminous telegraphic exchange of notes, offering to the two States a glorious opportunity of mutual calumniation. Nevertheless Paraguay forthwith sent messages over forests and oceans to assure that she would observe her international obligations, and Bolivia shortly followed suit, so that at the final session of the Council on the 15th of December Briand was in a position to congratulate them on their loyalty to the principles of the Covenant and to induce the Council to entrust him with the future observation of the affair. But before he entered the train to Paris a telegram arrived reporting fresh frontier incidents, and he was compelled to appeal to both Governments for calm. During the journey from Lugano to Geneva a number of League diplomatists, inspired by an equal lust for peace and conflicts, reached such a stage of excitement that the Secretary-General and some high officials cut short their stay at Geneva and proceeded to Paris in order to arrange an extraordinary meeting of the Council in order to prevent the worst. Happily Paraguay expressed her readiness to accept the good offices of the Pan-American Conference, while Argentina and the United States did their utmost to deliver the League from its nightmare. Meanwhile Briand was gravely and seriously negotiating with the ministers of the conflicting parties and the *chargés d'affaires* of the mediating States. Already he was threatening to call the Council together, when, on the 18th of December, the Bolivian Government concurred in accepting the good offices of the Pan-American Conference. On the 19th Briand could declare the extraordinary meeting superfluous, showering congratulations on the two States, accepting showers of congratulation for himself, and handing all the congratulations to the Secretariat for printing. The blue banner of the League was waving over the fort in the Gran Chaco—but had the conflict itself, in so far as it ever existed, been settled? It broke out again, quietened down, broke out once more, and quietened down yet again, with no one to take any interest in its belated convulsions. Fresh memoranda and fresh pamphlets were being drawn up celebrating the success of the League and the conflict itself had become superfluous. Can we blame the propagandists? After all, something had been gained if the League Powers paid lip worship to and consolidated their duties, rights and methods. In the exaltation or excitement of a night, by the light of the moon and to the song of nightingales, they had made their declaration of love to the goddess of peace. Now they were the prisoners of their declaration; the grey day had dawned, the clamour of the working week was around them, the exaltation was over, and gloom had taken its place; but if they refused to take notice of the girl, the world would know them for wicked adventurers.

We have been looking for evidences of League activity in two continents. Africa is a colony of Europe in practically the whole of its extent, and here the League could not shine. It had confined itself to open the columns of the *Journal Officiel* to the misgivings of Abyssinia, which felt herself threatened in her independence by Anglo-Italian economic agreements and to handing an Anglo-French dispute about the French decrees on Tunisian and Moroccan nationality to the Permanent Court, while the sanguinary wars waged by France and Spain in North Africa had to be ignored as internal affairs of these countries. Let us turn to Asia. We saw the League at work in Mossul. The events in the mandated territory of Syria, where the French butchered the warlike Druses, bombarded the population, and waged a brutal war with the aid of African savages and the Foreign Legion, could not be treated under the heading of "international" disputes, and had to be debated in the Mandates Committee after the event. The sanguinary civil war in China was an internal affair not concerning the League. The dreadful Chinese famine, which might easily have increased the national anarchy and turned it into an international menace, had to be left unchecked because the World League of Assistance formed out of League organs to deal with such disasters had not yet been ratified. On the outbreak of political complications between Russia and China, the Geneva officials urgently advised the Chinese not to embarrass the organs of peace by an appeal to them. For the League organization China was simply a field of propaganda in which League officials undertook costly journeys in order to prevent China from destroying the impressive diagram on the League map by deserting the League. Meanwhile the Chinese, despite occasional obstinacy designed to liberate them from the "inequitable treaties" and to win them back the non-permanent seat on the Council which had been lost in course of time, were reluctant to lose contact with the Powers ruling at Geneva, and consequently were usually willing to spare the Geneva institution serious difficulties. When the Assembly of September 1931 re-elected them to the Council, their gratitude was considerable.

But the well-disposed Chinese, no less than the cautious League officials, could not escape their fate. While Japan and China sat peacefully side by side at the Council and investigated current reports, while both were collaborating in the Assembly in dealing with the agreement on methods for strengthening the means to prevent war, and while a League committee for hygiene, communications and education was travelling in China, Japanese troops suddenly invaded Manchuria and bombarded and occupied Mukden. War broke out and knocked so loudly at the League doors that it was impossible to feign deafness. On the 21st of September China appealed to the Council under Article 11, requested it to prevent any aggravation of the conflict, to restore the *status quo*, and to provide for just compensation—a severe test for the League but also a fruitful opportunity for League activity. One of the Great Powers which had founded the League had infringed the Covenant while Council and Assembly were actually in session; and not only the Covenant, but also the Kellogg Pact, whose harmonious adaptation to the Covenant was actually under discussion, as well as the so-called Nine Power Pact guaranteeing China's independence. One of the leading permanent Council Powers which for years had been judging the smaller member States with strict impartiality, had launched an attack upon a neighbouring country—the only country with regard to which its League obligations could apply. Evidently the firmest energy was requisite if Assembly and Council would meet the danger threatening not so much China—whose experiences in the past had been unfortunate—as the League organization. The Covenant had been infringed—the Covenant must be applied; for only so would the organization and its methods draw fresh life and vigour from the penalty exacted for the transgression. The documents covering the Greco-Bulgar incident, which had been so loudly advertised throughout the world, were ready at hand; there were equally ready the details of the dispute between Bolivia and Paraguay, which everybody knew. Everything was ready and everything was exceedingly simple. What had been the procedure followed on those occasions? The President had requested both parties not merely to refrain from fresh military movements, but forthwith to withdraw troops behind their respective frontiers and within twenty-four hours to inform him that orders for withdrawal had been given and within sixty hours that this order had been complied with. A military commission was dispatched in order locally to supervise the withdrawal, and war having thus been prevented, it caused the dispute to be examined. The case was clear and there was nothing to prevent swift action.

Meanwhile Mr. Sugimura's sumptuous room in the political department seems to have undergone a sudden metamorphosis. The map, the Covenant and the filing cabinets seem to revolve around us, and it appears impossible to establish any relation between filing cabinets, Covenant and map. Can it be possible that the Assembly disperses after a few empty phrases from the President, and that a week of Council deliberations ends with the acceptance of a meaningless resolution in which no mention is made of withdrawal of troops, of a time limit for their withdrawal, or of any investigation of the dispute? Instead, notice is taken of the insolent communication from Japan in which she declares that she will withdraw in so far as the security of Japanese subjects in Manchuria permits. Thereupon the Council suspends its session and allows the Japanese to continue their warlike operations, not meeting again until the 13th of October, when another meaningless resolution is passed permitting the Japanese themselves to decide upon the conditions and period of their withdrawal. While the Japanese troops advanced and their aircraft were dropping bombs, the Council dispersed once again in order to reassemble at Paris for the third time on the 16th of November. Three weeks of deliberations followed, culminating in yet another meaningless resolution in which no mention was made of Japanese withdrawal either now or at any future date. The Japanese promises were accepted, and instead of the Supervisory Commission on which League praises had been lavished for so many years, a purely Informatory Commission was appointed containing Japanese representatives and having a composition actually approved by Japan. Hereupon the League dispersed.

Do we dream? From the 22nd of September to the middle of December the Council deliberated on the Chinese appeal without applying the Covenant sanctions to Japan. The proved methods were not applied although no less an expert on these methods than Monsieur Briand presided, although Wilson's country was represented at the second session by her Geneva Consul—the first appearance of the United States—and although the greatly respected American Ambassador Dawes was present behind the scenes at the third. The Council bowed to Japan, which invariably appeared as accuser and not as accused, and actually demanded political concessions on the part of China as the condition of the withdrawal of her troops.

Why did the Council yield; why did it forget all the rigorous rules for the prevention of war which had been drafted and sanctioned for its guidance? Certainly the Great Powers were uncomfortable; for they felt that an instrument which had rendered them excellent services was endangered, and that new and difficult propaganda would be required in order to give it its old edge. What were they to do? They were reluctant to oppose Japan, which was in a position to injure their own interests in the Far East, which at heart considered itself to have a perfect right to create "order" in the domain of the weaker Power, and which, above all, was a past accomplice and consequently not amenable to arguments inspired by League ideals. Every attempt to use the Covenant as an opiate was met with insolent and chilly words, although many obscure and angry remarks made by the Japanese delegates were in fact merely the expression of an indignant surprise. Surely—so the Japanese seemed to say—we loyally supported you when the Covenant had to be forgotten, circumvented, or infringed in your interest: remember Vilna, Upper Silesia, Mossul and Corfu. To-day Japan's turn has come. The League Covenant is an excellent arrangement, but the ancient Covenant by which the Great Powers can guarantee mutual support must have priority.

Thus it came about that Monsieur Briand's twenty-four hours and sixty hours turned into weeks and months, and that, while the Chinese appeal had been made on the 21st of September, 1931 ended and 1932 began, and the Japanese troops still continued to manœuvre and throw bombs in Manchuria. And thus, while the Press contained apposite reports from Hottop's Information Department on the beneficent co-operation of the League in the hygienic endeavours in China, the same issues contained equally apposite reports on the Far East referring to Japanese offensives and the unfortunately inevitable but unhygienic deaths resulting thence.

Alas, Mr. Sugimura, we had suspected all along that the organization provided by Articles 1 and 2 and the methods of Articles 3 and 4 and 11 to 17 were not likely to change your map of the world into a League map. The will to create a League would be requisite in order to work such a miracle; and it was in vain that we looked for this will in all your mysterious continents and in all those scattered, humble and terrible places which a relapse into barbarism had suddenly rendered dangerous and which a triumph of the ideal of world community might have rendered famous. Nowhere did we perceive so much as the beginning of a front of those Wilsonian flags which were intended to accompany the progress of the triumphant ideal and to strengthen the faint blue of the League colours. Instead we discovered everywhere the will to nationalism, and found French or British, Polish or Lithuanian and Belgian or Italian colours outlining the lasting frontiers of war. One question, Mr. Sugimura: in the morning, when you mount guard before your world map, do you not find yourself obliged to overcome a desire to outline the Manchurian front of the Japanese troops with little flags—little red suns on a white background?

Mr. Sugimura smiles his Japanese smile—polite, thorough and a little theatrical. Silently he raises his hand and points upwards. Is he asking us to seek comfort in heaven? Not so: he merely means that a release from the tragic conflict which consumes him as he smiles his silent smile must be looked for on the second floor, where the disarmament department is housed. Not until disarmament.... We know it, we have known it for long, and we know it now better than before: not until disarmament.... We cast a last look on the warlike map, on the tragic documents, on the useless Covenant, and on the imposing and agreeable personality of Mr. Sugimura. Then we follow the call of duty and with a sigh move to the second floor.

CHAPTER XIX

HOW IS IT DONE?

WE have been warned that as yet there was no meaning in wasting our time up there; and even the bright lift boy who accompanies us to the door of the disarmament department snaps his fingers to show that there is nothing between them. "Empty" is the meaning of his gesture and he adds, "zero," *anglicè* "nothing."

So much we had known beforehand; on this occasion we have not been expecting the immediate realization of our dream. We have not yet forgotten the books we read on our journey; and, although during our voyage there were long stretches in which hardly a soldier entered our compartment, there were others where arms continued to rattle, where gloomy barracks fringed the line on either side, where soldiers were marching on the square, N.C.O.s shouted, and decorative heroes were prancing on shining steeds. Our minds are void of illusions, and are filled instead with a consuming curiosity. How is it done? we ask with mingled amazement and admiration. How was it brought about that there is nothing here—that all is empty, zero, *anglicè* nothing; and how long can they keep it up? The Covenant had come into force on the 10th of January 1920. Article 8 of the Covenant, which recommends disarmament, is a mediocre article, but still it exists. On the 10th of January 1920, the Treaty of Versailles came into force; and though the Preamble to its fifth part is possibly a fraud, yet it exists. Neither text has been altered or expunged; furthermore, Wilson's fourth point exists; it has been recognized by the Allies and was solemnly conceded to the Germans as the prize of their surrender. Clemenceau's solemn assurance is in existence, by which German disarmament was to be followed by general disarmament. Meanwhile all the events of the post-war period have confirmed the old truth that disarmament is an essential for peace and that no League can exist without disarmament, i.e. without equality of power and a sharing of power. The conditions imposed by the Allies before disarmament as enforced on Germany should become universal have long been fulfilled. The enemies of the Great War have been reconciled. The outcasts of Versailles have been admitted at Locarno to the Council table. The various agreements intended to confirm world peace ended with a solemn declaration that the enforcement of the treaties and agreements would considerably contribute to a moral *détente* between the nations . . . that, by confirming peace and security in Europe, it would prove a suitable method effectively to accelerate disarmament as provided in Article 8 of the League Covenant; and that the Powers undertook loyally to co-operate in the work for disarmament already undertaken by the League and to endeavour to bring about the realization of a general understanding. Germany had entered the League and had a seat at the Council table. Since 1921 the League building had housed a disarmament department controlled by a series of skilled and able persons, like the former Italian Under-Secretary of State, Attolico, later Ambassador in Moscow, the brilliant Spaniard de Maderiaga, later Ambassador in Paris, the Norwegian Colban, later Minister in Paris, and the Greek Aghnides, for whom a brilliant career could be foretold. A large number of organs had concerned themselves with disarmament; among them the Council, which continued to pass weighty resolutions; the Assembly, which continued to proclaim solemn principles and to stage vast debates in its yearly Disarmament Commission; the permanent Consultative Military Commission, with its three subordinate committees on military, naval and air questions where the soldiers of the Council Powers were represented; the temporary mixed committee, where soldiers, politicians, economists and even labour representatives participated; a special committee of the Council, a so-called committee of co-ordination; and a vast Preparatory Committee appointed in 1925 whose task it was to prepare the Disarmament Conference, having for members representatives of the Council Powers and certain invited Powers, including both members and non-members of the League, numbering at first eighteen and later thirty-two delegates, with their attendant hordes of experts. The work of this Committee was not hidden under a bushel; it possessed a military sub-committee, an economic sub-committee possessing a sub-sub-committee on budget questions and another on air questions, while a new mixed committee worked by its side possessing sub-committees on chemical warfare, on the problem of the private manufacture of arms, and, later, a special committee for this problem, and finally a committee of arbitration and security. Germany, the United States, Russia and Turkey, all non-members of the League, took part in these preparatory labours. The minutes of the meetings, the proposals and counter-proposals of the delegations would fill volumes. Hundreds of private memoranda and petitions flowed to Geneva. Was the result indeed to be nothing? How is it done? We have solemn Treaty obligations, we have firm maxims, we are faced by the earnest necessity of perfecting the League and by the demand of Germany, which has the right and, indeed, the bitter need of disarmament; we are faced by generous America and enthusiastic Russia. The longing of the world is united and all the prerequisites of disarmament are assembled; and yet the result is—zero. Such masterly inactivity commands respect: how is it done? We are consumed by burning curiosity.

We open the doors of the department, but discreetly halt at the entrance. Are we intruding? Two high officials of the department are shaking hands in friendly conversation. "Good morning, Captain," one of them is saying, a small, lively, dark little fellow. "Back in Geneva again?" "Yes," the other replies, a pleasant fair-haired boy with a monocle. "The Secretariat would give me leave to serve only until the beginning of the Disarmament Conference. At home they are very anxious for me to attend, because I know the ropes here." "But of course the War Office counts your service with the League?" "Of course—been promoted meanwhile. And how are you getting on, Captain?" "Nothing but trouble. They've taken my batman, who was completing his service in my quarters here, and now I have to train a new man. Confounded nuisance." He sighs and shrugs his shoulders. The man with the monocle sighs and shrugs his shoulders. We sigh and shrug our shoulders. Is this how they do it? Not too bad. We approach and forthwith discover a third officer, an ex-officer, and finally, thank God, two civilians. We watch high officers of every service coming from the various delegations to call on their comrades at the Secretariat, from whom nothing distinguishes them; and we gradually find that the idea dominating the work done in this department is not so much that of League as of military expertness. We curiously contemplate all these bold and worthy warriors and have only the one regret, that they are not allowed to wear the glittering uniforms and arms which are part of them and which none of them likes to miss for long, in the offices and debating halls. Soldiers in civilian's clothing—is that how they do it?

How else do they do it? For, whatever they do, there is a disarmament department, there is a Council, an Assembly, and there are numbers of committees; and while all these institutions exist, how is it possible to postpone disarmament? Alas, we all too soon discover that Council, Assembly and committees are much more efficient as the servants of procrastination than of acceleration. Here there is talk about disarmament, here new instruments and methods are devised, here there is the illusion of industry, here time is killed. One single concrete disarmament plan was devised by Lord Esher, following the pattern of the Great Powers' Naval Conference at Washington, by which a coefficient of armament was to be set up; but the project was rejected and it was discovered that disarmament was impossible without security, and that there must be security before concrete plans for disarmament could be considered. There was a two-fold advantage in working out

HOW IS IT DONE?

new systems of security which were allowed to break down in turn; on the one hand time was gained, and on the other it became possible regretfully to declare that the degree of security was not yet adequate. Meanwhile various subsidiary questions could be dealt with. The temporary mixed committee was allowed to draft a mediocre agreement to control international traffic in arms to take the place of the inchoate agreement of Saint-Germain dating from 1919, and a special conference was called in May 1925 to sanction it. Complicated and insincere preliminary labours were initiated to draft an agreement on the private manufacture of arms, which remained fruitless and were postponed until the general Disarmament Conference. The conference on the traffic in arms was allowed to draw up a protocol condemning gas and bacteriological warfare while every country was merrily pushing on preparations for both these types of war. After much preliminary work, rules covering the right of investigation were drawn up in 1924. The investigation was that to be exercised by the Council under the peace treaties after Allied supervision had ceased in the countries compulsorily disarmed, and in the process a permanent supervision was created instead of a temporary right of investigation, a flagrant infringement of the text of the Treaty since the investigation continued to rest with the Allies. After the Rhineland had been evacuated an attempt was made to introduce so-called stable elements in order to assure the permanence of French military influence, and it was not until Germany joined the League that certain modifications were introduced into the system similar to those by which other States compulsorily disarmed had benefited. But these modifications were fundamentally immoral because they merely confirmed the privileges of the victorious Powers and the subordinate part played by their servant the League.

Naturally all this industry could not deceive the world in the long run. After lengthy hesitations the Assembly of 1925 found itself compelled to arrange for the methodical preparation of a Disarmament Conference; care was taken, however, that no date was fixed for the Conference, and the preparatory work was arranged so methodically that all prospects of a conference soon vanished in a misty future. In December 1925 the Council drew up a questionnaire which, in May 1926, was placed before the new Preparatory Committee to serve as a basis of its activities. Its first cautious and innocent question was: what is the meaning of armaments? Next, is it possible to limit war armaments, or does this only apply to peace armaments? Further, what *is* restriction or limitation of armaments? Next, what rules must be followed to compare the armaments of various countries? Again, are there offensive and defensive armaments? Further, according to what principles should the relations between the armaments of the various countries be calculated, the following factors being taken into consideration: population, resources, geographical position, length and nature of sea communications, density and nature of railway system, exposed frontiers and centres of national life near frontiers, the varying periods required to change from peace armaments to war armaments and the degree of security? Yet another question: how can allowances be made for the facilitation and acceleration of the military and economic support provided for in Article 16? How is the difference between military and civilian aircraft to be calculated? Are spare parts of aircraft to be taken into consideration? What is the position of the mercantile marine? Is disarmament to be universal or regional? Each of these questions is attended by a mass of subordinate questions, and provides the Committee with the material of weeks and months of deliberations—a material which is admirably adapted for distribution among sub-committees and sub-sub-committees. We are now destined to witness the most absurd and ridiculous debates; more especially the military experts will complicate the questionnaire with political and economic arguments, and recur enthusiastically to that glorious invention, the *potential de guerre* which is hidden behind most of the questions and by whose help the "potential" military power of the disarmed nations is to be measured

HOW IS IT DONE? 299

against the "merely" effective military power of the armed nations.

Soon we realize that all these questions can be reduced to one single question: is disarmament permissible? and that the universal chorus answers "No; at any rate, not to-day, not to-morrow and not the day after to-morrow." The scandal was so considerable that, when the Preparatory Committee met for a brief second session at the end of September 1926, the American delegate Gibson found himself compelled to utter a warning against the methods of the Military Committee, and that the third session, which lasted from the end of March until April 1927, witnessed the application of a new method. Lord Robert Cecil deposited a complete British draft disarmament convention by the side of which Paul-Boncour deposited an equally complete French draft two days later. And now the game of the questionnaire was followed by that of the "synoptic tables," which caused such joy in the disarmament department of the Secretariat. Article by article, the French and the British plans were written down and drafted into each other; and the preparation of disarmament turned into an Anglo-French debate:—

> Two Pow'rs each other brave,
> For the whole world at stake;
> All countries to enslave,
> Trident and bolt they shake.

This was the conclusion which Schiller's countrymen might draw in melancholy silence. The result of this Anglo-French struggle was a draft agreement of the Committee which neglected trained reserves and war material and made no mention of any figures, these being left to the Conference; so that it was immediately clear that the methods of the Versailles Treaty had been abandoned, and that instead of a restriction or limitation of armaments it was at best a stabilization which was being prepared. Adorned with numerous reservations from several delegations, especially the German, the first reading of this draft was solemnly carried, whereupon the Committee dispersed on the 26th of April 1927, not to meet again until seven months later, on the 30th of November.

Why this long pause? Why not approach a second reading at the earliest moment? Had the monstrous discrepancy between the methods of the Committee and those applied to Germany by the Treaty of Versailles provoked an inevitable crisis? Had the Germans protested and, finding their security threatened by the plan, demanded negotiations to remove this contradiction and to increase their security? By no means. The fact was that the Anglo-French struggle had not yet ended. With all their armaments, the victorious Powers still differed on a subsidiary question. In limiting naval armaments the British desired to calculate tonnage by categories while the French insisted on global tonnage, their purpose being to obtain greater scope to build submarines, which the British regarded with dislike. So long as this question remained unsettled there was a further danger for the French lest the British should support Germany on the question of land armaments. A special conference called by President Coolidge in Geneva in the summer of 1927 remained fruitless, and in spite of all their armaments the victorious Powers continued to insist that their security was inadequate and must be more certainly guaranteed before the Committee could make any progress. "Last spring," so the imaginative President of the Committee, Loudon, the Dutch Minister in Paris, declared, when opening the third session, "it was found—and the Eighth Assembly has unanimously confirmed us—that the progress of our studies was hampered by the absence of that general feeling of security which is essential if a diminished standard of armaments is to be fixed." Consequently a new Committee, that of arbitration and security, had to be formed with the ostensible purpose of investigating the possibility of increasing security, and actually in order to assist the negotiations of the naval Powers in taking over the dilatory part originally played by the questionnaire and later by the synoptic table. It might have been assumed for a moment that

HOW IS IT DONE? 301

these manœuvres could be disturbed by the fact that the Russians, who hitherto had declined to enter Switzerland on the grounds of the acquittal of the murderer of the Soviet delegate Vorovsky, who had been shot during the Eastern Conference at Lausanne, were now taking part in the work of the Committee, and that their radical measures might be expected to embarrass the capitalist and militarist Powers. In fact the opposite came about. The Russian speeches and manifestos were allowed to kill time until the session closed, and on the 3rd of December 1927 the Committee dispersed without a second reading having been begun. The world was informed that if all went well the Conference would meet in 1928; and when the fifth session of the Preparatory Committee was opened by Loudon on the 15th of March 1928 he was in a position to declare that the Committee of Security had meanwhile obtained very satisfactory results. Perhaps the second reading would now take place. Unfortunately, however, it was not; for the differences between the naval Powers had not yet been reconciled, and in Mr. Gibson's words it would not have been wise to proceed forthwith to a second reading or to fix a date for the next session of the Committee, to say nothing of the Conference itself. There remained no other resource than to take full advantage of the proposals of the unhappy Russians in order to pass the time and to disperse a week later, on the 24th of April, without fixing a date for the Conference or for the continuation of the Committee's labours—in spite of all the Germans' insistence. True, a reassuring resolution had been passed, according to which the President would call a sixth session as soon as possible, and if possible before the next meeting of the Assembly, i.e. before September 1928. A year, however, was to elapse before the Committee met again; and when the sixth session was opened on the 15th of April 1929 by the President of the Preparatory Committee, the delegates were forthwith regretfully informed that the moment had not yet come to proceed to a second reading of the total text of the agreement and to formulate a definitive text, which would mean the conclusion of the preparatory work—the reason being the continued dissension among the naval Powers. Within three weeks, on the 6th of May, the Committee accordingly concluded what was modestly called the first part of the sixth session and decided to await agreement among the naval Powers without determining a date for the commencement of the second part. By now, however, it was generally thought that the Conference would meet in January 1929, and the natural conviction arose that the second part of the sixth session would quickly follow the first part. Once more the delegates possessed their souls in patience.

Eighteen months, however, were to elapse before (6th of November 1930) Loudon opened the second part and declared that agreement had been reached meanwhile at the London Conference of naval Powers. A second reading now commenced, and on the 9th of December the draft agreement was adopted in the final meeting of the Committee. Unfortunately the draft had gradually become worthless. Its regulations were in every detail the opposite of those imposed on Germany. Only the troops actually serving with the colours were considered, and the trained reserves, on which the power of the military States rested, were neglected. Only war material actually in use was limited, and even this only indirectly by budget limitation and not by restricting material actually in stock and ready for war. Altogether the chief criterion resided in the budgets. Conscription was not abolished, the number of divisions and other units was not fixed, the existence of a general staff was not prohibited and the various staffs were not limited. No fortresses were to be destroyed and there were to be no demilitarized zones. In all these points the draft differed from the provisions applied to Germany. While Germany had been forbidden to possess an air force, anti-aircraft guns, submarines, and naval vessels above a certain class, these were permitted to the contracting Powers. Above all there was to be no supervision, and the suggested Disarmament Committee was merely to collect information without possessing the right of

HOW IS IT DONE? 303

local investigation. Further, the draft, not satisfied with recommending methods rendering disarmament impossible, expressly attempted to perpetuate the difference in armaments which Versailles had intended to be temporary; and its 53rd Article provided that any previous obligation to disarm was not to be affected by the agreement and was to remain the basis of any limitations accepted by the other Powers.

This is the conclusion of the preparatory work. Twelve years had been wasted—twelve years in which none of the Powers had decreased its armaments, most had increased them and no useful material for the Disarmament Conference had been produced. In spite of Council, Assembly and a vast apparatus of subsidiary organs, the problem of disarmament not only remained unsolved, but had been made so much more difficult and complicated that the new Conference was faced by greater obstacles and scepticism than the Paris Conference of 1919. And indeed the Disarmament Conference had ceased to be dangerous. At the final session of the Preparatory Committee even the spokesmen of those countries which were generally thought to oppose the French policy of disarmament made it clear that, as Lord Cecil said, the first Conference and the first steps taken were no more than the prelude to later and more important advances to be reached in five or ten years, and that, as Mr. Gibson reassured the meeting, at least a stabilization of armaments would be brought about. Is this all? This is all. Every danger was now averted; it now sufficed to postpone the Conference, which was to have taken place in 1925, in 1928 and in 1929, for only one more year; for the best method to evade an issue now lay in the Conference itself. A sham solution lay ready at hand, and the *tempo* for the further treatment of the disarmament question had been fixed; a slow and cautious *tempo* which reckoned the intervals between the various conferences and their progresses in decades and perhaps in centuries. Now it was possible to find a place for the question of disarmament among the other questions, like those of opium, hygiene and communications, dealt with by the League in its periodical conferences. The League was no longer in danger of having bitten off more than it could swallow; it would succeed in masticating and digesting the dangerous lump. And thus at its session of the 25th of January 1931 the Council was enabled to accept the draft agreement as the basis of the future deliberations of the Conference and to call the Conference itself for the 2nd of February 1932. And the Assembly of September 1931 could make a noble gesture and, following previous practice, pass a non-binding resolution requiring the Governments not to increase their armaments until the end of the Conference. How is it done? This is how it is done.

And this is how they will continue to do it. All the committees, questionnaires, synoptic tables, *potentiel de guerre*, questions of security, naval discussions, draft agreements, and conferences—all these methods to postpone and strangle the question of disarmament—are ultimately merely so many different manifestations of one fundamental and grandiose method outlined in Article 8 of the Covenant and developed with consistency and even with genius from 1920 onwards. What has been done and what will be done in order to keep disarmament away from the League is simply to keep the League away from disarmament. This is the grand and impressive conjuror's trick which has been performed for so many years with so much virtuosity, and which is intended to hold the stage for good. The disarmament bargains are concluded without the League; when disarmament is discussed every problem is mentioned save that of the League. The questionnaire contains every conceivable question save that of the League. The reader may ask, What is disarmament? The question what the League is has never been asked at Geneva. The question should have been asked in what way disarmament must be undertaken to make the Council, not the organ of a few Powers, but that of all the Powers represented thereon, and to allow the Assembly to play its proper part. The question never was asked. The question should have been asked,

HOW IS IT DONE? 305

What should be the condition of world armaments, to allow the apparatus for the preservation of peace as contained in Articles 11 to 17 to function, and to allow the equal application of Article 16 in which the sanctions are contained? The question should have been asked, What must be the state of disarmament in order that a universal international security be substituted for a partial national security, and in order that a joint Power within the League, the essence of the League itself, should begin to exist? None of these questions was asked. The idea of the League which alone could give a purpose to any attempts at disarmament is looked for in vain in the questionnaire, in the discussions of the military and economic sub-committees, in the synoptic table, in the draft agreement and, apart from the phrases of a few enthusiasts and the polemics of the German delegation, in every debate of the League organs. Disarmament should have been the making of the League; the omissions of 1919 had to be made good; the technique of disarmament should have followed; not the requirements of the various States, but those of the new institution known as League of Nations which, some day, ought to deserve this name; but this idea, an idea which should have possessed absolute priority, was not so much as admitted into the debating halls. A committee had been appointed to submit plans for disarmament to the League Council; but it was obvious from the first day that its members recognized the mandate, not of the League, but only of their respective Governments, that none pleaded for the League and all for themselves, and that, if any groups and parties arose, the object of their zeal was never the League, but always the interest of a nation. We have never yet entered the League, not even the temporary and imperfect League of the Covenant; still less have we found any place where its ideal was embodied. The Preparatory Committee and every other committee, the Council and the Assembly alike, presented us with a traditional conference of Governments, a conference partly reminiscent of the Hague conferences and partly of the Paris Peace Conference, but in any case a conference which did not end with the conclusion of the preliminary work, but continued to exist in the international debates which exercised the world between the Committee and the Disarmament Conference, a Conference which, above all, possessed a will to live in the Disarmament Conference itself: the eternal conference without a League.

Let us quote an example of the spirit of this Conference—a single brief scene out of a tedious drama. During the first part of the sixth session the German delegate, Count Bernstorff, had suggested the prohibition of aerial bombardment on the ground that this form of warfare primarily endangered the civil population. It might surely have been assumed that this motion would be immediately and unanimously adopted; but in fact the Polish delegate Sokal declared that this motion had nothing to do with disarmament and properly belonged to the sphere of the codification of the laws of war, adding that such a codification was in itself impossible. And why indeed not? With lofty pathos he exclaimed: "Gentlemen, I challenge you to face public opinion by calling a conference to codify the laws of war now that the Kellogg Pact has been adopted. War has been outlawed; what would public opinion say if the League were now to engage in providing rules for warfare by codifying the laws of war?" Thus aerial bombardments must continue in order to spare public opinion. The French delegate, Monsieur Massigli, admitted that aerial bombs were a danger to the civil population, but went on to ask—a delicate allusion to Big Bertha—whether long-range guns did not also constitute a danger. Admitting that aerial bombardments possessed an aggressive character, he proceeded also to insist upon their defensive value. But in Massigli's opinion these different points of view did not really matter; the Germans were anxious to prohibit air forces; they wished to extend a prohibition applying to themselves alone. "Gentlemen," the Frenchman remarked with icy frankness, "this cannot be our task. It cannot be our role to abolish military aviation." The Spanish delegate, Señor Cobian, vehemently declared: "Bombing aircraft are an absolute essential for Spain as a defensive weapon, in view of the naval and geographical position of the country." The American delegate—his name happened to be Wilson—did not yet consider the moment ripe for the discussion of so complicated a problem. The British delegate, Lord Cushenden, insisted that the motion lay outside the competence of the Preparatory Committee, that aeroplanes and airships were perfectly legitimate weapons and that it was impossible to abolish them, adding that the employment of explosives was perfectly admissible. A new argument was discovered by the Canadian delegate, Riddell; according to him the function of the Preparatory Committee was merely to produce a skeleton draft, the figures for which were to be added by the Conference. Now if bombing aircraft were prohibited, the figure o would have to be placed against the words "bombing aircraft," and this would mean an interference with the prerogatives of the Conference. As it occurred to nobody to appoint a mathematical sub-committee to investigate whether o was a number, the German motion was immediately negatived by a large majority, not before a number of delegations, unable to escape a certain feeling of embarrassment, had unctuously declared that their attitude did not, of course, imply any approval of the bombardment of civil populations. A single brief scene out of a tedious drama! But it contains all its essential components: hypocrisy, brutality, national selfishness and diplomatic cunning. It is full of that sickening atmosphere of lies and cynicism which pervaded the disarmament debates from the beginning.

Such, then, was the result of twelve years of preparation. The League and the spirit of the League had been exorcized from the debates on the League's most important problem. The diplomats, jurists, generals and admirals, with their old opinions and their old arguments, sit in conclave as they have always sat at all times and at every conference. The group of victorious major Powers and their Allies represent the interests of victory. These are the Powers who, in 1919, prevented disarmament, who based the new order on their own military superiority, and who now deprecate any change. France, the main beneficiary of the present distribution of power, is still what she was at Versailles, a gambler who won after a series of losses because for once Fate had dealt her a glorious hand, and thereupon ordains that there is to be no more play for the time being but at the same time provides for a fresh deal in which all the trumps of the last game shall remain in her hand. With these trumps in hand she presides over disarmament committees, with these she attends the Conference, and with these she intends to go home. If she is informed that the League renders such games and such trumps superfluous or harmful, she angrily shrugs her shoulders. A surrender of her own power in order to be absorbed in a more universal power would mean that Wilson had triumphed over Clemenceau after all, whereas in fact the League itself was only a card in the French game, created in order to augment and not to supplant the power of France. During the first years of course the French did not venture to lay their cards on the table, and their skilled pleader, Paul Boncour, inadvertently admitted, while intoning a hymn of praise for peace, that the Preamble of Part V of the Treaty of Versailles implied a moral and legal obligation for the victors as well as the vanquished. But while Boncour was speaking the real leader of the French delegation, Colonel Requin, was grinning sarcastically in the background; and when the preparatory work was drawing to a close the French began with growing energy to deny their obligation. On the conclusion of the preparatory work at Geneva a memorandum was handed in, in which they declared with the obstinacy of despair that it had never been intended to apply the Versailles methods to universal disarmament, that France had disarmed years ago and that the conditions of the Preamble as well as of Article 8 had been fulfilled. Would they be able to play this game to the end? Occasionally they were in a state of moral isolation, but generally when it came to voting they were sure of a majority, for the majority of the world was no less conservative than France, and although different methods of disarmament were sometimes pursued, the lead was generally left to France. Her minor Allies followed her unhesitatingly. Britain occasionally had to consider certain tendencies at home, and would not have been sorry to see a certain decrease in the French military power; at the same time she did not intend to reduce her own power in order to augment that of the League, and supported Article 53, in which the exceptional position of Germany was confirmed, with a more than French brutality and cynicism. Italy, pursuing two aims, followed two different roads. She wished to maintain her power, and consequently for a time supported the main French contentions, a method also pursued by Japan; but she also wished to maintain an equal power with France, and consequently towards the end espoused the cause of the disarmed Powers. As for the League, its existence provided Italy with a number of useful pretexts in this second phase: its future did not interest Italy.

As at every conference, the neutral minor Powers supported disarmament in principle, by which they primarily meant reduction of armaments on the part of the Great Powers. But they were also accustomed to take the latters' force into consideration, were completely sceptical as to their will to disarm, and consequently examined all plans with an eye to making sure that they did not weaken themselves. Apart from certain Scandinavian Powers which were out-and-out supporters of disarmament, they preferred to utilize the obstinacy of the military Powers as an argument against inconvenient anti-militaristic tendencies at home. Their chief concern was not so much to bring about a better League by general disarmament, as to preserve the existing League, which they considered gravely endangered by any failure of disarmament.

What is the position of the United States? They, who had been invited and listened to with so much respect, excelled every other nation in close attention to their own interests, which were chiefly to be found in naval agreements with Britain and Japan. Naturally for reasons of moral prestige a generally pro-disarmament attitude was adopted; at the same time the United States never dreamt of supporting Germany against France or the League against the European major Powers. Occasionally they might support Germany in certain fundamental questions, as indeed the Russians, Turks, a number of neutrals, and the Latin-Americans occasionally did; at the same time they always kept a distance, and at the earliest opportunity ostentatiously resumed their place among the full-blooded Great Powers. Indeed nothing else could have been expected. The United States had a right to follow a national policy at Geneva. They were not and did not wish to be members of the League, and declined to be interested in the realization of the Wilsonian League. Accordingly their participation in the disarmament debates was more of a hindrance than a help to the League; for it provided a new pretext for dealing with the problem outside the League instead of treating it as a fundamental part of the League. Consequently the very debates which were to perfect the League revealed with impressive clarity what a misfortune it was for the League when Wilson's native country turned away from it and the one powerful nation which might have insisted upon its development had ceased to think of or believe in it.

If the United States were merely the United States, Soviet Russia was merely the Soviet State plus Russia. Whether she desired disarmament was doubtful, but there was no doubt that she desired disarmament propaganda. Her aim at Geneva was threefold; to irritate and confuse the imperialistic and consequently hostile Powers with ultra-radical disarmament plans; to embarrass the Second International, already sufficiently embarrassed by the bourgeois disarmament policy, and to seize an opportunity of emerging from her isolation; to take up her place among the other Great Powers, and to establish communications with France, Britain and, above all, the United States—a convenient and also a difficult policy. Russia formed a minority with Germany; but she was a great military Power, bound by no disarmament regulations and not aiming at any immediate goal, so that she was unhampered in her ample gestures of opposition. At the same time her delegates, while boldly preaching the cause of immediate and radical disarmament, had to take care to avoid the critical point where the *élan* of their own rhetoric, which failed to move a hostile audience, would raise themselves in the air and fling them through the window and back to Moscow. And thus we witness the spectacle of Litvinoff, while the wind of his own eloquence causes his coat-tails and sleeves to flutter, switching off the engine, sitting down pacifically and, with a smile, replacing the plan demanding one hundred per cent. disarmament in his right-hand trouser pocket, at the same time drawing from his left-hand trouser pocket a plan asking for five per cent. disarmament. The tactics of Russia consisted in making extreme demands but never sulking when they were rejected, in not withdrawing until withdrawal had become inevitable or more expedient than continued attendance, and in compromising the others without being compromised by collaborating with them; but although these tactics hampered the work of the enemies of disarmament, the latter found an answer to the Russian as they had found one to the German tactics. It was not the League that Russia knew or desired to serve: her aim was to oppose the League in its existing form in order to destroy and not to improve it. And it would require a world revolution to bring about the future League. . . .

As for the policy of the conquered and disarmed nations, its best formulation is that which Count Bernstorff produced at the third session, who declared, in words inspired by a Wilsonian rhythm, that the nature of disarmament must be such as to prevent any State from possessing the power to set itself up against the League. "On the other hand each State must possess sufficient armaments to allow the League, by the united action of diverse States, to assure the triumph of the common will." The real meaning of disarmament for the League was never formulated more clearly than in these words, and never was the identity of the interests of Germany and of the League more clearly demonstrated. Germany was indeed the only State which could save the League, for it is the only State in which even a national egotism contributes to promote a better League. The question remains whether Germany is likely to have a clearer understanding of this task. Hitherto her feeble and timid efforts have invariably been opposed, and the tendency was to render her more feeble and more timid; and yet the future of the League, no less than the national future of Germany, demands that Germany shall firmly insist on her rights and surrender them to no pressure nor barter them against any concessions. As long ago as 1918 the League was on the verge of collapse because Germany was on the verge of collapse; a second and decisive struggle is in progress now; and if on this occasion Germany insists on her rights, an insistence which implies the salvation of the world, she need fear neither her own isolation nor the superior power of other nations. The German seat in the Conference room, albeit isolated and a centre of controversy, will then become the spiritual home of the League ideal, which has been exiled elsewhere. On the other hand, if Germany gives in and taken her place among the other Governments oblivious of the League, we may abandon all hope that a better League will ever penetrate into Geneva. In that case the French plan will have triumphed definitively.

Will this plan triumph? "What will you do after the Conference?" the naval captain attached to the League disarmament department asked the military captain attached to the League disarmament department. The answer is simple: he will return to his barrack square when the other returns to his ship; he wants to become a general as much as the other wishes to become an admiral; and it would not appear probable that either will be offered the post of Director in said department even if Monsieur Aghnides should succeed in obtaining a diplomatic post elsewhere. For, once everything is over and there is no more danger that League and disarmament will become established facts, these officers will be more urgently needed at home than at Geneva. Then the moment will have come when it will be thought expedient to beckon one of the international pacifists, in whose faces the door had hitherto been slammed, to lead him to the director's desk and to address him with honeyed words: "Will you please take your seat? We have been waiting for you so long."

CHAPTER XX

A CURIOSITY

ONCE more, angry and despondent, we find ourselves in one of Hottop's corridors. The League has failed to provide us with the political workshop of the factory of peace; on the contrary, it is full of the aggressive and threatening rattle of armaments. The idea of the League, which was to have overcome armed force, was banished from the disarmament department on the first day. Where shall we find it now? Shall we find it at all, or is every search in vain? While we are asking, a door is opened silently a few yards away. "The Legal Department," we are invitingly informed. "You are just in time; the lecture will begin in a minute." Where are we? We hesitate at the threshold. "Legal Department," we repeat—the department where the principles of a new international mentality are being created. We draw a deep breath; can it be true after all that the warlike flags on Mr. Sugimura's map and the ambitious officers in Mr. Aghnides's department are the last visions of a dying epoch? Clearly a united force serving the cause of peace can triumph only through the triumph of the law, and if the law is victorious the sword will be struck from the hands of the politicians. We draw a deep breath and enter.

We are in a large and well-lit antechamber; the secretary is peacefully typing on her machine. As in every other office, big filing cabinets of iron and wood are ranged side by side, an ugly and clumsy assembly. We are preparing to leave them and enter the inner offices when we find the antechamber filling; behind us there is a throng of students and teachers, study leaders of international women's leagues, and tourists from America, Holland and Saxony. They eagerly press into the simply fiurnished room and with respect contemplate the wholly uninteresting filing cabinets. An address is being delivered by an official of the Secretariat; we listen, and sud-

A CURIOSITY

denly the dull room is filled with romance and poetry. Are we reaching our goal? It is clear in any case that we are face to face with one of the great curiosities of the House. It is here, so we are informed by the eloquent bureaucrat, that the behest of the Covenant is fulfilled which demands that international relations shall be public and based on justice and honour. We remember the tables of the Covenant—Article 18, which recognizes the validity only of such treaties as are registered at and published by the Secretariat, and Article 20, which refuses to recognize treaties incompatible with the provisions of the Covenant. At the threshold of this room secret treaties, alliances and military agreements must cease to exist.

Tourists and study leaders, teachers and students listen with eager joy; we mingle with them, and we behold the miracle with our own eyes. The drawers of these filing cabinets contain 2,800 treaties, folded like any other one of the myriad documents which fill the House to overflowing; 2,800 treaties which have been deposited by the Governments of the member States in compliance with their obligations, which have been registered and filed away by the zealous officials of the Secretariat, and which have been collected, printed and bound in the fat volumes which may be seen in the adjoining room. The originals rest in the simple and capacious filing cabinets. Each of them is enclosed in a large white envelope; and on each envelope we can read the reassuring and solemn words: "League of Nations." Each treaty bears its number; not necessarily the number which it has in its home archives, but the League number which may place a British treaty between a Spanish and a Chilian treaty; a number which removes it from the self-centred national policy of its country, with all its international complications, and its obscure and selfish aims; a number which removes it from nationalistic confusion and gives it a place in the new and higher harmony; a number which is a promise, a guarantee and a fulfilment. Treaties to the number of 2,800 are garnered here, and each is a blossom in the wreath of peace of the united nations. While the outside world is rent by anarchy, order dwells in this apartment and changes a commonplace hotel room into the festal temple of a new religion. The antechamber of the legal section is the antechamber of a new world.

We listen with credulous admiration and obediently give heed while the system of registration with its double entry is being explained to us. It is like a registry of births and deaths, with particulars of the parents concluding the treaty and of the name of the child. We reverently contemplate diverse original treaties in their gorgeous bindings which are dug out for our particular benefit; we look at Hindenburg's gigantic signature by which Germany ratifies her adherence to the obligatory arbitration of the Permanent International Court; and we turn away to gaze at the impressive library containing the 2,800 treaties whose number grows from year to year, to which a fresh item is added every two or three days, and in which treaties are embodied from every corner of the world only to vanish forthwith in the conmunal filing cabinets. Our eyes caress all these thorough and eloquent agreements on political, economic, mercantile and social questions; all manner of treaties, on every manner of problem, discussed by Governments, accepted by Parliaments, ratified by ministries and signed by Cabinets, and which now have reached the climax of their career: they have received their League number and are at rest. We see them and rejoice: we have discovered the guiding rule for the life of nations. If the League is not here, where else can it be found?

Around us there is an admiring chatter, and all are eager to make the most of the moment. We eagerly open the drawers, pick up some of the big envelopes, confidently open them and, placing the treaties with pious fingers on the table, turn them over, search in them and read. Our eyes skip over the numerous treaties of arbitration; our lips whisper the names of countries and of the subjects of the treaties. "League of Nations," we trustingly read, and the words are of a pleasant and gentle

A CURIOSITY

touch to the lips. "No. 588," we say, and the number melts on our tongue. In this lottery every number must be a winner. Let us look at No. 588; we cheerfully open the envelope, eagerly withdraw the treaty, spread it out happily and begin to read. "Treaty of Alliance and Friendship between France and Czechoslovakia." Treaty of alliance? These words must give us pause, and we scrutinize the envelope again. It clearly bears the words "League of Nations" and the number 588. A treaty of alliance? We look around us. The reverential chatter of students and tourists, teachers and study leaders, fills the room with a religious murmur. We return the treaty to its envelope, dash our hand across our brow, and continue our search. We draw a new envelope, read the inscription "League of Nations No. 154" and discover the title: "Treaty of Alliance between the Kingdom of the Serbs, Croats and Slovenes, and the Republic of Czechoslovakia." Do we dream? Are we destined to draw yet more blanks? Not without apprehension we take up No. 155 and read: "Treaty for a Defensive Alliance Between the Kingdom of Roumania and the Republic of Czechoslovakia." Thoroughly frightened, we open No. 175 and read: "Treaty for a Defensive Alliance between the Polish Government and the Kingdom of Roumania." Where are we? We take up yet a further number of the quiet white envelopes and each time we find the old word "alliance" under the new "League of Nations." And while gradually the filing cabinets begin to revolve around us and the unctuous words of explanation addressed to students, teachers, study leaders and tourists become inaudible in our ears, we continue our search, although now we are filled with suspicion and a fierce desire to discover alliances even where they are not openly displayed as much. We find No. 58, a Franco-Belgian Correspondence on a Military Agreement; we discover No. 449, a "Political Agreement between France and Poland." We turn on, we read on, and our amazement grows. Where are we? We find nothing but alliances —treaties which are indistinguishable from those of the pre-war period and whose function is very different from that of the Locarno Treaty and other treaties of arbitration, which, of course, also have a place here. Their aim is not to regulate the relations between countries between which there is a possibility of wars or disputes, nor do they contain special agreements to eliminate the causes of wars or disputes and endeavour to prepare the pacificatory work of the League by regional agreements. The treaties which we find here are formally directed against third States; even in peace they double the power of each of the contracting parties and are intended to be employed against, or at any rate to weaken or threaten, a definite potential enemy; it is not their function to reconcile conflicting interests, but to form a common front between States having common interests against another State; they admit the possibility of war apart from League action, they are no less than the preparation for war and they enhance the spirit of aggression even when they bear the classical name of defensive alliance—treaties which in any case make superfluous and even ridiculous the League in which they should not themselves have a place as defensive measures—treaties which may possess a serial number in the League's system of peace, but which by virtue of their contents break out of this series.

Meanwhile, slowly and not without emotion, the studious League tourists are withdrawing; even at the door some of them, radiant but conscientious, are putting down their last note. "Public treaties," the amiable Englishwoman enthusiastically whispers, "public treaties mean peace."—"An end to mediæval secret diplomacy," the French teacher flutes, "and we shall have peace."—"A pity we didn't have this in 1914," the German visitor rumbles; "if we had, we might have had peace." Their murmuring voices die down the corridor; but their fading whispers leave behind one obstinate word which sticks in our ears, which forces itself into our ears like a thick piece of cotton wool, and which continues to hum in our brains: "peace." But we do not want to have cotton wool in our ears; we pluck it out and sit down before the filing cabinets, staring at the drawers and the documents they contain. Where

A CURIOSITY 319

are we? Angrily and despondently we realize that we are in the period after the last war—and in the period before the next.

Let it be acknowledged, then, that for the time being the League is a form of international co-existence to fill in the time between wars. The various Governments continue to conclude alliances with each other and against each other in defiance of the spirit of the Covenant. It might be considered an impertinence on their part if, in defiance even of the letter of the Covenant, they deposit their treaties of alliance in the present apartment and hand them in before the eyes of the world to be duly registered by double entry; but the fact is that, since the League is in existence, it is in their interest to give a legal form to a policy even if such a policy is alien or antagonistic to the League. The device necessary in order to cause such treaties to conform to the letter of the Covenant is, after all, a simple one: treaties containing no trace of the League spirit or of belief in or respect for the League contain the diplomatic phrase: "Nothing in the present treaty conflicts with the Covenant." Surely there is nothing difficult in this; and sometimes the desire to circumvent the new law is so powerful that the Covenant is mentioned in almost every article. But when it is so mentioned it is employed in the way in which children put into their secret letters special words which have only to be omitted in order to give a clear text. The League envelopes before us contain innumerable instances of this simple skill. Thus the political agreement between France and Poland of the 19th of February 1921, which was registered at Geneva in July 1923, and which is a regular Treaty of Alliance, contains in its first article the formula "In accordance with the League Covenant," by which means the old policy of alliances is introduced into the new secret language of the League. In the "correspondence" between the French and the Belgian Governments on the Franco-Belgian military agreement of the 7th of September 1920—and only the correspondence, not the agreement, was registered at Geneva—the object of the agreement (which was signed by Marshal Foch, General Maglinse,

Chief of General Staff of the Belgian Army, and by General Buat, Chief of General Staff of the French Army) the aim of the agreement was described as being to "strengthen the guarantees of peace and security resulting from the League Covenant." Other treaties piously point to the articles of the Covenant leaving open a recourse to war when they come to set out the provisions of the treaty in case of war. While discovering these diplomatic tricks we are led to ask which is more detestable—the existence of treaties which disregard the fact that it should be the equal endeavour of all members of the League to preserve peace, or the abuse to which the name of the League is exposed?

Yet there are times when this abuse seems almost like a last salute to the neglected ideal of the League: for there is no lack of other treaties where even this atrophied remnant of cynical respect is wanting, and the contracting Governments do not even pretend to attempt to take the League into their calculations. Let us glance at the Treaty of Alliance between the Kingdom of the Serbs, Croats and Slovenes and the Czechoslovakian Republic, registered at the League Secretariat on the 30th of August 1921. Article 1 plainly and simply informs us that in the case of unprovoked aggression on the part of Hungary against one of the high contracting Parties the other party undertakes to co-operate in the defence of the victim of aggression as laid down in the agreement provided for in Article 2 of the present treaty. Instinctively we expect that the provisions of Article 2 will be found to contain at least a formal proviso on the duties of States members and the rights of the League Council. But the agreement provided by Article 2 is wholly different: the "competent technical authority of the Republic of Czechoslovakia and the Kingdom of the Serbs, Croats and Slovenes"—i.e. not the organs of the League but the general staffs of the two countries—"will jointly arrange the necessary particulars"—i.e. military agreements—"to implement the present Treaty." And when Article 3 proceeds to deal with the right of the two countries to contract alliances no attempt is

A CURIOSITY

made to provide that the League's opinion on this system of alliances must first be obtained. Yet if there was to be no respect for the principles of the League, at least the blushes of its officials might have been spared. On the contrary, the central body is neglected and it is provided that neither of the high contracting Parties is to conclude a treaty of alliance with any other Power without previously consulting the other party. In other words, the aim is to prevent this particular treaty from being absorbed in a comprehensive treaty—the kind of League appeal so frequently brought forward by States contracting alliances—and to prevent one particular treaty from being neutralized by other particular treaties. The bilateral treaty has a unilateral purpose and a unilateral direction which it must not lose; and if other treaties are concluded to supplement it, how can this unilateral purpose and direction be guaranteed? As for the League, no mention is made of it until we come to the formalities. Thus according to Article 5 the agreement is to be reported to the League, and behind the word League we find the words, in brackets, League Covenant. Reported—why reported? For scrutiny and confirmation? By no means: the treaty is simply communicated to the League and the latter proceeds unemotionally to file it away in the cabinets and envelopes of the Legal Department, while we watch with open mouth and rounded eyes.

A similar wording is that of the treaties between Roumania and Czechoslovakia, entered at the Secretariat in August 1921; only here there is a special article by which, in order to coordinate their friendly endeavours, the two Powers are obliged to consult on questions of foreign policy touching their relations to Hungary. The defensive alliance between Poland and Roumania entered in the League Secretariat in October 1921 goes so far as to speak openly of a military agreement, forbids either State to conclude an armistice or a peace without the other, and prohibits any other treaties without previous consultation with the remaining contracting parties, herein resembling the other treaties. Nowhere is any mention made of any possible decisions of the League; but mention is made of the agreement concluded by Roumania to preserve the treaties of Trianon and Neuilly; it is magnanimously provided that these may be changed into treaties of alliance. The League knows this document merely in its quality as depository for alien documents. "The present agreement is to be communicated to the League": only on this occasion it was evidently thought that the reference to the Covenant would imply too much respect and consequently the words "League of Nations" are followed by the words "In conformity with the Treaty of Versailles." And why indeed not? For these high contracting Parties the Covenant obviously is identical with the Treaty of Versailles.

Altogether we have here a quaint collection of quaint treaties, designed not to assure peace, but the power of the powerful nations. Their methods are the old methods and the enemy at which they are aimed is not the unknown enemy of all, i.e. any State breaking the common law, the enemy which the inadequate articles of the Covenant seek to frustrate and against which the joint efforts of all the States should be directed. On the contrary, the enemy is a definite enemy, and though his name is not pronounced he plays a part in every treaty; he is plainly pointed at and the mere existence of the treaties constitutes a threat to him. We angrily ask on what grounds such a specialization of the pacificatory endeavours of the League should be permitted; but no sooner have we asked than we find that this specialization can be extended: not only are certain countries designated as potential enemies, but certain definite questions can be treated as causes for intervention and removed from the sphere of the League's care. It becomes perfectly permissible to interfere with the national sovereignty of other States. Thus Number 588 of the treaties entered at the League Secretariat, the treaty of alliance and friendship between France and Czechoslovakia, registered in March 1924, does not confine itself to obliging the two countries to consult jointly on all questions susceptible of infringing

A CURIOSITY

the order set up by the treaties of peace—although in any case Article 10 prohibits this interference and Article 19 permits it under certain definite conditions; but the treaty goes further, and provides that the two States are to agree on measures to be taken relating to the internal affairs of Austria and Germany. Had not the tourists and study leaders already been swallowed in the outside confusion we would like to call them back and supplement the able lecture they have heard by reading out in a loud voice Article 5 of League Document Number 588: "The high contracting Parties confirm that they are completely in accord on the insistent necessity, with reference to the preservation of the peace, of taking up a common attitude in view of any attempt to restore the Hohenzollern dynasty in Germany, and they undertake to consult together on the measures to be taken in such a contingency."

We continue to delve into the treasures of the Legal Department. Presently we came across two Italo-Albanian treaties. The first, concluded on the 27th of November 1926 and registered in February 1927, is described as a pact of friendship and security, while the second, signed on the 22nd of November 1927 and entered in Geneva in January 1928, is described as a defensive alliance. This discovery gives us pause. Why should Albania and Italy, a small and a Great Power, have recourse to Geneva? Can they come to an agreement on any other subject than methods for the settlement of conflicts between them; in other words, means to preserve the independence of the threatened minor Power as against the dangerous major Power—one of those reasonable agreements by which disputes between two Powers are eliminated and not, as in so many others, two States are united against a third? Yet we may ask why Article 1 of the first treaty—No. 1402 in the League series—should commence by earnestly declaring every disturbance of the political, juridical and territorial status of Albania incompatible with the interests of both States. Surely Albania is an independent member of the League, and as such can rely on the protection of the entire

Council including Italy, herself a permanent member, and this under more than one article of the Covenant, beginning with No. 10, which guarantees political independence and territorial integrity. Why, further, should Albania require a defensive treaty of alliance with Italy? Or can it be that, in spite or perhaps because of her power, Italy does not really trust the League, the Council and the Covenant, and imagines herself in need of protection from little Albania? In any case we are next faced by the defensive alliance between Italy and Albania, bearing League Number 1616, and requiring the two nations united in sincere and perfect friendship to support each other. And this postulate was not made with the diplomatic coolness of an unreliable ally who, in case of need, might remember his "sacred egoism" and exchange one alliance for another, but with such "zeal," as the treaty expressly states, as though either partner were safeguarding his own interests or advantages. It is impossible to read such a sentence without emotion or without horror. Can this be called an alliance? Is it not rather a marriage? In any case the treaty further provides that the two countries are to be united by an immutable defensive alliance lasting not less than twenty years, and that all methods are to be applied to guarantee a security of their States and to assure their mutual defence against foreign aggression. In their attempts to prevent the outbreak of a war provoked by an outside party they will always support a just compensation for the threatened party—as though the League had not already undertaken this task. And if peaceful methods are exhausted—which methods?—for we have not yet come across the League—either party is obliged to follow the fate of the other, just as in a regular marriage. Either must place at the disposal of the other all his military, financial and other resources and, of course, must renounce the right of concluding a separate armistice or peace. In six articles this forbidden alliance was confirmed—the forbidden subjection of one member of the League under another. Having completed these six articles the two parties evidently found that their

A CURIOSITY 325

work was good and rested in the seventh, in which they proclaim that the treaty is to be registered at the League after ratification. And so it happened. For here the treaty is before us in its white League envelope bearing League Number 1616, and in the adjacent room it forms part of the printed library; the Sales Department publishes it for propaganda purposes; it is a League publication, and as such has an honoured place in the libraries of Governments, historians and even of pacifists.

Where are we? Are we yet in the League? No: the old world of confusion is still at large in this Chamber of Horrors attached to the Government Museum named League Secretariat. A network of obscure and malignant treaties of the old style, having nothing to do with the League organization, ties the Balkan States to Poland, Poland to France, and France to Belgium; subordinates one system under the other, provokes an Italian counter-system, severs the unity of the League, supports the aggressive tendencies of certain States which the League was intended to abolish but which, in fact, constitute a heavy menace to it, and deprives the feeble apparatus for the preservation and the restoration of peace of its last support.

And so we must not be surprised to find that Germany too attempts by means of a treaty to regulate her relations with Russia before joining a League rendered practically worthless by such a mass of subsidiary treaties; for Russia is not herself a member of the League, is threatened by the policies of a number of member States, and is no less a potential danger than a friend. In fact no alliance was concluded, and the arrangement reached—not quite a defensive alliance and not quite a treaty of neutrality—was a kind of compromise which merely assured the neutrality of one State in the case that the other was attacked and demanded that it should take no part in any financial or economic boycott of the State in question. In taking these measures Germany was not so much influenced by the motive of other States, whose one anxiety was to be free to wage war despite their membership of the League, as by a wish to avoid dangers of war arising from her membership of the League. It was for this reason that she insisted in an exchange of notes with the Russian Government, that in its fundamental idea the League was destined to provide a peaceful and equitable settlement of international conflicts, and that the German Government was resolved to do its utmost in helping to realize this idea. It promised that it would energetically oppose any tendencies expressly directed against Russia in contravention of this fundamental idea of peace, and mentions the fact that German participation in any sanctions against Russia was limited by a declaration of the Locarno Powers, adding that a resolution of the Council designating Russia as aggressor would be binding on Germany only if she joined in the resolution; so that an unjustified accusation of Russia would not bind Germany to take part in any sanctions.

It is not perhaps an edifying spectacle to watch how the Government of a Great Power, at the moment when it is preparing to take up its permanent judicial function in the supreme world organ, begins by carefully explaining the special precautions and interpretation which it intends to bring to the exercise of this office in one particular case. And indeed the exchange of notes—not the Russo-German Treaty itself, which is the pattern of a security pact on League lines—comes close to the maximum by way of provisos compatible with the existence of any League. Yet it might be urged that it was the League itself which has unduly displaced and obscured its limits. Having been forcibly disarmed, Germany was unable to participate in League sanctions against the victorious Powers; and she was surely justified in making at least a theoretical attempt to prevent these Powers from making use of her troops or territory in any warlike actions undertaken under cover of the League. Thus it happened that a few months after the German application for admission to the League, and a few months before her entry, the Russo-German Treaty and the Russo-German exchange of notes were entered in the Legal Department and adorned with League Number 1268. Can we not hear the various treaties of alliance whispering

A CURIOSITY 327

in their League envelopes? "Who are you?" the old inmates ask the treaty of neutrality as it arrives, fully and carefully equipped with the entire armoury of the Pact. And while it is being placed in the drawer where it takes its place in this strange universe of paper it whispers back in sentences carefully edited and checked by Herr Gauss—and its words are half sighs and half laughter: "I am the herald of Germany in this house. I am Germany's suspicion . . . ."

After so many disappointments let us turn to a document lying on the table which may furnish evidence of the good work done by the League and of the Secretariat's loyal zeal. It is a fine stout volume with a brown cover, carefully planned, and bearing the date 1927; on examination we find that it is a second improved and amplified edition of a publication dating from 1926. Its title is "Arbitration and Security," and it bears the sub-title: "Systematic Survey of the Arbitration Conventions and Treaties of Mutual Security deposited with the League of Nations."

It is an official conspectus and digest produced by the Legal section and covering all the treaties serving the League as data for the study of the question of security which, of course, is a preliminary to the study of disarmament. We look through the book and examine its five chapters. Evidently the chapter dealing with treaties of guarantee and security is the most important, and by turning to it we can learn what are the principles of the League, or at any rate of its Legal section, with regard to international treaties. In this way we can recover from our melancholy voyage of exploration through the steel and wooden filing cabinets.

But what we find is the whole body of secret treaties as we discovered them in the drawers and volumes next door, copied in their serial order. It would be a mistake to believe, however, that they had been drawn up here in order to be tried and found wanting. In the eyes of the Legal section the Franco-Belgian and the Franco-Polish alliances, the treaties of the

Little Entente and the Italo-Albanian alliance, are so-called treaties of guarantee and security. The editor of the collection, van Hamel, at that time director of the Legal Department, coolly describes them as follows in his preface: "Most of these treaties express in one form or another the principle that it is the function of guarantees as between States to increase the respect felt for peace in the name of the League, by intensifying the sanctions to which a breach of the peace might lead"; and he does not blush to identify himself with the insincerity of certain Governments which, in their zeal to conclude treaties, insist that it is possible to see in these treaties an application of the principle of regional understandings mentioned in Article 21 of the Covenant. He insists that this chapter contains treaties expressly described as guarantee treaties, as well as alliances and other political arrangements, all of them embracing the principle of the enhancement of peace and security. Such are van Hamel's words. It seems natural to the Legal section not only to register and publish the treaties entered at the League without an examination, but actually to use them as the material for the new structure of security and for the further development of the League.

Where are we, and how can such an error be explained? Have the organs of the League forgotten Articles 18 and 20, the very foundations of the Covenant? If we examine the protocols of the League gathered in the offices of the Secretariat we soon discover that the League organs are fully responsible; they knew their duties and deliberately neglected them. When, in 1920, the Council had sanctioned a colourless report of the Secretary-General on the application of Article 18, various members of the Assembly realized that it was an essential part of the preliminary work upon the League to examine the scope of this article. But the Assembly of 1920 passed the problem on to that of 1921, and the latter handed it over to the Assembly of 1923. There were discussions and heated debates, but no resolution was reached, and nothing

A CURIOSITY

remained over save the report which was never adopted and never enforced, but which nevertheless continues to exist by virtue of the fact that it constitutes the legal interpretation of Article 18. In this way the dangerous principle is perpetuated that purely technical or administrative acts which do not touch international political relations, which are merely technical regulations and which, without effecting any changes, merely further define acts already registered, or endeavour to ensure the execution of such acts, need not be registered. Behind this screen of insincerity erected by the League jurists attached to the Great Powers we shall in hiding find military agreements and indeed any other agreements uniting States for common action. Even while the debates of the second Assembly were in progress the British representative, Lord Balfour, and the famous jurist, Sir Cecil Hurst, who was later to be a judge of the Permanent Court, successfully disputed the obligation to register financial agreements, in this way "neglecting one of the most important aspects of international life," as the French jurist Jean Rey puts it. Accordingly we shall not be surprised to find that the papers of the League reveal no trace of any serious examination of Article 20, which is the supplement to Article 18. Even at the time when the League Committee of the Peace Conference was deliberating it had been grasped that this article covered a fundamental problem of the League; but no sooner had the fact been realized than it was evaded. Wilson believed that it would suffice to leave it to public opinion to supervise the compatibility of treaties with the Covenant, while the Australian delegate, Sir Robert Borden, insisted that an examination by the Council should be the necessary preliminary to registration. The British, Portuguese and Greek representatives—Cecil, Reis and Venizelos—on the other hand wished the Secretary-General to be instructed to pass on to the Council any alliances conflicting with the Covenant. Certain advanced delegates, like the courageous Belgian socialist de Brouckère, later asked the Assembly to answer the question whether the

League was fulfilling its duty by registering all treaties submitted to it without satisfying itself that the obligation contained in Article 20 was being fulfilled; and other delegates pointed to the moral duty which this article implied for the League; while yet others formulated definite motions in different connections. But all these efforts remained unsuccessful and merely showed that the problem was perfectly well understood at Geneva. Everyone was fully aware that, as Jean Rey says, the real aim in insisting on the publicity of treaties was to permit public opinion and its organ, the League, to exercise a certain control, and that if the League was not required to criticize the treaties which it registered, its continued silence or inactivity constituted a heavy responsibility each time that a suspicious treaty was entered—for the precise reason that Article 20 placed certain duties upon the League in the event of its members forgetting their duties.

Nor, indeed, were members ignorant of their obligations; only unfortunately nobody dreamed of insisting on methods, commissions, expert organizations and rights of sanction which would strengthen and make effective the supervisory functions of the League. Simultaneously the greatest attention was devoted to a thousand matters lying outside its primary competence. No Government and no Parliament pointed accusingly at the abuse practised in Geneva for all these years, and even the Germans remained inactive, although before entering the League they had been voluble in their criticism and had promised Germany and the world that they would endeavour to improve its inadequacies; although it would have been in their interest to speak, they remained silent. And yet they might have quoted in their support not only Wilson, but even a greater than Wilson, Kant, who said, "All actions relating to the rights of others are wrong unless their maxims will bear publicity." The conspiracy of silence persisted among the authors as well as the victims of the policy of treaties; and thus no public conscience was formed which might have been outraged, and the treaties could continue to assemble at

A CURIOSITY

Geneva, to gather in the filing cabinets and to take a place within the innocent envelopes bearing the great name of the League. The labours of the learned officials of the Legal section confine themselves to checking the dates of the conclusion and ratification of the treaties. If they are formally in order, the document is given a number which makes it a part of the League. And in Countess Trani's room Sir Eric Drummond sits behind his orderly desk under the milky light of his reading-lamp and patiently sets an historical name beneath the letters of confirmation which the various Governments receive in exchange for registration.

No less than 2,800 times the Secretary-General has placed his signature under such a document, the only document which is not turned out by a typewriter but is written out on copperplate for the occasion. And on as many occasions this document has been the League's only reaction to a vital question.

Let us carefully examine these specimens of League calligraphy. Not only are they one of the most important curiosities of this Museum; they will also be one of the weightiest pieces of evidence on the day when the nations will rise against those who destroyed the League—a day whose imminence is proclaimed by the entire furnishing of this room. Then the furies of war will burst from the steel and wooden cabinets of the Legal section, will rend the League envelope, cast off the League number, rush past the chattering bureaucrats, the eager tourists and the study leaders and go raging down the corridors, waving their flaming torch above the house which so rashly offered them its hospitality.

CHAPTER XXI

THE WHALE

ONCE again the spirit of optimism which has accompanied us on our journeys seeks to reinspire and to console us. A mere antechamber could hardly be expected to be the temple of peace; and if the treaties of alliance in their steel and wooden cabinets block the entrance to a new world, there is yet an international law which points the way past these inevitable remanants of a pre-League epoch. For years other cabinets have been filled with evidence of a lasting endeavour to apply, to improve and to complete this international law, and as the life of the Covenant grows the ancient ghosts are gradually dispersed. If Articles 18 and 20 are insufficient, let us turn to the voluminous documents dealing with international justice, for there is no better evidence to show how much vital force the Covenant has meanwhile achieved. It is here that Article 14 is embodied: it is here that right is proved more powerful than might. This single article will bring fresh air and a broader light into the apartment and into the whole House.

Let us open the window and look out. In the distant Hague, far beyond the blue line of the Jura, the work created at Geneva is being developed. The first Assembly of the League had complied with the demands of Article 14 and had drawn up the rules for the new permanent International Court; and soon after the printed article had become a powerful reality. Elected in solemn simultaneous sessions of Council and Assembly, the college of international judges acquired a greater respect and a more solemn aspect than was possessed by the many shadowy structures deriving their vague existence from the paragraphs of the Covenant. Unrestricted by the considerations of national policy hampering the diplomats who elected them, the Hague judges were physically and morally free to rise into a sphere of international independence.

Their competence and their field of activity might be restricted; but the very fact of their existence sufficed to make them the symbol of a better League and to approximate them more closely to the ideal; nor was it a coincidence that the United States, obstinately resisting any attempt to draw them into the other organs devised by Wilson, felt the attraction of the Hague Court, a body which Wilson himself all but forgot. Eight years after the formulation of Article 14 Elihu Root, the American champion of the idea of an International Court, collaborated in a revision of the article, and a special Protocol of the League enabled the United States to join the Court.

Indeed we have but to examine the facts to find that the fairest of our dreams has already been realized. In the Legal section the Minutes of the Hague Court are filed in heaps. Among them we find the judgments rendered on the strength of so-called unilateral *démarches* under the peace treaties, e.g. in the case of the Anglo-French munition steamer *Wimbledon*, where Britain, France, Italy and Japan took joint steps against Germany. Other judgments were rendered under particular treaties, e.g. under the Upper Silesian agreement, when Germany proceeded against Poland in the matter of the appropriation of the Chorzow nitrogen factory; others under so-called compromises between parties, e.g. in the Franco-Turkish dispute relating to the collision of a Turkish steamer with the SS. *Lotus*, and in the Franco-Swiss dispute on the Geneva free zones. Such rulings are within the competence of the Court. More important still is the vast body of so-called consultative opinions rendered by the Hague Tribunal at the request of the Council, by means of which abstract right frequently penetrates into current politics, as in the minorities dispute between Germany and Poland, the conflict between Danzig and Poland, in the various interpretations of the international labour code, in the Franco-British dispute on nationalities in Tunis and Morocco, in the Mossul case and in the question of the Austro-German Customs Union. Further, we can here find the solemn documents in which by the end of 1931 no less than thirty-seven States had recognized the so-called optional clause recognizing the compulsory arbitration of the Court, among them the German document of ratification, the first one to witness the adhesion of a Great Power. Here there is hope for the future, no less than when Walther Schücking joined the world tribunal. He was the first German representative, and surely it was a symbol of peaceful progress that this representative should be a liberal exponent of international law, a champion of the International Court, and a joint author of the German League plan presented at Versailles as well as of the first scientific commentary of the Covenant.

Such considerations are certainly relevant. We admit that the documents provided at the distant Court contain the future of the League and remember the emotion we experienced when we heard the clear note of Article 14 among the gloomy mutterings of the rest of the Covenant. We are not, however, interested in the literal application of the article: what matters is its promise. Unless its scope is extended it cannot act as a leaven within the Covenant. At present the judges of the Hague are permitted to render their verdicts only if a request from the lower spheres of diplomacy reaches their exalted heights: the scope of their jurisdiction depends upon the politicians. Far from being placed above the League they are hardly within it; rather they only stand and wait. Indeed it may be doubted whether they are judges at all: their judgments and opinions more frequently betray the advocate than the judge. All too frequently they are compelled to follow the narrow cunning of the questions asked by the Council and thus to support purely political operations with the armament of Law. Are their ears never open to the arguments suggested by their own or by friendly Governments? At any rate, it was a memorable spectacle when the question of the Austro-German Customs Union divided the Court into two almost equal political groups, and the verdict was settled by the casting vote of the Cuban judge, Bustamente. And it was a scandal that the same legal advisers with whom we grew familiar at the tables of the Council and the League committees, where they attended on the peace delegates, whispering suggestions for a useful trick to adopt or pressing a skilfully drafted note into their hands, should be discovered more and more frequently in the robes of the International Court. We begin to suspect that behind the blue line of the Jura a second Geneva is being built up, and that a second Council meets in its Court. But if the tribunal is further to be infected and enslaved by politics, is it likely that its verdict will be accepted more readily than the compromises devised by the Secretariat? Even the compulsory arbitration of the Court is a disappointment, for the temporal restrictions and numerous provisos applied to it make it practically meaningless. The signatures under the Protocol grow more numerous; but the members of the League persistently decline to follow the only way which will genuinely realize compulsory arbitration, which would consist in giving the Court a part in the Covenant and in admitting its validity in political disputes. It was certainly a matter for congratulation that the United States eventually was attracted by the Court; but this very possibility cost the Court and the League heavy sacrifices in prestige and power. Admittedly Schücking was an ornament of the international tribunal: but nobody knew better than he that, although his journey was completed, the League's journey must go further. The culminating point of his career stands far beneath the level which the life of the nations ought to reach. We have not yet forgotten the premature jubilation raised by the judge of the new tribunal when the old tribunal was founded at the Hague. What has happened since then? A Court has been founded and indeed it is the centre of our hopes; but its hour has not yet come and we may doubt whether it will ever come. The case is, not that Article 14 can improve the Covenant, but that an improved Covenant is required to improve Article 14. Might must be eliminated from the rest of the Covenant before there is room for right, and the question is whether any steps are actually being taken in this direction.

We turn to a fresh document, and we learn that a Committee to suggest alterations in the Covenant was appointed within a year of its inauguration. In the course of years almost every page of the Covenant received its share of marginal notes and footnotes. But it does not follow that there is any desire to solve the fundamental questions and to eliminate the predominance of the Council over the Assembly, the preponderance of the major Powers over the small States, and the more intolerable survivals of the Allied origin of the Covenant. A few attempts were made to seize the real nature of the League; but other attempts were merely intended to support certain national plans, while others still were entirely unimportant. The result of all these laborious, methodical and uninspired labours can be perceived if the latest edition of a Covenant is compared with the 1919 version. Only five articles will be found to have lost their original form, and the creative spirit of the nations has added to the Paris version three brief sentences and nineteen words—the latter identical in some of the articles. The alteration of Article 4 is merely a technical explanation of the method by which the non-permanent members of the Council are elected; in Article 6 the alteration merely explains the proportions in which the expenses of the League are borne by the various members; while the sentences added to Articles 12, 13 and 15, in which the various methods of arbitration are enumerated, allow for the fact that the Permanent Court has come into existence since the Covenant was drawn up. This is all, or at least the only noticeable alteration in the Covenant; unless we consider it worth while to mention that since 1926 the various paragraphs within the different articles are numbered—by virtue of a special resolution of the seventh Assembly. The Covenant of 1932 is that of 1919; and 1919, which had been intended to be the modest beginning of the progressive realization of the idea of the

THE WHALE 337

League, has gradually become its solemn climax. We turn to yet another document. A timid attempt is made to interpret the Covenant, i.e. to insert between its immutable paragraphs loose sheets not requiring unanimous resolution or ratification. Most of these interpretations, which in fact are substitutes for failures to bring about alterations (as in Articles 10 and 16), never attain any practical importance. An interpretation of Article 16 formulated by one of the Locarno Powers failed to win the approval of the members not interested in the agreement. Interpretations of Articles 12 and 15 drafted after the Greco-Italian conflict of 1923 by a committee of jurists at the request of the Council never achieved any practical importance. Interpretations of Article 19 drafted in connection with the dispute between Bolivia and Chili and at the later request of China, as well as the interpretation of the Monroe Doctrine in Article 21, by which, in 1928, it was intended to facilitate the return of Costa Rica to the League, are so many jugglings with the text without political value. In short, the tendency towards the interpretation of the articles died down as rapidly as that towards their alteration; and in its place we find a growing endeavour to facilitate the application of the Covenant by providing the organs of the League with directions for the execution of their obligations under the Covenant; it is not the Covenant but the competence of its organs which is now extended. But these legal investigations between the lines of the League are soon pushed aside by the nationalistic tendencies represented by the leading member States which, far from intending to place the League apparatus above their system of alliances, mean to exploit it simply for the extension of this system.

Meanwhile a murmuring of many languages is heard: the language of the jurists attempting to explain and render practicable the Wilsonian Covenant, the language of the diplomats whom the Covenant does not interest, but who wish to exploit its organs in their own interests, and the language of the soldiers who are anxious to dispatch the nations on a wild-goose chase after a perfect peace in order that they may perfect the instruments of war undisturbed. And this murmuring gradually grows into a vast clamour from which louder and more commandingly there emerges the word security. Is it the nations who have cause for anxiety, the smaller members or the disarmed nations who cause this noise? By no means. The deafening call for increased security comes from the mouth of the victorious creators and masters of the League, who had fashioned the Covenant in accordance with their own needs and had placed at its beginning the words: "The High Contracting Parties in order to promote international co-operation and to achieve international peace and security . . . agree to this Covenant of the League of Nations." It is they who now insist that the High Contracting Parties must come to complementary arrangements in order to guarantee peace and security; and, instead of developing the Covenant, they render it valueless by heaping up in its midst, and especially between Articles 10 and 16, and the old Treaties of Alliance, a pile of documents containing a mass of complicated obligations. If we would read these new provisions and take a part in their creation we must not, however, remain inactive in the rooms of the Legal section. On the contrary, we must pursue the messengers who carry the documents from the Legal to the Political Department, from the Political to the Disarmament Department, from the Disarmament Department to Countess Trani's room, and thence back into the Legal section, where, however, their stay is not a permanent one; for all that is done there is to effect a formal revision of the work effectually done by soldiers and diplomats.

The next document we examine is an ostentatious one—the result of the disarmament labours. It is a resolution of the temporary mixed committee which had been intended to prepare the reduction of armaments, coupled with a later resolution of the third League Assembly, a resolution destined to become famous in League literature as Resolution Number 14. These two documents state that in view of the need of security felt by a number of States disarmament must be combined with a special agreement on defence. A French and a British plan were stirred up together; to the thesis of the beatific virtues of the general agreement is added a tendency towards the supposedly more practical regional arrangements, and the result was that in 1923 the draft of a treaty for mutual assistance was evolved. The preamble declared: "The High Contracting Parties being desirous of establishing the general lines of a scheme of mutual assistance with a view to facilitate the application of Articles 10 and 16 of the Covenant of the League of Nations, and of a reduction or limitation of national armaments in accordance with Article 8 of the Covenant to the lowest point consistent with national safety and the enforcement by common action of international obligations...."

The contracting Powers were further bound by the treaty individually and collectively to assist any State which might be attacked, provided that it had agreed to the disarmament arrangements contained in the Treaty; it instructs the Council to determine within four days after notification of hostilities which States had been attacked and whether they had any claim on assistance; it enumerated the various methods of support, some of them formulated with a good deal of reticence and it provided for the possibility of support under special agreements without any previous resolution of the Council, as well as for demilitarized zones and for steps towards the reduction of armaments. The great merit of the draft was seen in Article 1, which makes good the deliberate omissions of the Covenant. We are at length informed that "aggressive war is an international crime, and [the High Contracting Parties] undertake that no one of them will be guilty of its commission." But these merits are cancelled by the capital faults contained in Article 14. "Nothing in the present Treaty shall affect the rights and obligations resulting from . . . the Treaties of Peace signed in 1919 and 1920 . . . or from the provisions of treaties . . .

registered with the League of Nations and published by it at the date of the first coming into force of the present Treaty." In this way the world created by the peace treaties is confirmed, as well as the alliances which, in spite of Article 20, have found a home in the Chamber of Horrors of the Legal section. The plan suffered from a fundamental insincerity and was approved by no more than eighteen States, some of which took exception to parts of it; but it was wrecked by the idea to which it owed its inception, namely, the French desire to resurrect the plan of a Franco-British-American alliance—which had failed during the Peace Conference—in the shape of a powerful Franco-British alliance. In the League as it is, mutual support amounts to an alliance so long as armaments are unequal, and it was thought that the League would provide a suitable international framework for such a national alliance. But although Lord Robert Cecil adopted the draft, it was turned down by the British Government under Mr. Ramsay MacDonald on the ground that it meant an enormous complication of international relations.

A fresh document, however, arises out of the ashes of the treaty of mutual support, and this too was the product of the League's political factory. At the Assembly of 1924, which was held under the auspices of a new Franco-British *rapprochement*, after the completion of the Ruhr struggle, the conclusion of the Conference of London and Poincaré's resignation following the success of the French Radicals, the so-called Geneva trilogy was invented jointly by MacDonald and Herriot. It consisted in the three magic words: "Arbitration, Security, Reduction of Armaments." For weeks subtle and eager deliberations took place in committee, all of them under the charm of these words, culminating in a so-called protocol for the pacific settlement of international disputes, which, after statesmanlike and brilliant speeches by the Czechoslovakian delegate Benes and the Greek delegate Politis, was adopted by the plenary Assembly in an apotheosis of wild enthusiasm. Geneva was drunk with bliss and for a few days the world shared its intoxication. In a glowing preamble the Powers radiated their love of peace.

"Animated by the firm desire to secure the maintenance of general peace and the security of nations, whose existence, independence or territories may be threatened; Recognizing the solidarity of the members of the international community; Asserting that a war of aggression constitutes a violation of this solidarity and an international crime; Desirous of facilitating the complete application of the system provided in the Covenant of the League of Nations for the pacific settlement of disputes between States and of ensuring the repression of international crimes; and for the purpose of realizing, as contemplated by Article 8 of the Covenant, the reduction of national armaments to the lowest point consistent with national safety and the enforcement by common action of international obligations. . . ."

By virtue of the various articles of the Protocol the Powers bound themselves not to declare war on States conforming with its provisions and to acknowledge the competence of the Permanent Court as obligatory, with the exceptions of various permissible provisos. In this way the famous gap in Article 15 of the Covenant is filled; for hitherto the member States had been left free to act as they wished in default of a unanimous resolution of the Council. Further, the sanctions were rendered more complete, and finally an international disarmament conference was called for the 15th of June 1925, which was intended to draw up a general plan of disarmament after whose adoption the Protocol itself would come into force. We are further provided with important details on the subject of wars of aggression, a dangerous and ambiguous term rendered suspect by its associations with the old defensive treaties. It is Article 10 of the Protocol which provides us with the definition hitherto lacking by declaring that any States are to be treated as aggressors who wage war in defiance of the Covenant or the Protocol, who enter a demilitarized zone, who refuse, once hostilities have commenced, to submit the issue to one of the systems of arbitration provided, who disregard a resolution of the Council or any verdict, who disregard the provisional measures provided for in the Protocol to safeguard the *status quo* during the period of negotiation, who reject or infringe an armistice, or finally—and this is the most dangerous part of the definition—who reject a verdict by which the subject of a dispute is described as an internal affair of the opponent. In his report before the fifth Assembly Benes lyrically exclaimed that the great gap in the Covenant had been filled. Such an utterance may be regarded with scepticism: the gap will not have been filled until armaments have been equalized and it has become practical politics to punish as well as to define the aggressor. . . . And further, only one gap among several has been filled: war and defiance of the treaties have been prohibited; but peace in defiance of justice remains. If Article 15 is without a gap, the gap in Article 19 has become all the more noticeable. No methods and no obligations are provided to assure the revision of treaties which themselves constitute a menace to peace. The Protocol might have provided the beginnings of a better League had it been based upon a just peace or contained an apparatus for providing a better peace; with its faulty Article 19 it was useless for the League.

And in fact the Protocol soon shared the fate of the treaty of mutual assistance. The chief resistance to what would have amounted to an alliance with France within the League system emanated from Britain and the British Dominions; and although Mr. MacDonald had adopted the Protocol, his successor, Sir Austen Chamberlain, destroyed it six months later at the Council meeting of March 1925. He saw in the provisions of the Protocol a military method and feared that in future the aim of the League would not so much be the development of friendly collaboration and a deliberate harmony in the prosecution of international affairs as the preservation of peace by the organization of war, and possibly of war on a greater scale. He innocently asked whether a world system was necessary, and meant a Franco-British system. He declared that the natural approach for the consolidation of peace consisted in separate agreements between the States whose conflicting interests constituted the chief danger for peace; and in so saying he had in mind the future treaties of security already under negotiation and intended to eliminate all possible causes of war along the German, French and Belgian frontier.

We turn to yet another bundle of documents. The Protocol had died—Long Live Locarno. After the Messianic exaltation of the fifth Assembly nothing remained for the sixth, which met in the autumn of 1925, except to adopt the resolution of the Spanish delegate, Quiñones de Leon, to welcome the attempts made by the future Locarno Powers "in the spirit of the Covenant and in harmony with the principles of the Protocol" to recommend their extension to the rest of the world, and to resolve on the preparation of a Disarmament Conference, the date being left blank. Despite the laurels with which the League crowned itself, it had not contributed much to the treaties concluded at Locarno in November of the same year; their origin lay outside the League. But although it might be doubted whether the treaties would help the League, they certainly were closely related to it. They allowed the Council important powers, they introduced Germany into the League (that being their *raison d'être*), they remain in force until the Council should resolve with a two-thirds majority that the League itself provides the Council Powers with adequate guarantees, and, in their final Protocol, they bind the signatory Powers to realize the idea of disarmament. These treaties might have introduced calm and quiet into the confusions of Geneva politics with their clamour for security, their exaggeration of the principle of sanctions, and their French system of alliances; for the spirit of these treaties set a barrier to the French endeavours, based as they were upon a principle of alliances, and shifted the centre of gravity of the endeavours for international peace from the principle of sanctions to that of arbitration. The faulty foundation of the League, however, could not be rectified by these treaties any more than by the Protocol; the Foreign Ministers of Germany, France and Britain shone for some months in an artificial illumination of reconciliation which threw a glittering light upon the joint winners of the Nobel Peace Prize; but the distribution of power in the world remained unchanged; and even if this distribution could be forgotten for a moment the injury they did to the harmonious development of the League was greater than the support they gave to the temporary harmony in the relations between Germany, France and Britain. The Covenant was not improved and, since Britain and Italy were made arbitrators and not allies of France, they failed to provide the latter country with a substitute for the Geneva Protocol. Friends of peace and of the League might be slow to sense the danger in which the League found itself; but the French were all the more quick to appreciate the danger for their traditional policy. At Locarno they took what was serviceable and would have definitely become theirs—a new recognition of the frontier of Alsace-Lorraine and of the demilitarized Rhine zone; but they neglected all the other innovations introduced by the treaties—the assurance of British and Italian support in the event of German aggression, the progress made in the application of methods of arbitration, and, above all, the spirit of Locarno. Soon the call for a fresh guarantee arose with redoubled vigour; soon it was proclaimed with fresh obstinacy that disarmament was impossible as yet; and soon the meetings of the Preparatory Committee were so thoroughly troubled by French disquiet, pessimism and fear that the eighth Assembly was compelled to revert to the examination of the remnants of the Geneva Protocol, and this despite the fact that the sixth and seventh Assemblies had proclaimed an extension of the principle of arbitration. Thus a new document was produced, a resolution unfortunately without practical value, which reverted to the Polish motion and yet again condemned wars of aggression, "which are prohibited and remain prohibited." As the result of French insistence, however, a special committee on arbitration and security was attached to the Preparatory Committee of the Disarmament Conference, and was entrusted with the production of fresh masses of printed matter. Its function was to be to investigate measures calculated to provide all States within the sphere of arbitration and security with the guarantee necessary for the reduction of their armaments to a minimum. The Committee of Security drew up various drafts for general or bilateral treaties of arbitration, and for general or particular treaties of security in the spirit of Locarno; it recommended that the arbitration of the Hague Court be recognized as compulsory, and it produced a mass of texts, some of which were combined into the so-called general Act by the ninth Assembly. They formed an external extension of the Protocol and received lavish praise for purposes of advertisement.

Perhaps this new instrument might promote the development of the League. Perhaps—only unfortunately its Article 28 implicitly confirms the peace treaties and thus rendered the whole instrument unacceptable to Germany. Again the instrument might have been useful had it presented the world with the accomplished facts of an equalization of armaments; but unfortunately the policy of France was not security through disarmament, nor even security and disarmament, but security through armaments and the maintenance of armaments through the appeal for security. The French recipe continued to be the following: clamour for security—take hold of the new guarantees thus secured—discreetly pocket them—hold out your empty hands again and ask for more. . . .

Meanwhile a new document was produced capable of conveying the impression that the League was abandoning the principles which had previously guided French policy. Instead of employing Articles 10 and 16 to enhance security, the new document attempted systematically to facilitate the application of Article 11 and to promote the preventative function of the League instead of elaborating sanctions, herein following the practice of the Council. This tendency, which had already found expression in certain passages of the Treaty for Mutual

Support (Article 3) and of the Geneva Protocol (Article 7) and which had been strengthened by the experiences in the Greco-Bulgarian conflict, found its first important expression in a statesmanlike paper handed to the League by the Belgian delegate, de Brouckère; it first received a binding form in a pamphlet drafted jointly by de Brouckère, Lord Robert Cecil and the Roumanian Titulescu, and accepted by the Council in 1927, on methods and rules to expedite Council decisions and to carry through effectively obligations arising from the Covenant.

Henceforward the plan was, that in cases of imminent war the President of the Council was to telegraph without delay to the parties concerned requesting them to refrain from warlike action, while the Council was to assemble forthwith to take steps for the preservation of the *status quo*, to prohibit movements of troops and mobilization, to dispatch local representatives in case of need, to express official disapproval if one of the parties failed to conform to its recommendations, to order, if necessary, the withdrawal of diplomatic representatives and to give instructions for naval and aerial demonstrations, and, in short, to take a number of measures calculated to identify the aggressor and thus to facilitate the application of Article 16. A complementary resolution was adopted a year later after the Szent-Gotthard case, by which the parties were definitively urged to avoid any steps capable of hindering a settlement of the dispute through the Council, provision being made for this resolution to be brought to the notice of the Governments in question, in all cases where a conflict came before the Council, by the Secretary-General. These ideas were adopted by Germany, which already had co-operated at Locarno in the elaboration of methods to prevent war. In the Committee of Arbitration and Security she further emphasized their value as contributing to the security of the world and facilitating disarmament as against the French endeavours in the direction of increased sanctions. The outlines satisfying the Germans gradually developed into a model treaty, which was extended into a

THE WHALE

general agreement for the development of means to prevent war on a British motion and was adopted by the twelfth Assembly (1931). The new measure provided steps for the evacuation of any occupied territories even in case the Council declined to admit the danger of war, as well as the establishment of lines of demarcation not to be crossed by the parties concerned, the dispatch of commissars to supervise the execution of these steps, and the publication of the deliberations, resolutions and recommendations of the Council; finally, any State infringing these measures was described as aggressor. Simultaneously the various competent organs of the League were urged by the Committee of Arbitration and Security to accelerate communications between the League authorities and the external world by a private air and wireless service in times of crisis; while a Finnish motion initiated discussions on an international agreement calculated to facilitate financial support for any State which should be the victim of aggression in case of war and in special instances in cases of grave danger of war. This support was to take the shape of an international loan under the auspices of the League; the motion was adopted by the eleventh Assembly.

Among other measures which might have increased the sense of security, once disarmament became a reality and the chaotic world of the peace treaties was left behind, were the developments of the means for preventing war adopted under Article 11; for their universal application in a just cause now became a possibility. But such developments were not to the taste of France; the only developments she desired were those supporting her power and her treaties. Inconsolable at the decay of the Protocol and still dreaming of the alliances aimed at during the Paris Conference, she continued to see her real security outside the League; despairing of Britain she attempted to win over the United States, but failed to achieve anything more than the conclusion of a general obligation to keep the peace, the so-called Briand-Kellogg Pact, which bound the majority of countries, including Russia, solemnly to outlaw war. This new document had its origin in the greater world outside the League, and it might have been feared that, although it contained no sanctions, it might overshadow the Covenant which had failed to outlaw war. At first, indeed, it had a galvanic effect, since it morally compelled the member States to accommodate the old Covenant to the new Pact, thus once again filling, at least theoretically, the notorious gap which had remained open since the failure of the Protocol. But although the Kellogg Pact guided the League along the correct path towards an alteration of the Covenant, the weary debates of the League organs also witnessed a resurrection of the longing for a simultaneous strengthening of the sanctions; all attempts at altering the Covenant, for which numerous drafts had already been prepared, were inhibited for the time being, and for the moment all that happened was that the various documents were not even looked at but were laid aside until the Disarmament Conference should have reached some result.

Meanwhile France undertook an excursion outside the sphere of the League, the result of which was yet another mass of papers. The Pact of Security under American auspices had proved a failure: what could be better than to circle half the globe and to base security on the United States of Europe? In 1929, during the tenth Assembly, Briand organized a European luncheon; the diplomats of the other States, taken by surprise, and anticipating nothing more than an economic alliance, were induced to appoint him their *rapporteur*; and in May 1930 the draft of a new Pact worked out in all its details was presented by Briand under the title "The Organization of a European League Order." The whole world was surprised: what did France want? The League of Nations had been planned to embrace every State; now, by its side, the French draft provided for an exclusively European League, with a Covenant of its own, an Assembly of its own—a "European Conference"; a Council of its own—the "Political" or "European Committee"; and a Secretariat of its own. Politics was given priority over economics, because "the possibility of every advance towards economic union" is wholly dependent on the question of security. The general development of the system for arbitration and security, the progressive application of the policy of Locarno to the entire European community and the arrangement of particular agreements and groups of agreements within a general system, was described as the aim of this new League. The object of bringing forward the old tendencies under a new name was to provide a foundation enabling the treaty for mutual support or the Geneva Protocol to be realized; for the resistance of Britain prevented the League proper from providing such a foundation, and an organization resembling the League was essential. Europe felt itself before a dubious adventure. But although most of the Governments acted as good and amiable Europeans, most of them also—and not only the opponents of the French policy of security and the former neutrals—opposed the creation of new organs, and in so doing gave evidence of a passionate affection for the League in its present shape which must be preserved from any encroachments. Once more it was Britain, on this occasion strongly supported by Italy, which was the chief opponent of the French plan; while Briand insisted on having the question further debated within the European circle, Britain succeeded in having it brought before the eleventh Assembly. None of the Governments, however—not even the German Government, which confined itself to prudent and skilful manœuvring—succeeded in realizing that, while the League was faced by a possible danger, it was also being presented with a unique opportunity to renovate itself by its own resources. Indeed, the stroke of luck with which it was presented was remarkable; one of the most powerful founders and beneficiaries of the League had not only declared it inadequate, as it had often done before, but in its blind zeal had gone so far as to undermine the entire system, to question principles which had long come to be regarded as fixed, and to shake the timorous respect with which the Paris structure had hitherto been venerated and preserved. In this way, albeit unconsciously, an opening was made after all the unrealities of the last years for a new and profound investigation of previous attempts to realize the ideal of the League; an opportunity never, perhaps, destined to return, was offered to revert to the undertaking which had been left inchoate in Paris. But the Governments of 1930 had no greater wisdom than those of 1919, and the new French security offensive, which might have become a universal offensive in support of the League, ended in a mediocre compromise. The League, threatened in its existence, swallowed and digested Europe, and the European Union turned into a League Committee of Studies for a European Union. The petty result was inflated by France; the Committee of Studies which had been destined simply to investigate the problem was treated like an independent organ and allowed to exercise certain functions of a predominantly economic nature as though it were a European sub-section within the League; sub-committees were added to it, and since it remained under French leadership, it was at the disposal of future French plans. But although the Protocols of the League expanded, its idea began to atrophy.

Gradually, however, in spite of years of successful procrastination, the day approached on which Article 8 had to leave the seclusion of the Covenant and enter into reality. The tenth Assembly—the same in which Briand undertook his Pan-European advance—declared that the existing conditions of security resulting from the Covenant, the peace treaties, and above all the limitation of armaments applied to certain countries by virtue of these treaties and resulting from the Locarno agreement, would permit a general agreement on the limitation and reduction of armaments. It expressed the opinion that Governments not satisfied with the degree of security obtained could find new means of security in the labours of the Committee of Arbitration and Security; and it even voiced the sound idea that the agreement on disarmament outlined would increase national security. But eighteen months after the adoption of this resolution, and six months before the prospective assembly of the Disarmament Conference, France gloomily produced a fresh demand for security. In a political memorandum addressed to the League Secretariat the French Government, although, like every other Government, it had been requested merely to produce technical information on its armaments, declared—as we saw on our visit to Monsieur Aghnides—that French armaments had already been reduced to the point provided by Article 8 of the Covenant, where they constituted the minimum compatible with existing conditions in Europe and the world. Accordingly in the French view the task of the future Disarmament Conference could only consist in taking note of actual limitations of armaments already imposed and in demanding equal endeavours in all countries, when it would be possible to examine under what conditions new limitations would be possible. These conditions were, of course, the old ones—enhanced security on the lines of the Geneva Protocol. Indeed, France went so far as to describe her system of alliances—a direct contradiction of the spirit of the League—as a manifestation of solidarity in the interests of international order, an order which, however, must now be completed by means of a general organization and the obligation of mutual assistance. The task of the Disarmament Conference was not to be disarmament so much as the production of fresh covenants. "The real task of the Conference of 1932 is the firm and lasting organization of peace."

Of which peace? 1932 did not represent any progress beyond 1919. Without disarmament peace was not assured—on this point a part of modern mankind was in agreement with the prophet of the past.—Disarmament is impossible until peace is assured, the rest of the world replies in antistrophe.—Only justice in international relations can ensure peace, one half of mankind avers; the present state is just, the others insist. And so it goes on. Peace is endangered because some consider it unjust, and we require security against this danger; justice, moreover, means a state laid down by treaty; and everlasting peace, the perpetuation of the conditions of peace. Thus the world is torn by a conflict admitting of no solution—the old conflict between Clemenceau and Wilson. And this conflict is supported by all the useless documents which the messengers have been carrying back and forth for years between the Legal section and the Political Department, between the Political Department and the Disarmament Department, and the Disarmament Department and Countess Trani's room. Annexes to the peace treaties or to the Covenant, ruins of systems of security or adopted reports, suggestions and memoranda—they all remain so much paper, scraps of paper scattered by children lost in the forest and blown away by the wind. The result is that we wander in meaningless mazes. Instructions on the interpretation of Article 11 become useless as soon as a serious conflict breaks out between Japan and China; methods of arbitration and pacts of security cease to exist if France refuses to disarm. Twelve years have been lost. Empty-handed we wander between the Legal section, the Disarmament section, and the Political Department. Snippets of paper slip between our fingers and are carried away by the wind.

We have found our way back to the antechamber with its filing cabinets and those dangerous treaties of alliance. The loquacious official who had been explaining the system of registration with such eloquence to the study leaders and students and the English and German tourists notices our oppressed demeanour and smiles at us encouragingly. "I am glad to see you back. Are you looking for the right that is to conquer might? But you must not grow anxious; we have been working here without cease for many years. A motion brought in at the fourth Assembly was adopted by the fifth, by which it was resolved to draw upon the League increasingly in the progressive codification of international law. A committee of experts proceeded to deal with a number of questions of international law—questions which it seemed particularly desirable to solve by international agreement. Admittedly the codifying conference of 1930 was something of a disappointment, but at the same time an international agreement on one of the most important questions of international law crowned the restless endeavours of the Legal section and of the most profound jurists of the nations in the course of the twelfth Assembly. It is a sound and practical piece of work; it is neither a confirmation of the peace treaties nor an unpractical collection of theoretical directions. The French do not make it a matter of sanctions, the British do not reject it in the eleventh hour, and the Germans do not make any provisos. A thoroughly sound document. Let me read it to you. Article 1 is as follows: 'The High Contracting Parties agree to take, within the limits of their respective jurisdictions, appropriate measures to ensure the application of the provisions of the present Convention and the punishment of infractions of said provisions.' Surely this is straightforward talking. Let me give you Article 2: 'The present agreement applies only to balene or whalebone whales.' You are surprised? Naturally the agreement is to apply only to whalebone whales and not to denticete whales. You see, the title of our document is 'Convention for the Regulation of Whaling.' Let me give you Article 3: 'The High Contracting Parties . . .' "

The High Contracting Parties! We put our hands to our ears, leave the office and slam the door behind us. Once again we are in the corridor: whither next?

We look around us nonplussed: whither next?

CHAPTER XXII

PRAYER ON THE ROOF

WHITHER next? We have hardly had time to ask ourselves this anxious question before we find it answered noisily and on every side. Urgently and from every side we hear the call: "This way." All the doors open: "This way." From every office on the third and fourth floors and from the annexe to which the wooden Bridge of Sighs lead us, we hear the enticing, the noisy, the inviting call: "This way." We are in the central hall of a vast exhibition; impressive gentlemen, elegant youths, dignified ladies and pretty girls invite us to their stands. We are surrounded by a confusing multitude of goods and overwhelmed by the cries of the salesmen, while right and left they pluck at our sleeves and thrust us forward into their vast bazaar. "This way for the minorities and administrative department, this way for the mandates section, humanitarian and social questions, communications and traffic, economics and finance, hygiene and information," are the calls which deafen us on every side. Every shop-door is opened and all the shopkeepers are crying their wares, while the typewriters rattle and the telephones shrill. "This way for the real League, this way for the real League."

For the moment we are numbed and deafened; but while we are yet hesitating they have buttonholed us and have begun to talk. "Don't be annoyed because there is not a prophet installed in Countess Trani's room." "Don't be annoyed because Mr. Sugimura's map shows so many battlefields and because the disarmament offices are a barracks." "Don't be dismayed by the wicked Italo-Albanian treaty of the Legal section and by the idyllic agreement on whales." There are even voices of rebuke: "It is your own fault if you are disappointed; you have allowed yourself to be misled by these various *salons* and offices. The world cannot be improved by theories and principles; and the Preamble to the Covenant, or Article 8, or Articles 11 to 17, or Article 18 or 20 should not be taken too seriously. The Governments cannot be expected suddenly to fall in love with the League; on the contrary it is the daily practical routine applied to everyday problems which will educate the nations to peaceful coexistence and implant this habit so deeply that every war-map will end by becoming a peace map every barracks a disarmament section, and every theory and principle a reality which nobody notices because it is taken for granted. For this very reason you see the League before you here. Even the articles dealing with mandates to which you object so much and which you regard as a betrayal of the principles of the League no less than those chapters in the peace treaties which annoy you so much by importing into the Covenant questions on the administration of the Saar Basin, Danzig, and the protection of minorities, afford a fruitful field for international collaboration. The meagre and incoherent suggestions on White Slave Traffic, opium and epidemics, and the vague suggestions on international trade relations contained in Article 23 provide sufficient material and sufficient occasion for international meetings and co-operation; for it is articles like these which provide a daily occupation for so many people that they cover the globe with a network of interests, with the result that the method of international collaboration is applied and tested even where they meet with slight response and negligible success. And even where the issue seems insignificant or even foolish it becomes an international question which may give birth to an international spirit—that international spirit which some day, when dealing with more serious questions, may serve you well indeed. Come in," they call to us. "This way," they entice us. "Here is the League." The doors are open, the typewriters rattle, the telephones shrill.

We cannot but pay a tribute to the shopwalkers and salesmen of the League stores who thus endeavour to turn their eight-hour day into a ceaseless intellectual feast. There is something seductive in the general principle with which the opponents of theories and general principles attempt to idealize their petty occupations. Were it otherwise the disappointments with which we met on the lower floors would prevent us from feeling the slightest desire to enter these noisy bargain departments, which the prospectus of the firm describes as the technical work of the technical departments of the Secretariat with their technical organization. But, although nearly deafened at first, we soon discount a considerable part of what the advertisements tell us. We are aware that the great uniting idea of a daily international co-operation gradually developing into a true pacific disposition is not contained in the evil articles dealing with mandates, in the unbalanced League provisions of the treaties, nor in the embarrassed utterances of Article 23. True, we are told that this idea will emerge as the result of daily work and will inevitably become its result if it was not its original aim; but it is equally true that success depends on the spirit in which the work is undertaken and that the wares purveyed by the League are themselves suspect. The claims of your advertisements must become more than a pretence, they must become the gradual application of the ideal of a world community, before we will venture to resume our wanderings through Hottop's hotel and recommence our chase of the flying phantom that has been leading us for so long from office to office and from corridor to corridor.

Let us look at the evidence; let us examine the documents. What has been the outcome of your system of mandates? Has there been any development of the hypocritical principles which were intended to provide a meagre excuse for the annexation of German and Turkish possessions? We think not. When it was modestly suggested before the Assembly that the principles of Article 22 were to be regarded as a comprehensive colonial pact the suggestion was rejected. When it was proposed that the Powers which had signed the agreement on slavery were to report to the Secretariat it was indignantly replied that this would compel certain colonies to be placed on the same level as the former German colonies, and that this was inadmissible. We are told that important advances have been made within the limited field of application of the existing mandates; to which we reply that the principles of the Mandate have been violated by the incorporation of the African mandated territories, in defiance of justice, a defiance against which Germany protested in vain. The transfer of the colonies to new masters was explained as taking place in the name of the sacred rights and interests of the population; have these rights and interests been fearlessly respected? Voluminous reports give details of the revolt of the Bondelzwards, the war in Syria, unrest in Samoa, fighting between Jews and Arabs in Palestine, and show that the disaffection and oppression of populations in the League colonies are as intense as in the districts administered by powers internationally unknown.

The Mandates Committee defied the principle of publicity inherent in all the League debates and habitually met behind locked doors and closed windows; and if a few courageous neutrals ventured on a honest criticism the representatives of the great colonial Powers beat down such rebellious words with as much energy as they employed in beating down their rebellious subjects. If a motion was made to extend the right of petition of the natives—their petition at present can come before the League only through the intermediacy of the respective mandatory Powers—such a procedure was unanimously rejected by these Powers, since any method admitting a two-sided debate might contribute to weaken their autocratic control. The League itself might have been expected to increase its influence and authority in the mandated territories by extending the powers of its Mandates Committee; but in fact the Council Powers suppressed every effort to perfect this instrument by insisting upon the merely consultative character of this organ. In such circumstances it was absurd to pretend that there was any support of international co-operation. There was no co-operation between the colonial populations and the ruling Governments, and any co-operation between the organs of the League and the mandatory Powers was manifested merely in modest bureaucratic obstruction on the one hand and authoritative insistence upon treaty rights on the other. Within the narrow circle of the Mandates Committee and the equally narrow circle of the Council, the colonial Powers formed a close clique firmly resolved to prevent the development of any progressive international colonial policy or even of any international colonial conscience. The Mandates Committee is not so much the League as a subsidiary branch of the various colonial offices. . . .

But the Vanity Fair of Geneva hums around us; and we continue to ask for evidence, to look through the records of international administrative activity and to examine the complaints of the one and the resolutions of the other side. For surely we have a right to ask whether the League protected the Saar district against France or the Free City of Danzig against Poland, and whether it developed the narrowly restricted rights of these regions in order to provide some kind of future for the compromise devised at Versailles. And we find that in fact the League has been wanting in even these narrow duties. It has permitted the illegal occupation of the Saar district by French troops; it has connived at the introduction of the French language in the schools; it has, year after year, confirmed and reconfirmed a hated foreign domination despite the clear will of the populace; it has turned a deaf ear to the protests of the national spokesmen; it has done nothing to prevent the economic and political penetration of the country by France; and it was not until Stresemann was face to face with Briand at the Council table, and an understanding between the two became possible, that the League ratified concessions which France had judged expedient. The League stood by inactive while Poland violated the independence of Danzig and laid hold of the railways, postal system and harbours of the Free City, and it abused its power in order to embarrass the weaker in its difficult negotiations with the great State; the instances where

PRAYER ON THE ROOF

the weak were protected against the strong were few indeed, while its capital crime was that it permitted Polish munitions to be stored in Danzig territory and remained practically inactive in assuring economic co-operation between the port of Danzig and Poland in the interest of the distressed Danzig community. Yet such a co-operation was the one excuse for the forcible solution adopted at Versailles. While the high commissioners had to manœuvre pitifully between the powerful besiegers and the besieged town not a single step was taken to strengthen them with the authority of the League—a body whose united will would have been superior to any questioning. In short, neither the Saar nor the Vistula has witnessed any successful international co-operation; and when the representatives of these political entities came before the League, their confrontation never assumed any other form than that of a struggle between threatened Germanism and superior foreign annexationism, with a conflict between the Council Powers chiefly affected for background. So far from promoting co-operation, the League has merely succeeded in inspiring a wish to banish, as far as possible, the question of the Saar and of Danzig from the Council deliberations; for these questions were a source of disruption rather than of unity.

Let us examine what the League has done for the protection of Minorities. The principle of protection was arbitrarily applied by certain treaties to certain restricted regions; has the principle meanwhile been extended towards universality? A recommendation passed by an Assembly in the early days of the League was never applied and soon forgotten. Have the meagre safeguards for the Minorities been extended? On the contrary. The League calmly adopted the dangerous theory of assimilation; and though this theory had later to be tacitly abandoned, the Minorities were simultaneously discouraged and hampered in their struggle by a dense barrier of red tape; the ideal of national rights was degraded to that of loyalty towards a Government, and the outbursts of an outraged conscience or of despair were stifled by a hypocritical demand for elegant and measured language in the case of complaints. When the League officials travelled over the world at the expense of the united nations, who was it who had their ear—the complaining minority, which too often never penetrated beyond the League's antechambers, or the Governments who arranged brilliant banquets and receptions? In the outer world there were at least courageous private organizations who supported, on principle, a powerful minorities' movement; but the League never followed this example nor did it so much as collect scientific material to throw light on one of the most dangerous of contemporary questions. Instead the League was almost invariably content with the data piled up in its offices—data restricted by a thousand precautions and measures of oppression, and supplemented by meagre newspaper cuttings, which were rarely intelligible until translated. For years the petitions of maltreated populations had vanished without trace and without reply in the League filing cabinets and wastepaper baskets, while the memoranda of the ruling Governments were dealt with with care and distributed with respect. The offices of the League contained a hundred organs for hygiene and transit; but the formation of a Minorities Committee was opposed with bureaucratic obstinacy, although the Committee's privileges were not to exceed those of the harmless consultative Mandates Committee. Shortly before the entry of Germany into the League new methods of procedure were astutely devised which were intended to hamper the Council Powers in championing their countrymen in the minority regions; while the courageous attempt by the Canadian delegate Dandurand, who tried to improve the methods of procedure, and the passionate assault of the German delegate Stresemann, who attempted to deepen and clarify the fundamental guarantees inherent in the League, were alike opposed with a chilly cunning. In this way it came about that the insincere deliberations of various committees produced meaningless reforms in procedure where a vivifying will was needed, and that the crushing effect of this anti-climax spread a cloak of discouragement over the feeble minorities and their feeble defenders. Nor is it easy to see where international collaboration could develop. Certainly not in the Committee of Three in the Council, in which the profoundest subject of international debate was reduced to small talk between bureaucrats; nor yet in the Council, where the new and the old masters of the minorities districts angrily opposed each other and the minorities were not represented; nor finally in the Assembly, whose competence was disputed and whose every suggestion was stifled. Indeed we may doubt whether an international discussion was considered desirable. We have looked through the evidence in every detail; and we conclude that the principles of the League officials —who dictated policy only to be influenced themselves unconsciously—were not so much anxious to have an international debate as to have silence. The desired aim is to produce a *non possumus* in the shape of the treaties which, as the propaganda brochures of the League phrase it, "do not in certain special spheres permit of the liberty of action possessed in certain other spheres of activity." But in that case why stand in the way while we are eagerly searching for the League? The treaties are not the League; close the door.

Let us examine another stall. The wares here displayed are not drawn from the peace treaties but have their *raison d'être* in the Covenant; they are its Article 23 come to life. Has anything been achieved here? The industrious statisticians, students and organizers of the finance section and the Finance Committee were anxious not only to serve the cause of a future peace by the practice of collaboration, but also by solving the most urgent problems of the day, to serve the cause of contemporary peace. The work done here is based on the discovery, voiced shortly after the first meeting of the Council, that the post-war financial difficulties of the world must attract the interest of the League. Its origins lie in the Brussels Conference which gave to the world so much good advice on balanced budgets, the cessation of inflation, the return to a gold currency, the removal of international obstacles to trade, improvements in communications, the international organization of credit and the restoration of real peace. An excellent programme: what, however, has been achieved? We are told that Austria has been saved. True, but since then she has collapsed more than once, and everybody knows that the financial support of the League was merely a screen behind which the Great Powers and the hostile neighbours of Austria could pursue an anything but altruistic financial policy; forced into an artificial independence in relation to Germany, German Austria was to be compelled to be permanently dependent upon her former enemies. Further, Hungary, Greece, Bulgaria, Esthonia and Danzig have enjoyed the technical and organizing assistance of the stall whose wares we are examining; Greek and Bulgarian refugees have enjoyed its support, and agreements to obviate double taxation, the escape from taxation, and the counterfeiting of money have been drafted; there have also been investigations on the purchasing power of gold. But what is the state of affairs after all these impressive League activities, not only in Hungary and Danzig, but in the whole world? Apparently this section of the League has heard no more than vague rumours of the reparations question, inter-Allied debts, the horrors of inflation in Germany, of French inflation, and of the fall of the pound. For twelve years it has accumulated papers in its Geneva Academy as high as the Salève, while in the outer world a meretricious prosperity was followed by an all-too-genuine depression. Forgetting the nations and by the nations forgot, it had been meditating at Geneva while Ministers were travelling from capital to capital in order to prevent, in the eleventh hour, the financial collapse of the world. For twelve years it had been studying on the edge of reality, so many studious professors collecting scientifically valuable data. It had pointed out more than one possible method and had been surprised when the day came when in every country and in every conference the advice had to be preached which had been familiar to it from the beginning: balanced budgets, economy, no more inflation, return to a gold currency, international organization of credit and the restoration of real peace. . . .

And if we turn to the economic section of the League, we find documents which, if piled upon each other, would reach beyond Mont Blanc. Here there are discussions on unfair business methods, the treatment of overseas undertakings of various States, on nationality, unification of customs formalities and customs nomenclature, commercial arbitration, on bills and cheques, commercial statistics, and the protection of foreign purchasers against a supply of inferior goods. For years these subjects have been the object of honest, straightforward work, without attracting attention or producing any change in an economically rotten world. But the day of glory came. During the Assembly of 1925, when the triad of security, arbitration and reduction of armaments had been found wanting and a substitute was being looked for, Loucheur began to preach the doctrine of the security of political through economic peace. In May 1927, 194 delegates and 157 experts representing 50 States assembled for a world economic conference and recommended freedom of trade, reduction of customs walls, the formation of international industrial cartels, and agricultural agreements. What was the result of these suggestions? The various Governments allowed the officials to perfect their own economic organization; but the conference on the abolition or restriction of import and export prohibitions resulted in a meagre agreement on hides and bones, while the endeavours to reduce customs barriers remained wholly unsuccessful. Hymans's demand for economic disarmament brought forward at the tenth Assembly, Stresemann's grandiose economic vision, which he intended to incorporate in Briand's Pan-European scheme, and Italy's old demand for a solution of the problem of raw material and populations all remained mere words. With respect to the treatment of foreigners and with respect to the British proposal of a tariff armistice, which faded away in a chaotic conference on common economic action, the conference was alike futile. Endeavours to assist the small agrarian countries in their difficulties remained equally futile; in spite of fine phrases all that was done for them was to invent an agrarian bank for their benefit. And while reports, investigations, memoranda and studies grow in bulk, the tariff walls grow even higher; at the end of twelve years the countries face each other with greater hostility than at the end of the war, and the economic anarchy of the world is even more desperate than its political confusion.

Nor are we helped by the fact that in the adjacent department for communications and transit, the mysterious offspring of the communications organs of the Peace Conference and the Conference of Barcelona, a vast organization has been built up, whose secretariat, committees and conference are acknowledged in every handbook to be patterns of technical co-operation on League lines. Without cease delegates and experts are gathered in every city of Europe to deal with seaports and railway communications, the distribution of electric power, the exploitation of water power, the marking of Plimsoll lines on river steamers, the fixing of buoys at sea, lighting of coasts, unification of signals in automobile traffic, transit tickets for emigrants, calendar reform, and the dropping of newspapers from air-craft, and to publish excellent agreements, well-meant recommendations and admirable memoranda on these subjects. But all these endeavours have failed to restore the free granting of passports and the freedom of travel of the pre-war period, and despite all the skill and ingenuity brought to the task, all this mass of deliberations and treaties has nowhere served to make the frontiers between nations less felt.

Again it is impossible to find any praise for the exhibits of the social and humanitarian stall, the atrophied remnants of Nansen's warm-hearted work, the work of repatriating prisoners of war from Russia and Siberia and of caring for refugees. A world union of assistance has been founded to render aid in the case of important catastrophes; but it remains a dead letter and could not prevent millions from starving in Russia and China. The campaign against slavery, against white slave traffic and against the traffic in opium and other poisons, has been organized; but whether carried through negligently or voluptuously or as a piece of national business, not one of the campaigns was carried through to a finish. Let us turn to the hygiene stall, where the successors of the temporary epidemic commission are at work with their forty Secretariat officials, their hygiene council, hygiene committee, seventeen other committees and sub-committees, the Geneva information department for epidemics, the information department at Singapore, the innumerable pamphlets, the expeditions to America, China and Poland, their exchange of sanitary officials and their worthy medical director who hides the reality of a skilful champion of Polish interests behind the pages of his "Bulletin on the spread of influenza." We grant that they do no harm, that they are of some use in certain backward countries and that in certain instances they assist science; but they are not the League. They are an appendix of an appendix of the League, and their weal and woe is independent of the League's weal and woe. They speak when the League is embarrassed for something to say; and the noise which they make is so insistent that it ceases to hide and eloquently begins to reveal the League's silence.

And all the worthies who, on the third and fourth floor and in the annexes, are busy writing, typing, telephoning, talking and debating, publishing statistics, appointing commissions, arranging for conferences and committees, and drawing and distributing salaries, may do some good by their zeal, but are in fact no more than a disappointing orchestra before a curtain which never rises; and their music contains more discords than harmony. Yet it is they who fill the building; it is they who are heard and seen, whose documents bulk largest in the publications of the Secretariat, and whose expenses form the biggest item in its budget. Their reports swamp the agenda of the Council and of the Assembly. But with all their delegates and experts these bodies are temporary occupants of the League palace where the permanent tenant has not yet moved in, and on the day when the house is completed and habitable, and its real masters appear, these others will be put in their proper place. Those who live on the pernicious treaties will be sent packing; for, once the house of the nations is perfect and habitable, it will have no room for even the best experts on bad treaties; while those whose function it is to restore the economics and the finances of the world will be recalled from their quiet studies and made to face the practical politics from which they shrink at present. Those finally who light our coasts, arrange for buoyage, inspect brothels, and supervise the distribution of drugs, will be relegated to modest offices in the rear where they can be found when they are wanted and can be forgotten when they are not wanted. Once such reforms have been completed we may perhaps be able to recognize and admire a League vigorously at work upon a definite aim—at work in the room of the Secretary-General, in the department for intellectual co-operation, in the disarmament section, the political section, and the Legal section. And then, our survey of the League completed, if we have the time and are not too tired we may perhaps peep in with smiling curiosity and discover with satisfaction that even the smallest details have not been forgotten in this House where so much important work is being done.

The doors close one after the other; the nightmare of the League disperses. We seem to be alone again. But stop; on the right a new wing opens its doors to us. Eager hands beckon and faces shine with zeal: "Have you forgotten the Information Section? We are the League. We are its living idea. We are its voice, we are . . ." Hush! a kindly silence here is best. We have not, and we hardly could have forgotten you. We had hoped and for a time we had believed that after a long and suspicious past under allied control an opportunity would here occur for real international work, and that this would be the centre where the principle of League publicity would be pursued and the diplomatic pre-war mentality dominant in the

PRAYER ON THE ROOF

elegance of the lower storys would be scattered and overcome. Hush! Let us observe silence; and above all let us carefully close the doors—they seem to constitute the majority in this section —behind which, despite the inscription "Press Offices," the secret and obscure diplomatic work is done which cannot be conveniently housed in the political section. As for those others, whose profession it really is to provide information, whose life is divided between diplomats and journalists, whose function it is to be journalists among diplomats and diplomats among journalists, and whose time is occupied in cross-tacking between them—we can sympathize with their difficulties, the more so because we can discover more than one secret candidate for a better future League among them. Their task is a hard one. They are officials whose business it is to produce propaganda on behalf of certain narrow post-war interests and to take the place of the free prophets of everlasting peace who have accompanied us on our journey, but who are not admitted here. They must declare that whatever is, is right, describe every petty institution as soon as it has become bulky as though it were great, forget and minimize everything great unless it suits their principals, keep dark the inconvenient truth, change defeats into successes, and, if they happen to be Poles, to take care that the Polish Minister's speech looks more impressive in the *communiqué* than the German Minister's, or, if they happen to be German, take care that this fact is not noticed. Their work is difficult and we owe them our gratitude. They supply us with cards which admit us to the debating halls, they organize the technical details of the Press in a masterly fashion, they do us a hundred little favours and, when they come to speak about the League, they allow us to learn—nor could there be any more useful information—what Paris thinks or what the people in Paris wish us to think. We know their difficulties, which are great. Hush! Let us close the door. We will observe discretion.

We have reached the silent corridor of the top floor. We have wandered through Hottop's hotel from office to office and from stair to stair, and our pilgrimage seems to be at an end, when suddenly we see a narrow stairway leading to the fifth floor, directly under the leads. Filled with curiosity we ascend, and discover the most modest and also the topmost workroom of the house. The door is closed, there is nobody to invite us, and only a low, monotonous hum reaches our ears. Who can be the lonely worker in this eyrie? Can it be that we have discovered some secret report being written in this hidden spot, some report profoundly affecting the future and the mystery of the whole confused system? Are we at the doors of the longed-for and essential archives of the League, unrealized as yet? Have we reached some great laboratory where the unsolved questions of the League are being investigated? Have we found some arcanum where fearless truths are hidden? Carefully we open the door; but we are not met by the tapping of a typewriter, nor by the melting glances of one of the ravishing young ladies of the House. A modest, comfortable old body is sitting at her sewing-machine; she looks a little grumpy and a little sad; with her big glasses over downcast eyes and with grey hair over a wrinkled brow, she sits in silence and keeps her machine humming. She is unaware of our presence; she never glances up, but simply treads her machine and follows her thoughts. Surprised and disappointed we hastily withdraw and close the door behind us. Soon we learn that she is the industrious sempstress of the League whose function it is to hem and repair its curtains and towels, tablecloths and napkins, dishcloths and dusters. All day long she is busy in her attic, and often late in the evening, when all is quiet below, when the lights are turned off, the offices are empty and the charwomen drag their brooms over the wide and now prosaic staircases, while the night porter is beginning his first round in the dark hall below, she still sits treading her machine in her lonely room. Is she one of the Parcae, spinning the fate of the world, that fate which we were pursuing so eagerly? Is she Penelope, weaving the bridal dress of peace until nightfall, and unravelling it at night when the noisy suitors of the nations are snoring at home? Or is she the sleeping beauty's wicked fairy waiting for the curse to be fulfilled? Is she waiting for the day when the Secretary-General will feel a sudden urge to escape the pomp of the first floor and when, disquieted and anxious for the future of his work, he shall go wandering through the offices of all his numerous assistants? And will those wanderings lead him to this poor and distant attic where he will affably bend over the modest sempstress and eagerly explore her humble task? If he does so, surely the needle will prick his white finger; a red drop of blood will fall; a hundred years' sleep will descend over the palace by the lake, with all its inhabitants, not to cease until the true knight cuts his way through the thicket of roses and with his kiss wakes us all from suspended animation.

The last staircase with its narrow steps and many turnings is groaning under our feet. We open the skylight. We have reached the leads of the palace of nations and are blinded by a flood of light. What kind of world is it that we perceive? Is it a vast, flat plate of some milky material, a mixture of fog and paper, on which geometrical figures are drawn out, Council, Assembly, Secretariat, International Labour Office, International Court—so many squares, circles and oblongs called organization for traffic, hygiene, finance and economics, permanent and temporary committee, institute for law and intellectual co-operation, cinematographs and agriculture, with offices in London, Paris, Berlin, Tokio and Rome? Is this the world? We are bathed in light; and it is only now, where we are in the presence of the grand blue-golden reality of Geneva, that we realize how narrow and dark have been our late surroundings. We see the little lake bordered by the park of Mon Repos, the gardens of Grange and Eaux Vives, the two stone breakwaters, the pines, the lighthouses and the fountains; we see it spreading beyond the castle of Nyon and the hill of Cologny, and we see the lateen sails gliding on its surface. We see the blue line of the Jura, the snowy chain of Mont Blanc, Calvin's cathedral and citadel of refuge, and the romantic landscape of Enlightenment; they lie wide around and yet close together, to be counted singly like the beads of a rosary and to be embraced at one glance like the heavens. The frontier between Switzerland and France is lost; Italy lies behind those snowy heights, and those wooded hills lead us to the German frontier. Between them we can trace exactly the railways which carried us to this promised valley. And suddenly in the centre of this landscape, behind the trees of the green Ariana park, we discover the lofty scaffolding and walls which are to house the League when the nations leave Hottop's palace to commence a real co-operation. The whole plan in its grandeur stands before us, and once again we are willing to believe in it.

For after all, what we have left behind us is, surely, the inevitable detail and machinery of a bureaucratic and diplomatic routine. It is here on the roof that we have a vision of fulfilment. Below us the wheels go round; it is here that we can sense the stream of power flowing towards us from a distance. Below we saw only officials of the Secretariat and officials of the Governments fulfilling their bureaucratic and diplomatic tasks at the request of traditional authorities and in compliance with arbitrary rules and monotonous regulations. Their origins lie in the Treaty and the Covenant; but surely their roots also lie in a life which lies much deeper than Covenant and treaties. In the beginning was the Treaty of Versailles; but before the Treaty came the war, and this war must needs have other consequences than the Treaty. In the beginning was the Covenant; but before the Covenant there was the old dream of a League; and necessarily something more must have survived than the Covenant. The officials whom we watched at work are also men, and the Governments in whose names they pursue the routine for the sake of which they are employed and paid, and which they consider an eternal law, at bottom represent nations. But nations and men cannot be wound up like machines and cannot be switched on and off to fulfil a limited function. Surely in the course of this activity the men must become aware of their humanity and the nations of their nationhood; surely the men will some day grow beyond their

PRAYER ON THE ROOF

national limitations and the nations beyond the treaties and covenants. Articles 8 and 10, Articles 22 and 23, are not everything; there is also such a thing as the life of nations and individuals, a life which, in spite of the most rigid regulations, must slowly begin to move, and burst into sudden activity. We know the strict commandments and the complicated dietetics of the journey through the Wilderness, but we also feel with a passionate conviction that the gloomy demand of an eye for an eye and a tooth for a tooth must some day change into the bright commandment of "Love thy Neighbour." Instinctively we repeat the prayer with which François de la Harpe crowned his famous essay on Peace:

"Father of Mankind—for it is under this name alone that we can exist before thee and that the needs of our weakness can touch thy greatness—extinguish in our hearts the destructive rage which honours thy work; to the end that men may no longer add to the curse of necessity the curse of their madness, that they may cease to devastate this earth which thou gavest them to till, and the harvest ripening under thy rays. Let them cease in the excess of their madness to pray thy blessing on their deeds of murder or to thank thee for their crimes. May this my prayer be a prayer of atonement for all the bloodthirsty wishes which they so often dared to offer thee in the rage of their barbarous hatred or the joy of their mad triumph."

We lower our hands and return; once again we weigh the merits of the House with its five floors. Once again we are surrounded by the twilight of every day. We descend, passing the pedantic department of hygiene, the industrious and perverse information apparatus, the heavy encyclopaedia of economics and finance, the heartless and dull drill for the souls in Danzig. We pass the Saar, the minority districts and the colonies, the useless abracadabra of disarmament, the cautious charity bazaar organized by the enemies of opium and vice, the offices of the bureaucratized international jurists, and the foolish hyper-organization of intellectual by-products; we pass the first floor where the various foreign offices are internationally concentrated for work in front of and behind the scenes, and turn to descend the big central staircase. The wide and gloomy hall faces us once again; but this time we are met by a loud and murmuring noise. We stop, and from our point of vantage we behold a picture of confusion. Our eyes grow dizzy; there is not a vacant place before us and the vast space is one single, grandiose movement of heads and shoulders and of eyes and hands. It is a vast and manifold voice, a sea stirred by a mysterious rhythm, whose notes belong to no language and ascend to us like a choral song. They are assembled beneath us and before us, they are waiting behind the closed doors of the debating rooms, all those who followed the great vision and left the capitals of the world for Geneva; all those who hoisted their national colours over the windows of their hotels on either side of the lake, who yesterday were no more than so many groups of men hastily nodding to each other at the station, but who now are merged in this waiting-room—Italians and French, Germans and Spaniards, British and Portuguese, Chinese and Dutch, Greeks and Japanese, Poles and Abyssinians, white men and brown, and yellow and black, a nameless but a friendly multitude. Is it Governments they represent, or is it nations? It is no longer the one and not yet quite the other. The sea, moving and rumbling before us, is a community of men in no way differentiated from each other, and jointly waiting for a joint experience to commence.

Before we descend the last steps to be merged in this sea, we absorb the strange picture before us for a last time, and for the last time taste the precious minute. A passionate desire seizes us to trust, to embrace them all, and to forgive the folly of their sins which stand registered above in their documents, the poisonous hatred which they have inscribed upon the map of the world, their petty fears, and the cruelty of their foolish plans; for they are men; and as men we see them before us, speaking and laughing, shaking their heads, frowning, shrugging their shoulders or adjusting their ties. England is smoking a pipe, Germany a cigar, France is rolling a cigarette,

PRAYER ON THE ROOF

Italy is standing hands in pockets, and Spain, who has just seen a Roumanian joke, is laughing enthusiastically in the direction of Norway. Finland, bright and youthful, is coquetting with India, Canada is wearing an avuncular white beard, and Chili—or is it Sweden?—carries a fair round belly. They all are men; nothing has yet been lost; men are about to speak to men.

Where are we? Desperately but in vain we had been searching for the League in every corner of the house. Have we found it at last? We descend the last step: shall we find the League in the League's ante-chamber?

CHAPTER XXIII

"AFRIQUE DU SUD, ALBANIE, ALLEMAGNE..."

SUDDENLY a violent commotion draws the multitude in one direction. The talking groups of smiling, vivacious men coagulate, advance, and in a dense and slowly moving queue move from the wide and cheerful hall into the narrower and more austere corridors.—Around them, now stopping and now hastening their advance, stand the attendants.—They press past the doors, divide, and enter the different halls. The great fraternal community is divided into a number of working teams. Those who flow into E hall, encircling the long table and filtering into the chairs, bear the joint name of Committee of Communication and Transit. Those others who fill D hall are the Finance Committee, while yet others call themselves Committee of Studies for the European Union or Committee of Jurists, Editorial Committee, or Committee of Co-ordination. In every *salon* of Hottop's hotel they are to be found sitting between the white panelled doors and the lofty black marble of the chimney-pieces, before wide windows opening on terraces, gardens and the lake; and their heads—those fair, black, grey or white heads—are for the moment only so many points of which the geometric devices of the League are composed—one of the many squares, oblongs or circles in this vast and complex structure of organized co-operation.

At the extreme end of the corridors, halls and terraces where the delegates are followed by the densest throng of curious visitors, strenuous journalists, important League officials, and worried experts we find the smallest but also the most important of these devices. In the midst of the blue, green and white interplay of sky, lake, trees and hills—in the midst of a light and odorous world, a world clear, dreamy and unlimited—we discover the big square and sober glass hall like a bird-cage in a garden. In the midst of this transparent box, whence lake, clear air, white mountains and waving branches can be seen, a wide, horse-shoe-shaped table covered with a blue cloth is erected on a dais. Around this table fourteen Prime Ministers, Ministers or diplomats, sit under the chairmanship of the Secretary-General. These fifteen points between them compose the device known as the Council. The gap between the two wings of the semicircle is occupied by the translators, who sit half underground, jump up when their turn has come, hastily render a speech and vanish again while the fourteen members speak across the gap—at nobody. Often they would like to begin a conversation—a round-table conversation; but soon, involuntarily, they look and speak past each other, addressing the open side of the blue semicircle where perhaps an invisible semicircle has become visible. Clearly these elect ones lead a different life from the more modest creatures who sit at real tables between real walls and debate a real subject, while the members of the Council sit like so many members of a board before a meeting whose opinion is not asked; only with them it is a world which lies before them in compulsory silence. They constitute the well-known figure called Council, but as soon as they have been in session for a time it is clearly felt that the whole affair is a cabalistic one. Nobody knows whether the exact semicircle will wax and girdle the globe or whether it will meet with a sudden eclipse or dissolve into nothing.

Meanwhile the vast figure called Assembly, and composed of the entire multitude who came to Geneva, spreads before us in reassuring calm. It overflows the walls and glasses of the hotel, its dining-rooms, *salons* and luncheon-rooms. Consequently, until the quarrelling League architects have completed the monster building in the Ariana park, there will be turmoil in the various hired annexes on the other bank far from the lake and its parks. For ten years the Assembly could be watched in the gloomy, grey, barnlike and sparsely furnished hall of the Reformation, which was erected more than fifty years ago as a tribune for the exposition and defence of evangelical truth and which stands under Calvin's protection. Later it was housed in the massive white modern Geneva electoral building over whose doorway the parting words are carved which old Rousseau addressed to his son: "Jean Jacques," he said, "love your country." But after all, it is indifferent whether the hall is gloomy or bright, and whether it bears a message to the members meeting in it at the League's General Assembly, so long as it is big enough to hold the meeting. The requisite is that it has sufficient desks and seats and that the President's and speaker's tribunes have a conspicuous position, for the men who meet in the League Assembly do not wish to sit at a circular or a semicircular table, but, like every other parliament, on benches ranged behind each other, having a Speaker to whom to look; and every member rising to address the House is to belong to them all. They do not want lake or sky to look in on them; for their walls of stone or wood will in any case be more transparent than glass, and their horizon wider than that of the Geneva landscape. If they will it their meeting can transcend all limits, rising above Article 3 of the Covenant by virtue of which they assemble and each State member is granted three delegates with a joint vote, as well as above Article 1, which governs the number of members; indeed above the whole of the Covenant, above the order of the day, and above the rules of procedure and tradition devised by the Secretariat. For the moment all these men constitute merely the Assembly which plays a definite part within the structure of the League and whose members, in the reality of politics, have very different rights and powers; but they are also a gathering of the nations. And when representatives of a number of nations are gathered together yearly, the fact of their gathering is more important than the name under which they are gathered, and the natural law resulting from their joint debates has a more binding force than the rules which organized their first meeting. The nations are gathered together, and that in a time where every hour appeals for the realization of the ideal of the League. The Assembly exists and the ideal of the League exists; and that being so, surely the Assembly and the ideal will be brought together despite the faults of organization and of method which we witnessed and criticized.

The bell sounds; the delegates leave the corridors and gather in the hall. The public takes its places and the Press representatives of all the nations appear in the galleries; they have already booked their first calls and are looking down impatiently on the delegates. We all look down and watch the space below filling, watch the men beneath us exchanging greetings, only to separate again and join their countrymen on the benches which are their temporary home. And immediately, although enclosed within the same four walls, they have become separated from their colleagues; they are the same men as before but they bear a different name. Small labels are placed before their seats bearing these names: "Afrique du Sud, Albanie, Allemagne, Australie, Autriche, Belgique, Empire britannique" . . . these are now their names and the human faces sitting behind these labels are national faces; each bench is a nation.

Thus it immediately becomes evident that the bench entitled "Empire britannique," which we curiously contemplate from the gallery, is itself the British Empire. In the course of time many different men were seated on this bench; but all of them in every detail of face and voice were British Empire. Years ago we could see Balfour here—lofty, superior, cool but not without fire—a statesman with a rosy, youthful face under his white hair, and a man whose every gesture and word bespoke a representative of Empire. Next we saw Sir Austen Chamberlain, tall, dull and gentlemanly—blue and vacant eyes in a supercilious face; next MacDonald, with the head of a thinker and dreamy glances, a perfect demagogue, a secret aristocrat and a potential tyrant. With him Henderson, a fellow Labour man, friend and opponent of MacDonald, a workman who for years has been a bourgeois, a bourgeois who might become a peer, and, in any case, a man of the masses who has gradually come to represent the high political culture of a great and proud nation. But almost always the face of Britain was that of Lord Robert Cecil, a pale, intellectual face which, seen in full, might have been that of a salvationist, in profile that of a vulture, and in half-profile that of a Roman, but which commands many other expressions, reflects a dozen and hides a dozen opinions—the face of a man who, like the State he represents, can effect compromises with equal ease between others, with others, and with himself.

Meanwhile the French bench has gradually been filling. France; years ago France meant Léon Bourgeois, the mild, wise and slightly sentimental patriarch; René Viviani, the brilliant speaker and typical representative of the French Left, who one day would discard the pre-war shibboleths of the party and strike the attitude of a conqueror of Huns; with him a more frail and paler figure, that of Monsieur Noblemaire; next the historian Hanotaux, a survival from a distant past, Foreign Minister, dry, quarrelsome, thin and meagre like his beard; later Loucheur, whose keen olfactory sense and darting eyes under heavy brows would one day show him that Geneva was an excellent platform for French internal politics: for a number of sessions Loucheur socially dominated Geneva. France again is Paul-Boncour, the great pleader and actor, fond of playing the part of an inflexible but lyrical revolutionary; Henri de Jouvenal, one of the most persuasive and intelligent representatives of his country, a logical but charming speaker, an agreeable beast of prey with velvet paws; it is Herriot whose *embonpoint* and pipe announce the man of the people, whose sound works and carefully prepared speeches the intellectual, and whose massive brow and angular nose betray the keen realist hungry for success. France is the French Labour leader Jouhaux, a huge man with a little black beard at the tip of a full chin, dressed with elaborate carelessness after the fashion approved by French workmen in their intellectual leaders, and endowed with a praeterhuman voice which forms each word on a slow but gigantic scale, and with tremendous gravity, a gravity threatening world revolutions, thunders over his unmoved colleagues periods of wholly pacific import. But above all the bench of France is Briand's bench, and whoever occupies it, it will for long remain his.

He would come slowly through the rows of benches, dragging his feet, and would wearily drop into his seat. There he would sit with his traditional rounded back, grey unkempt hair, thick and drooping moustache and eyes generally half-closed in a big face with vague features and twisted mouth, whence a cigarette could usually be seen pendant, and from which next moment the full, charming violoncello notes would be heard. His pose as he sat was modest; his dress almost careless; his movements slow and gentle. He did not know how to pose because he hardly knew his body; what was most important in him were his eyes, as soon as he opened them, his slim hand, and his voice. Was he as intelligent as his surroundings maintained? At any rate he was probably much more intelligent than his collaborators suspected and much more skilful than his enemies believed; for he possessed a liberal and intelligent skill in the treatment of individuals and of groups of individuals—a skill compounded of native finesse, common sense, wide experience and a contempt for every kind of pettiness. He knew little of national psychology—less perhaps than the average Frenchman; but he knew men, and knew them well; and for this reason he was in a position to triumph in an institution where nations were represented by individuals. Having returned home, on the other hand, he was all the more apt to commit dangerous blunders in dealing with the abstraction of a Cabinet. Was he the great idealist whom friends and enemies praised and condemned? He was no more an idealist than the rest of France, and yet although mankind agreed in calling him a sceptic he was probably less so than most of his countrymen. At the same time the ideal which he meant even when he spoke of mankind was France, and he knew no other ideal; the pacifism which gradually caused many a hard and chauvinistic utterance of the war and post-war period to be forgotten was simply an instrument of foreign policy. He desired peace because peace meant France's victory. Above all he was the traditional enemy of Clemenceau and Poincaré, and it was his aim to supersede their policy of national aggrandisement by a policy of deliberate internationalism in the interests of France. This policy was not to imply any sacrifice for France; sacrifices were still to be the privilege of other nations; but for a method of cold force he desired to substitute one of persuasion and cunning. Was he an idealist, a dreamer? His lyrical exclamation "down with the cannons, down with the machine guns," did not imply any real intention to abolish machine guns and cannons; but he preferred to refrain from using them because at the moment he considered his eloquence and diplomatic skill to be more powerful weapons. The engines of destruction were to be pushed behind that broad back in order to be less conspicuous. Was he a knave? No; he was merely an old politician, an old man and an old Breton in whom the realism of the working day mingled with the poetry of the ever-breaking sea. It was his art always to be identical with victorious France and yet to invest this role with a charm. The result was that he fascinated Geneva; and it was not the nations before whom he played this part and whom he made willing slaves by his quiet address in the Council and his eloquence in the Assembly, but his own country which, fearing that the skilful player would at length become the prisoner of his own skill, felt it necessary one day to diminish his stature, defeat him and banish him from the Assembly of the nations.

We now look at the German bench, at one time the haunt of Under-Secretaries of State and Foreign Office officials, as well as of clever parliamentarians like Dr. Kaas and Dr. Breitscheid. By virtue of the French alphabet, the bench has a conspicuous position in the front, although many years had to elapse before a spectator looking down from the gallery saw any German bench; Afrique du Sud and Albanie were followed immediately by Australie, while the name of Germany was to be found only at the table of a few conferences. For years Germany was represented by a modest but pertinacious Dr. Ernst, by an intelligent Minister, von Eckard, or his energetic colleague

Seeliger, by the learned and shrewd opium expert Anselmino, or an impressive Minister like Schiffer, or a zealous Minister like Simons, by an intelligent professor like Dr. Kaufmann, or a man of the world like Dr. Lewald. Other typical representatives were the efficient officers of the new army who had this first opportunity of measuring their strength, with prudence and dignity, against their late enemies. Again, Germany in those days meant a gentleman like Count Bernstorff; it meant the various Ministers, Secretaries of State and economists dispatched to the World Economic Conference and the Labour Conferences; it meant the German Consuls at Geneva, and it meant the courageous Labour leader Wissell, who was the first to champion the German language in the International Labour Organization. Germany meant all those Germans who never found a place in the conferences, and had to remain in the corridors or in the public galleries, whence they followed the debates which decided their fate; Germans from Poland, Upper Silesia, from Danzig, from Memel, from the Saar district, from Sudetia—bold and energetic men who desperately tried to obtain justice, pursued high politics of their own, were guided by their impulses and obeyed common sense—workmen, clerks and officials who often called forth admiration by the way in which they cast off the petty atmosphere of their rural or urban administrations and proved themselves fit to grapple with the highest national and international problems.

But things have changed since then, and now the bench labelled "Allemagne" stands in the forefront of the Assembly. From the first day it was Stresemann's preserve. A day was to come when the Chancellor Müller or the Foreign Secretary Curtius unshrinkingly took over his heavy burden; but it is impossible to look down on this bench without seeing before us the broad, lively and jovial face, a face gradually to grow pinched, pale and nervous, of Gustav Stresemann. It is perhaps because he was so true a representative of Germany that we cannot forget his face; and in any case the Assembly could never have been presented with a better Germany than Stresemann's Germany. For it was Stresemann who embodied German courage when he undertook to lead his country back from capitulation into the concert of Powers, and who revealed the unfettered quality of the German mind when he entered this hall without a trace of the complex of defeat which had weakened and intimidated so many of his colleagues but like a triumphant victor, and the unshakable German belief in the German mission when he hoped by a rapid series of successes to overcome a terrible past. His brow was illuminated by the unconquerable intelligence which thinks itself superior to adversity; and his eyes shone with that confidence in the world which is not intimidated by the complexity of problems or the cunning and superior force of enemies. He embodied the will to fight of the German citizen which had been forgotten at Geneva; he embodied the profound and noble humanity which captious enemies declined to see in the German people, and the healthy raciness which delegates at Geneva had forgotten to look for in *gauche* and timid diplomats. He presented the world with a living, a struggling but also a friendly Germany; and when he enthusiastically quoted Goethe everyone felt that he was thinking of Bismarck, and felt the courage and ambition to become the Bismarck of a defeated nation. All those who wished to flatter Germany identified Germany with Stresemann, and he himself thought that he was a faithful portrait of his country. Yet we may ask whether he always did portray Germany. We dimly felt at that period what now we definitely know, that he truly represented Germany at a great and dramatic moment of her national life. He was Germany at the moment at which she cast aside the confusion of defeat and invested herself with the pride of a great nation. In those dangerous and critical moments, when confusion and self-esteem lay in conflict with each other, Stresemann met Briand, who was trying to embody a France which was discarding victorious insolence for the will to reconciliation. But the moment was missed. Germany continues to suffer and to struggle and to bear the imprint of suffering and struggling; and in the Assembly Hall the German bench continues to be a symbolic object recalling a scene from the life of a people.

Was Germany represented also on the benches of Austria? At the time when the former Ambassador, Count Mensdorf-Pouilly, was representing the new republic, Austria meant an aristocrat, *ancien régime*, gentle, resigned, demanding sympathy and a brilliant French linguist. Later, when Monseignor Seipel lent his eloquence to the Austrian cause, it meant a skilful and impressive priest—corpulent figure, bald skull, vast hooked nose, keen eyes behind spectacles, and uttering international platitudes in an unctuous style couched in a forcibly popular High German. It was only Doctor Schober, whose healthy colour, trim white beard and upright carriage, revealed a representative of the German peasant and townsman of the Alpine regions. And at all times the face of Austria was that of her Geneva representative, Baron Pflügl, a swift and resourceful diplomat, equally at home in all times and places; and always a vigorous official like Herr Schüller had the sense of reality, adaptability and expert knowledge to keep a keen-eyed look-out for economic and financial ways and means to keep Austria above water.

We turn to the Hungarian bench. Towering high above his former half-countrymen, glancing with something akin to insolence above the multitude, absent-minded, with muscular hands folded behind his back, the lean and as it were crumbling figure of ancient Count Apponyi is observed advancing to his seat; an overpowering personality; magnificent beard, big hawk's nose, and wide open nostrils which appear to be organs of scent and hearing; a master of men, whose majestic dignity emphasizes and by emphasizing overcomes the tragedy of defeat. Behind him Dr. Benes works his way towards the Czechoslovakian bench, jerking his shoulders as he walks; the cleverest and most skilful man in Geneva, who, because he possesses a democratic appearance, and because he represents a new nation, wins the delighted applause of all who love a democratic diplomat, but who in fact is the admirable Metternich in an age of parliaments and Leagues of Nations. We see him calling a lively greeting to the Roumanian representative Titulescu, whose small Mongolian head dances on unexpectedly high and broad shoulders, and in whose restless lineaments a permanent struggle between keen judgment, passionate desires, coquettishness and a lust for domination is revealed.

The hall is filling from minute to minute. On the Italian bench Count Scialoja, a slight and elegant figure, in whom a remarkable, an almost cynical, adaptability is mingled with an honest sense of juristic truth, takes his seat by the side of the youthful Fascist Foreign Minister, Grandi.[1] Like Lord Robert Cecil, Scialoja is one of the few survivors of the Paris League Commission. A third member of this group, the Spanish Ambassador, Quiñones de Leon, whose comfortable and rotund figure could for years be seen shrewdly pleading the French cause on the Spanish bench, alike in Council and Assembly, is no longer seen at Geneva. The new republic has put in his place new ministers, and a former official of the Secretariat, an expert in every kind of Geneva business, and a man of brilliant parts and intelligence, de Madariaga. On the Belgian benches the Foreign Minister Hymans, the estimable President of the first Assembly, recalls early days; a youthful and lively old gentleman, with white hair and moustaches, sparkling eyes and vivid gestures, of polished appearance and address, and an intimate part of the House of which he has a unique knowledge. But we no longer find Vandervelde, who played so considerable a part in the Assembly during the Locarno honeymoon, a diplomat who in spite of his deafness could hear the grass grow; nor do we find the old and proved pacifist Lafontaine, who spoke so bravely in the course of the first assemblies and who, later, could be seen on the Press gallery where, resting his head upon his hands, he would stare

[1] Since these words were written, Signor Grandi has become Italian Ambassador in London.

"AFRIQUE DU SUD, ALBANIE, ALLEMAGNE . . ." 385

down into the House with burning eyes. Among the former neutrals, who are just finishing a private conversation among their various benches, we note the white head of the Norwegian representative Lange; a fine and intelligent head somehow reminiscent of Björnsen which might serve an artist for model; but at the desk in front of his we no longer find the old and ever youthful Nansen, of the brisk, athletic figure, the grand skull and the deep-set eyes, the legendary hero of our youth, and the youthful Siegfried of the early years of the League, where he remained active until he withdrew from international politics to international beneficence. The Swedish bench, too, is one which has always been occupied by wise and honourable men, and here too we remember the dead; for it is here that Branting had his seat, once a champion of the Entente, but also one of the first champions of the oppressed German races: a vast seal's head with pale eyes and huge moustaches; a courageous voice having a tearful cadence. The Dutch benches too have been occupied by skilful men of sound opinions; by Jonkheer van Karnebeek, an elegant and, in a way, a Southern figure; later by Beelaerts van Blokland, a progressive and mildly pro-German representative; and by van Eysinga, a diplomat as plucky as he is obstinate. And now President Motta is seen approaching the Swiss benches. Greetings meet him on every side, and from the galleries too the frank and friendly features of this man are looked upon with satisfaction; a man both lively and serene, and who seems a suitable representative for a country characterized equally by candour and finesse, democratic sense, an appreciation of intellectual values, and a tempered taste for festive eloquence. We feel that this man is as cautious as his nation, composed as it is of three races, and that he can also be as courageous as any one of them.

And now the President of the narrow Council, whose function it is to open the wide Assembly, enters upon the platform. He halts before his elevated seat, and exchanges a few words on the agenda with the Secretary-General. Now, too, the representatives of Latin America, who until the last have been negotiating fiercely in order to present the uninitiated with an appearance of national unity and to that end have been attempting hastily to overcome their various differences, come hurrying to their seats scattered throughout the hall. Impossible to retain the traits of all of them. Always in front of San Salvador or Paraguay or Venezuela, the full clean-shaven face of Cuba can be seen with its keen nose and keen chin, a face distorted by a hundred passionate and intelligent grimaces; for it is the ancient prerogative of Señor Aguerro y Bethancourt to prepare with dexterity and success the presidential elections, the elections for every kind of committee, and even the elections for the Council. In a moment we shall find him on the tribune, reporting in sound and nervous language on the powers of the delegates, in order to determine whether all the men on the various benches are in fact and unchallengably representatives of their nations. Meanwhile the President of the Council has assumed his elevated seat between the Secretary-General and the translator, and while these gentlemen are finishing a whispered conversation a few curious visitors in the galleries are spying out such exciting figures as those of a slim and resourceful Japanese, a small, stout Chinaman, or a dusky Persian, men of distinguished appearance whom old watchers from the galleries have long since ceased to differentiate from Europeans; or such figures as that of the noble negro of Haiti, or the solemn dark men of Abyssinia, with their picturesque black draperies and crumpled white trousers, or the Indian Maharajah, with his cunningly folded turban and with diamonds which draw looks of greedy admiration.

The hall is now completely filled and almost every State member of the League is represented. We recognize a number of Prime Ministers and numerous Foreign Ministers, as well as ex-ministers, ambassadors, and other diplomatic representatives. On every bench we see famous, or at least well-known, able, intelligent and successful men; and all are leaders of their nations, whether delegated by the Great Powers or by the lesser countries, and whether they have prepared for this international meeting in Paris or London, or in Athens, Helsingfors or Lisbon. In the Press gallery we salute excellent journalists, men of intelligence and conversant with every international problem. In the public galleries we recognize a number of progressive party leaders, modern-minded diplomats, famous authors, and eminent students of international law. And in the diplomats' box, among the wives and daughters of ministers and officials, we note, dressed in mourning and with an unmoved face, the widow of Woodrow Wilson—the widow of the man who had willed this meeting and who had called the first of these Assemblies. A unique spectacle, adorned with a wealth of fame, genius, authority, splendour and faith.

The President of the Council rises and, while the cinematograph operators kindle their dazzling suns, he strikes his little desk with his little hammer. The vast hall is silent, with its crowded benches and crowded galleries; only here and there a door creaks or a paper rustles. The President says: "The meeting of the League Assembly is open." Next follows his grand address; next the Assembly checks credentials and elects its own President. Next this President delivers his address, and next the Assembly appoints its officers and its six committees, distributes work, and arranges a time-table for their deliberations. The Assembly's time-table has already been printed, and its list of members distributed. The annual Assembly of the League has commenced. In the vast hall we hear the first words of a common interest and see the first gestures of a common life; nation is speaking unto nation.

CHAPTER XXIV

THE HAMMER

THE first day passes, other days pass, the weeks pass. Each morning and afternoon the presidents rise in the various rooms and halls to declare the meeting open; everywhere they deliver their brief speeches and call upon representatives of Canada, of France or of Norway to address the meeting. Unwearingly they call upon the translators. In the body of the hall the delegate called upon rises and rapidly ascends the tribune; while in the Council the speakers remain seated in their comfortable chairs and simply raise their head a little when speaking. In the committee the expert rises at the long table, pushes back his chair, bends forward, places his hands upon the blotting-paper and begins his address. Colleagues and officials of the Secretariat surround the speaker; at the Press tables the telegrams fly into the hands of the waiting messengers, and girls go skipping down the corridors with their shorthand notes to their typewriters and back from the typewriters to the debating halls. The League has become a grand festival with numerous side-shows, a vast revolving stage on which the most diverse scenes are simultaneously enacted. Under a dozen different names, and discussing a hundred different subjects, men are standing and sitting together, talking to each other morning, noon and night, and their need of joint conversation seems so insatiable that they call on each other between sessions at their hotels, lock themselves together in their dining-rooms, have luncheons and dinners in groups, and arrange banquets and receptions in each other's honour, which, being almost without exception held in the same hotel, with the same menu and the same waiters, and only a different Foreign Minister acting as host, produce the effect of a second League Assembly. Or again, they arrange joint excursions to the little restaurants by the side of the lake, or across the frontier into France. On other occasions again they are seized by the urge to have another than merely a national audience; at the end of a session, at the door, in the corridor, in the hall, or on the way to their cars, they hand themselves over to the journalists or assemble them in their hotels, or are thankful when they are invited to a banquet given by the united Press accredited at the League, where, after the ices, and while coffee and liqueurs are being sipped, they have yet another chance of speaking to the globe.

The nations are conversing with each other, a splendid and an eloquent phenomenon; indeed nations, represented by so many men, are conversing together, and surely this conversation must grow into a lasting collaboration such as could not have arisen out of a dead mass of methods and organizations. The nations have become men, and speak to each other, and no longer fight with each other as though they had become wild beasts. After all, the long programmes were laid on the tables so that they should have food for speech and to prevent that oppressive silence from arising which is more dangerous than the most incautious words; for silence is silver and speech is golden. The nations are speaking together. Surely the reality of the League must arise from such speech.

But how do they speak together, on what subjects, and why? For, if this conversation is to act as a binding cement and is to provide them with a common mental structure in place of the former cold geometry of their squares, circles, semicircles and rectangles, it is necessary that their language be honest and open, and warm and brotherly, and that, however much they struggle for national advantages, they have the common cause even closer at heart. It does not suffice for them to speak like men; they must speak like men who have something to tell each other, who like each other's conversation, and who have nothing more important than this conversation; who become more and more clearly aware that it is not a self-seeking individualism, but common consultation and deliberation which is the necessary prerequisite of the welfare of each.

A common conversation must change into a common life. So much, surely, goes without saying: else why assemble them all here—the Prime Ministers, the Foreign Ministers, Ambassadors and Secretaries of State?

We begin to listen to the adroit and intelligent words of the President, who is now delivering the address prepared beforehand in the Secretariat; to the famous and experienced statesman, who walks up and down the tribune while expanding his subject with lively gestures; to the industrious and esteemed expert as he bends in committee over his carefully drafted notes. What languages do they speak? Can it be that they are all French or English? Hardly—the accent of many of them is too odd for that; and yet all of them speak either English or French. Only a few Germans or Austrians make use of their native language; but if they do so they have no claim to translation into French or English, and it is left to them to see how they can deal with the numerous documents which, except those emanating from the Labour Office, are in French or English, and constitute the foundation and the result of the international conversation. Incredible as it may seem in this house of all the nations, the only official languages are French and English. Only the French and their Belgian friends, only the members of the British Empire and the representatives of the United States invited to attend conferences and committees are allowed on every occasion to speak their native language and to write and read the contributions to the international conversation in their own tongue. The other nations must speak a foreign language in which, as Goethe lets his own Werther say at Geneva, "it is impossible to express the impalpable essence of the moment swiftly, vigorously, in its own quality and with ease," while it becomes necessary "to have recourse on every occasion to fine stereotyped phrases." The attempt is made to justify the stupid rule making compulsory the use of two languages, which hampers the choice of delegates and puts a film before the face of the nations by pointing to the practical demands of international debate. But is it a coincidence that the languages of the League are those of the Treaty of Versailles, Trianon, St. Germain and Neuilly? Surely the practical requisites would have been met more effectively by a single official language with the various delegates' native language as alternative, as demanded by numerous champions of the League idea, than by the present system. The two official languages are all too clear a reminder that the object was not so much to facilitate a debate than to command a conversation by two Powers and two civilizations. Incessantly they recall the history of the foundation of the House in which the nations are to meet at last in brotherly converse; but if a German listens from the gallery and hears his countrymen, who are neither French, nor Belgians, nor Anglo-Saxons, speaking French or English, he feels, as we feel, that they do not enjoy full and equal rights, either when action is taken or resolutions reached, or even in the progress of debate.

But perhaps it is hardly fair to blame the foreign language for the "fine stereotyped phrases" heard on every occasion in the full-dress speeches delivered by a wise President or by experienced statesmen. The Frenchman who addresses the Assembly speaks French, and the Englishman who sits at the Council table speaks English; they are speaking their mother tongue, and yet the phrases which they utter, though well-sounding, are infinitely meaningless. The President of the Assembly is a Balkan statesman who speaks French like his native tongue; why is it that his retrospect on the activities of the last League year is full of the most worn-out and clumsy clichés? Without interruption a long series of swollen, stilted and grandiose words like "humanity," "progress," "trust," "success," "hope" and "triumph" passes through the speeches of the delegates, and it is only on rare occasions that the addresses of former neutrals, Germans or Hungarians, contain the more modest word "disappointment." Endless sleek and polished declamations unfold before us, declamations familiar in exhibitions, banquets, and unveilings of monuments, so many monologues with the speaker standing before a mirror, solemn yet trivial superfluities. When the speakers are also great artists and employ their native language, their sounding platitudes can naturally sometimes attain aesthetic merit, and this is enough to induce a state of enthusiasm in the hall and the galleries, and to evoke enthusiastic applause. Meanwhile, what are our own feelings while we sit by, charmed and applauding? Are we really convinced that nation is speaking to nation? Rather we are admiring an artist who is a good speaker and a good actor, and, at most, we congratulate his country upon the possession of a successful manipulator of words, capable possibly of winning successes for his country in the sphere of rhetoric and even in that of politics. At the same time, however, these speeches seem so irrelevant to the real purpose of debate that we are inclined to forget the nationality of the speaker—not so much because of the international flavour of his speech, as because of his fine speaking; we forget the meaning underlying the entire assembly and become oblivious of the fact that it is not an artistic or a social, but a moral institution.

What is the theme of their words? Let us only listen. Each time when they proceed to produce their monotonous and pretentious series of commonplaces, it is the League of Nations that is their subject, and indeed they cannot utter the name of the League without coupling it with commonplaces. The speakers are intelligent, shrewd and instructed, but as soon as they mention the League they forget their talents, personality and knowledge and become so many actors, good, bad or indifferent. On hearing their pompous banalities we cannot but feel surprised; have all these intelligent men nothing better to tell each other when the gravest problem of mankind is under discussion? We listen anxiously; but often we have to wait for days before a profound or honest word is heard, and we long in vain for a novel or exciting idea related somehow to the reality which constitutes the daily life of the populations outside Geneva. Fine and empty words arranged according to the

THE HAMMER 393

rules of French or English syntax—is this the language of the nations whose representatives we see before us—is this the official language of the League?

Our well-meaning neighbours in the gallery try to calm us and to explain the mystery. They urge us not to forget that the present and many other meetings take place in public and that so progressive an innovation naturally demands special precautions. We do not forget these facts, and we are ready enough to congratulate the speakers for having the courage to speak their mind in public. On the other hand we are equally far from admitting that the final purpose of the Assembly can be to deliberate in public; and quite equally we are far from blaming the delegates for having recourse to secret meetings of the Council and of various commissions in order to investigate and to settle those delicate and difficult questions which touch individual and national susceptibilities and can be carried to a successful conclusion only if dealt with in cautious preliminary negotiations. But we do expect of the speakers that everything said in public is worth saying in public, and that the Assembly to which we have been admitted is not used merely for an exchange of compliments or for the utterance of remarks calculated and prepared for the public and obscuring the actual relations between the nations. We have the right to demand that they tell the truth and not mislead us; if they are to speak in public, the principle of public speaking must be utilized to enhance the value of their speeches, and if the result of publicity is merely to render their speeches trivial without adding profundity or making full use of the opportunity inherent in the gathering of the nations, we would much prefer to be excluded from these deliberations. Better that secret meetings should become the rule and public meetings the exception, if these rare public meetings would only give an unequivocal and convincing expression to the solidarity of nations, secretly cemented. But we have a right to ask why, since the public is excluded sufficiently often in any case, the speakers should consider themselves obliged to cling to banalities and to a contemptible prudence when the public is admitted. After all, they need not fear to shock the susceptibilities of nations; their eyes and ears have not been spoilt in the present any more than in past centuries. The nations survived a public war, and are likely to survive a public peace of whatever kind.

And yet there are times when all the pompousness and ambiguity of the rhetoricians is forgotten and a human note is heard among the conventionalities of the debate; a discord pierces the harmonious melody which was tending to send us into a state of exaltation, or of somnolence; an angry gesture takes the place of the studied pose, grieved or threatening words are heard, and fine, conventional, stereotyped phrases become brutal and unequivocal cries from the heart. But it is rarely enough that we witness such an awakening of the nations, and when we do we rarely have cause for congratulations. When, in the dark period of the beginnings of the League, a Frenchman like Noblemaire found generous words of homage for the German and French soldiers who fell during the war, when Monsieur Motta spoke courageously on behalf of Germany, and when Lord Robert Cecil, during the Council debate on Corfu, emphatically read out Article 16 of the Covenant for the benefit of the Italian delegate Salandra, we might have felt that a conversation between the nations was no impossibility. And when Stresemann, already marked for the grave, stood on the tribune of the Assembly for the last time and suddenly laid down his manuscript and confessed his belief in a free League of Nations in words of an unstudied and convincing eloquence, we might have felt that here was an honest appeal to every heart. A year later, however, when Briand took the occasion of a Press dinner to call upon the spirit of dead Stresemann in words of impassioned eloquence, one soon felt —after wiping away one's tears—that his chief aim was to annoy Dr. Curtius, the successor of Stresemann.

And indeed on almost every occasion when the nations become human and speak a clear and honest language they are

THE HAMMER

not so much anxious to provoke the common debate as to voice their private wishes and passions. The Frenchman Viviani rudely interrupts the Swiss representative Motta because he cannot bear to see Germany a member of the League. The Czech Osusky speaks bitterly but sincerely about Hungary. The Hungarian Apponyi turns against the Little Entente with honest indignation. The Lithuanian representative Galvanauskas furiously strikes the table because he is inconvenienced by the protection of minorities. The German Stresemann strikes the table with equally unconcealed indignation because he is obliged to defend his isolated countrymen against Poland. The Japanese Adatchi becomes excited in the committee debating the Geneva Protocol and threatens to sabotage the entire work because Article 11 exempts from pacific settlement the troubles which might conceivably arise from Japanese immigration into America. The Frenchman Briand walks up and down the tribune fuming and tries to bully the German delegation because he dislikes Chancellor Müller's disarmament thesis. The little Spanish Councillor of Legation, Quer Boule, who was dispatched by his offended Government to the Council table when Spain resolved to withdraw, utters heartfelt words of farewell with a low and melancholy cadence. Mello Franco, the Brazilian, flings his veto from the tribune into the Assembly with a violent gesture. The Belgian Vandervelde, finding his country's application for re-eligibility to the Council rejected, delivers an address which is almost moving and containing elements of deep sincerity and generous melancholy. Even the Opium Conference is suddenly shaken by a cry from the deep when a Chinese representative inveighs against the British delegate with unexpected vigour. We lean over the gallery and watch and listen to the human voices of the nations: why is it that no note of sorrow or anger causes their voices to vibrate when they speak of the League? Why do they not strike the table to express their grief or their indignation to find their work so infinitely far removed from fulfilling the ideal of the League? Why is it that, whenever they leave the League, it is only because they are dissatisfied with the treatment accorded to their own country and never, since the withdrawal of the Argentine delegation, because they are dissatisfied with the community of nations? Almost invariably when they speak with honest candour, anger, or sorrow, the representatives of the nations are thinking of their own country or even of themselves; of the effect of their remarks in Parliament, at home, in the Press or with the public. How can contact be established between the nations if the great international conversation is to confine itself to the vocabulary of the lowest forms of human conversation, to conventional phrases and an eternal pre-occupation with self?

But let us have patience. For now that the meeting is gradually drawing to a close the *rapporteur* of the first committee mounts the tribune; in a few moments the Assembly will adopt a common resolution. He will be succeeded by another *rapporteur*, and another common resolution will be adopted: everywhere in the Council and in the committees reports will be read out and common resolutions adopted. Perhaps we have been unduly despondent, and perhaps the event for which we have been waiting is now about to take place, for it is only now that the hopes can be fulfilled which draw us into the debating rooms. The conversation between the nations is, while it lasts, a conflict or a game at hide-and-seek, and what is said by each nation in the course of the debate is of no great importance; for the language of the individual nations does not matter so much as the grand concluding sentence where they speak in chorus; it is not the preparatory co-operation but the final dispersal that matters, where, so we hope, each representative says what he has to say in the only way in which it can be said. For days and weeks the nations have recited their national monologues with an excess of caution or an excess of bluntness; at the end everything that is above individual interests and above the injustice and greed of individuals will resound in one common chorus of reason and courage.

The *rapporteur* stands on the tribune and reads out his report: "In view of the fact that . . .," he says; "In consideration of the fact that . . .," he reads out; "In recognition of the circumstance that . . .," he declares. Terrible contorted sentences are laboriously uttered, worse than anything we have heard hitherto. Every other main clause has a subsidiary restricting clause; every phrase is so formulated as to admit of three different interpretations, so that every delegation can provide the home Press with a different version and every jurist attached to the delegations can rub his hands with satisfaction. Almost invariably the report ends with suggestions, recommendations and wishes which are void of content and whose emptiness the public does not notice because it has been deafened by the pomp and circumstance which preceded the poor conclusion. The whole world is suffering from a vast economic and financial crisis, and the President raises his hammer, for a number of resolutions on the economic activity of the League Assembly have to be adopted.

"The Assembly . . .," so we vaguely hear, "declares that the normal exchange of goods among nations is seriously hampered by the continued changes in customs tariffs and in general by the lacking stability in commercial policy. . . ."—"In consideration," so we further hear, of the fact that a sub-committee of the Committee of Studies for European Union "considers that the inequality of tariffs hinders the efforts to stabilize currencies and organize credit," the Assembly resolves—listen, all you who are assembled in the hall, public and Press galleries—"to appeal urgently to all the nations" to do all in their power to avoid changes in tariffs and commercial policy, etc.

"In consideration"—the stuttering utterances recommence—"of the necessity of close economic co-operation to alleviate the present economic crisis, and of the fact that a report of the sub-committee of experts details the means to this end, and of the fact that the gravity of the crisis and the needs of the coming months demand the expeditious application of all measures useful and calculated to alleviate it, the Assembly takes note of the resolution of the Committee of Studies for European Union to invite the Governments of Europe to hand in if possible before the 1st of January 1932 their observations on this report...." What becomes of the considerations and resolutions of the sub-committee and committees of study on the gravity and needs of the time? Take heed, all who are assembled in hall and galleries: the Assembly *recommends* the Report to the notice of all the Governments.

Do our ears deceive us? Are the nations assembled at Geneva appealing to the nations, and the Governments assembled at Geneva drawing the attention of the Governments to various facts? Surely the nations and the Governments are mocking themselves as well as us. They are assembled together, they have been speaking together, and yet the conclusion of their long debate is simply that they appeal to themselves and draw their own attention to certain facts. They talk, they talk and they talk, and all the complicated sentences which contain the result of their talking amount to this: we nations and we Governments will draw the attention of ourselves, of nations and Governments who are here assembled or of the other nations and Governments our neighbours, to this and that fact. Is this the language which is calculated to raise us above the events of the past twelve years? The President suffers his hammer to fall on the table: the resolutions have been adopted.

We listen once again. The name of China has been mentioned, and we lean over the gallery, hand behind ear: "The Assembly trusts that the traffic organization will use every endeavour to ensure complete success in the collaboration between itself and the Chinese national Government with regard to the investigation of the question of public works." The President's hammer drops. Once again the name of China is heard: we hear that the unhappy country has suffered loss of human life, that a terrible catastrophe has visited the population, and that in consequence a humanitarian problem of the greatest importance and a question of international interest arises. What is the question at issue? Similar words have been heard at the beginning of the session when there was at least the appearance of quiet in the Far East. On that occasion they dealt with the disastrous floods in the valley of the Yangtse; on the present occasion, where China has already appealed to the League against Japan, the words must necessarily have a grimmer import and the question of "international interests" must necessarily be *the* great question of the League.

Sentence after tortuous sentence falls on our ears, and we realize that the conversation of the nations has made no progress to-day. Again the hammer falls: we have heard the last resolution of the subject of China to be adopted by the present Assembly. Is this the language of the nations? The Geneva organization is impotent to stop the economic crisis or to preserve peace and justice in the Far East, and we had suspected as much. But is this the language which Germany, France, Britain, Holland and Switzerland desires to hear in order to learn that their common labours have proved a failure? Surely, if the Geneva talks are to be the prelude of action at Geneva, the last word should be inspired by ruthless honesty and intelligent self-criticism; for in no other way the doom can be averted which hitherto has blighted the co-operation of the nations. If we listen to the words uttered beneath us, we need not feel, however, that the nations are doomed; for each time that the President's hammer drops it is to signify the adoption of a resolution in which the conversation of the nations is summarized in the jolliest terms; the men beneath us recognizing, considering and acknowledging in the most diverse phraseology that everything is to their satisfaction.

"The Assembly is happy...." Why happy? Happy, because the endeavours of the International Committee for Intellectual Co-operation continue progressively to prepare a knowledge of the League and a present understanding of the nations among the young.

"The Assembly congratulates itself...." Why? Because

preparations are being made to ensure the joint action of competent authorities for the protection of copyright.

"The Assembly notes with satisfaction. . . ." What? That the International Committee for Intellectual Co-operation has undertaken new work for the defence of culture and civilization.

"The Assembly congratulates itself upon the results obtained. . . ." Obtained by the Administrative Council of the International Institute for Educational Films. . . .

"The Assembly is happy to discover . . ."—that there has been a lowering of customs walls—for educational films.

"The Assembly expresses its satisfaction . . ."—on the increasingly satisfactory development of international periodicals on educational films.

And now the Assembly reaches the climax of joy. It is "happy" and "satisfied" at the same time—it expresses its happy satisfaction to find that a monument has been erected at San Domingo in honour of Columbus, who "perfected the globe."

Is this the language of the nations? Or is it the clause demanding unanimity—the explanation hastily suggested by our friendly neighbour—which compels the representatives of nations beneath us to conclude their conversation with such confused, such foolish, and such insincere utterances? To such a suggestion we reply that no clause can compel us to subscribe to meaningless or ridiculous remarks on petty and unimportant details while the world in its distress is eagerly waiting for intelligent recognition of facts and energetic measures of help. There is no article of the Covenant and no paragraph in the order of the House to compel the delegates to support a declaration of sympathy with the victims of Chinese floods, or to accept the report on Chinese communications, while remaining silent on the Sino-Japanese conflict. The fact is that the language which we hear beneath us is the secular language which we have heard before any clause demanding unanimity was devised; it is the language of which Wilson had attempted to cure the representatives of the nations and which they smuggled back into his Covenant, a language which twelve years of common conversations could not serve to eradicate or to correct, a language which, year after year, was carefully cultivated and gradually brought to perfection in successive meetings of Assembly, Council and Conference. It is the vague and obscure language of Article 8 and the peace articles of the Covenant, and it is the insulting and disingenuous language which we discovered in the course of our investigations in Article 22 of the Covenant, the article dealing with the colonial mandates, discovering simultaneously to our disgust that the struggle for the League is in fact a struggle against the language of this article.

Meanwhile the President has raised his hammer for a new resolution:

"The Assembly once more expresses its confidence . . ."

"The Assembly congratulates itself upon the work to be done . . ."

Whence this time the Assembly's enthusiasm? It is the Mandates Commission, the Mandatory Powers, the Council and the application of Article 22 that raise its enthusiasm. As thus:

"As in previous years the Assembly expresses the hope that, thanks to the further endeavours carried on jointly by the Mandatory Powers, the Council and the permanent Mandates Commission, the mandate system will continue to assure the realization of the cultural ideal outlined in Article 22."

The cultural ideal proclaimed in Article 22. Do we dream? Twelve years have passed since Versailles, and not even an attempt has been made to eradicate this language; and, more than that, it is actually held up to admiration. This language which means death to the League is to be the language of all the nations? The hammer of the President falls: this language has been unanimously adopted—and in the presence of a German delegation. . . .

No—as yet there is no conversation between the nations. It

was only for a brief moment that all these men, the would-be representatives of the nations, constituted a League; for that moment when they stood in the ante-chamber of the League, forming a dense mass without name, nationality or feature, but containing a hundred potentialities. A moment later they became figures within the main structure and bore the faces of men while symbolizing so many nations. But no sooner had they begun to talk than they became what they had always been, the diplomats and professional politicians of all times, pursuing their old business with a few new rules and methods, but without giving a thought to these methods and rules. Not even the agenda became the subject of a genuine international discussion: they were taken seriously, and it was pretended that they were the one important matter, and this pretence served as an excuse for silence on more important affairs. Eventually they withdrew into their hotel rooms, their secret sessions, their banquets, or their secluded restaurants, only because in their opinion the really serious matters immediately touching the interests of their respective nations had no use for international conversations, so that the old method of direct conversation between the parties interested in special questions seemed alone expedient. Already indeed it would seem that the time and place of this organized international conversation has ceased to provide a satisfactory opportunity for these private conversations; it would seem that the League organization acts as a disturbing element and as though they preferred to discuss their troubles in Paris, London, Rome and Berlin in the privacy and seclusion of traditional conferences and congresses. Once again they have reached the methods suitable perhaps for removing immediate difficulties but inadequate to assure a safe future or to prevent a war. But if the Geneva organization and its methods not only fail to create a League, but even to promote a conversation or a debate on the League, then the outlook is black indeed.

The President of the Assembly raises his hammer; in every

room of Hottop's hotel and in all the branches Presidents are raising their hammers. They are delivering gorgeous concluding addresses inspired by satisfaction and confidence in the future, and as soon as they have finished they will let fall their hammers and declare the session closed. Meanwhile our impulse is to beg them, so far from closing the meeting, to open it; to take one single point and place it in the Agenda of their Assembly and Council discussions, of the discussions of the Disarmament Conference and of the Committee; and to call this point the formation of a League of Nations. The attempt is worth making, for the framework is ready for the experiment. We have a city which is more suitable than Paris; we have an electoral building, a hall of the Reformation, the glass room of the Council, and the new building for the Disarmament Conference; and all are more propitious than the Hall of Mirrors at Versailles. There is no lack of documents awaiting emendation —the Covenant with its twenty-six articles, and the treaties of peace, with their hundreds of articles. Numerous important papers are to be found in the library, the pride of the collection, full of stimulating ideas, forgotten at Paris and Versailles—all the profound programmes from Dubois to Kant, and from Kant to Wilson await their attention. Nor is there any lack of capable, shrewd and industrious officials, of able statesmen, skilled diplomats and trustworthy experts. The nations too are assembled with their gradually growing suspicions and their eagerness to see something done; they display their wounds— wounds caused by peace no less than by war. Above all, there is the accumulated experience which has demonstrated in the course of twelve bitter years that the methods of Paris will not do and that there are others which will. Let then the session be opened without self-deception or deception of the nations. For, unless there is a rapid change of heart, the nations will lose their last hope for the realization of the League ideal. Why is it that the League declines to come into existence? It is because the present organization occupies the place which should be occupied by the League. It is you, the rulers at

Geneva, who have ousted the old prophets, and while you have ruled at Geneva no new programme for a League has been produced. And yet you must not simply vanish; for if your work is destroyed every enemy of the great ideal will exclaim that the impracticability of the League has been definitively established, and even its friends will look upon it as a mere Utopia. If the first attempt to realize the League coming at the end of six hundred years of endeavour proves a failure, before the new foundations for the true League have been laid, we shall have lost the ground gained in six hundred years and shall have returned to a stage earlier than that of Wilson, of Kant and of Dubois; and even if some enlightened ruler were to uphold the cause of the nations in a world war, such a championship would be useless. The cause of the nations is your cause: let the session be opened.

The hammer is raised in the President's hand: it falls: the session is ended.

CHAPTER XXV

THE WOMAN AT THE LEVEL CROSSING

WE have made our farewell visit in the Secretariat, have made our bow to the high officials, have shaken hands with Herr Hottop, have taken a last look at the negro girl with the round eyes and cast a last glance at the inscription in memory of President Wilson, an inscription which, so we hope, will be replaced some day by a monument of atonement in the garden of the new League building, some monument resembling that at Champel, where Calvin's error is recorded. We walk along the quay, with its white parapet fringing the luminous lake. Soon the *bise* will lash its waters, and a thick mist will cover its surface, placing a dense grey pall between Hottop's hotel and Calvin's citadel. The celebrations are over; another League year has become part of history.

Our hotel is wearing a quiet and gloomy air. The trunks and boxes of the delegation have been trundled down the back stairs and into the lorries. Here and there, in the inhospitable and unkempt corridors, a typewriter or a bundle of documents witnesses to the last hurried labours, while next door the secretary, whose desk, with the completion of her task, has almost become a dressing-table, is fitting her travelling hat on to her blonde coiffure. The commissionaires, mentally half at home already, hurry for a last time through the empty rooms, which a minute ago were disguised as Foreign Offices. Downstairs, at the desk, the secretary of the delegation is nonchalantly settling the bill.

Meanwhile in the hall the Minister rises from the big easy chair in a quiet corner, where he has been carrying on a last political discussion with the colleague from the hotel opposite. For the last time he accompanies his guest to the door, an amiable host, returns, and with his mind at ease shakes hands right and left, slips carelessly into his coat, takes his hat as though going out for a walk, and, smiling and gracious, walks under the flag which will be lowered in a few minutes, past the bowing hotel servants. He settles in his car. The air is easy; the afternoon sun is mild and gentle; the street is indifferent and wears its everyday face. The brief journey from the hotel to the station suffices to let the excitement of the last days vanish; already Geneva is beginning to be lost in the distance. The strange dream is resuscitated for a last time on the platform in the noisy confusion of travellers, where little trolleys with cigars, chocolate, oranges and newspapers are wheeled about. The other members of the delegation are waiting at the coach doors; the Consul and the associations are standing by, no less than the girl with the bouquet and the secret service agent. Colleagues from other countries are hurrying past the chattering group to other coaches; quick farewells and amiable good-byes are exchanged; then there is a silent patch in the noise of the station. The nations are gathered into groups. Journalists and photographers wait eagerly for a last phrase and a last gesture. Trivial words and exaggerated laughter, vainly attempting to fill the embarrassed minutes before the train leaves, are exchanged between coach and platform. Soon the travellers have settled in their compartments and, placing their hats in the racks, have taken possession of their moving home, and have left behind the strange world in which they have been domiciled for weeks.

What was the outward aspect of this world? From the station they can look down into the wide street which greeted their arrival, with the friendly confusion of boats and the rocky pile of the Salève for background. Trams and cars are moving below, people cross the street and enter shops, and the flags of the Swiss cantons and semi-cantons have long since vanished; for the rifle meeting, the automobile exhibition and the horse-races are over. We stand behind the half-lowered windows, listen abstractedly to the trivialities of the last conversation, and let our eyes roam over the empty lake, the empty hills and the town, empty too, in spite of its traffic.

THE WOMAN AT THE LEVEL CROSSING 407

Within a few minutes the train will leave. Meanwhile on our right hand, although invisible from our present point of vantage, there is the Hôtel des Bergues with its big blue-grey hall, a thousand tail-coats and a thousand evening frocks. Opposite, on the left, lies the *Beau Rivage* with the small private room where the ministers held their conferences. Behind the English garden is spread the bulk of the Hôtel Metropole, over which recently the German colours were hoisted: everything is in its place, and everything is left behind. The hall of the Reformation, the electoral building and, by the side of the lake, the Hôtel National, with its manifold and complex life, that same hotel in which we followed the growth and development of an idea from the room of the Secretary-General to the sempstress's garret, they all are in their place and they all are left behind. We leave behind the big building of the Disarmament Conference, the new growing domicile of the League, the cathedral in the Cité, the little restaurants in the town, the quiet inns on the lake's banks, and the villas and gardens once haunted by Rousseau, Goethe, Byron and Lamartine. Gradually they are all left behind and are gilded over by memory. A shining mystic blue-golden light covers this world for the last time—the blue-golden light of the unparalleled lake which is passing at our feet behind the moving screen of green vineyards and in front of the rigid background of lofty mountains.

Where were we? It grows dark, the curtains are drawn before the windows of our compartments, and the lamp at the ceiling severs us definitively from the regions we have left behind. A piece of work has been done, and a conversation concluded; speeches have been delivered, and documents compiled. Some of us take periodicals and books in hand, while others begin to study new documents and prepare new work. Gradually the journey changes its character. We have ceased to leave behind us a place—we are travelling into the future; curiosity has taken the place of regrets.

What is our destination? Are we so many excursionists or

hangers-on around a congress returning to every-day realities? The League is finished, so the travellers say; the Reichstag, or the Chamber, is about to begin. Are they exchanging a political holiday for normal and serious work?

Perhaps they are to-day, and perhaps they will to-morrow or the day after. For some time to come they will undertake this foolish and pleasant journey to the blue lake and back to the grey capital, and so back and forth until they have lost all sense of the meaning of their migration and even the most enthusiastic fails to see the significant signals which stand along our route and grows deaf to the voice of the prophets accompanying us. And for that reason we pray that the new use may not become an unthinking habit. For the last time, open the windows, turn off the light and look at the flying landscape—the last gleam of the lake or the last foam of the Rhône. Say farewell, but understand that you are taking with you nothing and are leaving behind nothing; that nothing is waiting for you, immovable and unchanged.

Where have you been?

You looked for the League in hotels, offices and debating rooms. You did not find it; for all that you saw around you were the familiar offices which you knew at home. You have looked for the grand conversation between the nations and you have not found it, for you never heard any but your own isolated voices. Where were you? If you have learnt or discovered anything, it can only be that Geneva is not your goal, but is only a stage on the way. Whither does this way lead? Unless you have wasted your time—unless you wish to waste your time—you must have the certainty that your journey will continue. Your journey back is not so much a return home as a journey towards a goal. For the League is at home with you; it is domiciled in Berlin, Paris, Warsaw, Brussels, Riga and Budapest; and it is only now—if you will it—that your journey, the deliberate and inspired journey to the League, commences. The woman at the level crossing little suspects what passengers are carried in your trains as they go rushing across

THE WOMAN AT THE LEVEL CROSSING 409

country, and she waves her flag with wonted indifference; the labourers in the fields look at the speeding pomp unthinkingly, and only the school-children on the embankment wave with joyous eagerness. But if you bear within you the secret symbol which differentiates you from other travellers, your train will carry you to the right goal. It is in your offices at home, at your own desk, where to-morrow the messengers with important air will inform visitors that you have returned from Geneva—it is there alone that the League can exist; there is no other soil in which it can grow, flourish or prevail. The League must form a part of your daily documents, and of your telephone conversations; it must become a part of the daily debate of the nation; and it is thus and only thus that it can spread from one Foreign Office to the next, from Paris to Berlin and from London to Rome, becoming the never-ceasing international long-distance conversation of the nations. The League must become an inspiration at home before we can rediscover it in the blue-golden fairyland of Geneva, in the house by the Quai Wilson and in the big halls of stone and glass. It is then and then only that it will form part of your baggage on your next journey, together with your file and Hughes machines, between the senior officials and the Press officers, and wrapped up with your swallow-tails and orders. Then only will it roll down the rue Mont Blanc in your car under the flags of Uri, Basle and Vaud, and past the reflective monument on the Rousseau island.

The trains rush through the valleys, past rivers and hills; west by way of Bellegarde, and east by way of Lausanne, the community of men and nations takes its way; by way of Paris, the gathering point of the western hemisphere, by the grand Rhône valley, by Feldkirch and by Basle, they are scattered over the four quarters of the European world. The pilgrims from Geneva are spilt from the stations in the capitals and from the harbours of the Mediterranean and the great oceans, so many sparks scattered over the globe; and Havas, Wolff, Reuter, Stefani, Pat and Fabra duly report: "On the conclusion of the League session the delegation left Geneva by train. There were present at the station. . . ." Some reports add that on the same day the Central Committee for the Supervision of Opium Traffic met at the League Secretariat, and that the information section published a *communiqué* on the registration of the new method of arbitration.

The trains go thundering through the night. Everything is quiet and empty in the corridors of the sleeping-cars, and only the conductor sits on his folding seat and counts the diplomatic passports. Cathedrals and stations flit past the drawn curtains. The journey continues.

ANALYSIS

The following list gives a general conspectus of the manner in which the League is dealt with in its various aspects in the course of the book.

CHAPTERS	
II	Antenatal History of the League up to the Great War
III, IV, V	President Wilson's idea of the League
V	Paris Peace Conference and the Foundation of the League
VI–XII	The Covenant of the League
VI	General Survey and Organization
VII	Disarmament (Articles 8 and 9)
VII	Safeguarding of Territorial and Political Independence (Article 10)
VIII	Preservation and Restoration of Peace (Articles 11 to 17)
VIII	The Treaty Policy of the League (Articles 18 to 21)
IX	The Mandates System (Article 22)
X	Saar, Danzig, Protection of Minorities (Peace Treaties and Special Treaties)
XI	International Labour Organization (Peace Treaties)
XI	Special Problems of International Collaboration (Articles 23 to 25)
XII	Revision of the Covenant (Article 26)
XIV	League Secretariat and League Officials
XV	The Heads of the Secretariat
XVI	Intellectual Co-operation
XVII	Extent and Political Importance of the League
XVIII	Political Disputes
XIX	League Activity in the Sphere of Disarmament
XX	The League and Treaties of Alliance
XXI	Juridical and Political Expansion of the League
XXII	Survey of the League's Activities in the following Spheres: Mandates System, Saar, Danzig, Minorities, Finance, Economics, Communications, Social Questions, Hygiene, Information
XXIII, XXIV	Significance of League Assemblies for International Collaboration and the Realization of the Ideal of the League
XII, XIII XXII–XXV	General Considerations

INDEX

Aaland dispute, 270, 271
Adatchi, 395
Aghnides, M., 294, 312, 314, 351
Aguerro y Bethancourt, Señor, 386
Angell, Sir Norman, 25
Angora, Treaty of, 281
Anschluss, 144, 145
Anselmino, Dr., 381
Apponyi, Count, 383, 395
Arenol, M., 220
Aschmann, Herr, 250
Attolico, Signor, 294

Baker, R. Stannard, 58
Balfour, Lord, 198, 199, 245, 279, 329, 377
Banffy, Count, 243
Barnes, Mr., 240
Benes, M., 241, 340, 342, 383
Bergson, Henri, 226, 236
Bernstorff, Count, 306, 311, 381
Bethmann-Hollweg, 38, 39, 40
Bolivar, Simon, 20
Borden, Sir Robert, 329
Bourgeois, Léon, 75, 82, 226, 378
Branting, Herr, 280, 385
Breitscheid, Dr., 380
Briand, Aristide, 41, 84, 251, 282, 283, 285, 286, 290, 291, 348, 349, 350, 358, 379, 382, 394, 395
Brockdorff-Rantzau, Count, 65
Buat, General, 320
Burritt, Elihu, 21, 22
Bustamente, Judge, 335

Cavell, Nurse, 72
Cecil, Lord Robert, 76, 77, 92, 112, 240, 277, 279, 299, 303, 329, 340, 346, 378, 394
Chamberlain, Sir Austen, 251, 275, 342, 377

Chinda, Viscount, 76
Clemenceau, Georges, 41, 72, 74, 80, 81, 83, 84, 143, 154, 226, 251, 252, 293, 352, 380
Cobian, Señor, 306
Colban, Dr., 294
Coolidge, President, 300
Corfu incident, 276, 277, 284
Curie, Mme, 227
Curtius, Dr., 270, 381, 394
Curzon line, 272
Cushenden, Lord, 307

Dandurand, Mr., 360
Danzig, 146, 147, 148, 156, 171, 263, 264, 268, 355, 358, 359
Dawes, General, 290
de Brouckère, M., 329, 346
de Jouvenal, H., 378
de la Harpe, François, 229, 371
de Maderiaga, 294, 384
de Maistre, Joseph, 20
Deputy Secretary-General, 218 *sqq.*
de St. Pierre, Abbé, 228
de Sellon, Count, 21
Drummond, Sir Eric, 192, 210 *sqq.*, 331
Dufour-Feronce, Herr Albert, 221, 225, 235
Dunant, Henry, 26

Ebert, President, 245
Einstein, Albert, 227
Ernst, Dr., 380
Erzberger, Matthias, 54, 59, 65, 84
Esher, Lord, 296
Eupen and Malmedy, 144, 264, 271, 272

Fisher, Lord, 279
Foch, Marshal, 64, 65, 109, 116, 242, 319

Fourteen Points, Wilson's, 52–55, 62, 99, 105, 107, 134
Frangulis, M., 279
Franklin, Benjamin, 20
Fried, Alfred, 26, 284

Galsworthy, John, 227
Galvanauskas, M., 395
Gauss, Dr., 78, 327
George, D. Lloyd, 41
Gran Chaco dispute, 285 sqq.
Grandi, Signor, 384
Grey, Viscount, 38

Hague Peace Conference of 1899, 25, 28
Hague Peace Conference of 1907, 25, 28
Hanotaux, M., 378
Henderson, A., 377
Herriot, M., 247, 254, 340, 378
Hertling, Count, 55, 56
Hottop, Herr, 192, 193
House, Colonel, 76, 77, 112
Hugo, Victor, 22, 172
Hurst, Sir Cecil, 77, 329
Hymans, M., 273, 363, 384

Intellectual co-operation, 226 sqq.
International Labour Office, 159, 162, 163, 164, 178

Jay, William, 21
Jouhaux, M., 378

Kaas, Dr., 380
Kant, Immanuel, 172, 228, 234, 235, 236, 330, 403, 404
Kaufmann, Dr., 381
Kellogg Pact, 123, 288, 347, 348

Ladds, William, 21
Lafontaine, Senator, 226, 278, 384
Lansing, Secretary of State, 111
League to Enforce Peace, 31
Lenin, 51, 73

Leroux, Pierre, 20
Lewald, Dr., 381
Litvinoff, 311
Locarno, Treaty of, 249, 250, 268, 318
Lotus case, 333
Loucheur, M., 363, 378
Luther, Dr., 250

MacDonald, J. Ramsay, 246, 247, 340, 342, 377
Maglinse, General, 319
Makino, Baron, 76
Manchurian dispute, 288
Mann, Thomas, 227
Mantoux, Professor, 237
Marx, Chancellor, 246
Massigli, M., 306
Max von Baden, Prince, 62, 64, 65, 79, 253
Mayer, Dr., 265
Mello Franco, 251, 395
Memel question, 266, 267, 271
Mensdorf-Pouilly, Count, 383
Miller, D. H., 77, 112
Monroe Doctrine, 78, 129, 130
Mossul question, 280, 281, 287
Motta, Herr, 239, 385, 394, 395
Müller, Dr. Adolf, 245, 381
Murray, Professor Gilbert, 227

Nansen, F., 279, 364, 385
Nicaragua, occupation of, 284
Nicolas II, Emperor of Russia, 25, 27, 37
Nine Power Pact, 288
Nobel, Alfred, 25
Noblemaire, M., 378, 394

Orlando, Count, 76
Osusky, M., 243, 395

Paderewski, 154, 272
Painlevé, M., 227
Palier de Saint-Germain, 112
Paul-Boncour, M., 299, 308, 378

INDEX

Paulucci di Calboli Barone, Count, 195, 221
Pequer, Constantin, 21
Pflügl, Baron, 383
Phillimore, Lord, 77
Pilsudski, Marshal, 271, 275
Poincaré, M., 340, 380
Political Department of the League, 237 *seq.*
Politis, M., 340
Pueyrredon, Señor, 239

Quer Boule, Señor, 395
Quiñones, de Leon, 343, 384

Requin, Colonel, 308
Rey, Professor Jean, 107, 329, 330
Roosevelt, President Th., 25
Root, Elihu, 127, 333
Ruhr district, 246, 267, 268, 269, 284

Saar district, 145, 146, 156, 158, 199, 253, 263, 264, 268, 355, 358
Salandra, 277, 394
Scheidemann, Herr, 79
Schiffer, Dr., 381
Schober, Dr., 383
Schücking, Walther, 26, 40, 78, 79, 81, 84, 125, 334, 335
Schüller, Herr, 383
Scialoja, Count, 76, 282, 384
Second International, 161, 310
Secretary-General of League, 210 *sqq.*
Seeliger, Dr., 381
Seipel, Dr., 383
Simons, Dr., 78, 381
Smuts, General, 76, 77, 137, 154
Sokal, M., 306
Stresemann, G., 194, 246, 250, 251, 253, 268, 269, 358, 360, 363, 381, 382, 394, 395
Sugimura, Mr., 221, 236 *sqq.*, 254, 258 *sqq.*, 291, 292, 314

Taft, President, 31
Thibaudet, M., 227
Thomas, Albert, 164
Titulescu, M., 346, 384
Trani, Countess of, 191
Trotsky, 51

Upper Silesia, 265, 271

Vacarescu, Helene, 235
Valéry, Paul, 227
Vandervelde, M., 384, 395
van Eysinga, 385
van Karnebeek, Jonkheer, 385
Venizelos, E., 329
Vilna dispute, 272, 273, 284
Viviani, R., 240, 241, 242, 378, 394
Voldemarus, M., 199, 272, 273
Voltaire, 229
von Blockland, Beelaerts, 275, 385
von Bülow, Dr. Bernhard, 264
von Eckard, 380
von Schubert, Herr, 250
von Suttner, Berta, 25, 26

Wehberg, Dr., 80, 84, 125
Weingartner, Dr., 227
White Slave Traffic, 165, 166, 167, 355, 365
Wilson, President, 32 *sqq.*, 36 *sqq.*, 40 *sqq.*, 45, 47–51, 54–58, 60–65, 67–71, 73–84, 93, 97, 99–101, 105, 107, 109, 111–114, 116, 124, 127, 128, 130, 133, 136 *sqq.*, 140, 143, 144–148, 151, 152, 154, 161, 175, 191, 226, 238, 251, 252, 255, 258, 268, 293, 329, 333, 352, 387, 400, 403, 404
Wimbledon case, 333
Wirth, Chancellor, 266
Wissell, Herr, 381

Zalesky, M., 199
Zeligovski, General, 272, 273
Zoka ed Duvleh, Emir, 279

For Product Safety Concerns and Information please contact our EU representative GPSR@taylorandfrancis.com
Taylor & Francis Verlag GmbH, Kaufingerstraße 24, 80331 München, Germany

www.ingramcontent.com/pod-product-compliance
Lightning Source LLC
Chambersburg PA
CBHW060549230426
43670CB00011B/1748